**(ọ'bri**
wine o

2002 has been action-packed fo
O'Briens. The Group continues to
new outlets, with Drogheda being
latest addition. Our staff are all enti
astically working through their wine e
cation programs and this year three or
our managers sat the 2nd year of their
W.S.E.T diploma exams.

David Whelehan, Brendan O'Brien
and T. P. Whelehan

We, the wine buying team, have once again clocked up the air miles. We have visited all the major wine shows, tasted at the wineries and really worked to find what we believe are some of the most exciting wines available. We are totally committed to offering the best range of wines in Ireland, while always paying particular regard to quality and value. We hope you will enjoy some of our latest award winning additions.

*T. P. Whelehan* TP Whelehan   *David Whelehan* David Whelehan

We are particularly proud to recommend the wines of:

Australia – Angoves • Tatachilla • Bethany • Xanadu • Rymil

Chile – St. Emiliana • Villard • Luis Felipe Edwards •
Laura Hartwig • Los Boldos

South Africa – Rust en Vrede • Guardian Peak • Delheim

Italy – Falesco • La Carria • Pervini • Pasetti

France – Chanson • Brocard • Château Beau Rivage •
Louis Bernard • Domaine des Anges • Gerard Bertrand •
and a huge collection of classified Bordeaux

Spain – Abadia Retuerta • Campo Borja • Sierra Cantabria

For any information on our range or any advice please contact us:

e-mail: info@obriensgroup.ie, www.obriensgroup.ie,
ph.1850 269777

# experience the difference

blackrock • bray: quinsboro road and vevay road • dalkey •
donnybrook • drogheda • dun laoghaire • greystones • glasnevin •
malahide • navan rd • navan town • newbridge • rathgar • rathmines •
sandymount • stillorgan • templeogue

# Add a little colour to Life

*Funky*
*Passionate*
*Sexy*
*Desirable*

# LUNA DI LUNA

Dazzle your customers, with the hotest new International wine range from Luna di Luna, distributed exclusively in Ireland by Woodford Bourne. Contact the sales team now, on 01 404 7300, and get ready for an altogether more colourful future.

*250 years of excellence*

# The Wine Guide 2003

*Edited by*
Barbara Boyle

A. & A. Farmar

© A. & A. Farmar 2002
© articles by the named contributors 2002

All rights reserved. No text may be reproduced in any medium or storage system without permission from the publishers. The database of which this book is an emanation is copyright of A. & A. Farmar Ltd.

British Library Cataloguing in Publication Data
A CIP catalogue record for this book is available from the British Library

ISBN 1-899047-93-X

Published by
A. & A. Farmar
Beech House, 78 Ranelagh Village, Dublin 6
Ireland
Tel: (01) 496 3625 Fax: (01) 497 0107
E-mail: afarmar@iol.ie
Web: www.farmarbooks.ie

Editorial director: Anna Farmar
Production director: Tony Farmar

Contributions by: Niamh Boylan, Barbara Boyle, Pat Carroll, Alan Crowley MW, Katherine Farmar, Tony Farmar, Sarah Furno

Cover design: Brosna Press
Text design and setting: Bookworks
Printed and bound by: GraphyCems

Sales: Mullett Fitzpatrick
Distribution: Columba Mercier Distribution

# Contents

Foreword *Anna and Tony Farmar* iv
Introduction *Barbara Boyle* 1

Wines of the Year shortlists 4
Wines of the Year 5
Great value wines 6
The tasting panel 8
Tasters' choices 10
The mystery of vintages *Alan Crowley MW* 22
Grape varieties *Pat Carroll* 25

*Wine and food . . . and beer*

Seasonal food and wine *Niamh Boylan* 35
Cheese and wine *Sarah Furno* 38
Matching wine to food table *Niamh Boylan and Barbara Boyle* 41
Matching food to wine table *Niamh Boylan and Barbara Boyle* 47
Premium beer *Tony Farmar* 51

*The wines*

Argentina 56
Australia 62
Austria 93
Chile 96
France–Alsace 114
France–Bordeaux 118
France–Burgundy 130
France–Loire 141
France–Rhône 146
France–South 157
France–South West 169

Germany 173
Greece 178
Hungary 180
Italy 181
Lebanon 201
New Zealand 202
Portugal 207
Romania 211
South Africa 212
Spain 226
USA 245

Rosé 254
Sparkling 257
Sweet 270

Participating importers' contact details 274
Glossary *Katherine Farmar* 280
Index of wines 285

# Foreword

Welcome to the eighth edition of *The Wine Guide—The Best of Wine in Ireland*. Last year's edition, edited by Barbara Boyle and Pat Carroll, was chosen by the Gourmand World Cookbook Awards held in Perigueux, France, as Best Wine Guide in the World, beating international competition from publishers such as Penguin and Mitchell Beazley, and writers such as Hugh Johnson. In the citation the organisers wrote: 'Ireland is well known as a healthy food and beer drinking paradise, It is now becoming also a wine country, due to the surge of a culinary culture, with excellent restaurants, good food and wine writers and publishers.' We believe that this eighth edition, edited by Barbara Boyle, will more than maintain the standard, and hope you agree.

The award would not have been possible without the support we regularly receive from tasters, importers and the wine trade generally. We would like to thank the members of the tasting panel for their commitment and generosity in giving so freely of their time and experience to evaluate the wines. Their enthusiasm and love for the grape is constantly rewarding and shines out in the tasting notes.

We would also like to thank especially the importers who support the book year after year by submitting samples and patiently answering our requests for further information. We are always happy to welcome new suppliers of interesting wines. If you would like to participate in the next edition, please contact us before March 2003.

And finally . . . we would like to thank all our readers and offer

### An invitation

Tell us what you think about this book—especially how you think it could be improved. The ten best suggestions will win a free copy of the next edition!

*Anna and Tony Farmar*
*September 2002*

# Introduction *Barbara Boyle*

## The tastings

### Selecting the wines to be tasted

The guide is based on the results of blind tastings conducted over an intensive two and a half month period between May and July 2002. The wines tasted were selected from importers' lists, after much discussion with them and with wine retailers. We focused on wines which are new to the Irish market, wines not previously tasted for the guide and new vintages of previous favourites. The wines were submitted by 48 importers, some of whom are new to the book this year (an important feature in reflecting the diversity of wines available). Our objective in making the selection was to represent the best of wine on the Irish market from every major wine region, across many different styles of wine and over a wide price range from as little as €6 to €40 (more for Champagne). Together these variables make this guide an invaluable resource in finding some of the best wines on the Irish market.

### How the wines were tasted

Each of the 1,288 selected wines was tasted blind by two members of the tasting panel, tasting first alone and then comparing notes. No prices were given and the tasters were asked to assess the wines purely on the basis of intrinsic quality and the pleasure the wines gave. Assessment therefore could not be based on price or label—it is easy to be indulgent towards a perky but cheap bottle or to be too harsh or overly impressed by an immature and expensive bottle. The tasters allocated marks out of 20 for nose, palate and overall quality taking into account, amongst other factors, the character, concentration and complexity of the wine. To qualify for inclusion a wine had to score at least 12 marks (representing a 60 per cent pass rate). Some 13 per cent of the carefully pre-selected wines were rejected at this point. Therefore *any* wine included in this guide comes with a strong recommendation.

### How the awards were determined

Six awards were made this year: Red Wine of the Year, White Wine of the Year, Best Value Red Wine of the Year, Best Value White Wine of the Year, Sparkling Wine of the Year and Sweet Wine of the Year. The winners emerged in a special tasting session held after the main round of tastings had been completed. This tasting session was also conducted entirely blind. The wines that had scored 16 or more points (140 wines in total) were retasted and reassessed. During this session some wines retained their scores, some were demoted and some were promoted. The highest scoring of these wines—22 in all—formed the shortlists for the awards and the winners were finally selected from these (all wines still blind) in a closely argued session. The Wines of the Year, and the shortlists from which they emerged, are listed on pages 4 and 5.

# The hunt for great value

## How we calculated value for money

In wine, as in so much of life, you get what you pay for. But sometimes you can be lucky and get more than you pay for. As in previous years we have tried to reflect this with the value ratings. These wines are indicated by the symbol €. In previous years our tasters made their own judgement as to which wines were particularly good value, but this year we've tried a more rigorous, objective approach. By not revealing the prices during the tastings, the quality rating became independent of the price. Thus we could combine the two statistically to determine the average score for wines in each price band, and hence the wines that delivered above-average quality for the price.

As one would expect there was a broad correlation between price and quality—the more you paid the better the wine. (The exception to this rule, the €20–€25 band, is discussed below.) Since we were looking for wines that bucked this trend, it is not surprising that most of the 'value' wines fell into the lower price bands. Just under 90 per cent of the 93 great value wines we identified cost between €7 and €12. There were 44 reds, 38 whites, 4 sweet, 6 sparkling and 1 rosé.

## Do you always get what you pay for?

Our results showed that on the whole the more you pay the better the wine. However, there was a notable dip in the quality/price ratio in the €20–€25 price bracket. This was the only price-band in which the quality ratings were not noticeably higher than the cheaper band. *Caveat emptor*—you could pay €24 for a bottle and get no better quality than from a different bottle for €18! This may mean that you have to spend more to hit the really high notes or, more encouragingly, that you can spend less and get something of similar or better quality.

## Where is the best value to be found?

The South and South West of France contributed 15 exceptional value wines—which is not a great surprise as we have come to expect good quality at an affordable price from those regions. More surprisingly, Alsace has 5 value wines. This region is often under appreciated and its white wines deserve much more attention. So France, with 27 great value wines in total, came first for value, closely followed by Australia with 22; Chile, Italy and South Africa were next, each with 8 great value wines.

## What was the most common grape variety?

No one grape variety dominated the value wines. In fact, the range of varieties is huge—from Aglianico to Viognier—offering an amazing array of tastes to be tried. Only 9 out of the 93 value wines are Cabernet Sauvignon varietals, 5 are Shiraz/Syrah varietals, 6 are Chardonnay varietals and 7 are Sauvignon Blanc varietals.

A few styles or regions really stood out. The Sauvignon Blanc varietals and blends from Rueda in Spain offered tremendous value for their price and Alsace whites were also very impressive. White wines dominated the value wines from Australia while Italy, Spain and Chile contributed many value reds. Perhaps not surprisingly, some of the best value sparkling wines come from Australia.

As might be expected, a number of the bigger brand names feature as value wines and luckily for us these are fairly widely available; they include Jacob's Creek, Peter Lehmann and Wyndham Estate from Australia and

Carmen, Santa Rita and Santa Carolina from Chile. However, the majority of the value wines are from smaller producers, some well known, others new to Ireland. Most should be readily available and, even if limited to one or two stockists, they are well worth seeking out.

## Some general trends

### *Sauvignon Blanc—the grape to be seen drinking*
Even though we tasted many more Chardonnays than Sauvignon Blancs, of all the white grape varieties tasted, Sauvignon Blanc consistently scored highest whether it came from the Loire in France, Chile, New Zealand, South Africa or Spain. The Best Value White Wine of the Year is a Sauvignon Blanc from South Africa and a number of other Sauvignons were short-listed for awards.

### *Cabernet still leads the red field*
More examples of Cabernet were tasted than any other variety, followed closely by Shiraz/Syrah varietals and blends. Cabernet Sauvignon and Cabernet blends continue to be the leading styles of red wine scoring consistently higher than other styles, whether as a varietal or as part of a blend.

### *Hottest region?*
The range of premium Australian wines in Ireland has widened and there are also more wines available from Puglia in southern Italy, Bergerac in South-West France and Languedoc-Roussillon in the South of France. These are some of the regions most likely to yield interesting results when you are looking for something new.

### *Which countries did well?*
Stars, value symbols and high marks were fairly evenly distributed given the relative size of each country or region. However, some regions had a higher than average proportion of the higher marks, notably Italy, New Zealand and Alsace. The Red Wine of the Year and the Best Value Red Wine of the Year are both Italian. While New Zealand's wines are generally a bit more expensive they really do deliver the goods when it comes to quality. More detailed comments on each country/region can be found at the beginning of each chapter.

# Wines of the Year shortlists

*White Wine of the Year shortlist*
- **Carl Ehrhard Riesling Auslese Trocken QmP 99** ☆☆☆☆
  *Germany, page 177 'The Winner'*
- Chatelain AC Pouilly-Fumé 01 ☆☆☆☆€
  *France–Loire, page 142*
- Dom. du Clos St Landelin Riesling
  AC Alsace Grand Cru Vorbourg 00 ☆☆☆☆
  *France–Alsace, page 117*
- Grove Mill Sauvignon Blanc 01 ☆☆☆
  *New Zealand, page 204*

*Red Wine of the Year shortlist*
- **Enzo Boglietti Roscaleto DOC Barbera d'Alba 99** ☆☆☆☆
  *Italy, page 200 'The Winner'*
- Cesari Il Bosco DOC Amarone della Valpolicella Classico 97 ☆☆☆
  *Italy, page 199*
- Ch. Maucaillou Cru Bourgeois AC Moulis 97 ☆☆☆
  *France–Bordeaux, page 129*
- Geoff Merrill Reserve Cabernet Sauvignon 97 ☆☆☆
  *Australia, page 88*
- Geyser Peak Reserve Cabernet Sauvignon 96 ☆☆☆
  *USA, page 253*
- Peter Lehmann Mentor 97 ☆☆☆
  *Australia, page 91*

*Sparkling Wine of the Year shortlist*
- **Green Point Vintage Brut 97** ☆☆☆€
  *Australia, page 269 'The Winner'*
- Comte L. de Ferande Brut nv ☆☆€ *France–Champagne, page 257*
- Bernard Depoivre Brut nv ☆☆ *France–Champagne, page 258*

*Sweet Wine of the Year shortlist*
- **Alois Kracher Neusiedlersee Beerenauslese Cuvée 2000**
  **Prädikatswein 00** ☆☆☆€ *Austria, page 271 'The Winner'*

*Best Value White Wine of the Year shortlist*
- **Clos Malverne Sauvignon Blanc 02** ☆☆☆€
  *South Africa, page 214 'The Winner'*
- Ch. Tahbilk Marsanne 98 ☆☆☆€ *Australia, page 64*
- Sipp Mack Pinot Blanc AC Alsace 01 ☆☆☆€ *France–Alsace, page 115*
- Viña Cascarela Sauvignon Blanc DO Rueda 00 ☆☆☆€ *Spain, page 227*

*Best Value Red Wine of the Year shortlist*
- **Archidamo DOC Primitivo di Manduria 00** ☆☆€
  *Italy, page 188 'The Winner'*
- Agramont Crianza DO Navarra 98 ☆☆€ *Spain, page 231*
- Blewitt Springs Cabernet Sauvignon 98 ☆☆€ *Australia, page 77*
- Comté de Mérinville AC Minervois 97 ☆☆€ *France–South, page 163*

# Wines of the Year

*White Wine of the Year (Germany, page 177)*

**Carl Ehrhard Riesling Auslese Trocken** QmP **99** ☆☆☆☆
Delicious, benchmark German Riesling, in a highly complex, big style with excellent length. Flavours of peach, mango, ripe apples, honey, lime and some leafiness with crispish acidity, perfect balance and lingering, classic Riesling finish. *Karwig Wines*

*Red Wine of the Year (Italy, page 200)*

**Enzo Boglietti Roscaleto** DOC Barbera d'Alba **99** ☆☆☆☆
Brilliant deep ruby in colour with chocolate, bitter cherry and rich, raisiny aromas. The seductively rich and spicy palate is vibrant and packed with dense berry fruit and plum flavours, with a memorable length. *WineKnows*

*Sparkling Wine of the Year (Australia, page 269)*

**Green Point Vintage Brut** **97** ☆☆☆ €
Burnt toast with nut and strawberry shortcake aromas followed by rich mouth-filling red berries, honeyed, nutty hints and tons of tangy, fresh, citrus fruits. Excellent mousse and long length of flavour. *Febvre*

*Sweet Wine of the Year (Austria, page 271)*

**Alois Kracher Neusiedlersee Beerenauslese Cuvée 2000** Prädikatswein **00** ☆☆☆ €
Divine classic style of silk, satin and spice. Intense aromas of orange blossom and honey with lovely, spicy nuances. Full-bodied palate with ripe nectarine and orange flavours. *Searsons*

*Best Value White Wine of the Year (South Africa, page 214)*

**Clos Malverne Sauvignon Blanc 02** ☆☆☆ €
Wonderfully intense, layered bouquet displaying nettles, cut grass and tropical fruit. Explosive palate with classic flavours of green fruit, black-currant leaf and nettles and lusher pineapple and mango. Great texture and superb length. *Dunnes Stores*

*Best Value Red Wine of the Year (Italy, page 188)*

**Archidamo** DOC Primitivo di Manduria **00** ☆☆ €
Smooth and wonderfully warming vanilla, chocolate and liquorice aromas. Smoky, dark chocolate palate oozing cherry and red berry flavours, with a concentrated texture and a lengthy finish. *O'Briens*

# Great value wines under €12

## White under €9

**Australia**
Cudgee Creek Colombard Chardonnay 01 *see page 62*
Jacob's Creek Dry Riesling 01 *see page 63*
Peter Lehmann The Barossa Chenin Blanc 00 *see page 63*

**Chile**
Las Casas del Toqui Chardonnay 01 DO Cachapoal Valley *see page 97*

**France**
Charles Koehly & Fils St-Hippolyte Gewürztraminer 99 AC Alsace *see page 114*
Ch. Peyragué 00 AC Graves *see page 118*
Cuvée Orélie 01 VdP des Coteaux de l'Ardèche *see page 146*
Dom. de Joy 01 VdP des Côtes de Gascogne *see page 169*
Laurent Miquel Chardonnay Viognier 01 VdP d'Oc *see page 157*
Michel Laroche South of France Terret 01 VdP d'Oc *see page 157*
Thomann Riesling 01 AC Alsace *see page 114*
Virginie Chardonnay 01 VdP d'Oc *see page 158*
Virginie Viognier 01 VdP d'Oc *see page 158*

**Hungary**
Chapel Hill Irsai Olivér 99 Minoségi Bor *see page 180*

**South Africa**
Bellingham Sauvignon Blanc 01 *see page 212*
Kleinrivier Chardonnay 00 *see page 213*

**Spain**
Con Class Sauvignon Blanc 01 DO Rueda *see page 226*
Viña Cascarela Sauvignon Blanc 00 DO Rueda *see page 227*

## Red under €9

**Argentina**
Etchart Rio de Plata Malbec 00 *see page 57*
Santa Rosa Estate Malbec 00 *see page 58*
Simonassi Lyon Malbec 98 *see page 58*

**Australia**
Cudgee Creek Cabernet Sauvignon 00 *see page 75*
Jacob's Creek Cabernet Sauvignon 00 *see page 75*

**Chile**
Carmen Cabernet Sauvignon 00 *see page 101*
Carmen Merlot 00 *see page 101*
Quiltro Merlot 00 *see page 102*

**France**
Ch. Salauze 99 AC Minervois *see page 160*
Côtes du Rhône des Papes 01 AC Cotes du Rhône *see page 148*
Didier Picot Cabernet Sauvignon 99 VdP d'Oc *see page 160*
Laurent Miquel Cabernet Syrah 01 VdP d'Oc *see page 161*
Virginie Syrah 00 VdP Catalan *see page 161*

**Greece**
Mirambelo 99 VQPRD AO Peza *see page 179*

**Italy**
Fantini Primitivo 00 DOC Salice Salentino *see page 187*
Rocca 98 IGT Rosso Salento *see page 187*

**Portugal**
JP Barrel Selection Red Wine 96 VR Terras do Sado *see page 208*

**South Africa**
Hutton Ridge Pinotage 00 WO Riebeekberg *see page 217*
Hutton Ridge Shiraz 00 WO Swartland *see page 217*
Long Mountain Merlot Shiraz 00 WO Western Cape *see page 218*
Vaughan Johnson's Good Everyday Cape Red nv *see page 218*
**Spain**
Agramont Crianza 98 DO Navarra *see page 231*
**USA/California**
Vendange Cabernet Sauvignon 98 *see page 248*

## White €9–€12
**Australia**
Ch. Tahbilk Marsanne 98 *see page 64*
Honey Tree Semillon Chardonnay 01 *see page 65*
McGuigan Bin 6000 Hunter Valley Verdelho 01 *see page 66*
Peter Lehmann The Barossa Semillon 01 *see page 66*
Tyrrell's Old Winery Chardonnay 01 *see page 67*
Wakefield Clare Valley Chardonnay 99 *see page 68*
Wakefield Clare Valley Semillon 00 *see page 68*
**France**
Ch. Court-les-Mûts 00 AC Bergerac Sec *see page 170*
Hugel Cuvée Les Amours Pinot Blanc de Blancs 99 AC Alsace *see page 114*
Sipp Mack Pinot Blanc 01 AC Alsace *see page 115*
**Italy**
Terlan Pinot Bianco 01 DOC Alto Adige Terlano Classico *see page 182*
**South Africa**
Clos Malverne Sauvignon Blanc 02 WO Stellenbosch *see page 214*
Delheim Sauvignon Blanc 01 WO Stellenbosch *see page 214*
**Spain**
Con Class Vendimia Excepcional 01 DO Rueda *see page 227*
Mantel Blanco Verdejo-Sauvignon Blanc 01 DO Rueda *see page 227*
**USA-California**
Canyon Road Chardonnay 99 *see page 245*

## Red €9–€12
**Australia**
Angove's Classic Reserve Shiraz 00 *see page 76*
Blewitt Springs Cabernet Sauvignon 98 *see page 77*
Peter Lehmann Clancy's 00 *see page 79*
Wyndham Estate Bin 888 Cabernet Merlot 00 *see page 81*
Wyndham Estate Bin 555 Shiraz 00 *see page 80*
**Chile**
Miguel Torres Santa Digna Cab Sauv 00 *see page 104*; **Rosé** 01 *see page 255*
Santa Carolina Merlot Reservado 99 *see page 105*
Viña Tarapacá El Tranque Cabernet Merlot 99 *see page 106*
**France**
Ch. de Ruth 99 AC Côtes du Rhône *see page 150*
Ch. d'Or et de Gueules 98 AC Costières de Nîmes *see page 162*
Comté de Mérinville 97 AC Minervois *see page 163*
Les Maîtres Vignerons 98 AC Côtes du Rouss. Villages Tautavel *see page 165*
**Italy**
Archidamo 00 DOC Primitivo di Manduria *see page 188*
Tormaresca 99 IGT Puglia *see page 189*
Millesimato Riserva 99 DOC Teroldego Rotaliano *see page 189*
**USA-California**
Talus Cabernet Sauvignon 98 *see page 249*

# The tasting panel

*All the members of the tasting panel are professionally qualified, holding the WSET Diploma or equivalent, with many years' experience of tasting.*

**Niamh L. Boylan** is a food and wine consultant. She lectures for the Wine Development Board and the Restaurants Association of Ireland and is a council member of the Irish Guild of Sommeliers.

**Barbara Boyle** turned to wine after ten years as a tax and financial consultant. She gained a distinction in the WSET Diploma and is Chairwoman of the WSET Diploma Students' and Graduates' Wine Club. She was joint editor of *The Wine Guide 2002* and contributes on wine subjects to various publications.

**Pat Carroll** is a food and wine editor. She was joint editor of *The Wine Guide 2002*, has lectured for the Wine Development Board and is Secretary of Premier Cru Wine Club.

**Tony Cleary** has worked for twenty-five years in the wine trade. He now works for Barry & Fitzwilliam in the sales division and lectures to trade groups and wine clubs. He covers all wine areas but specialises in Central and South Eastern Europe.

**Colm Conaty** is a sales representative with TDL.

**Willie Dardis** is Regional Manager for TDL, a member of the Irish Guild of Sommeliers and Vice-Chairman of the WSET Diploma Students' and Graduates' Wine Club.

**Martina Delaney** has been sommelier at L'Ecrivain restaurant since 1993.

**Bairbre Ennis** works for On the Grapevine and lectures for the Wine Development Board.

**Sheila Gahan** is a director of Wilson Hartnell Public Relations. Outside the day job, her wine interests include researching and sourcing wines for Corbally Wines, a family business. She is a member of the WSET Diploma Students' and Graduates' Wine Club.

**Catherine Griffith** is a wine consultant to Molloy's Liquor Stores and lecturer for the Wine Development Board.

**Hilary Hough** is an accountant and financial consultant who has worked most of his life with Bank of Ireland. Describing himself as 'a lover and collector of wines' he organises regular tastings and trips for the Elm Park Wine Club, one of the largest and most active wine clubs in the country.

**Evelyn Jones** is the proprietor of The Vintry wine shop, Rathgar, and winner of the Gilbey/Noffla Irish Off Licence of the Year Award 2002. She is a member of the Champagne Academy and runs wine appreciation courses as well as a wine club.

**Jacinta Kennedy**, is Off-Licence Specialist with Banesto Group comprising the Super-Valu Cellars in Raheny, Killester, Stockwell Lane, Drogheda and Custom House Quay, Wexford.

**Sinead Lewis**, formerly of Searsons Wine Merchants and the Wine Development Board, is an independent wine consultant. She won the Maggie McNie Tasting Cup in 1998.

**David Lonergan** is manager of The Vintry wine shop in Rathgar. He lectures for the Vintry Wine Club, where his particular forte is the Rhône Valley. He is a member of the Champagne Academy.

**Canice McCarthy** is a freelance consultant. He has written for the People Group of newspapers. He is a member of the Guild of Sommeliers and runs wine appreciation courses in Malahide Community School.

**Cathal McHugh** has worked in the wine trade for seven years and is the proprietor of McHugh's Off Licence. He also runs a wine club in Sutton.

**Julie Martin** is an award-winning sommelier and has represented Ireland; she is ranked Commandeur in the Association Internationale des Maîtres Conseils en Gastronomie Française, has worked at Ashford Castle and Restaurant Patrick Guilbaud, and is Secretary of the Irish branch of the Champagne Academy.

**Ben Mason** runs and owns the Wicklow Wine Co. with Michael Anderson.

**Robert Mooney** works for Superquinn, Sutton.

**Anne Mullin** is co-founder of WineOnline and a council member of the Irish Guild of Sommeliers. She travels extensively to source, taste and buy wines from world suppliers.

**Monica Murphy** of Febvre is a professional wine and cheese consultant, lecturer and writer.

**Ciaran Newman** is a Director of Cheers! Take Home and a council member of the Licensed Vintners' Association.

**Maureen O'Hara** is brand manager with Findlater Wine Merchants.

**Alan O'Toole** works for Searsons Wine Merchants.

**Lorna Jean Poulot** is a wine consultant for O'Brien' Wine Off-Licence and lectures for the Wine Development Board.

**John J. Quinn** owns a management training company, Priority Management, and conducts wine appreciation courses and American wine evenings.

**Douglas Stewart** works with wine importer Kelly & Co.

**Kevin Summons-Walsh** is a confirmed wine hobbyist, being a member of five wine clubs. He lectures on sherry, and also teaches tasting to Dublin WSET Diploma students.

**John Wilson** is an independent wine consultant. He has wide experience of the wine trade in Ireland and the UK.

# Tasters' choices

Here is an interesting selection of favourite wines from members of our tasting panel. They were invited to write about wines (from firms other than their own if they are in the trade) tasted within the last six months or so. There was no limit to the price, and wines could be chosen from among those blind-tasted for this book or tasted on other occasions.

*Niamh Boylan*

## Cannonau di Sardinia 'Le Bombarde' DOC Sardinia 00
*Italy, Sardinia €12–€15*

This smoochy Italian was given to me as a present a few months ago and I've been in love with its easy-drinking style ever since. Cannonau is the local Sardinian name for Grenache, that lovely fruity, spicy grape of Southern France, also much used in Australia and Spain. In fact, this wine, though from the Old World has a New World appeal to it. It is soft, smooth and spicy with flavours of wild mountain herbs and some good gamey flavours. I love the individuality of these local wines. This is so versatile when it comes to food and is particularly good with anything cooked with olive oil and garlic. *Sardinia Wines*

## Casa Rossa di Mizzole IGT Rosso di Verona 98
*Italy, Veneto €15–€18*

This smashing wine from the north-eastern region of Verona has a very enticing garnet hue. It is bursting with ripe redcurrants, loganberry and cherry fruits with some subtle hints of spicy peppercorns and violets. I kid you not—many classy Italian reds have a delightful whiff of violets. It tastes delicious, like a good cherry fruit tart with a refreshing lick of zesty citrus. Lots of class at a great price. Like all Italians this is a foodie's delight—try it with polenta and chicken or a wild mushroom risotto, or anything else you fancy! *TDL*

*Barbara Boyle*

## Dom. d'Auphilac Blanc VdP du Mont Baudie 00
*France, Languedoc-Roussillon €18–€22*

This is exactly the kind of white wine that I particularly like—an interesting blend of grape varieties and extra dimensions added through oak. Made from Ugni Blanc, Grenache Blanc and Chardonnay in the proportions 40/40/20, a quarter is fermented in barrel and the wine is aged for one month in oak. The colour is a deep lemon; the nose has mineral qualities as well as lemon and lime aromas; the palate is fantastically flavoured with candied peel, grapefruit, apple and apricot with the wood adding a very light and subtle toasty dimension. *Wicklow Wine Co.*

## Dutschke St Jakobi Shiraz 99
*Australia, Barossa Valley €30–€35*

Over the past year I seem to have drunk quite a bit of Shiraz/Syrah. In the process I found a large number of wines that I would recommend. One of these is St Jakobi from Dutschke, although for my own personal taste, I admit to drinking it far too young and intend waiting a year or two before approaching another bottle. It is a huge but elegant wine, with a nose of menthol, plum and some vanilla spice and a rich and concentrated palate which is very plummy with liquorice, spice, chocolate, leather and tarry flavours and a bitter or herbal twist on the finish. This is a real treat; decant it if you drink it over the next year as this will definintely open it out even more. *WineKnows*

## Zaca Mesa 96
*USA, California, Santa Barbara County €35–€40*

With 20 per cent Viognier added to Syrah, this is a Côte Rôtie lookalike. The nose is very big and when it opens out it is also quite developed with aromas of strawberry, black fruits, smoke with sweet tobacco and is just a touch rubbery. The palate is very juicy with grainy tannins and Rhône-like pepperiness, chocolate, plum and fruitcake flavours and a terrifically fruity finish. *Terroirs*

*Pat Carroll*
## Champagne Gervais Gobillard Brut nv
*France, Champagne €25–€30*

This wine proves that good Champagne doesn't necessarily have to cost a fortune. It has a rich nose of ripe pears, baked almonds and strawberries. The palate is full of flavour, with lively acidity, bags of fruit with a hint of strawberry and a long, toasty finish. It's delicate, yet rich, fantastic value and much better quality than most Champagnes in this price range. Great as an apéritif.
*French Wine Unlimited*

## Sandalyn Verdelho 00
*Australia, Hunter Valley €18–€22*

Although Verdelho was introduced to Australia in the 1820s, Hunter Valley Verdelho isn't seen here very often. If you're looking for something quite different, this is one to try. It has an aromatic nose of flowers, peaches, honey and a little marzipan. A dry wine, with rich, peachy fruit, well-integrated alcohol and medium acidity, it's full bodied and mouth-filling, with flavours of apricots and tangerines. With its touch of spice, it can stand up to quite strongly flavoured food. Food match: Chicken, scallops, monkfish. *Inis Wines*

## Ch. Court Les Muts AC Saussignac 97
*France, South West €15–€18 (50cl)*

Though vines have been grown in Saussignac since the eleventh century, the area wasn't awarded AC status until 1982. Saussignac is beside Monbazillac and, if this wine is anything to go by, produces lovely sweet wine. Made from Sémillon it has a wonderful nose of butterscotch, toffee and honey, with extra layers of aroma from *Botrytis cinerea* ('noble rot'). This special fungus thrives in areas near rivers, where morning mists and afternoon sun encourage its growth, which results in shrivelled grapes with concentrated sweetness and flavour. The palate is sweet, with delicious flavours of marmalade, cream and oranges. The wine has enough acidity to counter the sweetness and has wonderful length. It's remarkably good value—try it with foie gras. *Wicklow Wine Co.*

*Tony Cleary*
## Lustau Manzanilla Fino
*Spain, Sanlúcar de Barrameda* €9–€12 (50cl)

Once again I return to my favourite pre-dinner drink. I try and keep a half-bottle in the fridge at all times. Ignore the hype from 'marketing types' of Jerez (home of Fino sherry) who try and deny the salty tang of Manzanilla, it is there. Available from most good off-licences, where good turnover is guaranteed, thus ensuring freshness. Drink at one year old maximum. Just as uplifting as a 'G and T' but far less damaging to the old liver. *Mitchells*

## Ornellaia VdT 98
*Italy, Tuscany* €60–€80

The neighbour to the Supertuscan Sassicaia. A Supertuscan in its own right, but, even though the price is high, it is nowhere near the superstratospheric price of Sassicaia, which is almost impossible to find. During a trip to Tuscany this summer (2002), a visit to an 'enoteca' (literally a wine bottle library) in Florence produced two shocks. One, Sassicaia was not available, and two, Ornellaia was more expensive than at home, at around €120. Share the expense with some like-minded friends and try this superb wine. It is a perfect combination of fruits, spices, vanilla and woodland flowers. It has the longest velvety finish of any wine I have ever tasted.
*Woodford Bourne*

*Willie Dardis*
## Viña Casablanca Sauvignon Blanc 01
*Chile, Casablanca* €12–€15

From an area in Chile that is renowned for producing great Sauvignon Blancs, this producer has been acclaimed for producing one of the best examples. Vina Casablanca is owned by leading producer Santa Carolina. This wine is both subtle and complex with exquisite aromas of gooseberry and cut grass. Full flavoured and refreshing, it has a crisp, zippy, sweet lime and grapefruit palate, finishing with long, delicious and exotic overtones. It would be good with white meat or fish. *James Nicholson Wine Merchant*

## Zenato Ripassa DOC Valpolicella Superiore 99
*Italy, Veneto* €15–€18

One of Italy's most uniquely delicious wines made from a special process, affectionately known as 'baby' Amarone, this is a classic. The Valpolicella is passed over the post-winemaking skins of the Amarone which adds depth, concentration and complexity, thus making the new wine 'Ripassa'. A full- bodied, yet elegant wine it has pretty aromas of liquorice, berry and rosewood, surprisingly soft tannins, a palate of delicious berry flavours with some fruitcake and a soft vanilla finish. *Searsons*

*Sheila Gahan*

## Dom. Zind-Humbrecht Gueberschwihr Riesling AC Alsace 97

*France, Alsace €22–€25*

You only have to look at this wine to get a sense of its quality. It is beautifully clear, almost glossy, with a delicate and sustained nose of honeyed citrus fruit. For a wine that is over five years old, it is wonderfully fresh with only very faint hints of the petrolly characteristics that can over-power Riesling. On the palate it is lively with a burst of apples and lemon. The acidity is well integrated with the fruit and there is an elegant finish. Try it with fish, shellfish or oriental food. *Comans*

## Con Class Sauvignon Blanc DO Rueda 01

*Spain, Castilla-León €9–€12*

Once you get over the awful name ('with class'), this is a great example of a good value Sauvignon Blanc. From Rueda, one of Spain's best areas for quality white wine, in style Con Class is somewhere between the more austere Sauvignon Blancs of the Loire and the very aromatic New World Sauvignons. It is bursting with ripe gooseberries and tropical fruits. Dry and aromatic with a lovely lively finish. Great with rich shellfish like crab. *Searsons*

## Guelbenzu Azul VdM Ribera del Queiles 99

*Spain, Navarra €12–€15*

Spicy, almost meaty on the nose with fruits of crushed dark cherries and ripe plums. The aromatic characteristics of the dominant Tempranillo grape are much in evidence on the palate. This wine is dry, with integrated tannins and loads of ripe spicy dark fruits. It is a very attractive blend with a great structure and a finish of ripe cherries and blackcurrants that would go well with meat, especially lamb, and cheese. *Searsons*

*Hilary Hough*

## Alvaro Palacios Les Terrasses DO Priorat 99

*Spain, Catalonia €18–€22*

Les Terrasses 99 gives a very good and reasonably priced introduction to the superb winemaking skills of Alvaro Palacios and to the unique attractions of the growing number of excellent wines emerging from the Priorat region, south west of Barcelona. This is a wine with a dark brooding colour, an intense nose of fruit and spice and a palate that bursts with layers of blackcurrant fruit, liquo-rice and spices. It is an excellent example of a great coming together of terroir and fruit with a skill that extracts all that's best from both in a wine that packs a big impact and lingers for a long time on the palate. The almost burning level of alcohol evokes vivid memories of the searing sunshine experienced on a recent visit to the remote hilltop town of Gratallops where Alvaro Palacios crafts this wine and its more famous and massively expensive cousin L'Ermita. *Approach Trade*

*Evelyn Jones*

## Castello Banfi DOC Rosso di Montalcino 00

*Italy, Tuscany €22–€25*

'Rosso di' implies a wine in the style of Brunello but lighter, therefore faster maturing. This wine offers the chance to experience this classic wine style without having to wait ten years and at half the usual price. Do not be misled by the use of the word light. This is a rich, concentrated wine, with that stylish signature of good Italian wine in the form of black cherry with hints of cacao and smoke and a lovely foil of tartness. Try it with chargrilled lamb chops now, or lay it down for three to five years and experience the added dimension of bottle age. *Febvre*

## Marc Brédif Réserve Privéee AC Vouvray 97

*France, Loire €22–€25*

Made from Chenin Blanc, this is a dry Vouvray with a lovely, tangy sweet sour influence of lime and good waxy wild honey. It is elegant, yet it has power and concentration with lovely weight in the mouth and a refreshing yet rich finish. Even though it is over five years old it has barely started to acquire bottle age and will easily keep and improve for another five. Chill lightly and try it with some sweet shellfish like crab or lobster. *Morgans*

## Sarget de Gruaud-Larose AC St Julien 97

*France, Bordeaux €25–€30*

The second wine of Ch .Gruaud Larose this is a classic and classy Bordeaux drinking really well now. Blackcurrant, plums, cedar and smoke combine with a stylish structure and ripe tannins to give a taste experience one normally associates with a classed growth. Yet this wine does not have a classed growth price. Worth every last cent! *Comans*

*Jacinta Kennedy*

## Ruinart Brut 95

*France, Champagne €55–€60*

The house of Ruinart was established in 1729 making it the oldest Champagne house. Dom Thierry Ruinart, a priest in Reims and well known scholar, observed the work of his friend and fellow Benedictine monk Dom Perignon from whom he learned the secret of 'the wine that sparkles'. Ruinart is a unique Chardonnay style Champagne house. The 95 is considered the first real vintage since 1990 and many of these Champagnes are just about appearing on our shop shelves. This Champagne is almost half Chardonnay, all from premier cru sites, and half Pinot Noir. It has an excellent complex nose, creamy brioche with gentle hints of fresh tropical fruits and a very slight toasted aroma. The palate is full bodied, refined and restrained with an elegant mousse. Hints of apples and pears with a lovely mineral finish. A beautiful glass of Champagne now but will definitely develop more toasty complex flavours with further ageing. *Taserra*

## Ch. Vignelaure AC Coteaux d'Aix-en-Provence **97**
*France, South €18–€22*

Ch Vignelaure 97 is a wine I consume on a regular basis, particularly because I had a hand in making the wine by picking grapes on a visit to Vignelaure in that year. Provence is my favourite spot in the world and I understand entirely why the O'Brien family swapped training horses for making wine. David O'Brien has certainly established La Source de Vignelaure as being one of the best rosé wines made in France, winning Gold Medals at the Concours Générale in Paris on a number of occasions. The 97 red Ch Vignelaure is such a good expression of the Provence terroir by virtue of its blending of Cabernet Sauvignon and Syrah. Grapes are hand picked ensuring that only the best quality grapes get vinified. The wine was matured in new partially toasted American oak barrels. Wood ageing is very evident on the nose of this wine with fresh pencil shavings immediately evident and quite dominant. The palate has warm berry fruit flavours, Cabernet's blackcurrant mixing quite well with quintessential peppery Syrah flavours. These combine with a strong tannic grip giving a full-bodied mouth feel and good, medium length.
*James Nicholson*

*David Lonergan*
## Laurent–Perrier Brut Rosé nv
*France, Champagne €40–€50*

This is one of the best known pink Champagnes produced, and certainly has a keen following on the Irish market. There is only one problem with this wine – it is too easy to drink! One of the most memorable nights of my life was dinner at Laurent-Perrier's country house during the summer of 2001 in Tours–Sur-Marne, where the hospitality and ambience were unforgettable, and since then I have always had an extremely high regard for this family-run house. Full of ripe strawberry, raspberry and red fruits of the forest, the Champagne has lovely balance with freshness of acidity and layers of flavour, altogether a classy wine. It is a joy to drink on its own as an apéritif or with red fruit desserts it is a real treat. *Gilbeys*

## d'Arenberg d'Arry's Original Shiraz Grenache 00
*Australia, McLaren Vale €12–€15*

This is a wine made in an old-fashioned style; in other words, it's allowed to make itself. Made from old, low-yielding vines, the grapes are hand–harvested and gently crushed, then open fermented, where traditional foot treading takes place. It is aged in oak barrels for 18 months. This wine is neither fined nor filtered, which keeps the heart in the wine, and results in a harmless deposit in the bottle. I feel a lot of Australian Shiraz can be overly heavy, but here the Grenache softens it nicely. The wine is full of spicy, earthy, ripe cherry, mint and dark fruit flavours, plenty of extract, concentration and a fair bit of tannin – which will allow it to age nicely in bottle, giving even further complexity. A hearty winter wine, best with food. Spiced lamb dish would be good. *Taserra*

### Candido Duca d'Aragona IGT Salento Rosso 96
*Italy, Puglia €18–€22*

Another little gem from Southern Italy, where wine making standards have come on in leaps and bounds in recent years. This, combined with an array of local grape varieties, each having its own special characteristics, is resulting in wines with unique, complex flavours, not matched anywhere else in the wine making world. This wine from Puglia is made from Negroamaro and Montepulciano grapes. It has intense, complex aromas of earthy, spicy, chocolate raisin and dried cherry and black fruits; on the palate it is rich and full with the dried fruits spice and chocolate coming through, and a good backbone of tannin—all beautifully balanced. A nice accompaniment to a good pepper steak. *Findlaters*

*Canice McCarthy*
### Bethany Schrapel Family Vineyards Grenache 00
*Australia, Barossa Valley €9–€12*

Soft, very attractive, ripe, stewed fruit nose with lovely cherry and eucalyptus flavours. Palate is full and warm with mouthfilling spicy fruit flavours, almost chewable. Full, warm feeling on the long, fruity finish from the higher than usual alcohol. *O'Briens*

### Pepperwood Grove Zinfandel 99
*USA, California €9–€12*

Soft, warm, fruity nose with full flavours of strawberries and soft fruit. The palate has plenty of soft stewed fruit flavour with the strawberries much in evidence, also nicely integrated hints of spice, and all these flavours carry forward onto the long finish with just enough tannins. *Gleesons*

### Chanson Perè et Fils AC Viré-Clessé 01
*France, Burgundy €12–€15*

Soft, fruity nose with hints of minerals and of butter and citrus. Palate is full and smooth with an underlying crispness and freshness with clean fruit flavours and a persistent, almost mellow, smoothness. The wine could be described as similar to a Macon but with the fullness and sweetness of a Pouilly-Fuissé. *O'Briens*

*Julie Martin*
### Nepenthe Lenswood Riesling 00
*Australia, Adelaide Hills €15–€18*

An elegant example of displaying everything harmoniously, and nicely viscous in the glass. A fresh and lively wine with a bouquet of exotic dulcet notes, exuding honeyed melon and papaya along with some steely, ripe green kiwi and lime fruit aromas. Exuberant bossy flavours mingle and expand on the palate, all these fruits coming through with the added nuance of wax and lanolin. Its fresh acidity can be matched with turbot in a tomato cream on pasta with snipped chives. A lovely quality wine with a great tangy finish. *Barry & Fitzwilliam*

## Villa Maria Private Bin Riesling 01
*New Zealand, Marlborough €12–€15*

I was at the tasting table when the Villa Maria Private Bin Riesling 01 was awarded star status. It's another stunner, and being from New Zealand comes from a cooler maritime climate than Australia. This and the Nepenthe are fabulous examples of Riesling, so get out there and see what you're missing. *Allied Drinks*

## Campillo Reserva DOC Rioja 95
*Spain, Rioja €18–€22*

This is old style, traditional Rioja. Definitely not a beginner's red wine, more for the connoisseur. First and foremost it needs roast beef, but if you are of the vegetarian, non-vegan variety fine cheeses will suffice. It's definitely a winter warmer to be savoured. During this so called summer I noticed it warming up my legs and feet, arms and hands that I hadn't realised were cool. It made me laugh to be captured by its glow in this mad weather. The Campillo bodega has 50 hectares of mature Tempranillo vines growing in the Laguardia region. After the harvest it had two years in oak and three years bottle age leaving it to mellow and fine. Ruby, turning garnet in colour, with a fading brick rim indicating age. Smooth and velvety, with warm wafts of old oak, supporting tannins and still some baked plum compote fruit in a robust and silky palate.

The front label tells how many bottles were made in the 95 vintage, which is 757,968 and this is number 405151. It has 13 per cent volume alcohol and comes with the Rioja DOC seal over top foil. *Barry & Fitzwilliam*

## Mateus Rosé Sogrape
*Portugal Under €9*

This country mansion is an historic palace and is featured on the never changing Mateus Rosé label. It dates back to to the begining of the 18th century, and is a masterpiece of baroque architecture. The brand is one of the best selling in the world and most appealing of all, it is available everywhere and has been for as long as I remember. For those of you sticking fingers down throat the fact remains that this has been the first stepping stone for many a wine drinker, and it is extremely versatile. Sogrape's founder Fernando van Zeller Guedes is responsible for the famous bottle. It is vinified by a method they call 'bica aberta' which is a long fermentation, under controlled tempratures yielding the fresh and fruity wine. Basically what they do is white wine vinification with red grape varieties. Believe it or not it is a perfect match with Chinese and Thai food, and should feature more as house wine in these restaurants.

Nicely chilled as an apéritif before going out, great for barbecues and picnics for sailing, lunch box for the golfer etc., etc. It doesn't mind having the odd splash of sparkling water or lemonade to dilute down the alcohol for the mostly forgotten but most important grannies and grandads. (My granny thinks it's just lovely, she's 96.)

A Pimmless Pimms can be achieved if you're having a party, made with one third Mateus, one third red or white lemonade and one third vermouth. Lots of sliced juicy fruit excluding bananas and a ladle to serve. *Dillons*

*Ben Mason*

## Angelo Gaja 'Promis' IGT Toscana 99
*Italy, Tuscany €25–€30*

Angelo Gaja Piedmont wines are legendary; no producer in Italy scores consistently higher marks, or fetches higher prices. Until recently I had never tried one of Gaja's wines primarily because a starting price for one of his basic Nebbiolos is nearly €40, while his top end stuff stretches to €250. 'Promis' actually comes from Gaja's newer vineyards in Montalcino, Tuscany. You can pick it up for about €27, and it is a blend of Sangiovese (25 per cent), Merlot (45 per cent) and Cabernet Sauvignon (30 per cent). I think this is a sensational wine with rich, smoky aromas combined with black cherry and plum fruit. The palate is dense and structured with concentrated, spicy blackcurrant fruit. With firm ripe tannins and a long soothing finish, it should age very well. Available in specialist Italian selection shops such as Michael's Wines, try it out now, while it remains good value for a Gaja wine.

## Ch. de Gourgazaud Réserve AC Minervois La Livinière 99
*France, Languedoc-Roussillon €12–€15*

To me this is the quintessential Languedoc wine with full powerful aromas of baked black fruits, hot dusty earth, olive, and aniseed. Its complex aromas really draw you in. Despite its sturdy tannins and high acidity it remains an elegant wine with lovely enticing spice laden fruit. With a little more bottle age it should mellow out nicely in time for Christmas.
*Kelly & Co.*

*Maureen O'Hara*

## Ch. Court-les-Mûts AC Bergerac Sec 00
*France, Bordeaux €9–€12*

A Sauvignon/Sémillon blend, with a bit of oak I thought this wine was a cracker. When you tire of big, blowsy New World wine styles, this one refreshes the parts that other wines cannot reach. It is dry, with a lovely rich rounded palate, and has a soft, rich almost oily texture. The fruit flavours include herbaceous/green apples, nicely softened with apricot flavours. The palate seems to go on forever.
*Wicklow Wine Co.*

## Mount Pleasant Elizabeth Hunter Valley Semillon 95
*Australia, Hunter Valley €15–€18*

Another white worthy of a detour to a good off-licence, who will often have an older vintage available,sometimes (if you're lucky) back to 94. Depending on the age of the wine, it develops succulent, oily, petrolly flavour, and a rich golden colour as it matures. It's a real eye-opener for someone who has never tasted a mature white wine before. The flavours are quite complex, from honey, to hazelnuts, to lemon, to buttered toast to petrol. Superb. *TDL*

*Lorna-Jean Poulot*

## René Michel AC Viré-Clessé 99

*France, Burgundy €15–€18*

This new appellation was created in November and was formed by combining the Mâcon-Viré and Mâcon-Clessé sub-appellations and recognising the wines from Viré-Clessé in their own right, above and beyond Mâcon-Villages. Here, René Michel presents a unique and interesting wine full of intrigue and flavour. It has a complex, pungent, developed nose with aromas of oranges, apple peel and smoked cheese that follow through to the palate and are enhanced by a fat, waxy mouthfeel with a good backbone of acidity and pleasant kick of alcohol. The wine finishes on a lingering, spicy note. *Searsons*

## Ch. Kafraya Les Breteches 00

*Lebanon €12–€15*

Here is a super red from the Lebanon full of character and oozing with flavour. There is a touch of volatile acidity on the nose often encountered in wines from this part of the world. Baked fruit and raisins aromas, with complex, developed vegetal and meaty undertones, lead to a sumptuous palate of juicy, sweet dried prunes, mingling with stewed blackberries, dark chocolate and appealing autumnal forest tones of wild mushrooms and damp earth. *James Nicholson*

*John J. Quinn*

## Reichsgraf von Kesselstatt Josephshöfer Riesling Kabinett 99 *Germany, Mosel-Saar-Ruwer €15–€18*

When you consider that Reichsgraf von Kesselstatt only use the Riesling grape variety for their yearly production of 14,000 to 20,000 cases of wine, and that they have been making wine since 1349, you could assume that they are very, very good at what they do. And you would be absolutely correct. When I visited them, I had the opportunity to taste a wide range of their wines from the 99 and 00 vintages, from various sweetness ranges from Kabinett to Auslese and from a variety of their vineyard sites. Although both vintages were good, the 99s seemed just that extra bit fuller and richer. And of all of those, I liked the one from their Josephshöfer vineyard the best (although I also enjoyed wines from their other vineyards such as Piesporter Goldtröpfchen). This wine has got a lovely nose of grapefruits and lime. On the palate, it's just as youthful and fruity with very crisp acidity, balanced with just the right amount of residual sugar. This is just the right partner for rich Asian cuisine such as Thai coconut curries, Chinese sweet and sour dishes, or Indian dishes such as korma. The sugar and fruit is a match for the richness, while the acidity helps cut through the sauce. Another benefit is that it is only 8.5 per cent alcohol! If your only familiarity with German wines is Liebfraumilch, try this—you'll be hooked!

*Searsons*

*Kevin Summons-Walsh*

## Boekenhoutskloof Semillon WO Franschoek **00**
*South Africa, Paarl €15–€18*

OK, so Franschhoek Boekenhoutskloof isn't exactly the easiest wine to ask for. But this is a mouthful in more than just the name. The oaky nose (unusual in a Semillon) combines aromas of lemon sponge pudding, honey and lanolin. On the palate it scores with mouthcoating flavours of egg yolks and lemon curd, balanced by a refreshing acidity. Ending with a long, lemony, eggy finish, this is a serious white wine that needs minimal chilling. Try it with turkey or fried pork. More, please! *Oddbins*

## Vignaioli Asti DOCG Asti **nv**
*Italy, Piedmont €9–€12*

Asti (they've dropped the 'Spumante') has one of the naffest reputations in the wine world. It's definitely not cool to be seen drinking it. However, put your prejudices aside and just taste this wine outdoors in the heat of a summer's day. The aromas of ripe grapes and fresh strawberries jump out of the glass and are echoed on the medium sweet, fizzy palate. It even looks fun in the glass! The typically low alcohol content (7.5 per cent ABV) means you can drink more, without the hangover. Not all wines are meant to be 'serious'; for a dash of summer frivolity, this is hard to beat. Simply crack this open and add strawberries, sunshine and friends. *Dunnes Stores*

## Gonzalez Byass Apostoles Palo Cortado DO Jerez
*Spain €15–€20 (1/2 bottle)*

For those who think that sherry is sweet, sticky stuff fit only to be given to maiden aunts and vicars, this wine is a revelation. Yes, that's not a typo—sherry is wine. And, just like other wines, most of the best sherries are dry. This has a beautiful amber/mahogany colour. Aromas are of brazil nuts and real, creamy toffee—the sort your grandmother used to buy. The palate is dry, intensely nutty, with caramel and toffee tones and a huge, lingering finish. Consider: for around €15 you can drink one of the world's classic wines. If you don't appreciate it—fine; but do yourself a favour—you have to try this. Have some mature hard cheese or any type of nuts, on hand, for nibbling. And remember—a sherry is not just for Christmas.
*Barry & Fitzwilliam*

*John Wilson*

## Ch. Cheval-Blanc AC St Émilion 1er Grand Cru Classé **59**
*France, Bordeaux €900–€1,000*

I did not pay anything like the price above, but bought it more than a decade ago at the still expensive £50 a bottle. However, this was one of the greatest wines I have ever tasted. Superb, fragrant nose, with beautiful, amazingly youthful, very ripe fruit, intermingled with intense barnyard aromas, and great depth. All there on the palate, rich, full, sweet fruit, supple, almost lush, with classic Bordeaux acidity keeping it alive. Good length. Improved as the evening went on. Sublime.
*Corney & Barrow*

## Dom. de Trevallon AC Coteaux d'Aix en Provence **88**
*France, Provence €40–€45 (98 vintage)*

I paid about €19 for the 88 eleven years ago. Trevallon has always been one of my favourite wines. The price may have risen over the years, but I still believe it to be a relative bargain compared to many Bordeaux. Made from a blend of 50 per cent Cabernet and 50 per cent Syrah. Lovely nose, developed, complex ripe fruit, with herbs, barnyards; The palate similar, no sign of fading, but fully mature; lovely, pure, classy ripe plums, and cassis, with some barnyards, and a touch of garrigue; excellent length. A wine that sang to the heavens. The 98 will need about ten years. *Karwig Wines*

## Rockford Barossa Valley Local Growers Semillon 98
*Australia, Barossa Valley €12–€15*

Robert (or Rocky) O'Callaghan is one of the great characters of the Barossa. The key to his success is old vines, and very traditional methods. They are wines made without compromise. Most young Semillon is difficult to taste. This one wasn't. My wife and I nearly came to blows over the last few drops. Very closed at first, then a lovely, very distinctive nose, a hint of cloves with limes; absolutely delicious, lemon-lime fruit with a touch of lanolin and lots, lots more, carried along on a superb creamy texture. Even the tasting note on the back label is great—'a traditional full-bodied white which time will massage into a slippery yellow wine that just invites itself to lunch.' Need I say more? *Arbutus Wines*

# The mystery of vintages *Alan Crowley MW*

Part of the mystique of wine is which are the better or lesser vintage years? The importance of the vintage is the variability from year to year of weather conditions during the growing seasons. As an agricultural product, the effect is of particular importance on the potential quality of the final wine, especially in European wine regions. Thus, in good vintage years, grapes can be produced of a better quality to make a superior wine.

Wine regions with more regular weather conditions produce wines where vintages assume less importance. Such regions include the vineyards of South Africa, California, Australia and Chile. However, even in these regions knowledge of the vintage and wine style is important to ensure the optimum time for drinking the wine.

The following quick reference vintage chart is only a general guide as the best producers can make a good wine in 'off' years, and in good years a winemaker, or part of a wine region, can experience local problems resulting in an inferior wine. So the chart can only be viewed as a general guide and my opinion of when that wine is at its best.

# Vintage chart

AEach region for each year is given a mark out of ten for its vintage (revised September 2002).

**Key:** ↑ = Keep    ↗ = May be drunk—best will keep    → = Drink now    ↘ = Possibly past their best

| Region | 00 | 99 | 98 | 97 | 96 | 95 | 94 | 93 | 92 | 91 | Classic Vintages |
|---|---|---|---|---|---|---|---|---|---|---|---|
| Bordeaux Red | ↑10 | ↑7 | ↑7 | ↗7 | ↗8 | ↗8 | ↗6 | ↑6 | ↗3 | ↗4 | 90, 85, 82 |
| Sauternes | ↑7 | ↑8 | ↗7 | ↗8 | ↗8 | ↗7 | ↗4 | ↗4 | ↗3 | ↑3 | 90 |
| Burgundy Red | ↑6 | ↑8 | ↑7 | ↑7 | ↑8 | ↑8 | ↗6 | ↗8 | ↗6 | ↗7 | 90, 89, 88, 85, 83 |
| Burgundy White | ↑7 | ↑7 | ↗6 | ↗7 | ↑9 | ↑8 | ↗6 | ↗7 | ↗7 | ↘5 | 90, 89, 85, 83 |
| Rhône | ↑8 | ↑9 | ↑8 | ↗9 | ↗7 | ↗8 | ↑7 | ↗3 | ↑4 | ↑7 | 90, 89 |
| Champagne | ↑8 | ↑8 | ↑8 | ↑8 | ↗8 | ↗6 | ↑6 | ↑7 | ↗5 | ↗8 | 90, 85, 79 |
| Germany | ↗4 | ↗8 | ↗7 | ↗8 | ↑7 | ↗8 | ↑8 | ↑7 | ↑6 | ↑4 | 76, 75 |
| Spain | ↑7 | ↑8 | ↑7 | ↑8 | ↑7 | ↗9 | ↑7 | ↗6 | ↗7 | ↗8 | 82, 64 |
| Italy | ↑7 | ↑7 | ↑8 | ↑9 | ↗8 | ↗7 | ↗8 | ↑6 | ↗5 | ↑9 | 90, 85, 78, 71 |
| Port | ↑10 | ↑7 | ↑7 | ↑8 | – | ↑7 | ↑10 | – | ↑7 | – | 85, 77, 70, 66, 63 |
| Australia | ↑7 | ↑7 | ↗9 | ↗7 | ↗8 | ↑7 | ↑8 | ↑7 | ↑7 | ↑8 | 82, 79 |
| California | ↑8 | ↗9 | ↗7 | ↗6 | ↗6 | ↗7 | ↑8 | ↑7 | ↑8 | ↑9 | 74 |
| South Africa | ↗9 | ↗7 | ↗6 | ↑8 | ↑7 | ↑6 | ↑7 | ↑7 | ↑8 | ↑5 | |
| Austria | ↑8 | ↑9 | ↗8 | ↑7 | ↑7 | ↑8 | ↑8 | ↑8 | ↑8 | ↑7 | 90, 86, 85, 83, 79 |

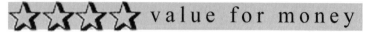

★★★★☆ value for money

# WHY WAKEFIELD?

## london
international wine & spirit competition 2002

GOLD MEDAL
promised land shiraz cabernet

## sydney
international wine competition 2002

GOLD MEDAL
wakefield merlot
wakefield shiraz

# why not?

australia's most awarded wine maker

# Grape varieties *Pat Carroll*

Most people like variety and winemakers are no exception. Their quest for something new and their desire to push back the boundaries mean that the range of wines from different countries grows each year. Unlike EU countries, where experimentation is often curtailed by regulations, winemakers in 'New World' countries such as Australia, South Africa, USA and South America can plant grape varieties and blend them more freely. The only limitation is that people must want to buy (and drink) them.

Freedom to plant what they want where they want allows New World winemakers great scope. California, which had only 27 ha of Syrah in 1990, now has nearly 6,100 ha. Such flexibility is impossible in Europe. In France, for instance, Pinot Noir has Appellation Contrôlée status only in certain areas. A Bordeaux producer cannot include it in an AC wine. Many New World producers, however, like the challenge of growing this tricky grape, with the result that many interesting (and steadily improving) Pinots are coming on to the market from countries such as New Zealand, South Africa, California and Chile. Another example is Viognier, which comes from the Rhône, but is now a fashionable choice for producers in Australia and South Africa.

But not all the interesting varieties we are increasingly seeing come from the New World—wines such as Salice Salentino from Italy (Negroamaro grape), various Portuguese wines (e.g. Touriga Nacional, Trincadeira grapes) and Greek wines (e.g. Aghiorghitiko grape) have been made for many years. The difference now is that winemaking techniques have improved so much that these wines are much more attractive to consumers than they were a number of years ago.

Of the thousands of grape varieties grown world wide, Cabernet Sauvignon and Chardonnay are still the best known, followed closely by Syrah/Shiraz, Sauvignon Blanc, Pinot Noir and Merlot. This year the grape varieties section has been expanded to include varieties that are becoming more popular—for example Aglianico and Primitivo from the south of Italy, Trincadeira from Portugal, Aghiorghitiko from Greece and Verdejo from Spain. As more wine drinkers try different wines, extending their experience, we can expect to see a wider range of lesser-known varieties on off-licence shelves over the next year.

> **How to use this book**
> *The wines are listed in order of country/region, colour (red or white), price band, then by name. If you can't quickly find the wine you are looking for try the index, which we have expanded for this edition. There are separate chapters for rosé, sparkling (including Champagne) and sweet wines. Since wine prices are not fixed the price bands are guidelines only. The dates suggested for when to drink the wines do not indicate their expected life but the period over which our tasters thought they would enjoy them most.*

# White

### Albariño/Alvarinho (Galicia, Spain; N Portugal)

| | |
|---|---|
| Dry, aromatic, lemon/peach aromas, full flavours of citrus and peaches, firm backbone of acidity; can become honeyed with age but usually drunk young | *Rías Baixas, Vinho Verde* |

### Chardonnay (originally from Burgundy but now grown everywhere)

| | |
|---|---|
| Chameleon—ranges from very dry, light, minerally, high-acid, citrus-dominated wines from cooler climates to dryish oaked heavyweights full of butterscotch, peaches, melons and pineapples from hotter regions; affinity with oak cask ageing | *Champagne, white Burgundy, including Chablis, Mâcon, Marsannay, Meursault, Montagny, Montrachet, Pouilly-Fuissé and Rully; varietal from Argentina, Australia, Bulgaria, California, Chile, New Zealand, South Africa* |

### Chenin Blanc/Pineau/Steen (Loire; South Africa; California)

| | |
|---|---|
| Dry to sweet, pale lemon in youth maturing to pale gold in older sweet wines, honey, wet wool and damp straw flavours, possibly nuts and marmalade in mature sweet wines; high acidity ensures that Loire sweet wines will age for decades | *Dry: Savennières, South African varietals, mass-produced Californian blends* |
| | *Dry/medium dry/sweet: Vouvray* |
| | *Sweet: Bonnezeaux, Coteaux du Layon, Montlouis, Quarts de Chaume* |
| | *Sparkling: Saumur Mousseux* |

### Cortese (Piedmont, NW Italy)

| | |
|---|---|
| Dry, crisp wines with fresh acidity, slightly floral, lemony aromas and steely lemon fruit | *Gavi* |

### Furmint/Mosler/Zapfner (Hungary, mainly Tokaji region; Burgenland, Austria)

| | |
|---|---|
| Dry or sweet, very high in acidity, high in alcohol, long lived, rich, fiery flavours—smoke, pears and citrus for dry wines, apricots, marzipan, citrus and spice for sweet wines | *Principal ingredient of Tokaji, Hungary's ancient sweet wine; Hungarian dry wines; Ausbruch (sweet) wines from Austria* |

### Garganega (Veneto, NE Italy)

| | |
|---|---|
| Dry, aromas of lemon and almonds in the best wines, fresh and fruity; drink very young | *Soave (with Trebbiano—dry), Recioto di Soave (sweet)* |

### Gewurztraminer/Gewürztraminer
(Alsace; Germany; Austria; Chile; New Zealand; Australia)

| | |
|---|---|
| Medium dry to sweet, colour can be deep; very characteristic perfumed aromas of lychees, roses and spice, flowery flavour but lacking the acidity of Riesling; classic accompaniment to spicy food | *Try a dry Gewurztraminer from Alsace for pure flavour; available as a varietal from Germany, Austria and the New World* |

### Gros Manseng (SW France)

| | |
|---|---|
| Dry but occasionally sweet, high acidity, floral, apricot and spice; character changes, depending on soil | *Béarn, Irouléguy, Jurançon, Pacherenc du Vic Bilh* |

### Grüner Veltliner (Austria)

| | |
|---|---|
| Dry, occasionally sweet, not much aroma in youth, complex, grapefruit, peppery, spicy flavours, ages well, taking on honey tones | *Grüner Veltliner varietals* |

### Macabeo/Maccabéo/Viura (Spain; S France)

| | |
|---|---|
| Nearly always dry, floral character, lowish acidity, resists oxidation well, sometimes blended into red wines | *In Spain whites from the DOs Alella, Bullas, Campo de Borja, Penedès, Rioja, Rueda, Utiel-Requena, part of Cava blends; in France white Corbières, rosé Coteaux du Languedoc, white Côtes du Roussillon, Fitou, and Minervois, vins doux naturels* |

### Malvasia/Malmsey (Friuli, NE Italy; central Italy; Sardinia; Madeira)

| | |
|---|---|
| Ancient grape, making dry to sweet styles, pale lemon (dry) to deep amber (sweet), nuts, cream and apricots, slightly spicy; early drinking or long ageing | *Collio, Isonzo, blended with Trebbiano in Frascati and central Italian whites; sweet wines in Sardinia; Madeira* |

### Marsanne (Rhône; Australia)

| | |
|---|---|
| Dry, deep coloured, full bodied, peach, honeysuckle and almond aromas (melons and mangos in Australia), quite heavy, usually matured in oak, often blended with Roussanne | *White Coteaux du Tricastin, white Côtes du Rhône, white Crozes-Hermitage, white Hermitage, white St Joseph, St Péray; varietal in Australia, e.g. Ch. Tahbilk* |

### Melon de Bourgogne/Muscadet (Loire)

| | |
|---|---|
| Very dry, light, fresh, crisp, some green apple flavours but often fairly neutral; best examples are 'sur lie' (matured in barrels containing yeast sediment); classic seafood wine | *In ascending order of quality—Muscadet, Muscadet de Sèvre et Maine, Muscadet de Sèvre et Maine Sur Lie* |

### Müller-Thurgau/Rivaner (Germany)

| | |
|---|---|
| Usually off-dry to medium-sweet wines, light in colour, not much aroma or acidity; not a quality grape; drink young | *Liebfraumilch blends and some varietals* |

### Muscat (Alsace; Rhône; Italy; Australia; Greece)

| | |
|---|---|
| Dry to very sweet, pale lemon (dry) to deep amber (sweet), marked grape and musk aromas, scented fruity flavours, touch of spice, moderate acidity | *Dry: Muscat d'Alsace* |
| | *Sparkling medium sweet: Asti Spumante* |
| | *Sweet: vins doux naturels from France, e.g. Muscat de Beaumes de Venise, liqueur Muscats from Australia and Greece* |

### Palomino (Jerez, Spain; South Africa; Australia; California)

| | |
|---|---|
| Low acidity, low sugar levels and its tendency to oxidise make Palomino the perfect grape for dry, medium or sweet sherry | *All styles of sherry—manzanilla, fino, amontillado, oloroso, palo cortado* |

### Parellada (Spain)

| | |
|---|---|
| Dry, lemon and flower aromas, zesty acidity, apple fruit; drink very young | *Blended in Spanish sparkling wine Cava and white Costers del Segre; 100% in Torres' Viña Sol* |

### Pinot Blanc/Pinot Bianco/Weissburgunder (Alsace; Italy; Germany; Austria)

| | |
|---|---|
| Mostly dry, some apple aromas, almonds in Austria, soft, quite full bodied, moderate/high acidity; usually for early drinking | *Alsace varietal, Italian varietal or blend, e.g. Colli Orientale del Friuli, Collio; Italian sparkling wine; dry wines from Pfalz and Baden; sweet and dry wines from Austria* |

### Pinot Gris (formerly Tokay d'Alsace)/Pinot Grigio/Ruländer/Grauburgunder
(Alsace; NE Italy; Germany; Austria; Australia; New Zealand; Oregon)

| | |
|---|---|
| In Alsace styles range from dry to sweet, with fairly deep colour and quite full body, slightly spicy, floral, perfumed aromas, peach fruit that develops buttery flavours with age—rich and spicy wine; drier, lighter, crisper and not so aromatic in Italy | *Varietal in Alsace, varietal in Italy or part of the blend in Collio; varietal elsewhere* |

### Riesling (Germany; Alsace; Austria; Australia; New Zealand; USA; South Africa)

| | |
|---|---|
| Dry to sweet, pale straw with green hints to deep gold in older sweet wines, floral and honey aromas when young, developing petrol-like notes on ageing; apple or peach flavours in Europe (depending on sweetness), limes in New World, piercing acidity, rich fruit on the palate; can age for decades | *Made usually as a 100% varietal, from dry to sweet, in Germany (Mosel-Saar-Ruwer, Rheingau, Pfalz, Nahe), Alsace, Austria, Australia, New Zealand (Marlborough and Central Otago), California, Oregon, Washington State, South Africa* |

### Roussanne (Rhône; Languedoc-Roussillon)

| | |
|---|---|
| Dry, aromatic, herbal aromas, elegant, good acidity, often blended with Marsanne | *White Châteauneuf-du-Pape, white Coteaux du Tricastin, white Côtes du Rhône, white Crozes-Hermitage, white Hermitage, white St Joseph, St Péray, whites from S France* |

### Sauvignon Blanc (Loire; Bordeaux; New Zealand; Chile; California; South Africa)

| | |
|---|---|
| Dry or sweet, grassy, herbaceous, gooseberries, green apples, even cat's pee aromas, with citrus and green apple flavours, steely acidity; mostly for early drinking | *Sancerre, Pouilly-Fumé, part of the blend in white Bordeaux and Sauternes; varietal from New Zealand (especially Marlborough), Chile, California (oaked), South Africa* |

## Peter
# LEHMANN
### The Barossa

### Grenache
A soft and smooth Australian red wine
with flavours of soft ripe berry fruits.
A fruit driven, easy drinking wine with
a mellow finish.

### Chenin Blanc
An Australian white wine with flavours
of apple and tropical citrus fruits.
A well balanced wine crisp, zesty and
easy to drink with no oak flavours.

## UNDURRAGA®
### EXCELENCIA EN VINOS DESDE 1885

### CABERNET SAUVIGNON
100% Cabernet Sauvignon from the
Colchagua valley. An intense ruby red colour
with ripe blackcurrant & vanilla flavours and
softening tannins perfectly balanced.

### SAUVIGNON BLANC
An excellent example of new world
Sauvignon. A fresh crispy wine with
zesty citrus fruit flavours and a long finish.

COMANS WHOLESALE LTD,
BELGARD ROAD, TALLAGHT, DUBLIN 24.
TEL: 01 - 451 9146. FAX: 01 - 451 9772.

### Sémillon/Semillon (Bordeaux; Australia; South Africa)

| | |
|---|---|
| Dry to sweet, light in colour to deep gold, not much aroma when young, perhaps some toast or wax, lowish acidity, but matures to nutty, waxy, honeyed aromas in Australia and honey and marmalade in Sauternes and Barsac; citrus and nuts on the palate in drier wines, marmalade and honey in sweet wines; very long-lived wines | *Most important grape in Sauternes, Barsac and white Bordeaux; varietal in the Hunter Valley and Barossa Valley; often blended with Chardonnay or Sauvignon Blanc in Australian wines; blended or varietal in South Africa* |

### Tocai Friulano (Friuli-Venezia Guilia, NE Italy)

| | |
|---|---|
| Dry, light colour, floral aroma, apple or almond flavours, should be drunk young | *Colli Orientale, Collio, Grave del Friuli, Isonzo* |

### Torrontés (Argentina; Spain)

| | |
|---|---|
| Dry, with distinctive flowery, Muscat-like fragrant nose, zesty acidity, rich, peachy fruit, some citrus; early drinking | *Blended or varietal* |

### Trebbiano/Ugni Blanc (Italy; SW France)

| | |
|---|---|
| Dry, light, high acidity, quite neutral flavour, medium body, workaday grape; early drinking | *Found in Trebbiano d'Abruzzo, Trebbiano di Romagna, Orvieto, Frascati, Soave, Lugana, Galestro, Vin de Pays des Côtes de Gascogne; base wine for French Cognac and Armagnac* |

### Verdejo (Spain)

| | |
|---|---|
| Dry, aromatic, slightly grassy character, pear flavours, good body; most drunk young but can age well, developing slightly nutty, honeyed nuances | *Rueda (blended with Viura or Sauvignon Blanc), Toro, Cigales* |

### Verdelho/Godello/Gouveio (Portugal; Spain; Australia; Madeira)

| | |
|---|---|
| Dry, fresh, lively, lemony wines of good quality; good ageing potential | *Dry whites from the Douro Valley, Spain and Australia; Madeira* |

### Verdicchio (Marches, central Italy)

| | |
|---|---|
| Dry, pale straw with green tinge, crisp, lemony acidity, nutty flavour with a mineral, salty edge, slight bitter almonds finish; drink young, though best can age for five years; good with seafood; semi-sweet and sweet wines also made | *Verdicchio dei Castelli di Jesi, Verdicchio di Matelica (white and sparkling)* |

### Vernaccia (Italy, especially Tuscany)

| | |
|---|---|
| Dry, crisp acidity, steely, citrus flavour, good body | *Several different Vernaccia wines in Italy, but the best is Vernaccia di San Gimignano* |

**Viognier** (Rhône; Languedoc-Roussillon; Australia; California; South Africa)

| | |
|---|---|
| Dry, pale straw developing to pale gold, apricot, peach and spring blossom aromas becoming honeyed with maturity, deep, rich palate with apricot and peach flavours, quite high alcohol; drink young, less than eight years old; moderate to low acidity | *Condrieu (vast majority dry, but a few producers make demi-sec wines), Ch. Grillet; can appear in Côte Rôtie; increasingly used in white Côtes du Rhône; vins de pays from Languedoc-Roussillon; varietal elsewhere* |

**Xarel-lo/Pansá Blanca** (Spain, especially Penedès)

| | |
|---|---|
| Dry, aromatic, fairly high acidity, vegetal, strong, earthy flavours | *Part of the blend in white Alella, Cava, white Costers del Segre, white Penedès, white Tarragona* |

# Red

**Aghiorghitiko/St George** (Greece, mainly on the Peloponnese in Nemea)

| | |
|---|---|
| Versatile grape, rich colour, very fruity, with spice, plums, blueberries, lowish acidity, soft tannins, full bodied, blends well with Cabernet Sauvignon; best wines from higher altitudes, as acidity retained | *Sole constituent of Nemea, ranging from fruity, early-drinking wines to meaty wines with longevity; also makes good rosés* |

**Aglianico** (S Italy, particularly Campania and Basilicata)

| | |
|---|---|
| Deep colour, aromatic, concentrated smoky berry fruit, tobacco tones, good acidity, very tannic in youth | *Taurasi, Aglianico del Vulture, Aglianico del Taburno* |

**Barbera** (Piedmont, NW Italy; Argentina; Australia; California)

| | |
|---|---|
| Deep ruby, fruity, full bodied, high acidity, not very tannic; for early drinking | *Barbera d'Alba, Barbera d'Asti, Barbera del Monferrato; varietal elsewhere* |

**Bonarda** (Argentina; N Italy)

| | |
|---|---|
| Dense, fruity, plummy, full-bodied, soft wines | *Rising star in Argentina; Oltrepò Pavese in Italy* |

**Brunello** (Tuscany, central Italy)

| | |
|---|---|
| Relative of Sangiovese, but with more flavour and body; plums, prunes and spice, fair bit of tannin, ages well | *Brunello di Montalcino* |

**Cabernet Franc** (Bordeaux; Loire; Australia; California; Washington State)

| | |
|---|---|
| Fragrant, lighter in colour and less tannic than its relative, Cabernet Sauvignon; redcurrant fruit, medium body | *Blended in Bordeaux, playing a more important role on the right bank of the Gironde in the St Émilion/Pomerol area; on its own or blended in Loire reds— Saumur-Champigny, Bourgueil, Chinon, Anjou-Villages; blended or varietal in New World* |

## Cabernet Sauvignon (originally from Bordeaux but now planted world wide)

| | |
|---|---|
| Deep ruby with a purple tinge, blackcurrants, chocolate, violets, green peppers, cigar-box aromas when mature, firm tannins; capable of very long ageing; good affinity with oak-cask maturing | *Blended in Bordeaux clarets, ranging in quality from AC Bordeaux through crus bourgeois to crus classés; on its own or blended in Australia (with Shiraz), California (with Merlot etc.), Chile, Italy (Supertuscans), South Africa, Spain, Romania, Bulgaria—everywhere* |

## Carignan/Cariñena/Mazuelo (S France—most widely planted grape variety in France; Sardinia; Priorat, Tarragona and Rioja)

| | |
|---|---|
| Lots of colour, tannin, alcohol and bitterness, but little fruit or aroma; some good examples from old vines in S France, but mostly blended with Cinsault and Grenache | *Part of the blend in many Languedoc-Roussillon wines such as Corbières, Costières de Nîmes, Coteaux du Languedoc, Côtes du Roussillon, Faugères, Fitou, Minervois, St Chinian; Carignano del Sulcis from Sardinia; can be part of blend in Rioja, Priorat and Tarragona* |

## Carmenère/Grande Vidure (Chile; Bordeaux)

| | |
|---|---|
| Deep ruby, red berry fruit aromas, soft red fruit flavours, mulberries, hint of chocolate, grilled meat, full bodied, similar to Merlot but less ageing potential | *Grown and bottled with Merlot in Chile for years, Carmenère is now produced as a varietal in its own right; rarely used in Bordeaux* |

## Cinsault/Cinsaut/Hermitage (S France; Lebanon; South Africa)

| | |
|---|---|
| Pale, soft, light, quite perfumed and fruity; used a lot for rosé in France | *Blended in Languedoc-Roussillon wines such as Corbières, Costières de Nîmes, Côtes du Roussillon, Faugères, St Chinian; blended with Cabernet Sauvignon and Syrah in Ch. Musar (Lebanon); crossed with Pinot Noir in South Africa to produce the Pinotage grape* |

## Corvina (Veneto, NE Italy)

| | |
|---|---|
| Light in colour, cherry and floral aromas, fruity wines with a hint of almond, lively acidity, low tannin; thick skins make it suitable for drying | *Up to 70% of the blend in Valpolicella, Recioto and Amarone Valpolicellas, Bardolino* |

## Dolcetto (Piedmont, NW Italy)

| | |
|---|---|
| Deep purple-ruby colour, soft, gentle wine with a touch of liquorice; drink young | *Dolcetto varietals, e.g. Dolcetto d'Alba* |

## Dornfelder (Germany; UK)

| | |
|---|---|
| Good colour, juicy, red berry flavours, can age for two to three years; variety developed for the German climate | *Dornfelder varietals* |

31

### Gamay (Beaujolais; Loire)

| | |
|---|---|
| Pale in colour with a bluish tinge, light wine with juicy red fruit aromas; some people find bananas and boiled sweets; drink very young | *Beaujolais, Beaujolais crus (Brouilly, Chénas, Chiroubles, Côte de Brouilly, Fleurie, Juliénas, Morgon, Moulin-à-Vent, Regnié, St Amour), Cheverny, St Pourçain* |

### Grenache/Garnacha/Cannonau (Rhône; S France; Spain; Sardinia; Australia; California)

| | |
|---|---|
| Fairly light colour, fruity, juicy, slightly sweet raspberry fruit, lowish tannin and acidity, high alcohol; can be spicy if not overcropped; huge variation in quality | *One of the ingredients in Châteauneuf-du-Pape; S France reds and rosés, vins doux naturels such as Rivesaltes and Banyuls (great with chocolate desserts), Spanish Priorato and Rioja; Cannonau di Sardegna; blended or varietal wines in Australia and California* |

### Malbec/Cot (Argentina; Cahors, SW France)

| | |
|---|---|
| Dark-coloured, ripe, tannic wines with good concentration and blackberry flavour; can be austere, peppery, spicy; wines age well | *Argentinian varietal; part of the blend in Cahors and other wines from SW France* |

### Merlot (Bordeaux; S/SW France; Italy; California; Washington State; South America; Bulgaria; Romania; Australia; New Zealand)

| | |
|---|---|
| Deep ruby, smooth, plummy, maturing to rich fruit cake flavours—velvety texture, with less colour, tannin and acidity than Cabernet Sauvignon; softer and earlier maturing | *Generic Bordeaux, St Émilion, Pomerol, Buzet, Cahors, vins de pays from S France, N Italian varietal, US varietal or 'Meritage' (a blend of Cabernet Sauvignon, Merlot, Cabernet Franc, Malbec and Petit Verdot); varietal elsewhere* |

### Molinara (Veneto, NE Italy)

| | |
|---|---|
| Pale colour, high acidity, juicy, easy drinking | *With Rondinella, up to 30% of the blend in Valpolicella, Recioto and Amarone Valpolicellas, Bardolino* |

### Montepulciano (central Italy, mainly Abruzzo)

| | |
|---|---|
| Deeply coloured, rich, brambles, cherries, pepper, spice, zesty acidity, firm tannins, best can age well | *Montepulciano d'Abruzzo, Rosso Conero, Biferno, Rosso Piceno (NB: Vino Nobile di Montepulciano is made with Sangiovese, not Montepulciano)* |

### Mourvèdre/Monastrell/Mataro (Provence; S Rhône; Languedoc-Roussillon; Spain; Barossa Valley, Australia; California; Chile)

| | |
|---|---|
| Lots of blackberry fruit, fleshy, high in alcohol and tannin, slightly meaty flavour in youth; blends well with Grenache or Cinsault, giving structure | *Blended in Bandol, Côtes du Rhône, Côtes du Ventoux, Vacqueyras, Costières de Nîmes, Côtes du Roussillon, Faugères, Fitou, Minervois, St Chinian; used in many Spanish DOs, e.g. Alicante, Almansa, Jumilla, Valencia, Yecla; varietal or blend elsewhere* |

## Nebbiolo (Piedmont, NW Italy; Argentina; Australia; California; South Africa)

| | |
|---|---|
| Not very deep colour, but powerful truffle, raspberry, liquorice, chocolate and prune aromas—even violets; high acidity, very firm tannins; usually needs long ageing | *Barolo, Barbaresco, Gattinara, Nebbiolo d'Alba, Valtellina; varietal elsewhere* |

## Negroamaro (Puglia, S Italy)

| | |
|---|---|
| Deep colour, high alcohol, rich, robust red wines, some of which can age well | *Salice Salentino, Rosso di Cerignola* |

## Nero d'Avola (Sicily)

| | |
|---|---|
| Dark colour, soft fruit, rich texture, responds well to barrel maturation and oak ageing | *Nero d'Avola* |

## Petit Verdot (Bordeaux; California)

| | |
|---|---|
| Rich colour, hint of violets on the nose, concentrated tannic wines with a touch of spice | *Used as a small part of the blend in Bordeaux clarets and Californian Meritage wines* |

## Petite Sirah (California; South America)

| | |
|---|---|
| Inky, quite tannic, firm, robust, full-bodied wines | *Unrelated to the Syrah of the Rhône; traditionally blended with Zinfandel in California, now offered as a varietal as well; varietal in South America* |

## Pinot Meunier (Champagne; Australia; California)

| | |
|---|---|
| Gives freshness, fruitiness and crisp acidity to sparkling wines | *Champagne; sparkling wines from Australia and California* |

## Pinot Noir/Pinot Nero/Spätburgunder (Burgundy; Champagne; Loire; Alsace; Austria; Germany; Italy; California; Oregon; Australia; New Zealand; South Africa; Romania)

| | |
|---|---|
| Light in colour and low in tannin, quite high acidity, magical sweet aromas of strawberries or cherries, turning to mushrooms, truffles and even farmyards as it ages; velvety texture; long ageing; used in sparkling wines to give body and fruit; best in cool, marginal climates | *Red Burgundy from basic Bourgogne to Grand Cru; blended in Champagne, used in sparkling wines from the New World; red Menetou-Salon, red Sancerre; varietal elsewhere* |

## Pinotage (South Africa)

| | |
|---|---|
| South African crossing of Pinot Noir and Cinsault, deep colour, strong tannins; best have good body and juicy berry fruit, but can have a paint-like aroma (seen less often nowadays) | *South African varietal and Cape blends* |

## Primitivo (Puglia, S Italy)

| | |
|---|---|
| Deep colour, early maturing, berries, liquorice, spicy fruit, good body, making full-bodied wines high in alcohol; related to California's Zinfandel | *Primitivo di Manduria, IGT wines* |

### Rondinella (Veneto, NE Italy)

| | |
|---|---|
| Robust grower, yields well, but a fairly bland variety, with less aroma and flavour than Corvina | *With Molinara, up to 30% of the blend in Valpolicella, Recioto and Amarone Valpolicellas, Bardolino* |

### Sangiovese (central Italy, especially Tuscany; Australia; Argentina; California)

| | |
|---|---|
| Slightly pale colour, very dry, cherry and possibly farmyard aromas, cherry and plum flavours, high acidity, robust tannins, slightly bitter finish; good for ageing, can be austere in youth | *Part of the blend in Chianti, Carmignano, Vino Nobile di Montepulciano, Torgiano and the Supertuscan Tignanello; varietal elsewhere* |

### Syrah/Shiraz (Rhône; Languedoc-Roussillon; Australia; South Africa; new plantings in California, Washington State, Chile)

| | |
|---|---|
| Deep colour, aromas of black fruits becoming gamey and leathery with age; intense blackberry, raspberry, earthy, spicy, pepper, burnt rubber flavours, more black cherries and chocolate in Australia; tannic, rich, needs time to soften | *Hermitage, Crozes-Hermitage, St Joseph, Châteauneuf-du-Pape, vins de pays from Languedoc-Roussillon; on its own or blended with Cabernet Sauvignon in Australia; varietal in South Africa; varietal or blend in the US; varietal in Chile* |

### Tannat (SW France; Uruguay)

| | |
|---|---|
| Very dark, very tannic, raspberry aromas, needs time in bottle; can age well | *Part of the blend in Madiran and Cahors; varietal in Uruguay* |

### Tempranillo/Tinta Roriz/Aragonez (Spain; Portugal)

| | |
|---|---|
| Deep colour, strawberry and tobacco aromas, low acidity and tannin, good for early drinking or ageing | *Blended or varietal in Rioja, Costers del Segre, Navarra, Penedès, Ribera del Duero, Somontano, Valdepeñas; Portuguese red wines; part of the blend in port* |

### Touriga Nacional (Portugal; Australia)

| | |
|---|---|
| Deep colour, mulberry aromas, concentrated fruit, high tannins; in port, very long ageing potential | *Part of the blend in port, Douro and Dão wines; Australian port* |

### Trincadeira Preta/Tinta Amarela (Portugal, mainly Alentejo and Ribatejo regions)

| | |
|---|---|
| Deep colour, strong tannin, good body, sturdy structure, plum and blackberry fruit, pepper and herbs | *Borba, Douro, Redondo, Reguengos, many IPR wines* |

### Zinfandel (California)

| | |
|---|---|
| Varies in style from very dark, alcoholic, bramble-flavoured reds to mass-produced sweetish 'blush' wines; can make excellent reds in the right hands | *Zinfandels in all shades from palest pink to deepest red* |

# Seasonal food and wine *Niamh Boylan*

Hailstones in July, heatwaves in October—global warming has run amok and made our seasons much less seasonal. However, our primal body clock still thinks 'spring', 'summer', 'autumn', 'winter'—the seasons provide a sort of framework for the year and condition the mind. And despite being able to eat strawberries in December and turkey in May, many foods are truly seasonal. So match the food and wine to the seasons and you won't go wrong. Don't forget the golden rule when matching food and wine— light wine with light delicate dishes and richer styles with more flavour- some foods.

On a miserable winter evening nothing appeals more than a flavoursome hotpot with a bowl of steaming mash and, of course, a glass of gutsy red wine such as a rustic Portuguese red or a deep, brooding Malbec from Argentina. Comfort food is the order of the day from traditional cottage pie, beef and Guinness stew or bangers and mash (posh ones, of course, as an excuse to open a hearty Shiraz). A good cheesey vegetable gratin or bean ragout with a Minervois or St Chinian from the Languedoc, a Salice Salentino from Puglia or a Cannonau from Sardinia will keep out the cold. Winter nights can be whiled away with pizza and Valpolicella, a cheesey pasta bake with an oaked Chardonnay or a more serious Saturday special of steak with a decent Cabernet or Merlot. Take your pick—traditional Bordeaux, Chilean or Aussie—red meat needs a structured red wine. Finish your meal with some good cheese and the wine.

We're also looking forward to the silly season—Christmas/New Year and parties galore. Both white and red wines work with turkey. Try a full-bodied white Bordeaux, or if you prefer red, choose something with moderate tannins—a Rioja Reserva or a good Merlot. Duck and goose are very rich and really need a biggie—think Shiraz, Supertuscan or a fine South African or Napa Cabernet Sauvignon.

If you're having ham I suggest Pinot Noir. The grape's acidity helps cut the fat. Beaujolais, too, works well; one of the Crus such as Morgon or Moulin à Vent would be a great choice. Alternatively, be daring and have a crisp Mosel Riesling—always good with ham or turkey.

New Year's Eve suggests Champagne. There's nothing quite like it to get the festive spirit going. It's the perfect apéritif, producing a frisson of anticipation, that enticing bubbly freshness getting the tastebuds going, but it can also be a wonderful match with food.

In spring whatever about young men's fancy etc. our eating habits change. We crave something light—lots of fish and new season's lamb with all those delicious new season vegetables. There's a sense of looking for- ward, an opportunity to try some exciting new wines such as those from Greece. You'll soon get your head around those difficult sounding grape varieties like Aghiorghitiko (red) and Roditis (white). You don't have to be a classical scholar to appreciate these great tastes.

Greek whites have plenty of rich flavour which perfectly complement many fish and light chicken dishes, particularly if onion and herbs are used in the cooking. They can stand up to food cooked in olive oil, so our spring resolution for healthy eating can extend to wine, too.

That delicious classic French dish, *Navarin d'agneau* (lamb stew to you and me) cries out for a nice red Côtes du Rhone or perhaps something soft

35

from Navarra. Irish stew can be a bit more difficult to match successfully: a medium weight Aussie Verdelho or a Vin de Pays Merlot would fit the bill. Australian Verdelho also goes well with roast vegetable dishes and mild Indian foods.

Fish cakes are a favourite family dish in our house and are perfect once the bright evenings arrive. Serve them with a light tomato sauce, crunchy sugar snap peas and a squeeze of lemon and choose a New Zealand Sauvignon Blanc or Riesling to drink. Quiches, too, are great at this time of year, whether it's the traditional partnership of Quiche Lorraine with ham and cheese and a Riesling, Pinot Blanc or Pinot Gris from Alsace, or a vegetable quiche such as broccoli and sweetcorn with a simple Vin de Pays, red or white. I had a fabulous pear and blue cheese quiche in South Africa— it was a delicious combination and went very well with an unoaked young Chardonnay, local of course.

Summer conjures up fantasies of sunshine. We may not get a lot of it, but we can certainly brighten up the long evenings with some delicious wine. Summer food is lighter with easy salads, lots of barbecues (hopefully) and tasty colourful dishes which are quick and simple to prepare. The golden rule of thumb certainly applies here—match the body and weight of the dish to the body and weight of the wine.

Many reds suitable for summer drinking benefit from light chilling which accentuates the fruity character of the wine. Italian reds such as Valpolicella and Bardolino are good candidates for chilling. So, too, are Beaujolais and some Loire reds and the lighter style of Zinfandel. Rosé wines come into their own now and are great with many salad dishes such as Salade Niçoise and poached salmon.

Barbecued meats take on a smoky caramelized flavour, so the accompanying wines need to have quite a punchy character. Avoid young wines with assertive oak or tannin. Reds with some spicy, smoky flavours will do the trick and really complement your best barbecue endeavours. Think light Shiraz, good Zinfandel or perhaps Pinotage from South Africa. Forget any prejudice about Pinotage. There has been a huge change in quality and style resulting in some very attractive easy-drinking wines, just right for barbecues. The South Africans, after all, are masters of the 'brai' as they call barbecues. Well-flavoured oaked Chardonnays, Marsanne and Pinot Gris are all whites which can take on barbecued fish and chicken. So, keep it cool and keep it light.

For a real summer treat try a bowl of ripe, luscious strawberries and cream or rich rhubarb mousse with a glass of sweet dessert Champagne Doux— what a wonderful climax to a special meal!

'Season of mists and mellow fruitfulness'—Keats' fruity reference gives us plenty of vinous scope. I love autumn—that dark leaf smell (mature Burgundy) smoky peat fires (Nebbiolo) and, of course, Hallowe'en's fruit and nuts. They bring to mind Chilean Cabernet, Aussie Grenache blends or a warming glass of good dry amontillado sherry. It's not cold yet but those darkening evenings need a cheering glass.

Start off with some tasty chicken or duck pâté or game terrine with a schooner of sherry. The warm nutty flavours go so well with pâté. It's time to revive sherry but do buy a good name such as Lustau or Domecq. There are some cheapies which taste pretty tacky and are best avoided.

Oysters, fish, game, pork and tasty pastas all come into their own at this time of year. One of the enduring great classical matches is oysters with Chablis. Heaven! For a more everyday meal try grilled mackerel smeared with Dalkey mustard and baby spuds for a quick and healthy supper which tastes even better with a zippy, clean Muscadet (remember Muscadet?), Soave or unoaked New World Chardonnay. Keep it light and crisp. Pork goulash is less heavy than the traditional Hungarian beef dish and is particularly tasty if you use smoked paprika in the sauce. Lots of flavour here so go for a robust rustic red from Cahors. Pasta calls out for Italian partners—Chianti, Barbera, Valpolicella.

If game is your thing, autumn is your season. Wonderful pheasant, widgeon, and wild duck all make their annual appearance. These birds love to be cooked with fruit—apples, dried apricots, prunes—and positively demand a fine wine. To keep it classical, indulge in a mature Barolo or Châteauneuf-du-Pape. Alternatively try a sexy Napa Cabernet. Wild mushrooms, too, are in season and add excitement to many dishes—chicken, guinea fowl, rich risottos. The earthy flavours are well suited to red Burgundy—it doesn't have to be a top *cru*. Rioja is another good choice.

It's all too easy to get in a rut where food and wine are concerned. Boring! By all means, have your old reliables, but take a chance and try some new flavours. I love the excitement of finding a great new taste combo. Recently I enjoyed a very simple garlicky roast chicken with a new favourite wine of mine, Fiano di Avellino. This is a vibrant, deeply flavoured Italian white with lots of rich, warm, nutty and wild herbal nuances. It comes from Campania in south-west Italy and shows the great variety of wines now coming to us from the Italians. Nothing wimpy or anonymous, just lots of taste and magic with the sweet garlicky flavour of the bird.

From the simple classics and everyday staples to the exotic and ethnic, there are wine choices for all tastes! There's no need to be pompous, just follow the suggestions in the tables on pages 41–50 and have fun finding your own favourites.

# Cheese and wine   *Sarah Furno*

Cheese and wine is a classic partnership. However, given the varieties of styles of both it is not surprising that matching them successfully requires some understanding of their different characteristics. The various types of cheese need wines that complement their flavours and textures—the wrong match can have disappointing results. Remember, too, that cheese, like wine, varies in quality (and price). The best matches come about when the qualities mirror each other.

There are seven broad categories of cheese: blue, fresh or curd, goats', hard, smoked, wash rind and white bloom or mould.

**Blue cheeses** such as Roquefort, Danish Blue, Gorgonzola and Cashel Blue, vary in flavour but all young blues are salty. Salt, like the rind of a mature, bloom ripened cheese, is a foe of tannin, resulting in off-flavours. Riper blue cheeses are far less salty and partner certain wines admirably. However, bear in mind that strongly-flavoured cheese demands a strongly-flavoured wine, possibly a fortified wine. Such burly partnerships are unlikely to leave room for the appreciation of the subtleties of either wine or cheese but do result in great length and richness of flavour as exemplified in the classic partnership of port and Stilton.

Salt in moderation and balance as in crumbly, slightly creamy yet tangy sheeps' blue works well with the sweetness of a botrytised Semillon or traditional, less fruit-driven style, Tokaji. If you are not a fan of sweet wines and find port too heavy, a fruit-driven Bordeaux blend or New World Merlot can also work well.

**Fresh** or **curd cheeses** include Ricotta, cottage cheese and cream cheese. These cheeses, as the name indicates, are not ripened and are therefore straightforward in flavour. The wine chosen should mirror the cheese's youthful characteristics. Sauvignon Blanc, Pinot Grigio, Lugana or zesty New World Riesling are all possible partners.

**Goats' cheese** may be soft or hard, fresh or matured, but always has a high level of acidity. Fresh and younger goats' cheeses tend to work better with white wines with marked acidity. Sauvignon Blanc is a good match for goats' cheese logs and the drier texture and sharp tang of miniature cheeses. Dry Vouvray complements slightly creamier styles. Hard goats' cheese is more difficult to match, though successful partners can be found for semi-hard versions among the Loire reds, and for the harder cheeses among medium-bodied Syrah/Shiraz.

When matching wine and **hard cheese**—Gruyère, Emmenthal, Cheddar, Parmesan, Comte—a lesson can be drawn from the old wine merchants' maxim: 'buy on an apple and sell on cheese'. The acidity of apples highlights a wine's thinness whereas the richness of protein in hard cheese balances the astringency of young tannins thus creating a pleasing, softer and fuller impression in the wine. However, young and tangy hard cheeses, such as Cheddar or Caerphilly, do not usually make particularly interesting combinations with wine and are better placed on brown bread with chutney and served with a glass of ale. Certain hard cheeses such as Comte, Gruyère or Gouda, can be surprisingly fruity in flavour; over-burly reds would overpower this characteristic. A well-oaked Chardonnay with a nutty edge would be a better choice here. If you decide to include a matured hard cheese on a cheese board you should treat it as you would a blue, balancing the strength of the cheese to the strength of the wine. Australian Shiraz, South African Cabernet or a robust Southern Rhône red can all work well, as can port or Tokaji, depending on the occasion.

While soft cheeses have a high level of acidity when young, hard cheeses have a higher level when old. This can be seen in the classic Italian partnership of Parmesan, a cheese aged for between two and four years, and the Nebbiolo-based wine, Barolo, known for its acidic character.

There are two types of **smoked cheese**, according to the method used, traditional or artificial. Artificial versions are easily recognisable by their overpowering, almost sweet, smoky taste, which is a not a good partner for wine of any quality. Cheese traditionally smoked under a haze of oak smoke retains a subtlety of flavour, and fidelity to its origins, and is well partnered by a fruity Gewurtztraminer.

**Wash rind** is the most difficult style of cheese to match to wine. Identifiable by their soft texture and orange to reddish, sometimes sticky rind, which is often edible but is rarely eaten, these cheeses tend to be fruity and chalky when young, developing a more pungent flavour and creamy texture with time. Examples include Reblochon, Gubeen, Milleens, Ardrahan, Munster, Époisses and Pont l'Évéque. Like fine wines, they should be allowed time to mature and develop complexity with flavours ranging from spicy to nutty with mushroomy notes. Irish makers of this style of cheese often feel that their cheeses are happier with beer rather than wine. Regional French combinations include the strongly flavoured, creamy Époisses with aged Burgundian Pinot Noir, and pungent Munster cheese with a fruity Gewurztraminer from Alsace.

**White mould cheeses,** e.g. Brie, Camembert, Cooleeney, are also difficult to match successfully with wine. They tend to coat the palate in a creamy film, reducing the ability to perceive flavours and they also highlight the acidity in younger wine. In addition, the edible rind of mature farmhouse Camembert is one of the greatest enemies of wine and it can result in a distinct bitterness when combined with a slightly tannic red. Successful partners tend to be either light and fruity reds such as a Beaujolais Cru or a New World Pinot Noir or, for the more adventurous, a delicately and roundly oaked Chardonnay with balanced acidity. It is usually better to stick to moderately mature cheeses as distinct from the style that run off the plate!

A single cheese in good condition partnered with a suitable wine is often better at the end of a dinner party than a complex **cheese board**. For less formal occasions, a cheese platter may form a substantial part of a picnic-style meal among friends. Light- to medium-bodied fruity reds work well, not only with a wide range of cheeses, but also with other elements of the meal such as salamis and cold meats. If you prefer white wine, the most versatile grape variety is Chardonnay, which can work not only with goats' cheese but also with young wash rind and fruity harder cheeses.

For a quick guide to matching cheese to wine see the following table. There is also a cheese section in our Matching Food and Wine table, pages 49–50. These are suggestions only, not rules, and are by no means exhaustive.

| Cheese style | Suggested wine style | Classic partnerships | Word of warning |
|---|---|---|---|
| **Blue**<br><br>cows' milk<br>e.g. Cashel Blue<br><br>sheeps' milk<br>e.g. Crozier Blue | *Medium-bodied fruity reds which aren't too tannic, mature St Émilion*<br><br>*Botrytised Semillon, Tokaji, Vin Santo* | *Roquefort and Sauternes* | *Avoid salty young cheeses*<br><br>*The acidity needs to balance the sweetness to avoid overpowering the combination* |
| **Fresh or curd**<br>e.g. cottage cheese | *Young fruity unoaked whites with good acidity* | | *Avoid fresh cheeses blended with garlic or herbs* |
| **Goats'**<br>(other than hard matured versions)<br>e.g. St Tola | *Sauvignon Blanc, dry Vouvray, unoaked cool climate Chardonnay* | *Crottin de Chauvignol and Sancerre* | *Wines from warmer climates may overpower the cheese with their fruit* |
| **Mature hard**<br>e.g. farmhouse Cheddar | *Cabernet Shiraz, Barbera d'Asti, Gigondas* | *Parmesan and Barolo* | *Tannins should not be overly assertive* |
| **Smoked**<br>e.g. smoked Gubeen | *Gewurztraminer, fruity Shiraz* | | *Avoid artificially smoked cheeses* |
| **Wash rind**<br>e.g. Ardrahan | *Mature Pinot Noir, aged Hunter Valley Semillon, Gewurztraminer, white Burgundy* | *Munster and Gewurztraminer* | *Flavours in the rind of ripe cheese may react badly with the cheese; it is advisable to remove the rind* |
| **White mould or bloom**<br>e.g. Cooleeney | *Lightly oaked Chardonnay, Beaujolais Cru, or fruity Pinot Noir* | *Chaource and Champagne* | *The rind of very ripe cheeses may react with tannin in red wines causing off-flavours* |

# Matching wine to food

*Compiled by Niamh Boylan and Barbara Boyle*

Grape varieties in *italics*.

| White | |
|---|---|
| *Albariño/Albarinho* **medium bodied** | *Shellfish, oily or smoked fish* |
| Bergerac **medium bodied** | *Fish and chips, vegetable soufflé, salads* |
| Bianco di Custoza **medium bodied** | *Light seafood, linguine with clams, risotto* |
| Bordeaux Blanc **medium bodied** | *Roast cod, chicken, pasta primavera* |
| Chablis, see also *Chardonnay*, **medium bodied** | *Oysters, simply cooked fish, soft creamy cheeses* |
| *Chardonnay* | |
|    unoaked **medium bodied** | *Chicken, fish, cheesy dishes* |
|    oaked **full bodied** | *Roast duck, coconut curry, barbecued salmon, fish pie* |
| *Chenin Blanc*, see also *Savennières*, Vouvray **light bodied** | *Fish terrine, vegetable quiche, creamy chicken, risotto, goats' cheese dishes* |
| Condrieu, see also *Viognier*, **full bodied** | *Crab, lobster, roast pork* |
| Entre-Deux-Mers **medium bodied** | *Simple seafood, crab soufflé, salads* |
| Frascati **light bodied** | *Shellfish, chicken noodles, pasta carbonara* |
| Fumé Blanc **medium bodied** | *Char-grilled fish, vegetarian dishes, chicken, mushroom based dishes* |
| Gavi **medium bodied** | *Polenta, veal, prawns* |
| *Gewürztraminer* **medium bodied** | *Fusion/pan-Asian, rich pâté, spicy food* |
| Graves | |
|    **medium bodied** | *Simple seafood, fish and chips, vegetable soufflé, salads* |
|    **full bodied** | *Guineafowl, turkey, richly sauced fish* |
| *Grüner Veltliner* **medium bodied** | *Fish, scallops, vegetarian dishes* |
| Jurançon **medium bodied** | *Fish, cheese fondue, salads* |
| Lugana **medium bodied** | *Pasta pesto, roasted vegetables* |
| Mâcon **full bodied** | *Creamy pasta dishes, roast chicken, seafood, cod* |
| *Marsanne* **medium bodied** | *Stir fries, Asian, chicken, shellfish* |
| Meursault see also *Chardonnay*, **full bodied** | *Lobster, monkfish, roast turkey, dishes with nuts* |

## White (continued)

| | |
|---|---|
| Muscadet **light bodied** | *Oysters, mussels, smoked mackerel, herb omelette* |
| *Muscat* (dry) **light bodied** | *Whitebait, Chinese, noodles, Indian* |
| Orvieto **light bodied** | *Fish, creamy pasta dishes* |
| *Pinot Blanc* **medium bodied** | *Quiche Lorraine, Thai dishes, fish, pesto* |
| *Pinot Gris/Pinot Grigio* **medium bodied** | *Light pork and bacon dishes, veal, fish, quiches, salads* |
| Pouilly Fuissé **medium bodied** | *Creamy pasta dishes, roast chicken, seafood* |
| Pouilly Fumé, see also *Sauvignon Blanc*, **medium bodied** | *Trout, smoked salmon, goats' cheese* |
| Puligny-Montrachet see also *Chardonnay*, **full bodied** | *Rich seafood, roast turkey, dishes with nuts* |
| *Riesling* | |
| (dry) **light bodied** | *Charcuterie, grilled fish, salads* |
| (off-dry) **medium bodied** | *Fusion, curries, dim sum* |
| Rhône **full bodied** | *Creamy curries, pork, mature cheeses* |
| Rueda **medium bodied** | *Salads, grilled fish, crab soufflé* |
| Sancerre, see also *Sauvignon Blanc*, **medium bodied** | *Avocado, smoked salmon, Japanese dishes, goats' cheese* |
| Savennières, see also *Chenin Blanc*, **medium bodied** | *Fish, cheese soufflé, mussels* |
| *Sauvignon Blanc* **light bodied** | *Thai dishes, mullet, asparagus, tomato dishes* |
| *Semillon* **medium bodied** | *Fish pie, shellfish, chicken stirfry* |
| Soave **light bodied** | *Light chicken, fish, risotto, pesto, prawns* |
| *Torrontés* **medium bodied** | *Asian cuisine, chicken Véronique* |
| *Verdelho* **medium bodied** | *Spicy foods, Indian dishes* |
| *Verdicchio* **light bodied** | *Fish, cream-based pasta sauces* |
| *Vermentino* **light–medium bodied** | *Fish, cheese-sauced dishes, quiches* |
| *Vernaccia* **light–medium bodied** | *Fish, swordfish* |
| *Viognier*, see also Condrieu, **medium bodied** | *Seafood, root vegetable dishes, chicken, pork, mild curries, dishes with rosemary* |
| Vouvray (dry), see also *Chenin Blanc*, **light bodied** | *Sole, light fish dishes, goats' cheese* |

## Red

| | |
|---|---|
| Amarone **full bodied** | *Game, beef, rich meat dishes* |
| Bandol **full bodied** | *Liver, roast lamb* |
| Barbaresco **full bodied** | *Veal, risotto* |
| *Barbera* **medium bodied** | *Antipasti, spaghetti Bolognese, tomato dishes, lasagne* |

| Red (continued) | |
|---|---|
| Barolo **full bodied** | Venison, peppered beef, goose |
| Beaujolais **light bodied** | Cold meats, mushroom dishes, pork chops |
| Bordeaux **full bodied** | Roast lamb, beef, duck, goose, pheasant |
| Bergerac **medium bodied** | Chicken, lamb |
| Burgundy, see also *Pinot Noir*, **light–medium bodied** | Fish, tuna, ham, light game, vegetable gratin, risotto, kidneys |
| *Cabernet Franc*, see also Chinon, Saumur-Champigny, **medium bodied** | Tuna, mullet, cheese gratin, turkey |
| *Cabernet Sauvignon* **medium–full bodied** | Red meat, lamb, beef, barbecues, cheddar cheese |
| Cahors, see also *Malbec*, **full bodied** | Stews, shepherd's pie |
| *Carmenère* **full bodied** | Beef, steak, steak and kidney pie |
| Châteauneuf-du-Pape **full bodied** | Lamb, beef, venison, game, chicken, goose, stew |
| Chianti **medium bodied** | Rich pastas, beef dishes, grilled pork, veal |
| Chinon, see also *Cabernet Franc*, **medium bodied** | Light meat dishes, red mullet, cheese salad |
| Corbières **medium bodied** | Lamb shank, bean casserole, meatballs, chilli con carne |
| Côtes de Bourg **full bodied** | Steak and kidney pie, cheese |
| Côtes du Rhône **medium bodied** | Sausages, spicy food, vegetarian dishes |
| Crozes-Hermitage, see also *Syrah*, **full bodied** | Turkey, spicy sausages, vegetable gratin |
| *Dolcetto* **light bodied** | Pizza, cheese fondue, baked peppers, salads |
| Fleurie, see also Beaujolais, **light bodied** | Grilled chicken, salami, summer salads |
| Fitou **medium bodied** | Sausages, simple chicken dishes |
| Gigondas **medium–full bodied** | Stews, duck, lamb |
| Greek reds **medium bodied** | Grilled lamb chops, moussaka, dishes with olive oil and herbs |
| *Grenache/Garnacha* **light bodied** | Vegetable dishes, lamb kebabs, couscous, squid |
| Hermitage **full bodied** | Rich game and beef |
| Loire reds, see also *Cabernet Franc*, **medium bodied** | Tuna, mullet, roast chicken |
| Madiran **full bodied** | Rich cassoulet, duck, strong cheeses |
| *Malbec*, see also Cahors, **full bodied** | Confit, steak and kidney pie, bean casseroles, macaroni cheese |
| Médoc **full bodied** | Traditional beef or lamb, Brie, Camembert |

| **Red** (continued) | |
| --- | --- |
| *Merlot* **medium bodied** | *Sausages, cottage pie, lambs' liver, spicy chicken wings, meatballs* |
| Minervois **medium bodied** | *Lamb, spicy sausages, pork* |
| *Montepulciano* d'Abruzzo **medium bodied** | *Lasagne, pizza, simple chicken dishes* |
| *Mourvèdre/Monastrell* **medium–full bodied** | *Lamb stews, spicy sausages, ratatouille* |
| *Pinotage* **full bodied** | *Spare ribs, barbecues, smoked cheese* |
| *Pinot Noir,* see also Burgundy | |
|    Alsace **light bodied** | *Red mullet and snapper, salmon, roast chicken, veal* |
|    New World **medium bodied** | *Tuna, ham, light game, vegetable gratin, risotto* |
| Pomerol **full bodied** | *Roast lamb, wild mushroom dishes, cheese* |
| Portuguese **full bodied** | *Chorizo, aubergine dishes, pork* |
| Ribera del Duero **full bodied** | *Roast lamb, duck* |
| Rioja, see also *Tempranillo,* **medium–full bodied** | *Lamb with garlic or rosemary, poultry, truffles, beef* |
| Salice Salentino **full bodied** | *Aubergine, moussaka, stews* |
| Sardinian reds **full bodied** | *Vegetable stew* |
| Saumur-Champigny, see also *Cabernet Franc,* **medium bodied** | *Lamb, mushroom risotto, salmon* |
| Southern Italian **full bodied** | *Irish stew, tomato-based dishes, casseroles* |
| St Émilion **full bodied** | *Beef, lamb, duck, cheese* |
| *Syrah/Shiraz* **full bodied** | *Rich spicy stews, duck, chillies, goose* |
| *Tempranillo,* see also Rioja, **medium–full bodied** | *Lamb, poultry, hamburgers* |
| Valdepeñas reds **medium bodied** | *Meatballs, bean casseroles, seabass* |
| Valpolicella **medium bodied** | *Roasted vegetables, stir-fries, bresaola* |
| *Zinfandel* **full bodied** | *Soy-sauced dishes, roast turkey, confit, steak, barbecued meats* |

## Rosé

| | |
|---|---|
| Bordeaux rosé | *Seafood risotto, bouillabaisse* |
| Cabernet d'Anjou | *Apéritif, pizza, light summer salads* |
| Chilean rosé | *Swordfish, grilled sardines* |
| Rosé de Provence | *Salade Niçoise, pissaladière, pizza, dishes with anchovies, squid, spicy chicken wings* |
| Spanish rosé | *Salmon, seatrout, smoked fish pâté* |
| Tavel | *Couscous, seabass* |

## Sparkling

| | |
|---|---|
| Asti Spumante | *Christmas pudding, mince pies, fruit salad, meringue* |
| Cava | *Apéritif, smoked salmon, guacamole* |
| Champagne | |
|   Blanc de Blancs | *Apéritif, smoked salmon, Chinese, Japanese, fish and chips* |
|   Demi-sec | *Cake, desserts* |
|   Non vintage brut | *Apéritif, oysters, salmon* |
|   Rosé | *Prawns, chicken, Indian dishes* |
|   Vintage | *Smoked duck, salmon, scallops* |
| Crémant | *Picnic, smoked trout, pâté* |
| New World | *Spicy food, fish, Parma ham and melon* |
| Prosecco | *Apéritif, Parma ham and melon* |
| Sekt | *Kedgeree* |

## Sweet

| | |
|---|---|
| Banyuls | *Chocolate cake, blue cheese* |
| Bonnezeaux | *Fruit puddings, marzipan, strawberries* |
| Eiswein | *Peaches, sweet fruit tarts* |
| Malaga *Moscatel* | *Chocolate puddings* |
| Maury | *Chocolate desserts, nutty puddings* |
| Monbazillac | *Blue cheese, foie gras, fruit and custard tarts* |
| *Muscat* (sweet) | *Mince pies, chocolate desserts, ice-cream, nut-based puddings, cheesecake* |
| Muscat de Beaume de Venise | *Fruit crumbles* |
| Sauternes | *Blue cheese, foie gras, crème brulée, pineapple, strawberries* |
| *Semillon* (sweet) | *Pecan pie* |
| *Riesling* (sweet) | *Fruit puddings* |
| Tokaji | *Crème caramel, sticky toffee pudding, blue cheese* |
| Vin Santo | *Cantucci biscuits, panforte, nuts, apple desserts* |
| Vouvray (sweet) | *Apple tart, baked fruit desserts* |

| Sherry | |
| --- | --- |
| Amontillado (dry) | *Consommé, chicken liver pâté, mushroom dishes, cold roast turkey, trifle* |
| Cream | *Mince pies, Christmas pudding, vanilla ice cream, crème brulée, marzipan desserts* |
| Fino | *Tapas e.g. olives, salted almonds, anchovies; light tempura prawns or tempura vegetables* |
| Manzanilla | *Tapas, e.g. salted almonds, cured ham, rocket and parmesan salad; prawns, fried fish* |
| Oloroso | *Rich fruit cake, mature hard cheese* |

# Matching food to wine

*Compiled by Niamh Boylan and Barbara Boyle*

| Seafood | Wine |
|---|---|
| Cod | Mâcon, *Semillon, Vermentino* |
| Crab | New World *Sauvignon Blanc*, Rueda, Bordeaux Blanc, *Viognier* |
| Hake | Soave, *Verdicchio, Chenin Blanc*, Mâcon |
| Lobster | Meursault, Puligny-Montrachet, *Viognier* |
| Monkfish | *Chardonnay* especially Burgundy—Meursault, Puligny-Montrachet—or California |
| Mullet | *Sauvignon Blanc, Pinot Noir* |
| Mussels | Muscadet, Chablis, Bianco di Custoza |
| Oysters | Muscadet, Champagne Blanc de Blancs, Chablis |
| Plaice | Orvieto, Rueda, light-bodied *Chardonnay, Pinot Grigio* |
| Prawns | *Albariño*, dry Vouvray, Gavi, dry *Muscat*, sherry—manzanilla or fino |
| Salmon | *Chardonnay*, Loire red—Chinon, Saumur-Champigny—New World *Pinot Noir* |
| Scallops | Chablis, *Grüner Veltliner*, Champagne, dry Vouvray |
| Seabass | Soft reds made from *Merlot* or *Grenache* |
| Seafood chowder | Oaked *Chardonnay* |
| Sole | Soave, dry Vouvray |
| Smoked fish | Fumé Blanc, Champagne, *Riesling* Spätlese, Pouilly Fumé, Sancerre |
| Swordfish | *Vernacchia, Semillon*, Rhône whites |
| Trout | *Sauvignon Blanc*, Pouilly Fumé, *Pinot Gris* |
| Tuna | *Semillon*, light-bodied *Pinot Noir*, New World *Merlot* |
| Turbot | Napa *Chardonnay*, Condrieu, Meursault |

| Pasta | Wine |
|---|---|
| Arrabiata | Salice Salentino, Côtes du Rhône, South African *Shiraz* |
| Bolognese | Valpolicella, Chianti, Chilean *Merlot, Dolcetto* |
| Creamy sauces | *Verdicchio*, Mâcon |
| Seafood | *Chardonnay, Verdelho*, Gavi |
| Tomato sauces | *Sauvignon Blanc, Pinot Grigio* |

| Poultry and game | Wine |
|---|---|
| Chicken | |
| roast/grilled | Rioja, Côtes de Bourg, white Burgundy |
| with creamy sauces | Chenin Blanc, Valdepeñas reds |
| Duck | Cahors, Malbec, Shiraz, Pinot Noir, oaked Chardonnay |
| Goose | Bordeaux reds, Cabernet Sauvignon, Merlot, Shiraz, Shiraz/Cabernet blends, Pinot Noir, Riesling |
| Guineafowl | New World Pinot Noir, fine Burgundy, Ribera del Duero, Tempranillo |
| Pheasant | Merlot, especially Californian, Bordeaux, Châteauneuf-du-Pape |
| Pigeon | Chianti Classico, Bordeaux, Loire red, Montepulciano d'Abruzzo |
| Turkey | Full-bodied Chardonnay, Zinfandel, Crozes-Hermitage |
| Venison | Shiraz, especially Barossa, Hermitage, Barbaresco, Barolo |

| Meat | Wine |
|---|---|
| Beef | |
| barbecued | Pinotage, Malbec, Australian Shiraz, Zinfandel |
| hamburgers | Chilean Cabernet, Tempranillo, Montepulciano d'Abruzzo |
| steaks/roasts | Barolo, Bordeaux, New World Cabernet, Amarone, Zinfandel, Shiraz |
| stews | Madiran, Southern Italian reds, Australian Cabernet |
| Ham | Riesling, white Rioja, Barbera, Pinot Noir, Valpolicella |
| Lamb | |
| chops/roasts | Rioja, St Émilion, Californian Merlot |
| kebabs | Greek or Portuguese reds |
| stews | Corbières, Mourvèdre, Shiraz |
| Pork | |
| chops/roasts | Dolcetto, Beaujolais, Chianti, Loire reds |
| ribs | Châteauneuf-du-Pape, Shiraz |
| stews | Pinotage, Southern French reds, Greek or southern French reds |
| Salami | Côtes du Rhône, Grenache/Garnacha, Barbera |
| Veal | Chardonnay, Chianti, Pinot Noir, Barbera |

| Vegetarian | Wine |
|---|---|
| *Bean dishes* | *Malbec, Zinfandel,* Southern French reds |
| *Cheese and vegetable gratin* | Mâcon whites, Lugana, *Sauvignon Blanc/Semillon* blends, *Montepulciano* d'Abruzzo, Côtes du Rhône |
| *Mushroom dishes* | Châteauneuf-du-Pape, *Pinot Noir*, Sardinian reds |
| *Provençale vegetables* | Rosé, Bandol, *Cabernet Sauvignon*, Corbières |
| *Rice, couscous, risotto* | *Pinot Blanc, Grenache/Garnacha,* simple reds |

| Ethnic | Wine |
|---|---|
| *Chinese* | Champagne, Cava, *Sauvignon Blanc, Torrontés, Gewurztraminer* |
|    *meaty soy dishes* | *Zinfandel* or *Côtes du Rhône* |
| *Indian* | New World oaked *Chardonnay,* German *Riesling,* dry *Muscat, Grenache/Garnacha* |
| *Japanese* | Champagne or sparkling wine, fino sherry, dry *Riesling* |
| *Thai* | Champagne, *Riesling,* Fumé Blanc, *Sauvignon Blanc, Vermentino* |

| Cheese | Wine |
|---|---|
| *Ardrahan* | Mature *Pinot Noir*, aged Hunter Valley *Semillon, Gewürztraminer* |
| *Brie* | Beaujolais, light and fruity *Pinot Noir* |
| *Camembert* | Subtly oaked *Chardonnay,* Beaujolais Cru, aged Bandol |
| *Cashel Blue* | St Émilion, medium-bodied fruity reds, Gigondas, Chilean *Merlot* or tawny port |
| *Chaource* | Champagne, demi-sec Vouvray |
| *Cheddar* | *Cabernet/Shiraz* blends, *Barbera* d'Asti, Gigondas, tawny port |
| *Comte* | Oaked *Chardonnay,* smoked *Semillon* or Vin Jaune |
| *Cooleeney* | Lightly oaked *Chardonnay,* Beaujolais Cru, fruity *Pinot Noir* |
| *Cottage cheese* | Young, fruity, unoaked whites, with good acidity, e.g. *Pinot Grigio, Sauvignon Blanc,* Rhône-style white blends |
| *Crottin de Chauvignol* | Sancerre, white Bordeaux |
| *Crozier Blue* | Botrytised *Semillon,* Sauternes, Tokaji, Vin Santo |
| *Époisses* | *Pinot Noir*, especially aged Burgundy |
| *Fondue* | Savoie or Jura whites, Bourgogne *Aligoté,* white Rioja |
| *Goats' cheese, soft* | *Sauvignon Blanc,* dry Vouvray, unoaked cool climate *Chardonnay* |
| *Gorgonzola* | Demi-sec Vouvray, light fruity reds, e.g. *Dolcetto* |
| *Gruyère* | Oaked, matured *Chardonnay* or *Semillon* |
| *Gubeen, smoked* | *Gewürztraminer,* fruity *Shiraz* |

| Cheese (continued) | Wine |
|---|---|
| Milleens | Gewürztraminer |
| Munster | Gewürztraminer |
| Parmesan | Amarone, Barolo, port |
| Pont l'Éveque | Subtley oaked Chardonnay, Chiroubles, Arbois |
| Roquefort | Sauternes, Tokaji |
| Stilton | Vintage or tawny port or Madeira, Tokaji |

| Desserts | Wine |
|---|---|
| Apple tart | Eiswein, Vin Santo, sweet Vouvray |
| Bread and butter pudding | Monbazillac, sweet Austrian wines, sweet Semillon, Sauternes |
| Cheesecake | Asti Spumante, sweet Muscat |
| Chocolate cake | Banyuls, Malaga, Maury, sweet Muscat, Sauternes |
| Christmas pudding | Sweet Muscat, Tokaji, Vin Santo |
| Crème brulée | Sweet Muscat, Tokaji, Sauternes |
| Crème caramel | Sweet Muscat, Tokaji, Sauternes |
| Crèpe Suzette | Orange Muscat |
| Crumbles | Muscat de Beaume de Venise |
| Fruit-based desserts | Bonnezeaux, Eiswein, sweet Riesling |
| Fruit salad | Asti Spumante, Muscat, sweet Riesling |
| Meringue | Sweet Muscat, Vin Santo |
| Mince pies | Sweet Muscat, Asti Spumante |
| Pecan pie | Sweet Muscat, sweet Semillon |
| Strawberries | Bonnezeaux, Sauternes |
| Tiramisu | Sweet Muscat, Sauternes |
| Trifle | Amontillado sherry |

# And now for something completely different . . . premium beer *Tony Farmar*

Pliny the Elder, who was a snob, said Romans drank wine and barbarians drank beer. No doubt many readers of this book will agree. But the next time you visit your favourite off-licence, have another look at the shelf where the premium beers are stocked. Stimulated by people's enjoyment abroad of foreign beers, over the last four years or so this market has greatly expanded, and now those shelves hold some of the most exciting taste sensations in the shop.

Brewing is as old as winemaking and over the years has developed a similar density of understandings. But first a little jargon. We are not talking here of so-called 'session beers'—cheap, highly refined beers designed for happy hours with the lads. The beers described here are serious craft brews, with full, mouth-filling tastes, and alcohol levels mounting in the extreme case to 17 per cent. Their very intensity of flavours can force you to take them slowly, and like wine they are often best with food.

The beer world is divided into ales and lagers, the distinction being that in ales the yeast ferments at the top of the vat and in lagers at the bottom. Ales tend to be earthier and sweeter in flavour, lagers lighter, cleaner and drier. Stout is technically an ale, as is wheat beer; bock, on the other hand, despite its deep, dark colour, high alcohol and rich malt flavours, is a lager.

By way of an introduction to this exotic new world, I asked Wally Kearon (of Eurobeers) and Jimmy Redmond (of Redmonds of Ranelagh)to introduce me to some of their favourites.

## Where to find premium beers

Although most up-market off-licences increasingly stock a few premium beers, wide ranges can be found in Dublin at Redmonds of Ranelagh, McHugh's, Kilbarrack, the Porterhouse in Temple Bar, and the Drink Store, Manor Street; in Cork, the O'Donovan's chain is building up its beer range. (For further reading try *The Good Beer Book* by Timothy Harper and Garrett Oliver: American in orientation, but full of good information and tasting notes, which were helpful for this chapter.)

The beers are listed in order of weight and style.

## Fraoch Heather Ale

Made with wild organic heather; highly flavoured but not too challenging, plenty of body.

*Origin* **Scotland**
*Alc/vol* **5%**
*Bottle* **50cl**
*Price* **€3.50–€4**

## Kelpie

From the same stable as Fraoch Heather Ale, Kelpie is made from seaweed (before hops were introduced, many other elements were used to add bitterness to beer). Rich ruby red, hints of chocolate, very distinctive, but not overpowering.

*Origin* **Scotland**
*Alc/vol* **5%**
*Bottle* **50cl**
*Price* **€3.50–€4**

## Pilsner Urquell

The original pilsner, with a delicate floral flavour, smooth finish, rich aroma, and a complex, layered, hopfilled body. A great starting point, and obviously streets away from the 'quaffing' beers such as Budweiser or Heineken.

*Origin* **Czech Republic**
*Alc/vol* **4.4%**
*Bottle* **66cl**
*Price* **€3.50–€4**

## Liberty Ale

Intense nose with a good body and a long, dry finish. Slightly harsh at first, but on the palate an almost floral note comes through, with pine needles and grapefruit. Good with beef dishes.

*Origin* **USA**
*Alc/vol* **5.9%**
*Bottle* **35cl**
*Price* **€3–€3.50**

## Duvel

Another original which has inspired hundreds of imitators. A strong golden ale. A popular apéritif in Belgium with salads or perhaps soup. Nose with definite pear and almond notes, thick persistent head, naturally maintained. Strong but not overwhelming alcohol.

*Origin* **Belgium**
*Alc/vol* **8.5%**
*Bottle* **75cl**
*Price* **€7.50–€8**

## Schneider Weisse Original

This dark wheat beer has all the classic wheat beer elements. The natural carbonation is so high that it is best served into a dampened glass; by keeping to traditional brewing methods (not, for instance, using a lager yeast for the secondary fermentation) the beer keeps fuller, deeper flavours, a dark tanned appearance with peppery notes and spicy aromas with banana, cloves and smoke notes. The natural yeast sediment colours the beer to a rich tasty stew. Takes a bit of getting used to, but the critics all swear it's well worth it.

*Origin* **Germany**
*Alc/vol* **5.4%**
*Bottle* **50cl**
*Price* **€2.50–€3**

## Dublin Brewing Co's Revolution

Deep, rich mahogany colour, plenty of dimensions, full bodied, clean, hoppy character. Ideal with roast pork dishes.

*Origin* **Ireland**
*Alc/vol* **4.7%**
*Bottle* **50cl**
*Price* **€2–€2.50**

## Leffe Radieuse

Nice roast malt flavour, with underlying warmth from the alcohol. A great beer with strongly-flavoured cheese.

*Origin* **Belgium**
*Alc/vol* **8.2%**
*Bottle* **33cl**
*Price* **€3.50–€4**

## Aventinus

A remarkable beer—like a double strength wheat beer—from the same house as Schneider-Weisse; this tawny-brown double bock has a powerful aroma. Despite its relatively high alcohol, this drinks very light on the palate with fruity, citrusy flavours with a warm, spicy finish. Matches rich meat dishes and sausages.

*Origin* **Germany**
*Alc/vol* **8%**
*Bottle* **50cl**
*Price* **€3.50–€4**

## Fromboise Boon

Frank Boon is one of Belgium's best known premium brewers, specialising in lambic beers (double fermented with a mix of old and new beers). Produced with nearly 200 grams of fruit in every litre, this distinctive beer is crisp, light and refreshing—the rosé of beer—full of flavour and not at all sweet.

*Origin* **Belgium**
*Alc/vol* **5%**
*Bottle* **50 cl**
*Price* **€4–€4.50**

## Gueze Boon

Brewed by the most traditional methods, with deliberate use of wooden casks open at the beginning of the brew to natural wild yeasts. Designed to be laid down—the label reads 'best before 2021'! Nose starts with apple, lemon and wet wool. On the palate dry, Sherryish flavours. A notably challenging beer whose sour, even primitive, tastes get mellower as it matures.

*Origin* **Belgium**
*Alc/vol* **6.5%**
*Bottle* **50cl**
*Price* **€3.50–€4**

## Chimay Blue Label Grande Reserve

There are six Trappist monasteries making beer in Belgium, and Chimay is the best known. The monks who brew it suggest that the Grande Reserve should be cellared for at least three years to allow the dark fruit, nutmeg and rich peppery tones and Port-like characteristics to develop. (Interestingly, beer in corked bottles seems to mature better than those with caps.) A slightly sweet palate with an earthy backdrop of raisins and chocolate.

*Origin* **Belgium**
*Alc/vol* **9%**
*Bottle* **75cl**
*Price* **€8.50–€9**

## Bush

Amber coloured, full bodied, with a strong malt flavour, the perfect beer for quiet sipping in the evening.

*Origin* **Belgium**
*Alc/vol* **12%**
*Bottle* **25cl**
*Price* **€4–€4.50**

## Sam'l Adams Triple Bock

The strongest beer in the world. We tasted the 1995 vintage, brewed with a champagne yeast and hardly recognisable as a beer. Massive bouquet, rich, intense, black with liquorice, almost medicinal, notes. A memorable experience on the palate, but not for the faint-hearted!

*Origin* **USA**
*Alc/vol* **17%**
*Bottle* **25cl**
*Price* **€7.50–€8**

# The wines

The wines are listed in order of country/region, colour (red or white), price band, then by name. If you can't quickly find the wine you are looking for try the index, which we have expanded for this edition. There are separate chapters for rosé, sparkling (including Champagne) and sweet wines. Since wine prices are not fixed the price bands are guidelines only. The dates suggested for when to drink the wines do not indicate their expected life but the period over which our tasters thought they would enjoy them most.

The following table explains the symbols used throughout the book.

| The symbols | |
|---|---|
| 🌿 | *Organic* |
| € | *Exceptionally good value* |
| ☆ | *Accomplished, showing above average quality or character making it worthy of extra attention* |
| ☆☆ | *Excellent with great character, style and complexity* |
| ☆☆☆ | *Wonderful, showing terrific character and complexity, true to its origins* |
| ☆☆☆☆ | *Exceptional, with considerable complexity and classic balance. Rewards serious tasting.* |

# Argentina

Argentina's main grape varieties are Malbec for red wine and Torrontés for white, but good wines are also made from varieties introduced by Italian and Spanish settlers—Barbera and Tempranillo—and from Merlot, Cabernet and Syrah. Malbec consistently produces some of the best Argentinean reds and accounts for most of those recommended in this year's guide. It comes in a range of styles from straightforward and fruity to more full bodied and intense with ageing potential. Producer and price are probably the best indicators of quality. This year, we have seen an increase in the number of white wines from Argentina that we can recommend. Most of them are made from Chardonnay, with rich flavours of exotic fruit and oak. So if you like a little oak on your Chardonnay, try Argentina. Although much of the wine from Argentina is aimed at the value and price-conscious sector of the market some very high quality, premium red wines such as Trapiche Iscay, Finca Flichman Dedicado and Catena Alta are helping to establish the country's reputation for top quality.

## White

### Under €9

*Cafayete* is in the Northern province of Salta which is renowned for producing very good, aromatic, dry whites from Torrontés.

### Etchart Torrontés 00

More floral than fruity with rose petal aromas and orange peel flavours with hints of tropical fruit. *Irish Distillers*

| | |
|---|---|
| *Price* | **Under €9** |
| *Region* | **Cafayete** |
| *Grape* | **Torrontés** |
| *Alc/vol* | **13.5%** |
| *Food* | **Ethnic/Chinese** |
| *Drink* | **2002–3** |

### Picajuan Peak Chardonnay 00

Attractively fragrant with ripe pineapple and mango aromas and a deliciously fruity, creamy palate with flavours of nectarine, mango and lime. *Tesco*

| | |
|---|---|
| *Price* | **Under €9** |
| *Region* | **Mendoza** |
| *Grape* | **Chardonnay** |
| *Alc/vol* | **13%** |
| *Food* | **Ethnic/Indian** |
| *Drink* | **2002–3** |

### €9–€12

### Argento Chardonnay 01

Made by top producer Catena, this wine has a pungent, oily nose with peach stone and herbal aromas. The palate is fruity, with apple and nectarine flavours and crisp, citric acidity, finishing elegantly long. *Cassidy*

| | |
|---|---|
| *Price* | **€9–€12** |
| *Region* | **Mendoza** |
| *Grape* | **Chardonnay** |
| *Alc/vol* | **13%** |
| *Food* | **Pasta/seafood** |
| *Drink* | **2002–3** |

## Finca Flichman Chardonnay 00

Lovely, clear, leafy aromas of lime and lemon follow through on the palate with fresh green apples, figs and spice and a rich, ripe finish. *TDL*

| | |
|---|---|
| *Price* | €9–€12 |
| *Region* | Mendoza |
| *Grape* | Chardonnay |
| *Alc/vol* | 12.5% |
| *Food* | Poultry/chicken |
| *Drink* | 2002–3 |

## Finca Las Moras Reserve Chardonnay 00

Exotic nose—melon and nuts—and a toasty, oaky, vanilla palate with juicy pear, apple and peach flavours. *Comans*

| | |
|---|---|
| *Price* | €9–€12 |
| *Region* | San Juan |
| *Grape* | Chardonnay |
| *Alc/vol* | 13.5% |
| *Food* | Fish/monkfish |
| *Drink* | 2002–3 |

### €12–€15

## Alta Vista Chardonnay 00

Lovely balance between subtlety and richness. The refined nose with honeyed lemon peel and a hint of vanilla is mirrored in a fresh citrus palate with a buttery, creamy finish. *Mitchells*

| | |
|---|---|
| *Price* | €12–€15 |
| *Region* | Mendoza |
| *Grape* | Chardonnay |
| *Alc/vol* | 13.5% |
| *Food* | Fish/plaice |
| *Drink* | 2002–3 |

### €18–€22

## Catena Agrelo Vineyards Chardonnay 00

Substantial Dolly Parton style. Candied fruit, nutty, smoky and slightly charred aromas. Very ripe, almost sweet, juicy tropical fruit flavours—pineapple and peach—with a warm, peppery finish. *Cassidy*

| | |
|---|---|
| *Price* | €18–€22 |
| *Region* | Mendoza |
| *Grape* | Chardonnay |
| *Alc/vol* | 13.5% |
| *Food* | Fish/salmon |
| *Drink* | 2002–3 |

# Red

### Under €9

## Etchart Rio de Plata Malbec 00 €

A wine to accompany meat. Ripe aromas of raspberry and cherry with spicy undertones; chewy tannins with generous red fruit flavours. *Irish Distillers*

| | |
|---|---|
| *Price* | Under €9 |
| *Region* | Mendoza |
| *Grape* | Malbec |
| *Alc/vol* | 12.5% |
| *Food* | Meat/roasts |
| *Drink* | 2002–3 |

## Etchart Rio de Plata Merlot 00

Slightly vegetal and stalky aromas of green pepper and stewed plums belie much richer flavours of mint and juicy plum fruit on the inky, peppery palate. *Irish Distillers*

| | |
|---|---|
| Price | Under €9 |
| Region | Mendoza |
| Grape | Merlot |
| Alc/vol | 12.5% |
| Food | Meat/lamb |
| Drink | 2002–3 |

## Santa Isabel Barbera 99

Fragrant on the nose, this wine has a gentle, soft texture with summer berry flavours and hints of creamy toffee. *Dunnes Stores*

| | |
|---|---|
| Price | Under €9 |
| Region | Mendoza |
| Grape | Barbera |
| Alc/vol | 12.5% |
| Food | Pasta/Bolognese |
| Drink | 2002–3 |

## Santa Rosa Estate Malbec 00 €

Full, fruity, rustic style with ripe blackcurrant, blackberry and damson flavours, good structure and firm tannins giving a gritty texture. *Dillons*

| | |
|---|---|
| Price | Under €9 |
| Region | Mendoza |
| Grape | Malbec |
| Alc/vol | 12.5% |
| Food | Meat/steak and kidney pie |
| Drink | 2002–3 |

## Simonassi Lyon Malbec 98 €

Excellent nose of cherry, cigar box and white pepper. The extra age is evident in this wine's mellow, earthy flavours of spice, cherry and tobacco. *Gleeson*

| | |
|---|---|
| Price | Under €9 |
| Region | Mendoza |
| Grape | Malbec |
| Alc/vol | 12% |
| Food | Meat/ragout |
| Drink | 2002–3 |

## TriVento Malbec 99

Rustic, full-bodied style with good tannins, spicy blackberry and cherry flavours and a peppery finish. *Findlaters*

| | |
|---|---|
| Price | Under €9 |
| Region | Mendoza |
| Grape | Malbec |
| Alc/vol | 13% |
| Food | Vegetarian/bean casserole |
| Drink | 2002–3 |

### €9–€12

## Argento Malbec 00

Spicy, slightly floral aromas which follow through to the palate together with blackberry and ripe cherry flavours and easy tannins. *Cassidy*

| | |
|---|---|
| Price | €9–€12 |
| Region | Mendoza |
| Grape | Malbec |
| Alc/vol | 12% |
| Food | Meat/cassoulet |
| Drink | 2002–3 |

## Finca Flichman Syrah 00

Appetising, easy style with an inviting nose of
spice and caramelised black fruits. Ripe black
fruit on the palate with a dash of pepper and
vanilla toffee. *TDL*

| | |
|---|---|
| *Price* | €9–€12 |
| *Region* | Mendoza |
| *Grape* | Syrah |
| *Alc/vol* | 13% |
| *Food* | Meat/stews |
| *Drink* | 2002–3 |

## Finca Las Moras Reserve Malbec 99

Typical, gutsy Malbec, with lots of plummy
damson fruit, chocolate and spice, a good bite
and hints of aniseed, earth and leather. A real
steak wine. *Comans*

| | |
|---|---|
| *Price* | €9–€12 |
| *Region* | San Juan |
| *Grape* | Malbec |
| *Alc/vol* | 13.5% |
| *Food* | Meat/steak |
| *Drink* | 2002–4 |

## Picajuan Peak Malbec 00

Quality, classy Malbec with ripe dark fruit flavours of blackcurrant and cherries—Black Forest gâteau—with a touch of leather and some
mellow, smoky nuances. *Tesco*

| | |
|---|---|
| *Price* | €9–€12 |
| *Region* | Mendoza |
| *Grape* | Malbec |
| *Alc/vol* | 13% |
| *Food* | Poultry/duck |
| *Drink* | 2002–3 |

## Tierra Buena Reserve Malbec 99

A really fruity, tasty wine with a perfumed
blackberry nose. The palate has a good bite with
lots of sweet, ripe plum and berry flavours with
herbs, fennel and pepper. *Marks & Spencer*

| | |
|---|---|
| *Price* | €9–€12 |
| *Region* | Mendoza |
| *Grape* | Malbec |
| *Alc/vol* | 13.5% |
| *Food* | Ethnic/Indian |
| *Drink* | 2002–3 |

## Trapiche Malbec 97

A mahogany-coloured wine with some age,
drinking well now. The port-like nose shows
figs, orange peel, dates and prunes. The palate
has sweeter black fruit with spice and mocha
and velvety smooth tannins. *Gilbeys*

| | |
|---|---|
| *Price* | €9–€12 |
| *Region* | Mendoza |
| *Grape* | Malbec |
| *Alc/vol* | 13.5% |
| *Food* | Poultry/duck confit |
| *Drink* | 2002–3 |

## Viña de Santa Isabel Reserve Malbec 00

Deeply flavoured, classic Malbec, peppery and
toasty, with flavours of ripe blackcurrant and
blackberry, Christmas pudding and dark chocolate. *Dunnes Stores*

| | |
|---|---|
| *Price* | €9–€12 |
| *Region* | Mendoza |
| *Grape* | Malbec |
| *Alc/vol* | 12.5% |
| *Food* | Meat/barbecue |
| *Drink* | 2002–4 |

€12–€15

## Alta Vista Malbec 99

Attractive, intense perfumed nose of red fruits. The savoury palate has plum, mulberry and damson flavours, quite gripping tannins and a spicy kick. *Mitchells*

| | |
|---|---|
| *Price* | €12–€15 |
| *Region* | Mendoza |
| *Grape* | Malbec |
| *Alc/vol* | 13.5% |
| *Food* | Meat/lamb |
| *Drink* | 2002–3 |

## Altos de Temporada Reserve Malbec 96

Satisfying, maturing wine, still holding together really well. Earthy and rustic with berry fruit character and a nice bite of cherry. *Dunnes Stores*

| | |
|---|---|
| *Price* | €12–€15 |
| *Region* | Mendoza |
| *Grape* | Malbec |
| *Alc/vol* | 13.5% |
| *Food* | Poultry/chicken |
| *Drink* | 2002–3 |

## Altos de Temporada Reserve Cabernet Sauvignon 97

Mature, developed style showing good bottle age with vegetal, spicy and fruity aromas, intense, spicy fruit on the palate and lasting dry tannins. Pair with food for best results. *Dunnes Stores*

| | |
|---|---|
| *Price* | €12–€15 |
| *Region* | Mendoza |
| *Grape* | Cabernet Sauvignon |
| *Alc/vol* | 13.5% |
| *Food* | Meat/roasts |
| *Drink* | 2002–3 |

## Finca Flichman Reserve Malbec 00

Pure red fruit aromas have nuances of coffee. The palate is very smooth and big with ripe tannins and concentrated blackcurrant, plum and spice flavours. *TDL*

| | |
|---|---|
| *Price* | €12–€15 |
| *Region* | Mendoza |
| *Grape* | Malbec |
| *Alc/vol* | 13.5% |
| *Food* | Poultry/duck |
| *Drink* | 2002–4 |

## Santa Julia Oak-aged Tempranillo 00

A pleasant, fruity style with a silky, spicy texture and earthy, ripe strawberry, cherry and red-currant flavours. *Taserra*

| | |
|---|---|
| *Price* | €12–€15 |
| *Region* | Mendoza |
| *Grape* | Tempranillo |
| *Alc/vol* | 13.5% |
| *Food* | Meat/hamburgers |
| *Drink* | 2002–3 |

€18–€22

## Catena Lunlunta Vineyards Malbec 99 ☆

Attractive and full bodied. Soft, ripe blackcurrant flavours, with spicy oak, leather and cigar box. *Cassidy*

| | |
|---|---|
| *Price* | €18–€22 |
| *Region* | Mendoza |
| *Grape* | Malbec |
| *Alc/vol* | 14% |
| *Food* | Game/venison |
| *Drink* | 2002–5 |

# Cheers finest selection

## NORTHSIDE

| | | |
|---|---|---|
| Gibney's | Malahide | Tel: 8450606 |
| Baily Court | Howth | Tel: 8322691 |
| The Comet | Santry | Tel: 8427771 |
| Grainger's | Malahide Rd | Tel: 8332794 |
| The Jolly Toper | Finglas | Tel 8642454 |
| Martin's | Finglas | Tel: 8341307 |
| The White House | The Ward | Tel: 8342683 |
| The Goose Tavern | Drumcondra | Tel: 8064153 |
| Liz Delaney's | Coolock | Tel: 8474282 |

## SOUTHSIDE

| | | |
|---|---|---|
| The Burnaby | Greystones | Tel: 2874015 |
| Brady's | Shankill | Tel: 2821649 |
| The Playwright | Blackrock | Tel: 2887219 |
| Leopardstown Inn | Leopardstown | Tel: 2889189 |
| The Coach House | Ballinteer | Tel: 2963903 |
| The Old Orchard | Rathfarnham | Tel: 4930507 |
| The Missing Swan | Blackrock | Tel: 2888671 |
| Bakers Corner | Kill O'The Grange | Tel: 2302122 |
| Wicklow Arms | Delgany | Tel: 2871616 |
| Sea Bank House | East Wall | Tel: 8560095 |
| The Deer Hunter | Glenageary | Tel: 2851410 |

## WESTSIDE

| | | |
|---|---|---|
| The Silver Granite | Palmerstown | Tel: 6236135 |
| The Foxhunter | Lucan | Tel: 6235614 |
| Vesey Arms | Lucan | Tel: 6280248 |
| Cuckoo's Nest | Tallaght | Tel: 4626993 |

Cheers!
TAKE-HOME
Take Home Your Local
TAKE-HOME
The Way You Want It!

email: cheers@indigo.ie    website: www.cheers.ie

• Local • Convenient • Open Pub Hours • Party Service • Sale or Return • Delivery Service • Regular Wine Tastings • Exclusive Promotions every month • Wine Clubs • Monthly Competitions •

Pride.

Sinfully good wine.

### €30–€35

## Trapiche Iscay 97

Powerful style with inky black depths. Liquorice, violet and herbal aromas, weighty chocolate and vanilla flavours, with smoky wood and a fruity, black core. *Gilbeys*

| | |
|---|---|
| *Price* | **€30–€35** |
| *Region* | **Mendoza** |
| *Grape* | **Merlot/Malbec** |
| *Alc/vol* | **13.5%** |
| *Food* | **Meat/lamb** |
| *Drink* | **2002–6** |

### €35–€40

## Finca Flichman Dedicado 97 ☆☆

A worthy rival to Bordeaux, refined and smooth, with ageing potential. Rich, wood-influenced nose of tobacco, vanilla and toast. Delicious flavours of peppery currant, plum and chocolate with a persistent, generous finish. *TDL*

| | |
|---|---|
| *Price* | **€35–€40** |
| *Region* | **Mendoza** |
| *Grape* | **Cab Sauv/Syrah/ Malbec/Merlot** |
| *Alc/vol* | **14%** |
| *Food* | **Meat/steak** |
| *Drink* | **2002–6** |

# Australia

One message that emerged clearly from the tastings this year is that Australian wines have become more interesting, with a wider range of varieties, particularly in whites, more focus on regional differences and, most importantly, an increase in the number of wines from exciting producers now stocked in Ireland.

Some of the most interesting whites are made from Viognier and Marsanne (Rhône varieties) and the Rieslings just get better and better. Semillon styles are uniquely Australian but Sauvignons and Sauvignon/Semillon blends are also very promising. And of course there are lots of Chardonnays. Other white varieties include Chenin Blanc, Muscat, Verdelho and Pinot Gris and, in the true spirit of Aussie experimentation, Riesling has been blended with Marsanne, Gewurztraminer or Chardonnay with some interesting results. In reds, there is an increasing number of the more classic blends of Cabernet with Merlot and some stunning blends of Shiraz with Grenache and Mourvèdre.

The Australians have worked hard at producing consistently good quality and building up 'Brand Australia' so that consumers know what to expect—fruity, well-made, easily understood and fairly priced wines. The consistency is largely due to inter-regional blending which also delivers economies of scale to the big brand companies. South Australia, SE Australia or New South Wales on a label means that the wine may come from any or all of the regions in these vast areas. However, surveys have shown that consumers want to trade up and to be able to distinguish between regions and there is a growing emphasis on regional identification, with the Hunter Valley, Coonawarra, Barossa and Margaret River and newer regions, such as Orange, taking on a greater significance. The differences between the regions are subtle and it takes knowledge and time to understand and recognise them.

The most exciting development for Ireland is the increase in the numbers of wines from smaller producers that are making their way to our shores. Hewitson, Evans & Tate, Geoff Merrill, Greg Norman, Clos Clare, Grosset, Irvine, are just some of the names to look out for; their wines are available mainly from independent merchants. But it would be a mistake to overlook some of the terrific wines being produced by Peter Lehmann, d'Arenberg, Penfolds et al.

## White

### Under €9

### Cudgee Creek Colombard Chardonnay 01 €

A charming wine with a creamy texture. Substantial tropical fruit and floral aromas have a touch of vanilla. The ripe, exotic fruit flavours give an impression of sweetness. *Koala Wines*

| | |
|---|---|
| *Price* | Under €9 |
| *Region* | Murray Darling |
| *Grape* | Colombard/Chardonnay |
| *Alc/vol* | 12.5% |
| *Food* | Pasta/seafood |
| *Drink* | 2002–4 |

## Eaglehawk Chardonnay 01

Fragrant incense on the nose followed by a creamy texture with citrus fruits and dominant aniseed flavours. *Dillons*

| | |
|---|---|
| Price | Under €9 |
| Region | SE Australia |
| Grape | Chardonnay |
| Alc/vol | 12.5% |
| Food | Poultry/duck |
| Drink | 2002–3 |

## Hills View Vineyards Chardonnay Verdelho 00

An unusual mix of varieties gives a lovely blend of flavours—lemon, lime and honey, with apple skin and floral tones—really refreshing with a good length of flavour. *WineOnline*

| | |
|---|---|
| Price | Under €9 |
| Region | South Australia |
| Grape | Chardonnay/Verdelho |
| Alc/vol | 13.5% |
| Food | Fish/barbecue |
| Drink | 2002–3 |

*South Eastern Australia* includes the three most important wine states.
*South Australia*—the Barossa Valley, Clare Valley, Eden Valley, McLaren Vale, Coonawarra, Padthaway, Langhorne Creek, the Adelaide Hills and Plains.
*Victoria*—Rutherglen, Milawa, Glenrowan, King Valley, the Ovens Valley, the Pyrenees, the Grampians, the Yarra Valley, Mornington Peninsula, Geelong.
*New South Wales*—the Lower and Upper Hunter valleys, Mudgee, Orange.

## Jacob's Creek Chardonnay 01

Lemon, apple and apricot flavours and good length and concentration. A little touch of spice adds an extra dimension. *Irish Distillers*

| | |
|---|---|
| Price | Under €9 |
| Region | SE Australia |
| Grape | Chardonnay |
| Alc/vol | 12.5% |
| Food | Fish/fish pie |
| Drink | 2002–3 |

## Jacob's Creek Dry Riesling 01 €

A classic style, with lashings of tropical fruit, especially mango. The nose is pungent with typical kerosene, while the palate has a more unusual, slightly off-dry, stony character with limy acidity. *Irish Distillers*

| | |
|---|---|
| Price | Under €9 |
| Region | SE Australia |
| Grape | Riesling |
| Alc/vol | 11.5% |
| Food | Indian/curries |
| Drink | 2002–4 |

## Peter Lehmann The Barossa Chenin Blanc 00 €

Very moreish, apéritif-style wine with appealing aromas of red apple and honey, refreshing lemon acidity, apple flavours and some floral touches. *Comans*

| | |
|---|---|
| Price | Under €9 |
| Region | Barossa Valley |
| Grape | Chenin Blanc |
| Alc/vol | 12.5% |
| Food | Apéritif/starters |
| Drink | 2002–3 |

## Seppelt Moyston Unoaked Chardonnay 01

Classic Aussie Chardonnay—tasty, light and elegant with ripe melon and lime, creamy vanilla and good supporting acidity.
*Dunnes Stores*

| | |
|---|---|
| Price | Under €9 |
| Region | SE Australia |
| Grape | Chardonnay |
| Alc/vol | 13% |
| Food | Fish/salmon |
| Drink | 2002–3 |

### €9–€12

## Bethany Schrapel Family Vineyards The Manse Semillon Riesling Chardonnay 01

Plump and fruity, with a little bit of everything from the mix of grapes. Apple pie nose with flavours of apples, lemon and pineapple.
*O'Briens*

| | |
|---|---|
| Price | €9–€12 |
| Region | Barossa Valley |
| Grape | Semillon/Riesling/Chardonnay |
| Alc/vol | 11.5% |
| Food | Seafood/shellfish |
| Drink | 2002–3 |

## Brown Brothers Dry Muscat 01

Sweet aromas of honey and fresh lychees and an abundance of juicy fruit flavours, yet, at the same time, it is light, fresh and elegant.
*Woodford Bourne*

| | |
|---|---|
| Price | €9–€12 |
| Region | Victoria |
| Grape | Muscat |
| Alc/vol | 13.5% |
| Food | Ethnic/Indian |
| Drink | 2002–3 |

SHORTLIST
BEST VALUE WHITE

## Ch. Tahbilk Marsanne 98 ☆☆☆ €

A complex wine, made in a deliciously different style. Aromas of honey, orange oil and marmalade, flavours of orange and fig with some nuts. *Comans*

| | |
|---|---|
| Price | €9–€12 |
| Region | Victoria |
| Grape | Marsanne |
| Alc/vol | 13% |
| Food | Seafood/shellfish |
| Drink | 2002–3 |

## d'Arenberg The Stump Jump Riesling Marsanne 00

Pronounced developed aromas, oily and peppery, but the palate is much fresher with apple, lime and asparagus and good length of flavour.
*Taserra*

| | |
|---|---|
| Price | €9–€12 |
| Region | McLaren Vale |
| Grape | Riesling/Marsanne |
| Alc/vol | 12% |
| Food | Meat/pork |
| Drink | 2002–3 |

## Ferngrove Chardonnay 01

Floral and aromatic, with light buttery notes and a hint of citrus peel, this is a lively wine with flavours of lemon, melon and sweet pineapple, some spice and a tangy finish. A store cupboard essential and versatile standby.
*Oddbins*

| | |
|---|---|
| Price | €9–€12 |
| Region | Western Australia |
| Grape | Chardonnay |
| Alc/vol | 14% |
| Food | Seafood/cod |
| Drink | 2002–3 |

## Gold Rock Semillon Chardonnay 01

Smoky, spicy and mineral aromas; lively and refreshing palate with good tropical fruit flavours and hints of lemon and lime marmalade. *Koala Wines*

| | |
|---|---|
| Price | €9–€12 |
| Region | Hunter Valley |
| Grape | Semillon/Chardonnay |
| Alc/vol | 12.5% |
| Food | Seafood/crab |
| Drink | 2002–3 |

## Growers Chenin 01

Bottled by Coriole, this wine offers something a little bit different. Gentle aromas of green fruit and dill and a lightly perfumed palate with citrus, mandarin and some peach flavours and crisp acidity. *Wines Direct*

| | |
|---|---|
| Price | €9–€12 |
| Region | South Australia |
| Grape | Chenin Blanc |
| Alc/vol | 12% |
| Food | Poultry/chicken |
| Drink | 2002–3 |

## Hardys Nottage Hill Chardonnay 01

Ripe mango flavours with strong citrus notes and classic Chardonnay butteriness are kept fresh by crisp acidity. The oak doesn't dominate though it is obvious to the finish. *Allied Drinks*

| | |
|---|---|
| Price | €9–€12 |
| Region | SE Australia |
| Grape | Chardonnay |
| Alc/vol | 13% |
| Food | Seafood/chowder |
| Drink | 2002–3 |

## Hardys Stamp Riesling Gewurztraminer 01

Fleshy, generous, medium-dry style with perfumed aromas of honeydew melon and pineapple. Lighter flavours of lemon and apple with just a touch of honey and spice. *Allied Drinks*

| | |
|---|---|
| Price | €9–€12 |
| Region | SE Australia |
| Grape | Riesling/Gewurz-traminer |
| Alc/vol | 12% |
| Food | Chinese/spring rolls |
| Drink | 2002–3 |

## Honey Tree Semillon Chardonnay 01 ☆ €

Attractive, classic style with fruity aromas of melon and pineapple and generous, intense flavours of ripe tropical fruit—mango, apricot and lime—with a lovely touch of vanilla pod. *Marks & Spencer*

| | |
|---|---|
| Price | €9–€12 |
| Region | SE Australia |
| Grape | Semillon/Chardonnay |
| Alc/vol | 13.5% |
| Food | Poultry/chicken |
| Drink | 2002–3 |

## Jindalee Chardonnay 00

The very creamy vanilla and peach nose suggests a heavily oaked wine but the buttery palate is elegant and subtle with concentrated flavours of tropical and citrus fruits. *Koala Wines*

| | |
|---|---|
| Price | €9–€12 |
| Region | Murray Darling |
| Grape | Chardonnay |
| Alc/vol | 13.5% |
| Food | Poultry/roast chicken |
| Drink | 2002–3 |

## Lindemans Bin 65 Chardonnay 00

Toasty and full bodied, with aromas of caramel. Ripe, creamy texture and flavours of butter, tropical fruit and smoky wood tones. *Grants*

| | |
|---|---|
| *Price* | €9–€12 |
| *Region* | SE Australia |
| *Grape* | Chardonnay |
| *Alc/vol* | 13% |
| *Food* | Fish/salmon |
| *Drink* | 2002–3 |

## McGuigan Bin 6000 Verdelho 01 ☆ €

Full of character and style, this wine makes a real impression with its peppery, spicy, fruity nose, apple and spice flavours, balanced acidity and decent length. A wine to flummox your friends. *Barry & Fitzwilliam*

| | |
|---|---|
| *Price* | €9–€12 |
| *Region* | Hunter Valley |
| *Grape* | Verdelho |
| *Alc/vol* | 11.5% |
| *Food* | Ethnic/Indian |
| *Drink* | 2002–3 |

## McWilliam's Hanwood Chardonnay 01

Intense and quite exotic with ripe, tropical fruit aromas and nutty, oily hints. Dry on the palate, with rich flavours of mango, pineapple and kiwi. *TDL*

| | |
|---|---|
| *Price* | €9–€12 |
| *Region* | SE Australia |
| *Grape* | Chardonnay |
| *Alc/vol* | 13% |
| *Food* | Fish/cod |
| *Drink* | 2002–3 |

## Miranda High Country Chardonnay 00

In the style that made Australia famous. Oaky, toasty nose with plenty of ripe melon, vanilla, spicy ginger and cinnamon flavours. *Taserra*

| | |
|---|---|
| *Price* | €9–€12 |
| *Region* | King Valley/ Ovens Valley |
| *Grape* | Chardonnay |
| *Alc/vol* | 13.5% |
| *Food* | Cheese/Camembert |
| *Drink* | 2002–3 |

## Peter Lehmann The Barossa Riesling 01

Crisp and dry, with lime and lemon fruit, some oiliness and lovely length of flavour. Best with food to match the acidity. *Comans*

| | |
|---|---|
| *Price* | €9–€12 |
| *Region* | Barossa Valley |
| *Grape* | Riesling |
| *Alc/vol* | 12% |
| *Food* | Meat/salami |
| *Drink* | 2002–5 |

## Peter Lehmann The Barossa Semillon 01 ☆☆ €

Interesting, slightly oily nose, with dried apricot, nectarine and lemon peel. Fabulous mouthwatering palate with terrific weight and length and apricot and honey flavours. *Comans*

| | |
|---|---|
| *Price* | €9–€12 |
| *Region* | Barossa Valley |
| *Grape* | Semillon |
| *Alc/vol* | 12.5% |
| *Food* | Seafood/shellfish |
| *Drink* | 2002–5 |

## Peter Lehmann Weighbridge Chardonnay 01

An attractive, generous and warm wine with lemon, lime and red apple flavours overlaid with toasty oak. *Comans*

| | |
|---|---|
| *Price* | **€9–€12** |
| *Region* | **South Australia** |
| *Grape* | **Chardonnay** |
| *Alc/vol* | **14%** |
| *Food* | **Pasta/macaroni** |
| *Drink* | **2002–3** |

## Rosemount Estate Riesling 01

Australia meets Alsace. Crisp and almost austere—like freshly squeezed lemon and lime juice with herbal tones. Try it with food. *Grants*

| | |
|---|---|
| *Price* | **€9–€12** |
| *Region* | **SE Australia** |
| *Grape* | **Riesling** |
| *Alc/vol* | **12.5%** |
| *Food* | **Ethnic/Thai** |
| *Drink* | **2003–4** |

## Sacred Hill Semillon Chardonnay 01

The ripe, fresh nose with lightly toasted vanilla and lime fruit aromas is followed by pleasing, warm, tropical and zesty citrus fruit flavours. *Febvre*

| | |
|---|---|
| *Price* | **€9–€12** |
| *Region* | **SE Australia** |
| *Grape* | **Semillon/Chardonnay** |
| *Alc/vol* | **12.5%** |
| *Food* | **Poultry/chicken** |
| *Drink* | **2002–3** |

## Serentos Soft Press Chardonnay 99

An oaky Chardonnay, holding up and developing nicely. Quite toasty with tropical fruit flavours and a touch of gooey caramel slice. *Gleeson*

| | |
|---|---|
| *Price* | **€9–€12** |
| *Region* | **SE Australia** |
| *Grape* | **Chardonnay** |
| *Alc/vol* | **13%** |
| *Food* | **Poultry/turkey** |
| *Drink* | **2002–3** |

## Tesco Australian Reserve Chardonnay 00

Very well-integrated oak gives a subtle toastiness to this wine which complements the plentiful flavours of honey, melon and citrus. *Tesco*

| | |
|---|---|
| *Price* | **€9–€12** |
| *Region* | **SE Australia** |
| *Grape* | **Chardonnay** |
| *Alc/vol* | **13.5%** |
| *Food* | **Fish/monkfish** |
| *Drink* | **2002–3** |

## Tyrrell's Old Winery Chardonnay 01 ☆☆ €

Dramatic and sensual, well made and harmonious. Smoky aromas of vanilla and honeyed, intense, tropical fruit, lead to a huge burst of tastes on the palate—mango, pineapple and melon. *Maxxium*

| | |
|---|---|
| *Price* | **€9–€12** |
| *Region* | **Hunter/McLaren Vale** |
| *Grape* | **Chardonnay** |
| *Alc/vol* | **12.5%** |
| *Food* | **Meat/veal** |
| *Drink* | **2002–4** |

## Wakefield Chardonnay 99 ☆ €

A very pleasing wine showing good development. The
oily, luscious, tropical fruit
nose has vanilla tones which
appear on the palate as ripe
apple, peach, pear, lime and
butterscotch flavours.
*Koala Wines*

| | |
|---|---|
| *Price* | €9–€12 |
| *Region* | Clare Valley |
| *Grape* | Chardonnay |
| *Alc/vol* | 14% |
| *Food* | Poultry/duck |
| *Drink* | 2002–3 |

## Wakefield Riesling 01

Off-dry, yet lively acidity makes the wine very
fresh and zingy. Petrol and floral aromas are
followed by flavours of lemon curd and lemon
zest. *Koala Wines*

| | |
|---|---|
| *Price* | €9–€12 |
| *Region* | Clare Valley |
| *Grape* | Riesling |
| *Alc/vol* | 13% |
| *Food* | Fish/smoked fish |
| *Drink* | 2002–3 |

## Wakefield Semillon 00 ☆☆ €

Intense and delicious blend of spice, lime,
lemon, grapefruit and pineapple flavours with
full, rich, buttery vanilla notes. *Koala Wines*

| | |
|---|---|
| *Price* | €9–€12 |
| *Region* | Clare Valley |
| *Grape* | Semillon |
| *Alc/vol* | 12% |
| *Food* | Ethnic/Asian |
| *Drink* | 2002–5 |

## Wakefield Promised Land Chardonnay 01

Crisp, fresh, unwooded style with great concentration and length. Aromas and flavours are of
apples and warm tropical fruit yet there is a core
of zesty lime which really catches the palate.
*Koala Wines*

| | |
|---|---|
| *Price* | €9–€12 |
| *Region* | Clare Valley |
| *Grape* | Chardonnay |
| *Alc/vol* | 13% |
| *Food* | Fish/plaice |
| *Drink* | 2002–3 |

## Wakefield White Clare 99

Oaky yet crisp. The floral bouquet has a subtle
vanilla influence. The palate has refreshing,
zippy, limy acidity but is also quite creamy with
full, buttery flavours and ripe tropical fruits.
*Koala Wines*

| | |
|---|---|
| *Price* | €9–€12 |
| *Region* | Clare Valley |
| *Grape* | Chardonnay/ Crouchen |
| *Alc/vol* | 13% |
| *Food* | Fish/salmon |
| *Drink* | 2002–3 |

## Wolf Blass Chardonnay 00

An oaky style of Chardonnay, big and rich with
aromas of mango, melon, vanilla and toffee and
tropical fruit flavours. *Dillons*

| | |
|---|---|
| *Price* | €9–€12 |
| *Region* | South Australia |
| *Grape* | Chardonnay |
| *Alc/vol* | 13.5% |
| *Food* | Fish/turbot |
| *Drink* | 2002–3 |

## Wynns Coonawarra Estate Riesling 01

Light and crisp, with an exuberant elderflower
nose, lemon and lime pie flavours and just a
little kerosene. A good food wine. *Findlaters*

| | |
|---|---|
| Price | €9–€12 |
| Region | Coonawarra |
| Grape | Riesling |
| Alc/vol | 12% |
| Food | Fish/salads |
| Drink | 2002–3 |

### €12–€15

## Brookland Valley Verse 1 Semillon Sauvignon 00

Aromatic nose with sweet pea and primrose
gives way to flinty and smoky nuances. Flavours
of stewed apple and lemon peel and quite a rich,
luscious texture. *Oddbins*

| | |
|---|---|
| Price | €12–€15 |
| Region | Margaret River |
| Grape | Semillon/Sauv Blanc |
| Alc/vol | 13% |
| Food | Seafood/mussels |
| Drink | 2002–3 |

## Brown Brothers Pinot Gris 01

Lovely, pink-hued wine with a fruity and floral
bouquet, refreshing acidity and lots of lemon
and lime flavours. *Woodford Bourne*

| | |
|---|---|
| Price | €12–€15 |
| Region | Victoria |
| Grape | Pinot Gris |
| Alc/vol | 13% |
| Food | Meat/veal |
| Drink | 2002–3 |

> *Western Australia's* main regions are Margaret River, the Swan Valley and the Great Southern.

## Capel Vale Sauvignon Blanc Semillon 00

Concentrated, yet stylish, this is a big wine,
rich, spicy and honeyed. It is weighty with
peach fruit and a nice use of oak and has a
slightly sweet flavour. *Cassidy*

| | |
|---|---|
| Price | €12–€15 |
| Region | Western Australia |
| Grape | Sauv Blanc/Semillon |
| Alc/vol | 12.5% |
| Food | Poultry/turkey |
| Drink | 2002–3 |

## d'Arenberg The Dry Dam Riesling 01 ☆

A New World classic, honeyed and pungent
with spice, lime and melon on the nose and
tasty, peachy fruit on the palate with spice,
lemony acidity and good length of flavour.
*Taserra*

| | |
|---|---|
| Price | €12–€15 |
| Region | Fleurieu Peninsula |
| Grape | Riesling |
| Alc/vol | 12% |
| Food | Ethnic/Chinese |
| Drink | 2002–4 |

## d'Arenberg The Hermit Crab Marsanne Viognier 01 ☆

Youthful and engaging wine with a pungent
nose of honeysuckle and herbs and a full, ripe
palate with flavours of apricot and red apple.
Very well made with an excellent long finish.
*Taserra*

| | |
|---|---|
| Price | €12–€15 |
| Region | McLaren Vale |
| Grape | Marsanne/Viognier |
| Alc/vol | 14% |
| Food | Ethnic/Thai |
| Drink | 2002–3 |

## d'Arenberg The Last Ditch Viognier 01 ☆

Scented nose of jasmine and honeysuckle. Zesty, crisp, yet ripe and fruity palate with flavours of orange peel, apricot, pear and vanilla pod. *Taserra*

| | |
|---|---|
| *Price* | €12–€15 |
| *Region* | McLaren Vale |
| *Grape* | Viognier |
| *Alc/vol* | 14% |
| *Food* | Seafood/crab |
| *Drink* | 2002–4 |

## Evans & Tate Margaret River Chardonnay 01 ☆☆

One of the new wave of elegant, powerful, Chardonnays. Barrel fermented, with an impressive nose of hedgerow, honey and green apple with a floral touch. The fruit is really allowed to express itself with flavours of mango, lime and tart pineapple. *Comans*

| | |
|---|---|
| *Price* | €12–€15 |
| *Region* | Margaret River |
| *Grape* | Chardonnay |
| *Alc/vol* | 13.5% |
| *Food* | Poultry/chicken |
| *Drink* | 2002–4 |

## Gold Rock Chardonnay 00

Intense fruit-driven nose—very ripe, almost squashed banana aromas perfumed with vanilla. Ripe banana flavours. *Koala Wines*

| | |
|---|---|
| *Price* | €12–€15 |
| *Region* | Hunter Valley |
| *Grape* | Chardonnay |
| *Alc/vol* | 13.5% |
| *Food* | Cheese/Gruyère |
| *Drink* | 2002–3 |

## McWilliam's Hunter Valley Chardonnay 99 ☆

Big, fat, ripe nose with tropical fruit, butter and hazelnut aromas. The powerful palate has super-ripe tropical fruit and honey and a long, persistent finish. *TDL*

| | |
|---|---|
| *Price* | €12–€15 |
| *Region* | Hunter Valley |
| *Grape* | Chardonnay |
| *Alc/vol* | 13.5% |
| *Food* | Pasta/creamy sauces |
| *Drink* | 2002–3 |

## Pewsey Vale Riesling 00

Very fresh and crisp style, with aromas and flavours of Granny Smith apples, elderflowers and lime, needing food and a little time to open out fully. *Cassidy*

| | |
|---|---|
| *Price* | €12–€15 |
| *Region* | Eden Valley |
| *Grape* | Riesling |
| *Alc/vol* | 12.5% |
| *Food* | Fish/grilled fish |
| *Drink* | 2002–4 |

## Rufus Stone Sauvignon Blanc 01

Zesty and full of life, with aromatic, grassy, gooseberry and spring flower aromas and an intense, weighty, fruit-driven palate with ripe gooseberry, lime peel and hints of asparagus and nettles. *Oddbins*

| | |
|---|---|
| *Price* | €12–€15 |
| *Region* | McLaren Vale |
| *Grape* | Sauvignon Blanc |
| *Alc/vol* | 11.5% |
| *Food* | Fish/mullet |
| *Drink* | 2002–3 |

## St Hallett Barossa Select Semillon 98 ☆☆ €

This wine has the wow factor. It is complex and beautifully balanced, toasty, spicy, nutty and fruity, with oranges and apricots, a touch of honey, and terrific length. *O'Briens*

| | |
|---|---|
| Price | €12–€15 |
| Region | Barossa Valley |
| Grape | Semillon |
| Alc/vol | 13.5% |
| Food | Pâté/terrines |
| Drink | 2002–5 |

## St Hallett Eden Valley Riesling 00 ☆

Rich and full of flavour, showing some maturity with definite kerosene and oily elements as well as spice, red apple, lemon peel and lime, cleansing acidity and very good length. *O'Briens*

| | |
|---|---|
| Price | €12–€15 |
| Region | Eden Valley |
| Grape | Riesling |
| Alc/vol | 11.5% |
| Food | Ethnic/Japanese |
| Drink | 2002–5 |

## Yalumba Y Series Viognier 01

A classic Viognier with its fragrant nose, prickly mouth-watering acidity, and apple, peach, apricot and cream flavours. Best with food as it is still very young. *Cassidy*

| | |
|---|---|
| Price | €12–€15 |
| Region | South Australia |
| Grape | Viognier |
| Alc/vol | 13.5% |
| Food | Seafood/shellfish |
| Drink | 2003–4 |

### €15–€18

## Knappstein Riesling 01

Concentrated aromas of petrol on the nose and an excellent weight of flavours of grape and citrus with cleansing acidity. *Woodford Bourne*

| | |
|---|---|
| Price | €15–€18 |
| Region | Clare Valley |
| Grape | Riesling |
| Alc/vol | 12.5% |
| Food | Fish/salads |
| Drink | 2002–3 |

## Leeuwin Estate Art Series Riesling 00 ☆

Pronounced lime, apple, liquorice and herbs on the nose with a hint of kerosene—classic aromas. There are apricots in addition on the stylish palate, which has a lovely supple finish. *Searsons*

| | |
|---|---|
| Price | €15–€18 |
| Region | Margaret River |
| Grape | Riesling |
| Alc/vol | 13.5% |
| Food | Meat/ham |
| Drink | 2002–4 |

## Lenswood Vineyards Sauvignon Blanc 01

Juicy, fruity and tangy—this fine Sauvignon is made in a good chill-out style with oodles of flavour. Granny Smith apples, citrus fruit, nettles and grass on the nose with grapefruit, lime and green, grassy flavours on the palate. *Wines Direct*

| | |
|---|---|
| Price | €15–€18 |
| Region | South Australia |
| Grape | Sauvignon Blanc |
| Alc/vol | 12.5% |
| Food | Fish/smoked salmon |
| Drink | 2002–3 |

## Nepenthe Lenswood Riesling 00

Stony, dryish style with a hint of sweetness. Tropical fruit and candyfloss on the ripe nose, blackcurrant leaf and clementine flavours with a floral, rosewater hint. *Barry & Fitzwilliam*

| | |
|---|---|
| *Price* | €15–€18 |
| *Region* | Adelaide Hills |
| *Grape* | Riesling |
| *Alc/vol* | 13.5% |
| *Food* | Ethnic/Indian |
| *Drink* | 2002–4 |

## Nepenthe Lenswood Semillon 99

Attractive nose with lemon and apricot aromas and a little treacle. Opening out nicely in the mouth, the wine is quite limy with a very good lemon sorbet crispness and lovely length. *Barry & Fitzwilliam*

| | |
|---|---|
| *Price* | €15–€18 |
| *Region* | Adelaide Hills |
| *Grape* | Semillon |
| *Alc/vol* | 14% |
| *Food* | Seafood/shellfish |
| *Drink* | 2002–7 |

## Ninth Island Chardonnay 00 ☆

Elegant, with enticing aromas of mango, kiwi and lemon and a great depth of slightly nutty citrus and tropical fruit on the palate. *Irish Distillers*

| | |
|---|---|
| *Price* | €15–€18 |
| *Region* | Tasmania |
| *Grape* | Chardonnay |
| *Alc/vol* | 13% |
| *Food* | Fish/salmon |
| *Drink* | 2002–3 |

## Peel Estate Chenin Blanc 98

Wonderful golden colour with concentrated, buttery, tropical fruits on the nose. The palate is unusual: though dry, it has such ripe, honeyed, intense, buttered fruit that it appears richer. It needs food to match the intensity. *Waterford Wine Vault*

| | |
|---|---|
| *Price* | €15–€18 |
| *Region* | Western Australia |
| *Grape* | Chenin Blanc |
| *Alc/vol* | 14.5% |
| *Food* | Seafood/risotto |
| *Drink* | 2002–3 |

## Pierro LTC Semillon Sauvignon Blanc 01

LTC stands for 'Les Trois Cuvées', the wine's former name. It is a restrained style, with clear, crisp, lemon, pineapple and mango flavours, and a slight herbal twist with fresh, green citrus acidity. *Wines Direct*

| | |
|---|---|
| *Price* | €15–€18 |
| *Region* | Western Australia |
| *Grape* | Semillon/Sauv Blanc |
| *Alc/vol* | 13.5% |
| *Food* | Cheese/soufflé |
| *Drink* | 2002–3 |

## Rosemount Estate Show Reserve Chardonnay 00 ☆

An oily vanilla nose sets the palate up for a weighty mouthfeel of ripe tropical fruits with a touch of wood smoke and butterscotch. The surprise is the great zesty, lemony acidity. *Grants*

| | |
|---|---|
| *Price* | €15–€18 |
| *Region* | Hunter Valley |
| *Grape* | Chardonnay |
| *Alc/vol* | 13.5% |
| *Food* | Ethnic/Indian |
| *Drink* | 2002–4 |

## Somerset Hill Unwooded Chardonnay 00 ☆

Inviting aromas of vanilla and ripe fruit; rich, buttery palate with tropical fruit salad flavours and a delicious length of flavour. *Oddbins*

| | |
|---|---|
| *Price* | €15–€18 |
| *Region* | Great Southern |
| *Grape* | Chardonnay |
| *Alc/vol* | 13% |
| *Food* | Fish/monkfish |
| *Drink* | 2002-3 |

## Wolf Blass President's Selection Chardonnay 00

Tropical summer images are evoked by this wine's pineapple and light vanilla aromas and it tastes of summer, too, with its flavours of cara-melised pears and apples. *Dillons*

| | |
|---|---|
| *Price* | €15–€18 |
| *Region* | South Australia |
| *Grape* | Chardonnay |
| *Alc/vol* | 13% |
| *Food* | Fish/seafood |
| *Drink* | 2002-3 |

## Xanadu Semillon 99

A big, generous wine, nicely made and pleasing with fresh lemon and lime mingled with more luscious flavours, vanilla, orange marmalade and nuts. *O'Briens*

| | |
|---|---|
| *Price* | €15–€18 |
| *Region* | Margaret River |
| *Grape* | Semillon |
| *Alc/vol* | 13.5% |
| *Food* | Cheese/Ardrahan |
| *Drink* | 2002-5 |

### €18–€22

## Geoff Merrill Reserve Chardonnay 97

This high quality wine has aged really well and is showing nicely matured aromas and flavours of dried apricot, vanilla and nuts, with excellent intensity and length. From McLaren Vale (60 per cent), Coonawarra (26 per cent) and Padth-away (14 per cent). *Comans*

| | |
|---|---|
| *Price* | €18–€22 |
| *Region* | South Australia |
| *Grape* | Chardonnay |
| *Alc/vol* | 13% |
| *Food* | Poultry/chicken |
| *Drink* | 2002-3 |

## Greg Norman Estates Chardonnay 00

Slightly floral but restrained pea pod nose, fol-lowed by intense peach and citrus flavours and a long, warm finish. An interesting wine. *Cassidy*

| | |
|---|---|
| *Price* | €18–€22 |
| *Region* | Yarra Valley |
| *Grape* | Chardonnay |
| *Alc/vol* | 12.5% |
| *Food* | Fish/cod |
| *Drink* | 2002-4 |

## Grosset Semillon Sauvignon Blanc 00 ☆

Charming and classic, this wine shows finesse from the first. Aromas of lemon, gooseberry and grass with green vegetal and pea pod notes; spicy but lemony palate with asparagus and lime flavours. *Wines Direct*

| | |
|---|---|
| *Price* | €18–€22 |
| *Region* | Clare Valley |
| *Grape* | Semillon/Sauv Blanc |
| *Alc/vol* | 13% |
| *Food* | Fish/fish pie |
| *Drink* | 2002-5 |

## Hardys Tintara Chardonnay 00

An elegant wine showing some development, with an attractive, rich, tropical fruit nose and strong flavours of pink grapefruit complemented by crisp acidity and oak. *Allied Drinks*

| | |
|---|---|
| *Price* | €18–€22 |
| *Region* | South Australia |
| *Grape* | Chardonnay |
| *Alc/vol* | 13% |
| *Food* | Seafood/shellfish |
| *Drink* | 2002–3 |

## Katnook Estate Sauvignon Blanc 00 ☆

Exudes aromas of ripe gooseberries, lime, melon and apple. Delicious fruity palate with pineapple and mango, nettle and blackcurrant leaf flavours and a chalky underlayer.
*Woodford Bourne*

| | |
|---|---|
| *Price* | €18–€22 |
| *Region* | Coonawarra |
| *Grape* | Sauvignon Blanc |
| *Alc/vol* | 13.5% |
| *Food* | Salads/asparagus |
| *Drink* | 2002–3 |

### €22–€25

## Cape Mentelle Chardonnay 99 ☆☆

A wine full of character and interest. The nose is creamy, nutty and smoky with savoury and waxy lemon aromas. The very intense palate has juicy, tropical fruit salad flavours which, although big and full-bodied, finish elegantly lean and long. *Findlaters*

| | |
|---|---|
| *Price* | €22–€25 |
| *Region* | Margaret River |
| *Grape* | Chardonnay |
| *Alc/vol* | 14% |
| *Food* | Fish/smoked salmon |
| *Drink* | 2002–5 |

## Hewitson Riesling 01

More Alsace in style than Australia, this Riesling has a big nose with petrol and floral aromas, as well as honey and pineapple, and an off-dry palate with generous, juicy, stewed apple flavours and a crisp, zesty finish. *WineKnows*

| | |
|---|---|
| *Price* | €22–€25 |
| *Region* | McLaren Vale/ Eden Valley |
| *Grape* | Riesling |
| *Alc/vol* | 12% |
| *Food* | Meat/ham |
| *Drink* | 2002–4 |

### €25–€30

## De Bortoli Yarra Valley Chardonnay 99

Warm, big and spicy. Toasty and nutty aromas follow through on the palate together with luscious fruity flavours, harmoniously balanced with oak. *Febvre*

| | |
|---|---|
| *Price* | €25–€30 |
| *Region* | Yarra Valley |
| *Grape* | Chardonnay |
| *Alc/vol* | 13.5% |
| *Food* | Poultry/turkey |
| *Drink* | 2002–5 |

€30–€35

## Tyrrell's Vat 1 Hunter Semillon 95 ☆

Over its seven years of ageing this wine has developed aromas of luscious, ripe, honeyed fruits, caramel, nuts and lime. The palate is bone dry but quite tangy, with lots of life still and delicious grapefruit and marmalade flavours. *Maxxium*

| | |
|---|---|
| *Price* | €30–€35 |
| *Region* | Hunter Valley |
| *Grape* | Semillon |
| *Alc/vol* | 11.3% |
| *Food* | Fish/tuna |
| *Drink* | 2002–6 |

## Tyrrell's Vat 47 Pinot Chardonnay 96 ☆

A big but elegant wine with aromas of pineapple and spice. The very fruity palate has nice tart pineapple flavours with an oily, oaky influence. *Maxxium*

| | |
|---|---|
| *Price* | €30–€35 |
| *Region* | Hunter Valley |
| *Grape* | Chardonnay |
| *Alc/vol* | 13.5% |
| *Food* | Fish/John Dory |
| *Drink* | 2002–3 |

# Red

Under €9

## Cudgee Creek Cabernet Sauvignon 00 €

Full and fruity with redcurrants and bramble fruit on the agreeable nose. Rosehip, cherry and redcurrant flavours, with some heat and pepper. *Koala Wines*

| | |
|---|---|
| *Price* | Under €9 |
| *Region* | Murray Darling |
| *Grape* | Cabernet Sauvignon |
| *Alc/vol* | 13.5% |
| *Food* | Meat/lamb chops |
| *Drink* | 2002–3 |

## Eaglehawk Merlot 00

Lightly perfumed, fruity aromas. Silky textured with plum jam and ripe black fruit flavours and just a little touch of mint. *Dillons*

| | |
|---|---|
| *Price* | Under €9 |
| *Region* | SE Australia |
| *Grape* | Merlot |
| *Alc/vol* | 13% |
| *Food* | Fish/tuna |
| *Drink* | 2002–3 |

## Jacob's Creek Cabernet Sauvignon 00 €

A good example of Cabernet with super blackcurrant leaf aromas and generous blackcurrant flavours. There are also hints of herbs, mint, earth and cedar. *Irish Distillers*

| | |
|---|---|
| *Price* | Under €9 |
| *Region* | SE Australia |
| *Grape* | Cabernet Sauvignon |
| *Alc/vol* | 13% |
| *Food* | Meat/hamburgers |
| *Drink* | 2002–3 |

### Lindemans Cawarra Shiraz Cabernet 00

Straightforward and easy drinking with fruity and vegetal aromas and blackcurrant flavours. *Grants*

| | |
|---|---|
| *Price* | Under €9 |
| *Region* | SE Australia |
| *Grape* | Shiraz/Cab Sauv |
| *Alc/vol* | 12.5% |
| *Food* | Meat/stew |
| *Drink* | 2002–3 |

### Yellow Tail Shiraz 01

Sweet blackberry aromas, with some tar, are followed by pleasant, ripe, spicy red fruit flavours and lots of black pepper. *Oddbins*

| | |
|---|---|
| *Price* | Under €9 |
| *Region* | SE Australia |
| *Grape* | Shiraz |
| *Alc/vol* | 13.5% |
| *Food* | Meat/spicy dishes |
| *Drink* | 2002–3 |

€9–€12

### Angove's Classic Reserve Shiraz 00 ☆ €

Attractive fruity, earthy nose with spice and mint. Wonderful weight of blackcurrants on the palate with nuances of mushroom and fennel; all the flavours are held together in a firm, tannic structure. *O'Briens*

| | |
|---|---|
| *Price* | €9–€12 |
| *Region* | South Australia |
| *Grape* | Shiraz |
| *Alc/vol* | 13.5% |
| *Food* | Meat/ribs |
| *Drink* | 2002–4 |

## Blewitt Springs Cabernet Sauvignon 98 ☆☆ €

A classic—big, rich and intense. Eucalyptus
and mint aromas and a spicy, oaky palate with
assertive tannins and layers of flavours of
earthy blackcurrant fruit and coffee.
*WineOnline*

| | |
|---|---|
| Price | €9–€12 |
| Region | McLaren Vale/ Langhorne Creek |
| Grape | Cabernet Sauvignon |
| Alc/vol | 13% |
| Food | Meat/beef |
| Drink | 2002–4 |

## d'Arenberg The Stump Jump Grenache Shiraz 99

A summery red, with a pronounced nose of
raspberry and intense, ripe, juicy red fruit on
the spicy palate. *Taserra*

| | |
|---|---|
| Price | €9–€12 |
| Region | McLaren Vale |
| Grape | Grenache/Shiraz |
| Alc/vol | 14.5% |
| Food | Meat/lamb kebabs |
| Drink | 2002–3 |

## Half Moon Shiraz 00

Smoky and leathery with intense, ripe blackcurrant and raspberry aromas, and a smooth,
creamy palate. There are some medicinal notes
to the flavours of blackberry fruit compote.
*Mitchells*

| | |
|---|---|
| Price | €9–€12 |
| Region | Cowra NSW |
| Grape | Shiraz |
| Alc/vol | 12.5% |
| Food | Pasta/arrabiata |
| Drink | 2002–3 |

## Hardys Stamp Cabernet Merlot 00

Fruit pudding aromas, with a touch of oak,
matched by a smooth and supple palate with
blackcurrant and plum flavours and softening
tannins. *Allied Drinks*

| | |
|---|---|
| Price | €9–€12 |
| Region | SE Australia |
| Grape | Cab Sauv/Merlot |
| Alc/vol | 12.5% |
| Food | Meat/lamb |
| Drink | 2002–3 |

## Hills View Vineyards Cabernet Merlot 99

Jam-packed with plums, blackcurrants and a
hint of fig, with an earthy, spicy edge.
*WineOnline*

| | |
|---|---|
| Price | €9–€12 |
| Region | Langhorne Creek |
| Grape | Cab Sauv/Merlot |
| Alc/vol | 13% |
| Food | Meat/beef |
| Drink | 2002–3 |

## Hills View Vineyards Shiraz Cabernet 00

Big and approachable, full of juicy fruit and
very easy to drink with its sweet background of
ripe blackcurrants and damsons, green pepper
and fig flavours, soft tannins and gentle finish.
*WineOnline*

| | |
|---|---|
| Price | €9–€12 |
| Region | Langhorne Creek |
| Grape | Shiraz/Cab Sauv |
| Alc/vol | 13% |
| Food | Meat/barbecue |
| Drink | 2002–3 |

## Jindalee Cabernet Sauvignon 00

A hot-climate Aussie style, ample and full bodied with generous sweet Ribena aromas and spicy, earthy, black fruit flavours. *Koala Wines*

| | |
|---|---|
| *Price* | €9–€12 |
| *Region* | Murray Darling |
| *Grape* | Cabernet Sauvignon |
| *Alc/vol* | 13.5% |
| *Food* | Meat/steak |
| *Drink* | 2002–4 |

## Jindalee Merlot 00

Soft and easy drinking with fruitcake aromas, and rich damson and plum flavours with a toasty character. Warm, peppery finish.
*Koala Wines*

| | |
|---|---|
| *Price* | €9–€12 |
| *Region* | Murray Darling |
| *Grape* | Merlot |
| *Alc/vol* | 14% |
| *Food* | Pasta/Bolognese |
| *Drink* | 2002–3 |

## Jindalee Shiraz 99

Classic and rustic at the same time with aromas of rubber, tar and leather and fruity flavours of plum, blackberry and blackcurrant with a good dash of pepper and tobacco. *Koala Wines*

| | |
|---|---|
| *Price* | €9–€12 |
| *Region* | Murray Darling |
| *Grape* | Shiraz |
| *Alc/vol* | 14% |
| *Food* | Meat/stew |
| *Drink* | 2002–4 |

## McGuigan Bin 4000 Cabernet Sauvignon 99

A rich, creamy, fruity nose is matched by appetising flavours of sweet blackcurrant fruit, with a nice lick of liquorice and fennel. Good, persistent finish. *Barry & Fitzwilliam*

| | |
|---|---|
| *Price* | €9–€12 |
| *Region* | SE Australia |
| *Grape* | Cabernet Sauvignon |
| *Alc/vol* | 13% |
| *Food* | Pasta/lasagne |
| *Drink* | 2002–3 |

## McGuigan Bin 3000 Limited Release Merlot 00

A wine with character, showing some nice development. Aromas of fruitcake and a fine inky palate with ripe tannins, peppery nuances and mellow dark fruits. *Barry & Fitzwilliam*

| | |
|---|---|
| *Price* | €9–€12 |
| *Region* | SE Australia |
| *Grape* | Merlot |
| *Alc/vol* | 14% |
| *Food* | Meat/meatballs |
| *Drink* | 2002–3 |

## McGuigan The Black Label Merlot 01

Satisfying and pleasing pepper and tobacco character with blackberry and blackcurrant fruit and nuances of menthol. *Barry & Fitzwilliam*

| | |
|---|---|
| *Price* | €9–€12 |
| *Region* | SE Australia |
| *Grape* | Merlot |
| *Alc/vol* | 13.5% |
| *Food* | Poultry/chicken wings |
| *Drink* | 2002–3 |

## McWilliam's Inheritance Shiraz Cabernet 00

Lightly scented with raspberries and summer fruits. Much richer flavours of ripe fruit, spice and wine gums and an interesting, slightly burnt or earthy dimension. *TDL*

| | |
|---|---|
| *Price* | €9–€12 |
| *Region* | SE Australia |
| *Grape* | Shiraz/Cab Sauv |
| *Alc/vol* | 12.5% |
| *Food* | Meat/pork |
| *Drink* | 2002–3 |

## Oxford Landing Merlot 00

Light and feminine style, spicy and fruity with plum, damson and loganberry fruit and hints of violets. *Cassidy*

| | |
|---|---|
| *Price* | €9–€12 |
| *Region* | South Australia |
| *Grape* | Merlot |
| *Alc/vol* | 13% |
| *Food* | Meat/liver |
| *Drink* | 2002–3 |

## Peter Lehmann Clancy's 00 ☆☆ €

A generous wine, laden with aromas of toasty, spicy oak. More toasty oak, with baked blackberry and chewy, ripe berry fruit, on the palate with touches of warm, spicy clove and liquorice allsorts. *Comans*

| | |
|---|---|
| *Price* | €9–€12 |
| *Region* | Barossa Valley |
| *Grape* | Shiraz/Cab Sauv/ Merlot/Cab Franc |
| *Alc/vol* | 13.5% |
| *Food* | Pizza/pepperoni |
| *Drink* | 2002–3 |

## Tatachilla Partners Cabernet Sauvignon Shiraz 00

Lots of peppery, spicy black fruit flavours give good depth, intensity and warmth with a nice rustic edge. *O'Briens*

| | |
|---|---|
| *Price* | €9–€12 |
| *Region* | South Australia |
| *Grape* | Cab Sauv/Shiraz |
| *Alc/vol* | 13.5% |
| *Food* | Meat/mushroom-based dishes |
| *Drink* | 2002–3 |

## Wakefield Cabernet Sauvignon 00

Gentle and easy, with a perfumed, floral nose and fruity, blackcurrant flavour.
*Koala Wines*

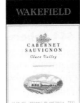

| | |
|---|---|
| *Price* | €9–€12 |
| *Region* | Clare Valley |
| *Grape* | Cabernet Sauvignon |
| *Alc/vol* | 13.5% |
| *Food* | Meat/barbecue |
| *Drink* | 2002–3 |

## Wakefield Promised Land Shiraz Cabernet 01

Classic, fruity, spicy style. Pure blackcurrant and white pepper on the nose, with intense blackberry and blackcurrant flavours and a firm tannic structure with a decent finish.
*Koala Wines*

| | |
|---|---|
| Price | €9–€12 |
| Region | South Australia |
| Grape | Shiraz/Cab Sauv |
| Alc/vol | 13.5% |
| Food | Cheese/Cheddar |
| Drink | 2002–4 |

## Wakefield Shiraz 01

A classic of its type. The aromas of rubber and black berry fruits, touched with pepper, are mirrored on the palate, with an extra dash of pepper. *Koala Wines*

| | |
|---|---|
| Price | €9–€12 |
| Region | Clare Valley |
| Grape | Shiraz |
| Alc/vol | 14.5% |
| Food | Meat/bacon |
| Drink | 2002–3 |

## Weandre Stream Shiraz 00

Full-bodied Shiraz with a smoky bramble fruit nose. Juicy palate with strawberry and raspberry flavours, some savoury elements and soft tannins. *Marks & Spencer*

| | |
|---|---|
| Price | €9–€12 |
| Region | Orange |
| Grape | Shiraz |
| Alc/vol | 12.5% |
| Food | Meat/pork |
| Drink | 2002–3 |

## Wolf Blass Red Label Shiraz Cabernet Sauvignon 00

Dry and firm tannins make this a winner with red meats. It's quite fruity with spice and green pepper flavours, and a finesse that's very appealing. *Dillons*

| | |
|---|---|
| Price | €9–€12 |
| Region | South Australia |
| Grape | Shiraz/Cab Sauv |
| Alc/vol | 13% |
| Food | Meat/beef |
| Drink | 2002–3 |

## Wyndham Estate Bin 444 Cabernet Sauvignon 99

Aromas of cherries, blackcurrants and cedar. Very good, chewy, complex palate with a tightly-knit structure and flavours of ripe blackcurrants, spicy currants, cigar box and tobacco.
*Irish Distillers*

| | |
|---|---|
| Price | €9–€12 |
| Region | SE Australia |
| Grape | Cabernet Sauvignon |
| Alc/vol | 13.5% |
| Food | Meat/lamb chops |
| Drink | 2002–3 |

## Wyndham Estate Bin 555 Shiraz 00 ☆☆ €

Smoky, inky and spicy, this generous wine has sweet cherry, leather and liquorice flavours, ripe tannins and mouth-filling richness.
*Irish Distillers*

| | |
|---|---|
| Price | €9–€12 |
| Region | SE Australia |
| Grape | Shiraz |
| Alc/vol | 13.5% |
| Food | Meat/steak |
| Drink | 2002–3 |

## Wyndham Estate Bin 888 Cabernet Merlot 00 ☆☆ €

An elegant style with aromas of blackcurrant, plum, toffee and spicy cedarwood. Hints of chocolate and tobacco give depth to the earthy fruit flavours. *Irish Distillers*

| | |
|---|---|
| Price | **€9–€12** |
| Region | **SE Australia** |
| Grape | **Cab Sauv/Merlot** |
| Alc/vol | **13%** |
| Food | **Meat/roasts** |
| Drink | **2002–3** |

## Xanadu Secession 00

Perfectly made, very fruity without being jammy, with good levels of soft, ripe, blackcurrant fruit, floral touches and some spice. *O'Briens*

| | |
|---|---|
| Price | **€9–€12** |
| Region | **Western Australia** |
| Grape | **Shiraz/Cab Sauv** |
| Alc/vol | **14%** |
| Food | **Pasta/pesto** |
| Drink | **2002–3** |

### €12–€15

## Baileys Glenrowan Shiraz 99

Satisfying, classic style. Spicy and peppery with fruity aromas and flavours of blackberry, dark cherry and plum and a really good, peppery finish. *Koála Wines*

| | |
|---|---|
| Price | **€12–€15** |
| Region | **NE Victoria** |
| Grape | **Shiraz** |
| Alc/vol | **13.5%** |
| Food | **Poultry/goose** |
| Drink | **2002–3** |

## Brookland Valley Verse 1 Cabernet Merlot 99

Reminiscent of Bordeaux from a ripe vintage, with dense blackcurrant and oak on the nose and intense cassis flavours with a touch of spice and tobacco. *Oddbins*

| | |
|---|---|
| Price | **€12–€15** |
| Region | **Margaret River** |
| Grape | **Cab Sauv/Merlot** |
| Alc/vol | **13.5%** |
| Food | **Meat/lamb** |
| Drink | **2002–3** |

## Brown Brothers Barbera 00

A very attractive example of full-bodied Barbera. Ripe blackberry, plum and cherry fruit with a hefty, spicy kick, firm tannins and crisp acidity. *Woodford Bourne*

| | |
|---|---|
| Price | **€12–€15** |
| Region | **King Valley** |
| Grape | **Barbera** |
| Alc/vol | **14.5%** |
| Food | **Pasta/Bolognese** |
| Drink | **2002–4** |

## d'Arenberg The High Trellis Cabernet Sauvignon 00

A generous wine with blackcurrant aromas, slightly floral and tinged with mint. The fruit-packed palate has blackcurrant and eucalyptus flavours. *Taserra*

| | |
|---|---|
| Price | **€12–€15** |
| Region | **McLaren Vale/ Coonawarra** |
| Grape | **Cabernet Sauvignon** |
| Alc/vol | **13%** |
| Food | **Meat/lamb curry** |
| Drink | **2002–4** |

## Evans & Tate Margaret River Cabernet Merlot 99

Distinguished, velvety style with a firm tannic backbone supported by very good fruit. Raspberry and blackberry fruit compote nose, plum and blackcurrant flavours with hints of chocolate. *Comans*

| | |
|---|---|
| *Price* | €12–€15 |
| *Region* | Margaret River |
| *Grape* | Cab Sauv/Merlot |
| *Alc/vol* | 14% |
| *Food* | Vegetarian/grilled vegetables |
| *Drink* | 2002–3 |

## Gold Rock Shiraz 00

The blackberry and blackcurrant nose has a floral, perfumed note, followed by ripe fruit flavours of plum and raspberry and a good dash of cassis. *Koala Wines*

| | |
|---|---|
| *Price* | €12–€15 |
| *Region* | Hunter Valley |
| *Grape* | Shiraz |
| *Alc/vol* | 12.5% |
| *Food* | Meat/steak |
| *Drink* | 2002–4 |

## Hardys Nottage Hill Cabernet Sauvignon Shiraz 00

Spicy, crushed red fruit aromas and a soft, fruity palate—blackcurrant and plum—quite spicy and peppery. *Allied Drinks*

| | |
|---|---|
| *Price* | €12–€15 |
| *Region* | SE Australia |
| *Grape* | Cab Sauv/Shiraz |
| *Alc/vol* | 12.5% |
| *Food* | Meat/shepherd's pie |
| *Drink* | 2002–3 |

## Hardys Nottage Hill Shiraz 98

Hearty Shiraz with a rich, spicy nose of vanilla, eucalyptus and mint aromas and an equally rich palate of mulberry and plum flavours, firm tannins and a savoury finish. *Allied Drinks*

| | |
|---|---|
| *Price* | €12–€15 |
| *Region* | SE Australia |
| *Grape* | Shiraz |
| *Alc/vol* | 14% |
| *Food* | Meat/pork |
| *Drink* | 2002–3 |

## Ironstone Shiraz Grenache 00

A weight of fruit waiting to be unleashed shows in the earthy nose of black hedgerow fruits. The flavours are of cassis and mixed black fruit jam with a touch of vanilla. *Findlaters*

| | |
|---|---|
| *Price* | €12–€15 |
| *Region* | Western Australia |
| *Grape* | Shiraz/Grenache |
| *Alc/vol* | 14.5% |
| *Food* | Meat/moussaka |
| *Drink* | 2002–4 |

## Jacob's Creek Reserve Shiraz 99 ☆☆ €

A big, warming wine with aromas of mint, eucalyptus and tons of spicy, black fruit. Smoky, peppery, sweet plum and damson flavours with mint and chocolate. *Irish Distillers*

| | |
|---|---|
| *Price* | €12–€15 |
| *Region* | South Australia |
| *Grape* | Shiraz |
| *Alc/vol* | 14% |
| *Food* | Meat/roasts |
| *Drink* | 2002–3 |

## Jamieson's Run Cabernet Shiraz Merlot 99

Chewy, with good tannic structure, perfumed with blackcurrants and infused with spicy pepper and smoke. *Gilbeys*

| | |
|---|---|
| Price | €12–€15 |
| Region | Coonawarra |
| Grape | Cabernet Sauvignon/ Shiraz/Merlot |
| Alc/vol | 13.5% |
| Food | Poultry/chicken |
| Drink | 2002–4 |

## Katnook Estate Cabernet Sauvignon 98

Fruit packed, big and beefy, with lots of juicy, ripe blackcurrant flavours and a hint of mint. *Woodford Bourne*

| | |
|---|---|
| Price | €12–€15 |
| Region | Coonawarra |
| Grape | Cabernet Sauvignon |
| Alc/vol | 13.5% |
| Food | Meat/stew |
| Drink | 2002–4 |

## Peel Estate Premium Red 99

Restrained, and more Old than New World in style. Plum, fig and raspberry flavours with some earthiness. *Waterford Wine Vault*

| | |
|---|---|
| Price | €12–€15 |
| Region | Western Australia |
| Grape | Merlot/Cab Franc |
| Alc/vol | 13% |
| Food | Meat/veal |
| Drink | 2002–3 |

## Peter Lehmann The Barossa Cabernet Sauvignon 99

The succulent nose—fruity, perfumed and rose-scented—really stands out. The rich chocolate and classic fruit palate is packed with blackcurrants and has great length of flavour. *Comans*

| | |
|---|---|
| Price | €12–€15 |
| Region | Barossa Valley |
| Grape | Cabernet Sauvignon |
| Alc/vol | 13.5% |
| Food | Meat/steak |
| Drink | 2002–3 |

## Peter Lehmann The Barossa Shiraz 00

Lovely flavours of soft, ripe blackcurrants, cherries and plums, backed by spice, with a long, warm, peppery finish. *Comans*

| | |
|---|---|
| Price | €12–€15 |
| Region | Barossa Valley |
| Grape | Shiraz |
| Alc/vol | 14% |
| Food | Poultry/duck |
| Drink | 2002–3 |

## Wolf Blass Merlot 00

Lots of flavour has been extracted here and given a good dollop of wood, resulting in a big, full, juicy, peppery and chocolatey style, with smoke, vanilla and caramel. *Dillons*

| | |
|---|---|
| Price | €12–€15 |
| Region | South Australia |
| Grape | Merlot |
| Alc/vol | 13% |
| Food | Meat/lamb |
| Drink | 2002–3 |

## Wolf Blass Shiraz 00

Soft, muted nose but plenty of ripe blackcurrant and black pepper flavours with some depth, supported by firm tannins. *Dillons*

| | |
|---|---|
| *Price* | €12–€15 |
| *Region* | South Australia |
| *Grape* | Shiraz |
| *Alc/vol* | 13% |
| *Food* | Meat/barbecue |
| *Drink* | 2002–3 |

## Yaldara Reserve Cabernet Merlot 99

Quite a classic style and all too easy to drink. Cassis and black fruit aromas on the forward nose; pure blackcurrant fruit flavours with toasty caramel and hints of woody spice. *Barry & Fitzwilliam*

| | |
|---|---|
| *Price* | €12–€15 |
| *Region* | SE Australia |
| *Grape* | Cab Sauv/Merlot |
| *Alc/vol* | 13.5% |
| *Food* | Meat/casseroles |
| *Drink* | 2002–3 |

## Yalumba Barossa Bush Vine Grenache 00

Warm and generous with a weighty mouth-watering palate of spicy fruitcake, luscious blackcurrant and redcurrant fruit, aniseed, clove and cinnamon. *Cassidy*

| | |
|---|---|
| *Price* | €12–€15 |
| *Region* | Barossa Valley |
| *Grape* | Grenache |
| *Alc/vol* | 14% |
| *Food* | Ethnic/Indian |
| *Drink* | 2002–3 |

## Yalumba Y Series Merlot 99

A good example of Merlot with its big, plummy, spicy nose, elegant, silky texture and plum, fig, spice and fruitcake flavours, lingering on the finish. *Cassidy*

| | |
|---|---|
| *Price* | €12–€15 |
| *Region* | South Australia |
| *Grape* | Merlot |
| *Alc/vol* | 14% |
| *Food* | Cheese/Gorgonzola |
| *Drink* | 2002–3 |

### €15–€18

## Baileys 1920s Block Glenrowan Shiraz 98 ☆

Rich and intense, yet elegant and restrained. Ripe blackcurrant and cigar box aromas are matched by concentrated, spicy flavours of red and black currants, plums and liquorice. *Koala Wines*

| | |
|---|---|
| *Price* | €15–€18 |
| *Region* | Victoria |
| *Grape* | Shiraz |
| *Alc/vol* | 14% |
| *Food* | Meat/char-grilled lamb |
| *Drink* | 2002–4 |

## Bethany Schrapel Family Vineyards Cabernet Merlot 99 ☆

Aromas are toasty and oaky with vanilla, coffee and pastille fruits; the flavours are of currants and chocolate. The tannins are firm but the very good fruit character complements this. *O'Briens*

| | |
|---|---|
| *Price* | €15–€18 |
| *Region* | Barossa Valley |
| *Grape* | Cab Sauv/Merlot |
| *Alc/vol* | 13% |
| *Food* | Meat/casserole |
| *Drink* | 2002–3 |

## Brokenwood Shiraz 99

More savoury than fruity in character with aromas of tobacco, tar and spice and big, but mellow, flavours of black fruit, leather and black pepper. *Oddbins*

| | |
|---|---|
| *Price* | **€15–€18** |
| *Region* | **McLaren/Padthaway** |
| *Grape* | **Shiraz** |
| *Alc/vol* | **13.5%** |
| *Food* | **Vegetarian/bean dishes** |
| *Drink* | **2002–3** |

## Cape Jaffa Mt Benson Shiraz 00

Intense nose with fruitcake and cherry aromas. Big, rich, juicy flavours of cherry and plum with a very smooth, soft texture. *Wines Direct*

| | |
|---|---|
| *Price* | **€15–€18** |
| *Region* | **South Australia** |
| *Grape* | **Shiraz** |
| *Alc/vol* | **13.5%** |
| *Food* | **Meat/stew** |
| *Drink* | **2002–3** |

## Coriole Redstone 99

Restrained style with interesting aromas of oriental spices, smoky bacon, ripe cherries, prunes and plums and a palate which is subtle, yet concentrated, with more plums and some leather. *Wines Direct*

| | |
|---|---|
| *Price* | **€15–€18** |
| *Region* | **McLaren Vale** |
| *Grape* | **Shiraz** |
| *Alc/vol* | **14%** |
| *Food* | **Meat/salami** |
| *Drink* | **2002–3** |

## d'Arenberg The Custodian Grenache 99

Soft, fruity, juicy style with blackberries and plums on both the nose and palate. Inky and peppery with noticeable tannins giving backbone—delicious with or without food. *Oddbins*

| | |
|---|---|
| *Price* | **€15–€18** |
| *Region* | **McLaren Vale** |
| *Grape* | **Grenache** |
| *Alc/vol* | **14.5%** |
| *Food* | **Indian/curries** |
| *Drink* | **2002–4** |

## Knappstein Cabernet Franc 98 ☆

Elegant, and wonderfully different, with an appealing floral character. The inviting nose of red and black currants has a distinct floral edge which also marks the palate with its flavours of redcurrants and blueberries. *Woodford Bourne*

| | |
|---|---|
| *Price* | **€15–€18** |
| *Region* | **Clare Valley** |
| *Grape* | **Cabernet Franc** |
| *Alc/vol* | **13.5%** |
| *Food* | **Poultry/chicken** |
| *Drink* | **2002–3** |

## Mamre Brook Barossa Cabernet Sauvignon 99 ☆

Powerful but supple, with a summer fruit nose and flavours of very ripe plums, blackcurrants and damsons with a minty character. *Gilbeys*

| | |
|---|---|
| *Price* | **€15–€18** |
| *Region* | **Barossa Valley** |
| *Grape* | **Cabernet Sauvignon** |
| *Alc/vol* | **14.5%** |
| *Food* | **Game/quail** |
| *Drink* | **2002–4** |

## Pipers Brook Vineyard Pinot Noir 00

With lots of warm, spicy, intense strawberry, cherry and sweet vanilla flavours, this is a relatively full-bodied style of Pinot Noir with fruit to the fore. *Irish Distillers*

| | |
|---|---|
| *Price* | €15–€18 |
| *Region* | Tasmania |
| *Grape* | Pinot Noir |
| *Alc/vol* | 13.5% |
| *Food* | Poultry/chicken |
| *Drink* | 2002–5 |

## Sandalford Margaret River/Mount Barker/Swan Valley Shiraz 98

Delicate and restrained, with spicy, smoky, sweet cherry aromas and peppery, fruity black-currant flavours. *Irish Distillers*

| | |
|---|---|
| *Price* | €15–€18 |
| *Region* | Western Australia |
| *Grape* | Shiraz |
| *Alc/vol* | 13.5% |
| *Food* | Meat/pork |
| *Drink* | 2002–3 |

## Sandalford Mount Barker/Margaret River Cabernet Sauvignon 97

With its intense, earthy nose of baked fruit and sweet oak, and generous flavours of plum and cherry, balancing soft tannins and gentle, oaky finish, this wine is mature and drinking well now. *Irish Distillers*

| | |
|---|---|
| *Price* | €15–€18 |
| *Region* | Western Australia |
| *Grape* | Cabernet Sauvignon |
| *Alc/vol* | 13% |
| *Food* | Meat/steak |
| *Drink* | 2002–3 |

## Wolf Blass President's Selection Cabernet Sauvignon 00

Big and warming with a spicy, peppery kick. Full, fleshy character. Cassis and blackberry flavours are held together with firmish tannins.
*Dillons*

| | |
|---|---|
| *Price* | €15–€18 |
| *Region* | South Australia |
| *Grape* | Cabernet Sauvignon |
| *Alc/vol* | 13% |
| *Food* | Meat/roasts |
| *Drink* | 2002–3 |

## Wolf Blass President's Selection Shiraz 00

Big, rich and spicy with aromas of tomato, fresh mint, menthol and cherry and a substantial, concentrated, spicy palate of plum and fig.
*Dillons*

| | |
|---|---|
| *Price* | €15–€18 |
| *Region* | South Australia |
| *Grape* | Shiraz |
| *Alc/vol* | 13.5% |
| *Food* | Meat/ribs |
| *Drink* | 2002–3 |

## Xanadu Cabernet Sauvignon 99 ☆

Rich and velvety with heaps of blackcurrants, spice, cedarwood and smoke and ripe, but noticeable, tannins. *O'Briens*

| | |
|---|---|
| *Price* | **€15–€18** |
| *Region* | **Margaret River** |
| *Grape* | **Cabernet Sauvignon** |
| *Alc/vol* | **14.5%** |
| *Food* | **Poultry/goose** |
| *Drink* | **2002–4** |

### €18–€22

## Greg Norman Estates Cabernet Merlot 98 ☆

Giving a lovely impression on the nose, this savoury wine has a muscular structure and lots of black fruit, coffee, pepper and chocolate flavours. *Cassidy*

| | |
|---|---|
| *Price* | **€18–€22** |
| *Region* | **Coonawarra** |
| *Grape* | **Cab Sauv/Merlot** |
| *Alc/vol* | **13%** |
| *Food* | **Meat/steak** |
| *Drink* | **2002–4** |

## Hardys Tintara Cabernet Sauvignon 98

Stylishly made, with ripe and substantial blackcurrant fruit to the fore along with some earthy, floral tones and a touch of mint and spice. *Allied Drinks*

| | |
|---|---|
| *Price* | **€18–€22** |
| *Region* | **South Australia** |
| *Grape* | **Cabernet Sauvignon** |
| *Alc/vol* | **13.5%** |
| *Food* | **Meat/lamb** |
| *Drink* | **2002–4** |

## Hardys Tintara Shiraz 98 ☆

From vineyards in Clare and Padthaway, this wine has a powerful nose with spice, spearmint and very ripe damsons and raisins. The palate is equally concentrated with a tremendous weight of raspberry fruit—not for the faint-hearted but great stuff. *Allied Drinks*

| | |
|---|---|
| *Price* | **€18–€22** |
| *Region* | **South Australia** |
| *Grape* | **Shiraz** |
| *Alc/vol* | **14%** |
| *Food* | **Poultry/turkey** |
| *Drink* | **2002–3** |

## Peel Estate Shiraz 98 ☆

Intriguing nose of liquorice, figs and black fruit. Velvety-smooth, savoury palate, combining violets, plums, spice and white pepper with robust tannins. Excellent, long, rich finish. *Waterford Wine Vault*

| | |
|---|---|
| *Price* | **€18–€22** |
| *Region* | **Western Australia** |
| *Grape* | **Shiraz** |
| *Alc/vol* | **14%** |
| *Food* | **Meat/roast pork** |
| *Drink* | **2002–4** |

## Penfolds Bin 128 Coonawarra Shiraz 98 ☆

Pronounced aromas of spice, vanilla, chocolate and lots of fruit are mirrored on the palate by concentrated fruit and spice flavours with layers of texture. Tannins are still firm and grippy. *Findlaters*

| | |
|---|---|
| *Price* | **€18–€22** |
| *Region* | **Coonawarra** |
| *Grape* | **Shiraz** |
| *Alc/vol* | **13.5%** |
| *Food* | **Poultry/coq au vin** |
| *Drink* | **2002–5** |

## Robertson's Well Cabernet Sauvignon 99 ☆

Very complex, with rich black cherry and chocolate aromas, a slightly floral touch and a chewy, ripe, spicy palate with heaps of blackberries and cassis. *Gilbeys*

| | |
|---|---|
| *Price* | €18–€22 |
| *Region* | Coonawarra |
| *Grape* | Cabernet Sauvignon |
| *Alc/vol* | 13.5% |
| *Food* | Poultry/chicken |
| *Drink* | 2002–4 |

## Rosemount GSM 99 ☆☆

Châteauneuf-du-Pape, Australian-style! The extra ripeness of fruit and the oak treatment make this a rich, warm and robust treat, with lots of tar and leather, sweet berry fruit, spice and vanilla. *Grants*

| | |
|---|---|
| *Price* | €18–€22 |
| *Region* | McLaren Vale |
| *Grape* | Grenache/Syrah/ Mourvèdre |
| *Alc/vol* | 14% |
| *Food* | Meat/beef |
| *Drink* | 2002–4 |

## Wynns Coonawarra Estate Cabernet 97 ☆

A wine with a warming heart and a really appealing, savoury nose with dense, spicy black fruit aromas. The flavours are concentrated and substantial—black fruit, plum, spice, pepper and cloves. *Findlaters*

| | |
|---|---|
| *Price* | €18–€22 |
| *Region* | Coonawarra |
| *Grape* | Cabernet Sauvignon |
| *Alc/vol* | 13.5% |
| *Food* | Game/pheasant |
| *Drink* | 2002–4 |

### €22–€25

**SHORTLIST RED WINE OF THE YEAR**

## Geoff Merrill Reserve Cabernet Sauvignon 97 ☆☆☆

With its fantastic nose scented with mint, cedar and blackcurrant, this is a complex wine with class and elegance. It has fine-grained tannins, ripe black fruit and tobacco flavours and a satisfyingly long finish. *Comans*

| | |
|---|---|
| *Price* | €22–€25 |
| *Region* | Coonawarra/ McLaren Vale |
| *Grape* | Cabernet Sauvignon |
| *Alc/vol* | 13.5% |
| *Food* | Meat/Szechuan beef |
| *Drink* | 2002–4 |

## Miranda Family Old Vine Reserve Shiraz 98 ☆☆

Powerful, yet silky textured, with a huge mass of fruit. Wonderful flavours of creamy vanilla, liquorice, dark chocolate, plums and blackcurrants. Drinking really well now. *Taserra*

| | |
|---|---|
| *Price* | €22–€25 |
| *Region* | Barossa Valley |
| *Grape* | Shiraz |
| *Alc/vol* | 13% |
| *Food* | Meat/game |
| *Drink* | 2002–4 |

## Nepenthe Adelaide Hills Pinot Noir 00

Fragrant, floral nose, with some liquorice and spice, and concentrated flavours of very ripe blackberry and red fruits. *Barry & Fitzwilliam*

| | |
|---|---|
| *Price* | €22–€25 |
| *Region* | Adelaide Hills |
| *Grape* | Pinot Noir |
| *Alc/vol* | 14.5% |
| *Food* | Meat/ham |
| *Drink* | 2002–4 |

## Nepenthe Lenswood Pinot Noir 99

A bigger style of Pinot Noir with aromas of rose oil and excellent fruity flavours of ripe dark cherries, spice and white pepper. The finish is long and satisfying. *Barry & Fitzwilliam*

| | |
|---|---|
| *Price* | **€22–€25** |
| *Region* | **Adelaide Hills** |
| *Grape* | **Pinot Noir** |
| *Alc/vol* | **14%** |
| *Food* | **Poultry/duck** |
| *Drink* | **2002–4** |

## Tatachilla Foundation Shiraz 98 ☆

Upfront fruity and spicy aromas are followed on the palate by a good depth of damson and plum flavours, with spice and pepper. *O'Briens*

| | |
|---|---|
| *Price* | **€22–€25** |
| *Region* | **McLaren Vale** |
| *Grape* | **Shiraz** |
| *Alc/vol* | **14.5%** |
| *Food* | **Meat/beef** |
| *Drink* | **2002–4** |

### €25–€30

## Ch. Reynella Shiraz 99 ☆

A Bruce Willis of a wine—big, heart-warming and chunky. It has muscle, body and some age, with a hot, earthy core and flavours of damson, cassis and vanilla. *Allied Drinks*

| | |
|---|---|
| *Price* | **€25–€30** |
| *Region* | **McLaren Vale** |
| *Grape* | **Shiraz** |
| *Alc/vol* | **14%** |
| *Food* | **Meat/stir fry beef** |
| *Drink* | **2002–3** |

## Clos Clare Shiraz 00

Aromas of leather and brambles. The palate has concentrated, ripe black fruit with cassis and pepper flavours and a firm tannic backbone. *WineKnows*

| | |
|---|---|
| *Price* | **€25–€30** |
| *Region* | **Clare Valley** |
| *Grape* | **Shiraz** |
| *Alc/vol* | **14.5%** |
| *Food* | **Ethnic/Indian** |
| *Drink* | **2002–3** |

## Craiglee Shiraz 98

The slightly closed nose has some savoury and red fruit aromas. The palate is a complete contrast with its wealth of dark, sweet flavours—damsons, fennel, spice, plums—that persist on a long, flavour-packed finish. *Wines Direct*

| | |
|---|---|
| *Price* | **€25–€30** |
| *Region* | **Victoria** |
| *Grape* | **Shiraz** |
| *Alc/vol* | **14%** |
| *Food* | **Pâtés/terrines** |
| *Drink* | **2002–4** |

## De Bortoli Yarra Valley Shiraz 99 ☆

Big, classic Shiraz nose full of spice, toast and black fruit and an impressive spicy, fruity palate. Lots of damson and blackberry flavours, with marked vanilla, pepper and spice. *Febvre*

| | |
|---|---|
| *Price* | **€25–€30** |
| *Region* | **Yarra Valley** |
| *Grape* | **Shiraz** |
| *Alc/vol* | **13.5%** |
| *Food* | **Poultry/turkey** |
| *Drink* | **2002–4** |

## Irvine Eden Crest Merlot Cabernet 99 ☆

Enticing aromas of leather, chocolate and black fruits. The palate has layers of earthy, ripe, luscious dark fruits, spice and coffee, a supple texture and a long, flavoursome finish.
*WineKnows*

| | |
|---|---|
| *Price* | €25–€30 |
| *Region* | Barossa Valley/ Eden Valley |
| *Grape* | Merlot/Cab Sauv |
| *Alc/vol* | 13% |
| *Food* | Meat/lamb |
| *Drink* | 2002–4 |

## Jim Barry McCrae Wood Shiraz 98

Wonderfully intense and upfront style with masses of blackcurrant and black fruit—a winter warmer. *Cassidy*

| | |
|---|---|
| *Price* | €25–€30 |
| *Region* | Clare Valley |
| *Grape* | Shiraz |
| *Alc/vol* | 13.5% |
| *Food* | Game/pheasant |
| *Drink* | 2002–3 |

## Lindemans St George Cabernet Sauvignon 98

Very rich, full nose with bags of fruit, mocha and chocolate aromas. The tannins are still gripping which makes the palate more subdued than the nose but it has a good plum and vanilla character. It should be drunk with food.
*Grants*

| | |
|---|---|
| *Price* | €25–€30 |
| *Region* | Coonawarra |
| *Grape* | Cabernet Sauvignon |
| *Alc/vol* | 13% |
| *Food* | Meat/beef |
| *Drink* | 2002–4 |

## McGuigan Shareholders' Shiraz 98

A few years in bottle have given this wine developed, mellow tobacco tones on top of the spicy black fruit, fig and vanilla flavours.
*Barry & Fitzwilliam*

| | |
|---|---|
| *Price* | €25–€30 |
| *Region* | SE Australia |
| *Grape* | Shiraz |
| *Alc/vol* | 13.5% |
| *Food* | Vegetarian/roasted vegetables |
| *Drink* | 2002–3 |

## Penfolds Bin 389 Cabernet Shiraz 98

Ripe damson and blackberry flavours with vanilla pod, spice, cedarwood and pepper, all nicely held together by firm tannins. *Findlaters*

| | |
|---|---|
| *Price* | €25–€30 |
| *Region* | South Australia |
| *Grape* | Cab Sauv/Shiraz |
| *Alc/vol* | 14.5% |
| *Food* | Poultry/goose |
| *Drink* | 2002–5 |

## Penfolds Bin 138 Old Vine Shiraz Grenache Mourvèdre 98 ☆☆

Rich, smooth and full bodied with great depth and character. Very dark and chocolatey, with juicy, ripe blackberry and plum flavours and an oak influence giving a smoky vanilla edge.
*Findlaters*

| | |
|---|---|
| *Price* | €25–€30 |
| *Region* | Barossa Valley |
| *Grape* | Shiraz/Grenache/ Mourvèdre |
| *Alc/vol* | 14% |
| *Food* | Meat/steak |
| *Drink* | 2002–5 |

## Tyrrell's Vat 8 Shiraz Cabernet 98 ☆

Vegetal and savoury, this maturing wine, with its massive damson and blackcurrant flavours, touched with spice and pepper, is drinking beautifully now. It has a rich texture and superb finish. *Maxxium*

| | |
|---|---|
| Price | €25–€30 |
| Region | Hunter Valley/ Coonawarra |
| Grape | Shiraz/Cab Sauv |
| Alc/vol | 13.8% |
| Food | Meat/pork |
| Drink | 2002–4 |

## d'Arenberg The Dead Arm Shiraz 98

Spicy, earthy aromas are quite pronounced. Plenty of blackcurrant and plum fruit on the palate which is also very spicy. Tannins are still firm but they are softening. *Taserra*

| | |
|---|---|
| Price | €30–€35 |
| Region | McLaren Vale |
| Grape | Shiraz |
| Alc/vol | 14.5% |
| Food | Meat/game |
| Drink | 2002–6 |

## De Bortoli Yarra Valley Pinot Noir 99

A pleasant, elegant style with soft, sweet berry compote, and some vegetal, aromas, and spicy, strawberry flavours. *Febvre*

| | |
|---|---|
| Price | €30–€35 |
| Region | Yarra Valley |
| Grape | Pinot Noir |
| Alc/vol | 13% |
| Food | Fish/salmon |
| Drink | 2002–3 |

## Peter Lehmann Mentor 97 ☆☆☆

Superb inviting aromas—a melange of fruits of the forest and damsons—reveal a mass of concentrated cherry and damson flavours on the palate with lots of chocolate, spice and pepper, still firm tannins and a very impressive finish. *Comans*

| | |
|---|---|
| Price | €30–€35 |
| Region | Barossa Valley |
| Grape | Cab Sauv/Malbec/ Shiraz/Merlot |
| Alc/vol | 13.5% |
| Food | Meat/venison |
| Drink | 2002–5 |

**SHORTLIST RED WINE OF THE YEAR**

### €35–€40

## Petaluma Coonawarra 99

Elegant, restrained blend of 60 per cent Cabernet and 40 per cent Merlot, with classic mint and blackcurrant aromas and a velvety texture. Abundant flavours of blackcurrant, pepper and vanilla and a long, ripe finish. *Woodford Bourne*

| | |
|---|---|
| Price | €35–€40 |
| Region | Coonawarra |
| Grape | Cab Sauv/Merlot |
| Alc/vol | 13.5% |
| Food | Meat/roast lamb |
| Drink | 2002–4 |

## Peter Lehmann Eight Songs Shiraz 98

Ripe nose with blackcurrant and violet aromas. The palate is quite rustic and tannic but is well integrated with a good depth of fruit and spice. *Comans*

| | |
|---|---|
| Price | €35–€40 |
| Region | Barossa Valley |
| Grape | Shiraz |
| Alc/vol | 14% |
| Food | Chinese/dishes with soy |
| Drink | 2002–4 |

## Rosemount Estate Balmoral Syrah 98

Big and rich with aromas of fruit, spice, vanilla and chocolate and a spicy, fruity palate—blackcurrants and plums. The concentrated texture has quite some grip. *Grants*

| | |
|---|---|
| *Price* | €35–€40 |
| *Region* | McLaren Vale |
| *Grape* | Syrah |
| *Alc/vol* | 14.5% |
| *Food* | Meat/beef Wellington |
| *Drink* | 2002–6 |

## St Andrews Shiraz 96

An example of what bottle age can do to Australian Shiraz with its mature nose—figgy, nutty, spicy blackcurrant aromas—and intense oaky, blackberry flavours with soft leather notes and long finish. *Koala Wines*

| | |
|---|---|
| *Price* | €35—€40 |
| *Region* | Clare Valley |
| *Grape* | Shiraz |
| *Alc/vol* | 13% |
| *Food* | Poultry/duck |
| *Drink* | 2002–3 |

## Trevor Jones Cabernet Merlot 98 ☆☆

A serious, earthy, spicy nose with plum and black fruits. The impressive palate has brooding dark fruits, tobacco, liquorice and a persistent, spicy length. *WineKnows*

| | |
|---|---|
| *Price* | €35–€40 |
| *Region* | Barossa Valley |
| *Grape* | Cab Sauv/Merlot |
| *Alc/vol* | 14% |
| *Food* | Meat/steak |
| *Drink* | 2002–6 |

| The symbols | |
|---|---|
| ❦ | *Organic* |
| € | *Exceptionally good value* |
| ☆ | *Very accomplished, showing above average quality or character making it worthy of extra attention* |
| ☆☆ | *Excellent with great character, style and complexity* |
| ☆☆☆ | *Wonderful, showing terrific character and complexity, true to its origins* |
| ☆☆☆☆ | *Exceptional, with considerable complexity and classic balance. Rewards serious tasting.* |

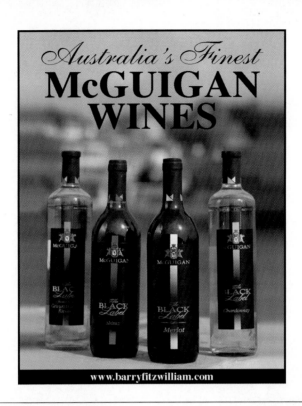

You can't talk about passion.
                    You have to taste it.

# CARMEN

Carmen, Winery of the year, 5th year in a row.
Wine and spirits magazine.

# Austria

Austria now has some of the strictest wine quality laws in the world. There are some very good, if expensive, Austrian wines on sale in Ireland (see page 94 for stockists). This year we recommend some affordable white wines, a red wine and, of course, the luscious Alois Kracher Beerenauslese Cuvée 2000 which is our Sweet Wine of the Year (see page 271).

## White

| €12–€15 |

### Johann Strauss Grüner Veltliner Kremser Sandgrube 00

A versatile style which could match most foods. Typical of Grüner Veltliner, it is peppery, and very spicy, with a bready, citric character and some pineapple flavours. *Karwig Wines*

| | |
|---|---|
| Price | €12–€15 |
| Region | Kremstal |
| Grape | Grüner Veltliner |
| Alc/vol | 12.5% |
| Food | Seafood/scallops |
| Drink | 2002–4 |

### Johann Strauss Rivaner Kremser Sandgrube 'Alte Reben' 00

Earthy and rustic with plenty of body and a pleasant finish. The flavours are of soft yellow fruits, toast, honey and spice. *Karwig Wines*

| | |
|---|---|
| Price | €12–€15 |
| Region | Kremstal |
| Grape | Rivaner |
| Alc/vol | 13% |
| Food | Fish/smoked fish |
| Drink | 2002–3 |

### Johann Kattus Nussberger Höhenweg Riesling Kabinett Trocken 98

Traditional style with a pungent, oily nose— smoky white pudding. Very spicy palate with lemony acidity and pear and citrus flavours. *Henry J. Archer*

| | |
|---|---|
| Price | €12–€15 |
| Region | Vienna |
| Grape | Riesling |
| Alc/vol | 12% |
| Food | Ethnic/Indian |
| Drink | 2002–3 |

### Wohlmuth Muskateller Summus 00

Distinctive and different, this wine is full bodied and concentrated with a strong aromatic and grapey character. Apple-flavoured and a touch oily, it also has a spicy warmth. *Karwig Wines*

| | |
|---|---|
| Price | €12–€15 |
| Region | Südsteiermark |
| Grape | Muscat |
| Alc/vol | 12.5% |
| Food | Seafood/crab |
| Drink | 2002–3 |

# Irish importers of Austrian wine

**SEARSONS WINE MERCHANTS**
Monkstown Crescent, Blackrock,
Co. Dublin
Tel (01) 280 0405 Fax (01) 280 4771
e-mail sales@searsons.com

Contact: Mr Frank Searson,
Managing Director

Alois Kracher Neusiedlersee
**WINNER Sweet Wine of the Year**

Beerenauslese Cuvée 2000

Freie Weingärtner Wachau

---

**BARRY & FITZWILLIAM LTD**
Glanmire, Cork
Tel (021) 432 0900 Fax (021)432 0910
also at: 50 Dartmouth Square, Dublin 6
Tel (01) 661 7133 Fax (01)660 0479
e-mail sinead@barryfit.iol.ie

Contact: Mr Michael Barry;
Mr Tony Cleary

Weinkellerei Lenz Moser

---

**TERROIRS**
103 Morehampton Road, Dublin 4
Tel (01) 667 1311 Fax (01)667 1312

Contact: Mr Seán Gilley;
Ms Françoise Gilley-Traineau

Johanneshof Reinisch

---

**MITCHELL & SON WINE
MERCHANTS LTD**
21 Kildare Street, Dublin 2
Tel (01) 676 0766 Fax 01-661 1509
e-mail wines@mitchellandson.com
website www.mitchellandson.com

Contact: Mr Peter B Dunne, Director

Domäne Müller Gutsverwaltung

---

**HENRY J. ARCHER & SONS LTD**
Ballymoney, Gorey, Co Wexford
Tel (055) 25176 Fax (055) 25842
e-mail paul.dubsky@oceanfree.net

Contact: Paul Dubsky

Erzherzog Johann Weine

Johann Kattus

Fritz Salomon

Jost Hoepler

---

**KARWIG WINES LTD**
Kilnagleary, Carrigaline, Co Cork
Tel (021) 437 2864/ 437 4159/437 3710
Fax (021) 437 2864
e-mail info@karwig-wines.ie
Website www.karwig-wines.ie

Contact: Mr Josef Karwig

Wohlmuth Wine Estate Est. 1903

Weinbau Johann Strauss

Kosher Wines

**www.winesfromaustria.com**

€22–€25

## Freie Weingärtner Loibner Loibenberg Riesling Smaragd Trocken 99

An elegant, stylish Riesling, quite fruity with peach, apricot and soft red fruit flavours and a very persistent finish. *Searsons*

| | |
|---|---|
| Price | €22–€25 |
| Region | Wachau |
| Grape | Riesling |
| Alc/vol | 13% |
| Food | Poultry/duck |
| Drink | 2002–4 |

# Red

€9–€12

## Wohlmuth Blaufränkisch 97

A perfect summer red, light and delicate and very tasty. Lots of attractive juicy red fruits—crushed raspberries and strawberries—and raw beetroot with some generous spices.
*Karwig Wines*

| | |
|---|---|
| Price | €9–€12 |
| Region | South Styria |
| Grape | Blaufränkisch |
| Alc/vol | 13% |
| Food | Poultry/chicken |
| Drink | 2002–3 |

*Blaufrankisch* is a good quality grape that can make very refreshing reds, similar to Loire reds made from Cabernet Franc. It is found mainly in Austria and Germany and in the USA where it is called **Lemberger** or **Limberger**. The best examples are intense and zesty with light, red fruit flavours, high tannins and acidity, and are not over-oaked.

# Chile

Chile is the third largest exporter of wine to Ireland, after France and Australia, ahead of many other great wine-producing countries, and thoroughly deserves this position. It offers lots of well-made, reliable red and white wines from a fantastic diversity of grape varieties, many for less than €9, as well as some stunning premium wines. But it is very clear from our tastings that Chile's great strength lies in its ability to deliver many different styles of above average quality in the €9–€15 price bracket (accounting for over half of the wines recommended this year). Only the South of France comes close to rivalling Chile for quality and variety in this category. Look out for super reds, often in a Bordeaux style, made from Cabernet Sauvignon and Merlot, and impressive examples of Carmenère, Shiraz and Pinot Noir. Whites with true varietal character are produced from Sauvignon Blanc and Chardonnay. Chile's excellent producers include Concha y Toro, Casa Lapostolle and Miguel Torres.

## White

*Under €9*

### Antu Mapu Sauvignon Blanc 01

Very pleasant and refreshingly crisp gooseberry and lime aromas. Zingy, zippy citrus fruit flavours in abundance with tangy pineapple and lemon sherbet. *Barry & Fitzwilliam*

| | |
|---|---|
| *Price* | Under €9 |
| *Region* | Maule Valley |
| *Grape* | Sauvignon Blanc |
| *Alc/vol* | 13% |
| *Food* | Cheese/cottage cheese |
| *Drink* | 2002–3 |

### Errázuriz Sauvignon Blanc 01

Slightly off-dry in style. The floral and zesty aromas are echoed in the sweet and sour flavours of sherbet and gooseberry, peach and nettles. *Allied Drinks*

| | |
|---|---|
| *Price* | Under €9 |
| *Region* | Curicó Valley |
| *Grape* | Sauvignon Blanc |
| *Alc/vol* | 13% |
| *Food* | Pasta/tomato sauce |
| *Drink* | 2002–3 |

### La Palmeria Chardonnay/Sauvignon 00

Agreeable fruity wine. Green apple aromas and a lemony and slightly floral palate with good acidity keeping it very fresh. *Grants*

| | |
|---|---|
| *Price* | Under €9 |
| *Region* | Rapel Valley |
| *Grape* | Chardonnay/ Sauvignon Blanc |
| *Alc/vol* | 13.5% |
| *Food* | Chinese/Thai |
| *Drink* | 2002–3 |

## Las Casas del Toqui Chardonnay 01 €

Attractive scented nose of tropical fruits, honey and jasmine. The palate has very good acidity and ripe citrus and melon flavours.
*Dunnes Stores*

| | |
|---|---|
| *Price* | Under €9 |
| *Region* | Cachapoal Valley |
| *Grape* | Chardonnay |
| *Alc/vol* | 13.7% |
| *Food* | Fish/plaice |
| *Drink* | 2002–3 |

## Montes Sauvignon Blanc 01

Classic example with all the hallmarks of Sauvignon Blanc: crisp acidity, aromas and flavours of lime, grapefruit and gooseberry and a pungent grassiness. *Grants*

| | |
|---|---|
| *Price* | Under €9 |
| *Region* | Curicó Valley |
| *Grape* | Sauvignon Blanc |
| *Alc/vol* | 13.5% |
| *Food* | Fish/trout |
| *Drink* | 2002–3 |

## MontGras Sauvignon Blanc 99

Fruity, flavoursome Sauvignon packed with tangy lemon and lime, elderflower and blackcurrant leaf flavours and fine, crisp acidity.
*Maxxium*

| | |
|---|---|
| *Price* | Under €9 |
| *Region* | Colchagua Valley |
| *Grape* | Sauvignon Blanc |
| *Alc/vol* | 12.8% |
| *Food* | Ethnic/Thai |
| *Drink* | 2002–3 |

## Sierra Grande Sauvignon Blanc 01

Light, aromatic aromas of nettles and green fruits. Fresh, dry palate with firm acidity and flavours of blackcurrant leaf, green capsicum, greengages and floral elements. A good choice for barbecues and outdoor eating. *Fields*

| | |
|---|---|
| *Price* | Under €9 |
| *Region* | Central Valley |
| *Grape* | Sauvignon Blanc |
| *Alc/vol* | 13% |
| *Food* | Fish/barbecue |
| *Drink* | 2002–3 |

## Tesco Chilean Sauvignon Blanc nv

Ideal party white. A gentle style with good zesty citrus and green pepper flavours backed with hints of elderflowers. *Tesco*

| | |
|---|---|
| *Price* | Under €9 |
| *Region* | Maule Valley |
| *Grape* | Sauvignon Blanc |
| *Alc/vol* | 12.5% |
| *Food* | Apéritif/fish |
| *Drink* | 2002–3 |

## Undurraga Sauvignon Blanc 01

Pleasant young wine with good classic aromas of grass cuttings and elderflowers and lime juice, apple and grapefruit flavours. Acidity is not too high making it very easy on the palate.
*Comans*

| | |
|---|---|
| *Price* | Under €9 |
| *Region* | Lontué Valley |
| *Grape* | Sauvignon Blanc |
| *Alc/vol* | 12.5% |
| *Food* | Vegetables/asparagus |
| *Drink* | 2002–3 |

€9–€12

## 35 South Chardonnay 00

Light, oaky, apple and pear nose. Easy, straight-forward palate with tropical fruit and a gentle fruity, toasty caramel finish. *Cassidy*

| | |
|---|---|
| Price | €9–€12 |
| Region | Central Valley |
| Grape | Chardonnay |
| Alc/vol | 13% |
| Food | Meat/veal |
| Drink | 2002–3 |

## Canepa Chardonnay 01

A decent glass with excellent balance between ripe, juicy mango and pineapple flavours, some toasty oak and crisp, steely acidity which keeps it on the light and refreshing side. *MacCormaic*

| | |
|---|---|
| Price | €9–€12 |
| Region | Rancagua |
| Grape | Chardonnay |
| Alc/vol | 13% |
| Food | Fish/monkfish |
| Drink | 2002–3 |

## Concha y Toro Casillero del Diablo Chardonnay 01

Zesty style with a lively, tingling palate of pine-apple and honeyed citrus flavours and an attrac-tive, fruity finish *Findlaters*

| | |
|---|---|
| Price | €9–€12 |
| Region | Casablanca Valley |
| Grape | Chardonnay |
| Alc/vol | 13.5% |
| Food | Vegetarian/gratins |
| Drink | 2002–3 |

## Concha y Toro Gewürztraminer 01

Fresh and light with good citrus fruit, a little vegetal and spicy, some white pepper and crisp green apple flavours. Good balance and a qual-ity finish. *Findlaters*

| | |
|---|---|
| Price | €9–€12 |
| Region | Rapel Valley |
| Grape | Gewürztraminer |
| Alc/vol | 13% |
| Food | Asian/fusion |
| Drink | 2002–3 |

## Montes Chardonnay 01

Beautifully poised and very stylish. Enticing smooth nose of pear and apple aromas with a decent concentration of lemon and pear fruit on the palate. *Grants*

| | |
|---|---|
| Price | €9–€12 |
| Region | Curicó Valley |
| Grape | Chardonnay |
| Alc/vol | 13.5% |
| Food | Apéritif/seafood |
| Drink | 2002–4 |

## Nostros Sauvignon Blanc 01

Honeyed nose with some lychees, melon and guava. Not at all dry, with an exuberant charac-ter—tropical fruit, rich, buttery flavours and enough acidity to balance the sweetness of the fruit. *Peter Dalton*

| | |
|---|---|
| Price | €9–€12 |
| Region | Maule Valley |
| Grape | Sauvignon Blanc |
| Alc/vol | 13.5% |
| Food | Seafood/crab |
| Drink | 2002–3 |

## Porta Reserve Chardonnay 00

Classic fruity, oaky Chardonnay with mango and tropical fruit character, citrus acidity and buttery richness. *Taserra*

| | |
|---|---|
| *Price* | €9–€12 |
| *Region* | Cachapoal Valley |
| *Grape* | Chardonnay |
| *Alc/vol* | 13.5% |
| *Food* | Fish/smoked |
| *Drink* | 2002–3 |

## Santa Carolina Reserve Chardonnay 00

Inviting, complex nose of nuts and tropical fruit aromas. Intense, ripe stewed apple on the palate with juicy, tropical fruit flavours. *TDL*

| | |
|---|---|
| *Price* | €9–€12 |
| *Region* | Rapel Valley |
| *Grape* | Chardonnay |
| *Alc/vol* | 13.5% |
| *Food* | Poultry/duck |
| *Drink* | 2002–3 |

## Santa Ines Sauvignon Blanc 01

Easy drinking with fruity aromas of lime, lemon and grapefruit peel and good, zesty citrus flavours with a slight salty tang. *Febvre*

| | |
|---|---|
| *Price* | €9–€12 |
| *Region* | Central Valley |
| *Grape* | Sauvignon Blanc |
| *Alc/vol* | 13.5% |
| *Food* | Cheese/goats' cheese |
| *Drink* | 2002–3 |

## Viña Tarapacá Piritas Vineyard Chardonnay 00

Beautifully proportioned with a depth of flavour, this is a rich mix of tropical fruit, lychee and citrus, underpinned by spicy oak, vanilla and pepper. *Gleeson*

| | |
|---|---|
| *Price* | €9–€12 |
| *Region* | Maipo Valley |
| *Grape* | Chardonnay |
| *Alc/vol* | 14% |
| *Food* | Pasta/seafood |
| *Drink* | 2002–3 |

### €12–€15

## Alto de Terra Andina Reserve Chardonnay 99

Crisp and steely with citrus and apple flavours together with some richer hints of peach and pear. *Irish Distillers*

| | |
|---|---|
| *Price* | €12–€15 |
| *Region* | Casablanca Valley |
| *Grape* | Chardonnay |
| *Alc/vol* | 13.5% |
| *Food* | Poultry/chicken |
| *Drink* | 2002–3 |

## Araucano Jacques et François Lurton Sauvignon Blanc 01

Lean, green fruit and nettle aromas with flavours of citrus and apple and an attractive, zesty lime peel finish. *Terroirs*

| | |
|---|---|
| *Price* | €12–€15 |
| *Region* | Central Valley |
| *Grape* | Sauvignon Blanc |
| *Alc/vol* | 13% |
| *Food* | Fish/Thai |
| *Drink* | 2002–3 |

## Carmen Reserve Chardonnay 98

Ripe, with a good depth of honey, apple and banana fruit, rich, toasty oakiness and crisp acidity which knits everything together perfectly. *Dillons*

| | |
|---|---|
| *Price* | €12–€15 |
| *Region* | Maipo Valley |
| *Grape* | Chardonnay |
| *Alc/vol* | 13.5% |
| *Food* | Poultry/chicken |
| *Drink* | 2002–3 |

## Casas del Bosque Sauvignon Blanc 00

A basketful of ripe green fruit and vegetable flavours: green plum, gooseberry, melon, grapefruit, asparagus and pea pod, with a tangy mouthfeel. *Waterford Wine Vault*

| | |
|---|---|
| *Price* | €12–€15 |
| *Region* | Casablanca Valley |
| *Grape* | Sauvignon Blanc |
| *Alc/vol* | 12.5% |
| *Food* | Cheese/goats' cheese |
| *Drink* | 2002–3 |

## Castillo de Molina Reserve Chardonnay 00

Very appealing, lively and fresh. Leafy salad aromas with a suggestion of coriander. The fruit is quite forward and tropical with an oaky richness. The kind of wine that justifies Chile's reputation. *Cassidy*

| | |
|---|---|
| *Price* | €12–€15 |
| *Region* | Lontué Valley |
| *Grape* | Chardonnay |
| *Alc/vol* | 13.5% |
| *Food* | Seafood/mussels |
| *Drink* | 2002–3 |

## Portal del Alto Reserve Chardonnay 00

Subtle New World style with baked apple pie and cinnamon toast aromas and a crisp, crunchy green apple palate. It would be great as an apéritif or a salad/starter wine. *Searsons*

| | |
|---|---|
| *Price* | €12–€15 |
| *Region* | Maule Valley |
| *Grape* | Chardonnay |
| *Alc/vol* | 13% |
| *Food* | Apéritif/salads |
| *Drink* | 2002–3 |

## Santa Rita Reserve Sauvignon Blanc 01 ☆

A very tasty, tangy style with energetic herbaceous and grassy aromas and oodles of crisp, green fruit flavours to get the gastric juices working. *Gilbeys*

| | |
|---|---|
| *Price* | €12–€15 |
| *Region* | Maule Valley |
| *Grape* | Sauvignon Blanc |
| *Alc/vol* | 13.5% |
| *Food* | Fish/mullet |
| *Drink* | 2002–3 |

### *€15–€18*

## MontGras Ninquén Chardonnay 97

Rich, fruity nose of guavas, mangoes and caramel. Zippy acidity balances ripe tropical fruits; the mouthfeel is oily, fat and buttery, with a lovely, creamy texture. *Maxxium*

| | |
|---|---|
| *Price* | €15–€18 |
| *Region* | Colchagua Valley |
| *Grape* | Chardonnay |
| *Alc/vol* | 12.5% |
| *Food* | Seafood/scallops |
| *Drink* | 2002–3 |

**€18–€22**

## MontGras Ninquén Barrel Select Chardonnay 97

Impressive nose with a wealth of aromas of pineapple, hazelnut and butter followed by a very concentrated, ripe tropical fruit palate and a full, spicy finish. *Maxxium*

| | |
|---|---|
| *Price* | **€18–€22** |
| *Region* | **Colchagua Valley** |
| *Grape* | **Chardonnay** |
| *Alc/vol* | **12.5%** |
| *Food* | **Fish/salmon** |
| *Drink* | **2002–3** |

**€25–€30**

## Amelia Chardonnay 00 ☆

Oak is very much to the fore on the nose which is intense, rich and toasty with a huge weight of tropical fruit. Everything comes together on the palate to give a full deep wine which will continue to develop with time. *Findlaters*

| | |
|---|---|
| *Price* | **€25–€30** |
| *Region* | **Casablanca Valley** |
| *Grape* | **Chardonnay** |
| *Alc/vol* | **13.5%** |
| *Food* | **Fish/turbot** |
| *Drink* | **2002–5** |

# Red

*Under €9*

## Carmen Cabernet Sauvignon 00 €

Concentrated and seductive with soft, plummy fruit and an underlay of pepper, set off by crisp acidity and a light touch of tannin. *Dillons*

| | |
|---|---|
| *Price* | **Under €9** |
| *Region* | **Central Valley** |
| *Grape* | **Cabernet Sauvignon** |
| *Alc/vol* | **13%** |
| *Food* | **Ethnic/Indian** |
| *Drink* | **2002–3** |

## Carmen Merlot 00 €

Very pure damson and plum nose with a cassis- and spice-flavoured palate. Quite a chunky texture, lively acidity and a dry finish. *Dillons*

| | |
|---|---|
| *Price* | **Under €9** |
| *Region* | **Central Valley** |
| *Grape* | **Merlot** |
| *Alc/vol* | **13.5%** |
| *Food* | **Meat/meatballs** |
| *Drink* | **2002–3** |

## Errázuriz Syrah Cabernet Sauvignon 00

Light, easy drinking with a juicy character and a good intensity of sweet, cassis-flavoured fruit. *Allied Drinks*

| | |
|---|---|
| *Price* | **Under €9** |
| *Region* | **Maipo Valley** |
| *Grape* | **Syrah/Cab Sauv** |
| *Alc/vol* | **13.5%** |
| *Food* | **Meat/shepherd's pie** |
| *Drink* | **2002–3** |

## La Palmeria Cabernet Sauvignon Merlot 00

Pure green pepper and plum fruit aromas and flavours, a touch spicy and earthy; well constructed with fresh acidity and a dry finish. *Grants*

| | |
|---|---|
| *Price* | Under €9 |
| *Region* | Rapel Valley |
| *Grape* | Cab Sauv/Merlot |
| *Alc/vol* | 13.5% |
| *Food* | Meat/ham |
| *Drink* | 2002–3 |

## Las Casas del Toqui Cabernet Sauvignon 01

Characteristic blackcurrant and vanilla aromas on the nose with a firm, tannic structure and a fruity palate of blackcurrant, plum and green pepper flavours. *Dunnes Stores*

| | |
|---|---|
| *Price* | Under €9 |
| *Region* | Cachapoal Valley |
| *Grape* | Cabernet Sauvignon |
| *Alc/vol* | 13.7% |
| *Food* | Cheese/Cheddar |
| *Drink* | 2002–3 |

## Quiltro Merlot 00 €

The palate delivers classic Merlot fruitiness of plum and red peppers though the nose is less typical with its stewed fruit character and earthy, rustic and toasty elements. *Oddbins*

| | |
|---|---|
| *Price* | Under €9 |
| *Region* | Maipo Valley |
| *Grape* | Merlot |
| *Alc/vol* | 14% |
| *Food* | Pasta/Bolognese |
| *Drink* | 2002–3 |

## San Pedro Merlot 01

Honest, well-made Merlot with ripe plums on the nose and earthy black fruit flavours with a spicy length. *Dunnes Stores*

| | |
|---|---|
| *Price* | Under €9 |
| *Region* | Central Valley |
| *Grape* | Merlot |
| *Alc/vol* | 13.5% |
| *Food* | Fish/tuna |
| *Drink* | 2002–3 |

## Sierra Grande Merlot 01

Sweet ripe berries on the nose. The pure fruit flavours carry through on the palate which reveals plums, damsons and a hint of Christmas cake. With gentle tannins and fruity, spicy flavours this is very easy to drink with food or on its own. *Fields*

| | |
|---|---|
| *Price* | Under €9 |
| *Region* | Central Valley |
| *Grape* | Merlot |
| *Alc/vol* | 13% |
| *Food* | Fish/tuna |
| *Drink* | 2002–3 |

### €9–€12

## 35 South Merlot 00

A delicious fruit bomb of very ripe blackcurrants with smoky and spicy oak; intensely concentrated with style, balance and length. *Cassidy*

| | |
|---|---|
| *Price* | €9–€12 |
| *Region* | Central Valley |
| *Grape* | Merlot |
| *Alc/vol* | 13.5% |
| *Food* | Cheese/Gorgonzola |
| *Drink* | 2002–3 |

## Canepa Merlot 00

Nicely complex and full bodied, to be enjoyed with a good steak. Big, bold tannins are backed by quite concentrated, warm, spicy, plummy fruit with cherry flavours and smoky tobacco and liquorice. *MacCormaic*

| | |
|---|---|
| *Price* | €9–€12 |
| *Region* | Colchagua Valley |
| *Grape* | Merlot |
| *Alc/vol* | 13% |
| *Food* | Meat/steak |
| *Drink* | 2002–4 |

## Concha y Toro Casillero del Diablo Merlot 01

Well made with lots of New World-style ripe fruit. The aromas are rich and plummy and the flavours are of dark black fruit backed by ripe tannins with balanced alcohol and a fruity finish. *Findlaters*

| | |
|---|---|
| *Price* | €9–€12 |
| *Region* | Rapel Valley |
| *Grape* | Merlot |
| *Alc/vol* | 13.5% |
| *Food* | Cheese/blue cheese |
| *Drink* | 2002–4 |

## Concha y Toro Casillero del Diablo Shiraz 00

Very expressive of the Shiraz grape. Aromas of cherries and damsons with a delightful earthiness; the full-flavoured palate yields ripe blackberries and plums with plenty of spicy flavour. *Findlaters*

| | |
|---|---|
| *Price* | €9–€12 |
| *Region* | Rapel Valley |
| *Grape* | Shiraz |
| *Alc/vol* | 13.5% |
| *Food* | Poultry/duck |
| *Drink* | 2002–3 |

## Concha y Toro Sunrise Carmenère 01

Full of flavour and personality with enticing aromas of baked red plums and a bigger palate which is a delicious mix of black fruits, spice and coffee. Gripping, firm tannins at present which need food or time to soften. *Findlaters*

| | |
|---|---|
| *Price* | €9–€12 |
| *Region* | Central Valley |
| *Grape* | Carmenère |
| *Alc/vol* | 13.5% |
| *Food* | Meat/roasts |
| *Drink* | 2002–4 |

## Concha y Toro Trio Merlot 99

Elegant but intensely concentrated, this is beautifully crafted with refreshing mint, blackcurrant and green pepper flavours and some spice. Bring on the lamb. *Findlaters*

| | |
|---|---|
| *Price* | €9–€12 |
| *Region* | Rapel Valley |
| *Grape* | Merlot |
| *Alc/vol* | 13.5% |
| *Food* | Meat/lamb |
| *Drink* | 2002–4 |

## Errázuriz Estate Merlot 00

Very agreeable and refreshing style with nicely defined damson, plum and white pepper flavours, lightly wooded with peppery tannins. *Allied Drinks*

| | |
|---|---|
| *Price* | €9–€12 |
| *Region* | Curicó Valley |
| *Grape* | Merlot |
| *Alc/vol* | 13.5% |
| *Food* | Meat/pork |
| *Drink* | 2002–3 |

> **How to find a specified wine**
> *If your local retailer does not stock a particular wine, contact the importer named in italic after the tasting note (contact details are on pages 274–279) for the name of your nearest stockist.*

## Las Casas del Toqui Reserve Cabernet Sauvignon 00

Punchy wine with fully ripe, fruity aromas of plum and black fruit and a spicy, warm texture with concentrated red and black berry fruit flavours. *Dunnes Stores*

| | |
|---|---|
| *Price* | **€9–€12** |
| *Region* | **Cachapoal Valley** |
| *Grape* | **Cabernet Sauvignon** |
| *Alc/vol* | **13.5%** |
| *Food* | **Vegetarian/peppers** |
| *Drink* | **2002–3** |

## Miguel Torres Santa Digna Cabernet Sauvignon 00 ☆ €

Concentrated style with true Cabernet character. Inviting aromas of spice, earth and squashed blackcurrants. Rewarding, rich, weighty palate with flavours of ripe berry fruit, hints of leather and tobacco and a smooth long finish. *Woodford Bourne*

| | |
|---|---|
| *Price* | **€9–€12** |
| *Region* | **Curicó Valley** |
| *Grape* | **Cabernet Sauvignon** |
| *Alc/vol* | **13.5%** |
| *Food* | **Meat/roasts** |
| *Drink* | **2002–4** |

## Montes Pinot Noir 00

A fruit-driven Pinot with sweet strawberry tart and red fruit flavours complemented by vanilla pod and a hot tarriness. *Grants*

| | |
|---|---|
| *Price* | **€9–€12** |
| *Region* | **Casablanca Valley** |
| *Grape* | **Pinot Noir** |
| *Alc/vol* | **13%** |
| *Food* | **Poultry/chicken** |
| *Drink* | **2002–3** |

## Nostros Merlot 00

A refined style of Merlot with a pleasing peppery and red fruit nose, plum skin and raspberry flavours, very firm tannins and a good defined finish. *Peter Dalton*

| | |
|---|---|
| *Price* | **€9–€12** |
| *Region* | **Rapel Valley** |
| *Grape* | **Merlot** |
| *Alc/vol* | **13.5%** |
| *Food* | **Meat/sausages** |
| *Drink* | **2002–3** |

## Porta Reserve Pinot Noir 00

Classic Pinot Noir characteristics with ripe cherries and redcurrants and vegetal and spicy flavours in a nicely constructed and supple style. *Taserra*

| | |
|---|---|
| *Price* | **€9–€12** |
| *Region* | **Bio Bio** |
| *Grape* | **Pinot Noir** |
| *Alc/vol* | **13.5%** |
| *Food* | **Vegetarian/gratins** |
| *Drink* | **2002–3** |

## Quiltro Reserve Cabernet Sauvignon 00

Dramatic and quite exotic with a sweet and sweaty nose of blackcurrants and leather and a great toasty palate of currants, spices and liquorice. *Oddbins*

| | |
|---|---|
| *Price* | **€9–€12** |
| *Region* | **Maipo Valley** |
| *Grape* | **Cabernet Sauvignon** |
| *Alc/vol* | **14%** |
| *Food* | **Meat/roast beef** |
| *Drink* | **2002–3** |

## San Pedro Reserve Cabernet Sauvignon 00

Warm and appealing with ripe berry fruit and vanilla pod aromas and a good chewy, weighty palate with spicy red fruit. *Dunnes Stores*

| | |
|---|---|
| Price | €9–€12 |
| Region | Lontué Valley |
| Grape | Cabernet Sauvignon |
| Alc/vol | 13.5% |
| Food | Meat/red meat |
| Drink | 2002–3 |

## San Pedro Reserve Merlot 00

Attractively upfront style with pure damson fruit, sweet cassis and vanilla extract as well as some pleasant vegetal and tomato flavours giving a savoury finish. *Dunnes Stores*

| | |
|---|---|
| Price | €9–€12 |
| Region | Lontué Valley |
| Grape | Merlot |
| Alc/vol | 14% |
| Food | Cheese/Cashel Blue |
| Drink | 2002–3 |

## Santa Carolina Cabernet Sauvignon 00 ☆☆

Easy drinking, with strong blackcurrant and green pepper aromas and generous, soft, punchy black fruit flavours with refreshing acidity cutting through. *TDL*

| | |
|---|---|
| Price | €9–€12 |
| Region | Rapel Valley |
| Grape | Cabernet Sauvignon |
| Alc/vol | 13% |
| Food | Meat/barbecue |
| Drink | 2002–3 |

## Santa Carolina Reserve Merlot 99 ☆ €

Smoky bonfire nose with heaps of blackcurrants, plums and cherries. Multi-layered palate with coffee, spice, damson and prune flavours. Softened, though still evident, tannins, make this an excellent food wine. *TDL*

| | |
|---|---|
| Price | €9–€12 |
| Region | Colchagua Valley |
| Grape | Merlot |
| Alc/vol | 13.5% |
| Food | Poultry/chicken |
| Drink | 2002–4 |

## Santa Ines Cabernet Sauvignon 00

Robust style with very ripe blackberry flavours and a minty and spicy character. Tannins are still quite firm but there is a rich texture to balance this. *Febvre*

| | |
|---|---|
| Price | €9–€12 |
| Region | Maipo Valley |
| Grape | Cabernet Sauvignon |
| Alc/vol | 13.5% |
| Food | Meat/lamb |
| Drink | 2002–3 |

## Santa Rita 120 Cabernet Sauvignon 00

Intense and warming with aromas of black fruit, mint, pepper and notes of rubber. Concentrated blackcurrant flavours with vanilla, smoky black pepper and softening tannins. *Gilbeys*

| | |
|---|---|
| Price | €9–€12 |
| Region | Central Valley |
| Grape | Cabernet Sauvignon |
| Alc/vol | 13.5% |
| Food | Meat/lamb |
| Drink | 2002–3 |

### Santa Rita Reserve Merlot 00

Generous and warm with a dense, creamy, oaky
nose, rich bramble fruit and a plummy character. Very good weight of blackberry flavours and
a decent smooth finish. *Gilbeys*

| | |
|---|---|
| *Price* | €9–€12 |
| *Region* | Maipo Valley |
| *Grape* | Merlot |
| *Alc/vol* | 14% |
| *Food* | Poultry/chicken wings |
| *Drink* | 2002–3 |

### Terra Mater Cabernet Sauvignon 00

Classic Chilean Cabernet with distinct aromas
of mint, tomato plant and blackcurrants. There
is a decent backbone of tannin which supports
the plum and blackcurrant flavours and makes
the wine a good match for meat dishes. *Tesco*

| | |
|---|---|
| *Price* | €9–€12 |
| *Region* | Maipo Valley |
| *Grape* | Cabernet Sauvignon |
| *Alc/vol* | 12.5% |
| *Food* | Meat/steak |
| *Drink* | 2002–3 |

### Tesco Chilean Reserve Cabernet Sauvignon 00

Upfront and fruity with pronounced blackcurrant aroma and flavour. Vanilla and coffee
flavours join the blackcurrant, giving a rich, soft
mouthfeel. Tannins are ripe and the finish is
long and fruity. *Tesco*

| | |
|---|---|
| *Price* | €9–€12 |
| *Region* | Curicó Valley |
| *Grape* | Cabernet Sauvignon |
| *Alc/vol* | 13.5% |
| *Food* | Meat/beef |
| *Drink* | 2002–3 |

### Undurraga Carmenère 00

Nice, light, stalky plum and blackcurrant fruit,
a touch vegetal, with good acidity which is very
refreshing. *Comans*

| | |
|---|---|
| *Price* | €9–€12 |
| *Region* | Colchagua Valley |
| *Grape* | Carmenère |
| *Alc/vol* | 12.5% |
| *Food* | Poultry/chicken |
| *Drink* | 2002–3 |

### Undurraga Pinot Noir 01

Attractive aromas of ripe strawberries and rose
petals. Light bodied with a pleasant red fruit
and raspberry character, some vegetal notes and
a good finish. *Comans*

| | |
|---|---|
| *Price* | €9–€12 |
| *Region* | Maipo Valley |
| *Grape* | Pinot Noir |
| *Alc/vol* | 13% |
| *Food* | Meat/ham |
| *Drink* | 2002–3 |

### Viña Tarapacá El Tranque Cabernet Merlot 99 ☆ €

A big and generous wine with an amazing array
of flavours, very concentrated black fruit and
iron mineral qualities. It is also extremely spicy,
rich and savoury. *Gleeson*

| | |
|---|---|
| *Price* | €9–€12 |
| *Region* | Maipo Valley |
| *Grape* | Cab Sauv/Merlot |
| *Alc/vol* | 14% |
| *Food* | Meat/lamb chops |
| *Drink* | 2003–4 |

## Viña Tarapacá La Cuesta Vineyard Cabernet Sauvignon Syrah 99

Substantial, larger than life style, with a very broad, attractive mouthfeel. Savoury, animal and vegetal flavours with stewed blackcurrants and oaky toastiness. *Gleeson*

| | |
|---|---|
| *Price* | €9–€12 |
| *Region* | Maipo Valley |
| *Grape* | Cab Sauv/Syrah |
| *Alc/vol* | 14% |
| *Food* | Pasta/arrabiata |
| *Drink* | 2002–4 |

---

### €12–€15

## Alto de Terra Andina Reserve Cabernet Sauvignon 99

Hot climate nose of warm, spicy, earthy aromas with stewed fruits; very upfront palate of peppery black fruit and a good depth of flavour. *Irish Distillers*

| | |
|---|---|
| *Price* | €12–€15 |
| *Region* | Cachapoal Valley |
| *Grape* | Cabernet Sauvignon |
| *Alc/vol* | 13% |
| *Food* | Meat/stews |
| *Drink* | 2002–3 |

---

## Araucano Jacques et François Lurton Cabernet Sauvignon 00

Blackberry and loganberry aromas with caramel notes matched by intensely juicy bramble fruit flavours. A generous wine but with a good cut of acidity running through making it very fresh. *Terroirs*

| | |
|---|---|
| *Price* | €12–€15 |
| *Region* | Rapel Valley |
| *Grape* | Cabernet Sauvignon |
| *Alc/vol* | 14% |
| *Food* | Meat/steak |
| *Drink* | 2002–3 |

---

## Canepa Carmenère 99

Big, yet elegant, with upfront aromas of black fruit, spice and dark chocolate following through as promised on the palate with flavoursome, soft, black berry fruit and a good backbone of tannin. *MacCormaic*

| | |
|---|---|
| *Price* | €12–€15 |
| *Region* | Colchagua Valley |
| *Grape* | Carmenère |
| *Alc/vol* | 13.5% |
| *Food* | Meat/beef |
| *Drink* | 2002–4 |

---

## Canepa Private Reserve Merlot 98 ☆

Seductive strawberry and spicy blackberry aromas; silky, fruity palate with warm spice, plum and damson flavours. *MacCormaic*

| | |
|---|---|
| *Price* | €12–€15 |
| *Region* | San Fernando |
| *Grape* | Merlot |
| *Alc/vol* | 13.5% |
| *Food* | Pasta/Bolognese |
| *Drink* | 2002–5 |

---

## Casa Lapostolle Cabernet Sauvignon 00

Ample, ripe, raspberry jam aromas and an equally substantial, broad palate which is spicy and earthy with a solid core of blackcurrant-flavoured fruit. *Comans*

| | |
|---|---|
| *Price* | €12–€15 |
| *Region* | Rapel Valley |
| *Grape* | Cabernet Sauvignon |
| *Alc/vol* | 13.5% |
| *Food* | Poultry/Chicken Kiev |
| *Drink* | 2002–3 |

## Castillo de Molina Reserve Cabernet Sauvignon 00

This wine would put many a Bordeaux to shame. It is very minty with delicious blackcurrant and eucalyptus flavours and a smoky, oaky character. *Cassidy*

| | |
|---|---|
| *Price* | €12–€15 |
| *Region* | Lontué Valley |
| *Grape* | Cabernet Sauvignon |
| *Alc/vol* | 13.5% |
| *Food* | Meat/lamb |
| *Drink* | 2002–4 |

## Dallas-Conté Cabernet Sauvignon 99 ☆☆ €

More Old than New World in character with fortifying iron tonic, rosehip and blackcurrant jam aromas and dry, peppery tannins with a green pepper and tart blackcurrant palate. *Koala Wines*

| | |
|---|---|
| *Price* | €12–€15 |
| *Region* | Rapel Valley |
| *Grape* | Cabernet Sauvignon |
| *Alc/vol* | 13.5% |
| *Food* | Meat/beef burgers |
| *Drink* | 2002–3 |

## Errázuriz Estate Syrah 00

Taut and serious with a pronounced nose of violets and tar and spicy damson fruit. Big, fruity flavours of plum and damson with some fennel and medicinal elements. Needs food to complement it. *Allied Drinks*

| | |
|---|---|
| *Price* | €12–€15 |
| *Region* | Aconcagua Valley |
| *Grape* | Syrah |
| *Alc/vol* | 14% |
| *Food* | Meat/pork |
| *Drink* | 2002–3 |

## Las Casas del Toqui Prestige Cabernet Sauvignon 99

Smooth and solid. The oaky nose with rich blackcurrant aromas is matched by very ripe blackcurrant flavours on the palate balanced by a fine, earthy dryness. *Dunnes Stores*

| | |
|---|---|
| *Price* | €12–€15 |
| *Region* | Cachapoal Valley |
| *Grape* | Cabernet Sauvignon |
| *Alc/vol* | 13.5% |
| *Food* | Vegetarian/ aubergines |
| *Drink* | 2002–3 |

## Los Robles Private Reserve Cabernet Sauvignon 99 ☆

Nicely oaked Cabernet, with a floral nose perfumed with cassis and vanilla and a toasty, spicy clove and fruitcake palate with a bitter cherry finish. *Papillon*

| | |
|---|---|
| *Price* | €12–€15 |
| *Region* | Curicó Valley |
| *Grape* | Cabernet Sauvignon |
| *Alc/vol* | 13% |
| *Food* | Meat/lamb |
| *Drink* | 2002–4 |

## Marqués de Casa Concha Cabernet Sauvignon 98

Reserved, herbaceous, tannic style with good balance and length and aromas and flavours of juicy plum tart and baking spices. *Findlaters*

| | |
|---|---|
| *Price* | €12–€15 |
| *Region* | Puente Alto Valley |
| *Grape* | Cabernet Sauvignon |
| *Alc/vol* | 13.5% |
| *Food* | Game/pigeon |
| *Drink* | 2003–4 |

## MontGras Reserve Cabernet Sauvignon 98

Full-bodied style with a rich, fruity mouthfeel and mild tannins. The aromas are of very pure blackcurrants and the flavour is blackcurrant with cinnamon spice and sandalwood. *Maxxium*

| | |
|---|---|
| *Price* | €12–€15 |
| *Region* | Colchagua Valley |
| *Grape* | Cabernet Sauvignon |
| *Alc/vol* | 13% |
| *Food* | Meat/hamburgers |
| *Drink* | 2002–3 |

## MontGras Reserve Carmenère 99

Blackcurrant and fig aromas with some earthiness, flavours of sweet blackcurrants, with an oaky background and a cedary finish. Tannins are ripe and approachable. *Maxxium*

| | |
|---|---|
| *Price* | €12–€15 |
| *Region* | Colchagua Valley |
| *Grape* | Carmenère |
| *Alc/vol* | 13% |
| *Food* | Meat/stews |
| *Drink* | 2002–3 |

## MontGras Reserve Merlot 99 ☆

Delicious, classic Chilean Merlot, soft, easy and plummy, with a rich, spicy vanilla and fruity nose and flavours of berry fruit, currants and plumcake. *Maxxium*

| | |
|---|---|
| *Price* | €12–€15 |
| *Region* | Colchagua Valley |
| *Grape* | Merlot |
| *Alc/vol* | 13 % |
| *Food* | Pasta/lasagne |
| *Drink* | 2002–3 |

## MontGras Quatro Reserve 99 ☆

Dramatic style with aromas of black fruit followed by a complex palate with black fruits, cedary overtones and tobacco leaves, good weight in the mouth and a velvety finish. It will benefit from decanting to open it up fully. *Maxxium*

| | |
|---|---|
| *Price* | €12–€15 |
| *Region* | Colchagua Valley |
| *Grape* | Cab Sauv/Merlot/ Carmenère/Malbec |
| *Alc/vol* | 13% |
| *Food* | Meat/liver |
| *Drink* | 2002–3 |

## Porta Select Reserve Cabernet Sauvignon 98 ☆

Ripe, perfumed nose of cassis and eucalyptus followed by blackberry jam and violet floral flavours with savoury and spicy elements. Very good structure and would be enhanced further by food or more time in bottle. *Taserra*

| | |
|---|---|
| *Price* | €12–€15 |
| *Region* | Aconcagua Valley |
| *Grape* | Cabernet Sauvignon |
| *Alc/vol* | 13% |
| *Food* | Meat/lamb |
| *Drink* | 2003–4 |

## Portal del Alto Reserve Cabernet Sauvignon 00

Textbook, flawless Chilean Cabernet, intensely fragrant with aromas of mint, blackcurrant, chocolate and spice matched with lots of cedar, spice, tobacco, mint and blackcurrant flavours on the palate. Tannins are firm but not hard. *Searsons*

| | |
|---|---|
| *Price* | €12–€15 |
| *Region* | Maule Valley |
| *Grape* | Cabernet Sauvignon |
| *Alc/vol* | 13% |
| *Food* | Meat/steak |
| *Drink* | 2002–5 |

### Santa Ines Carmenère 00

Fragrantly fruity wine with blackcurrant pastille aromas and a rich, creamy texture. Flavours of sweet black fruits, a definite spicy feel and an aftertaste of cinnamon sticks. *Febvre*

| | |
|---|---|
| *Price* | €12–€15 |
| *Region* | Maipo Valley |
| *Grape* | Carmenère |
| *Alc/vol* | 13.5% |
| *Food* | Pizza/pepperoni |
| *Drink* | 2002–3 |

### Santa Ines Legado de Armida Reserve Cabernet Sauvignon 99 ☆ ☆

This wine has great bite and depth and has won lots of international awards. There is mint and blackcurrant on the nose and a velvety mouth-feel which abounds in ripe blackcurrant fruit and mocha coffee flavours. *Febvre*

| | |
|---|---|
| *Price* | €12–€15 |
| *Region* | Maipo Valley |
| *Grape* | Cabernet Sauvignon |
| *Alc/vol* | 13.5% |
| *Food* | Meat/barbecue |
| *Drink* | 2002–4 |

### Santa Rita Reserve Carmenère 99

Lightly perfumed nose does not signal the concentrated palate with its inky intensity of plums, mulberry, black fruits, mocha and spice backed by rich velvety tannins. *Gilbeys*

| | |
|---|---|
| *Price* | €12–€15 |
| *Region* | Rapel Valley |
| *Grape* | Carmenère |
| *Alc/vol* | 14% |
| *Food* | Meat/steak |
| *Drink* | 2002–4 |

€15–€18

## Cousiño-Macul Antiguas Reservas Cabernet Sauvignon 99

Elegant and seductive style with fruit-filled aromas and mild vegetal character. The palate is richly concentrated and chocolatey with lots of blackcurrant flavour. *Woodford Bourne*

| | |
|---|---|
| *Price* | €15–€18 |
| *Region* | Maipo Valley |
| *Grape* | Cabernet Sauvignon |
| *Alc/vol* | 12.5% |
| *Food* | Meat/lamb |
| *Drink* | 2002–3 |

## Montes Alpha Cabernet Sauvignon 99 ☆☆

This excellent wine is drinking well now but will keep for 3–5 years. Classy, perfumed mint and cassis nose, powerful palate of mint and blackcurrant with wonderful balance and persistent finish. *Grants*

| | |
|---|---|
| *Price* | €15–€18 |
| *Region* | Colchagua Valley |
| *Grape* | Cabernet Sauvignon |
| *Alc/vol* | 14% |
| *Food* | Meat/leg of lamb |
| *Drink* | 2003–7 |

## Portal del Alto Gran Reserva Cabernet Sauvignon 99

Massively appealing, big and friendly, with lots of blackcurrant and vanilla spice on the nose and a good bite of acidity and tannin on the palate with ripe plum and minty blackcurrant fruit. Best with food. *Searsons*

| | |
|---|---|
| *Price* | €15–€18 |
| *Region* | Maipo Valley |
| *Grape* | Cabernet Sauvignon |
| *Alc/vol* | 12.5% |
| *Food* | Meat/cassoulet |
| *Drink* | 2002–5 |

## Portal del Alto Gran Reserva Carmenère 00 ☆

Intense raspberry fruit compote nose with a supple and flavoursome palate of spice and cinnamon, tobacco and earthy fruit flavours. Would be perfect with full-flavoured winter dishes. *Searsons*

| | |
|---|---|
| *Price* | €15–€18 |
| *Region* | Maipo Valley |
| *Grape* | Carmenère |
| *Alc/vol* | 13% |
| *Food* | Meat/roasts |
| *Drink* | 2002–4 |

## Santa Carolina Barrica Selection Carmenère 00 ☆☆

A distinctive wine with a rich, intense nose of damson jam and liqueur and a rich, black, peppery character to the palate which is flavoured by chocolate, plums and spice. *TDL*

| | |
|---|---|
| *Price* | €15–€18 |
| *Region* | Rapel Valley |
| *Grape* | Carmenère |
| *Alc/vol* | 13.5% |
| *Food* | Meat/pork |
| *Drink* | 2002–5 |

## Santa Carolina Barrica Selection Syrah 00 ☆

Mellow style with warm and intense aromas of pepper and leather, a rich black and red fruit character and a hint of iron or earthiness. *TDL*

| | |
|---|---|
| *Price* | €15–€18 |
| *Region* | Maule Valley |
| *Grape* | Syrah |
| *Alc/vol* | 13.5% |
| *Food* | Poultry/turkey |
| *Drink* | 2002–3 |

## Santa Rita Medalla Real Special Reserve Cabernet Sauvignon 99 ☆☆

A big wine with a solid depth of concentrated mint and blackcurrant aromas. Warm and full with ripe tannins it has dense, sweet, ripe, oaky blackcurrant flavours and a herbal note. *Gilbeys*

| | |
|---|---|
| *Price* | €15–€18 |
| *Region* | Maipo Valley |
| *Grape* | Cabernet Sauvignon |
| *Alc/vol* | 14.5% |
| *Food* | Meat/beef |
| *Drink* | 2002–5 |

## Villard Estate Reserve Pinot Noir 99

Excellent fruit and structure. Classic Pinot Noir aromas of raspberries and strawberries with a light spiciness. Good concentrated vegetal and earthy palate with red fruit character. *O'Briens*

| | |
|---|---|
| *Price* | €15–€18 |
| *Region* | Casablanca Valley |
| *Grape* | Pinot Noir |
| *Alc/vol* | 13% |
| *Food* | Fish/salmon |
| *Drink* | 2002–4 |

### €18–€22

## Miguel Torres Cordillera 00 ☆

Interesting wine in a smoky, charred and fruity style, classic in character and structure. The flavours are of heavily spiced currants with a lasting black fruit finish. *Woodford Bourne*

| | |
|---|---|
| *Price* | €18–€22 |
| *Region* | Curicó Valley |
| *Grape* | Cariñena/Syrah/ Merlot |
| *Alc/vol* | 14% |
| *Food* | Meat/casseroles |
| *Drink* | 2002–3 |

## MontGras Ninquén Barrel Select 97 ☆☆

Complex, rich and warm, this is a real charmer with inviting blackcurrant and plum aromas and a touch of mint. Full bodied with delicious layers of black fruits and pepper, supple tannins and smooth mouthfeel. *Maxxium*

| | |
|---|---|
| *Price* | €18–€22 |
| *Region* | Colchagua Valley |
| *Grape* | Cab Sauv/Merlot |
| *Alc/vol* | 13.5% |
| *Food* | Poultry/turkey |
| *Drink* | 2002–3 |

### €22–€25

## Concha y Toro Terrunyo Carmenère 99

Great fruity nose of damsons and loganberries, rich and sweet fruit palate of damsons, plums and Christmas pudding with yielding tannins and a dry, cedary finish. *Findlaters*

| | |
|---|---|
| *Price* | €22–€25 |
| *Region* | Peumo Valley |
| *Grape* | Carmenère |
| *Alc/vol* | 13.5% |
| *Food* | Fish/tuna |
| *Drink* | 2002–3 |

*€25–€30*

## Casa Lapostolle Cuvée Alexandre Merlot 99

Perfumed with ripe plum aromas with equally ripe, plummy fruit on the palate, mocha, spice and savoury elements and an underpinning of firm tannins. *Comans*

| | |
|---|---|
| *Price* | **€25–€30** |
| *Region* | **Colchagua Valley** |
| *Grape* | **Merlot** |
| *Alc/vol* | **14%** |
| *Food* | **Game/pheasant** |
| *Drink* | **2002–3** |

## Miguel Torres Manso de Velasco 96

Big nose showing ripe fruit, lots of sunshine and a touch of figs. Intense, full flavours in the mouth, fruity, vegetal and spicy. A wine with a strong character, maturing but drinking well. *Woodford Bourne*

| | |
|---|---|
| *Price* | **€25–€30** |
| *Region* | **Curicó Valley** |
| *Grape* | **Cabernet Sauvignon** |
| *Alc/vol* | **13%** |
| *Food* | **Meat/beef** |
| *Drink* | **2002–3** |

## Undurraga Founder's Collection Cabernet Sauvignon 98

Great intensity and finesse in a very impressive wine with aromas and flavours of blackcurrants and violets, together with savoury and earthy tones and an iron or metallic core. *Comans*

| | |
|---|---|
| *Price* | **€25–€30** |
| *Region* | **Maipo Valley** |
| *Grape* | **Cabernet Sauvignon** |
| *Alc/vol* | **12.5%** |
| *Food* | **Meat/lamb** |
| *Drink* | **2002–4** |

*€30–€35*

## Leyenda 99 ☆

Classic nose with creamy blackcurrant aromas. Seriously intense flavours of blackcurrant, vanilla, mocha and tobacco; full bodied, rich in flavour with excellent length. *Dunnes Stores*

| | |
|---|---|
| *Price* | **€30–€35** |
| *Region* | **Cachapoal Valley** |
| *Grape* | **Cabernet Sauvignon** |
| *Alc/vol* | **13.5%** |
| *Food* | **Poultry/goose** |
| *Drink* | **2002–4** |

*€35–€40*

## Ch. Los Boldos Grand Cru 98 ☆

Beautifully defined blackcurrant fruit, perfumed with vanilla pod and sweet spices. This is an accomplished style of some complexity, good tannic structure and long finish. *O'Briens*

| | |
|---|---|
| *Price* | **€35–€40** |
| *Region* | **Rapel Valley** |
| *Grape* | **Cab Sauv/Merlot** |
| *Alc/vol* | **13.5%** |
| *Food* | **Poultry/duck** |
| *Drink* | **2002–4** |

## Don Melchor 97 ☆☆

Superb wine with a very complex nose which takes time to open out giving savoury aromas with mineral and iron filings. Flavours are very elegant and concentrated—blackcurrant, spice and cedarwood—with a persistent finish. *Findlaters*

| | |
|---|---|
| *Price* | **€35–€40** |
| *Region* | **Maipo Valley** |
| *Grape* | **Cabernet Sauvignon** |
| *Alc/vol* | **13.5%** |
| *Food* | **Meat/roast lamb** |
| *Drink* | **2003–7** |

# France–Alsace

If you are looking for top quality wines, especially whites, then you have come to the right chapter. Alsace makes some astounding wines at very fair and often very good value prices. Of the nineteen wines listed in this section, thirteen were awarded stars. These include wines from the white grapes Riesling, Pinot Blanc and Gewurztraminer and one from the red grape Pinot Noir.

Alsace has had a very good run of successful vintages between 95 and 01. The 00 vintage was particularly good and wines from that year scored very well in the tastings. Most wines from Alsace are capable of ageing for several years and those with Grand Cru status can age for considerably longer. However, wines made from Pinot Blanc and Muscat should be drunk as young as possible so it's best to look for the most recent vintage.

## White

### Under €9

### Charles Koehly & Fils St Hippolyte Gewurztraminer
AC Alsace **99 €**

A more subtle Gewurztraminer than many others. Very pleasant and spicy with a decent weight of ripe red apples, some blackcurrant undertones and prickling pineapple acidity. *Irish Distillers*

| | |
|---|---|
| *Price* | **Under €9** |
| *Grape* | **Gewurztraminer** |
| *Alc/vol* | **13.8%** |
| *Food* | **Ethnic/Chinese** |
| *Drink* | **2002–3** |

### Thomann Riesling AC Alsace **01 €**

Taut, restrained style with lemony aromas and mineral hints. Full of crunchy, green apple flavours with crisp, refreshing acidity, very good concentration and length. A good food partner. *Dunnes Stores*

| | |
|---|---|
| *Price* | **Under €9** |
| *Grape* | **Riesling** |
| *Alc/vol* | **12%** |
| *Food* | **Cheese/goats' cheese** |
| *Drink* | **2002–3** |

### €9–€12

### Hugel Cuvée Les Amours Pinot Blanc de Blancs
AC Alsace **99** ☆ **€**

Aromatic and bready with apple pie aromas and a lovely rich, honeyed, apple fruit palate. Mature but still in good condition with crisp acidity and a tangy citrus finish. *Grants*

| | |
|---|---|
| *Price* | **€9–€12** |
| *Grape* | **Pinot Blanc** |
| *Alc/vol* | **12.5%** |
| *Food* | **Pasta/pesto** |
| *Drink* | **2002–3** |

## Hugel 'Gentil' AC Alsace 99

A blend of five Alsace varieties, Gewurztraminer, Pinot Gris, Riesling, Muscat and Sylvaner. Dry, spicy and pungent. Soft, apple and citrus fruit flavours with some herbal notes. A little slatey on the finish. *Grants*

| | |
|---|---|
| *Price* | **€9–€12** |
| *Grape* | **Alsace blend** |
| *Alc/vol* | **12%** |
| *Food* | **Meat/pork** |
| *Drink* | **2002–4** |

## Sipp Mack Pinot Blanc AC Alsace 01 ☆☆☆ €

A versatile wine, full of personality, with rich, fruity aromas of lemon and apricot, toast and honey and a stylish palate of ripe, crisp apple, mango and citrus fruit, with refreshing acidity. *Mitchells*

| | |
|---|---|
| *Price* | **€9–€12** |
| *Grape* | **Pinot Blanc** |
| *Alc/vol* | **12%** |
| *Food* | **Ethnic/Thai** |
| *Drink* | **2002–3** |

SHORTLIST
BEST VALUE WHITE

## Thomann Gewurztraminer AC Alsace 01

Attractive all-spice and peppery nose with Turkish Delight and rose petals and a matching grapey and spicy palate. Moderate acidity levels give a well-rounded, pleasing and just-dry style of Gewurztraminer. *Dunnes Stores*

| | |
|---|---|
| *Price* | **€9–€12** |
| *Grape* | **Gewurztraminer** |
| *Alc/vol* | **13%** |
| *Food* | **Cheese/Ardrahan** |
| *Drink* | **2002–3** |

### €12–€15

## Berrys' Own Selection Alsace Pinot Blanc AC Alsace 00

Made by Dom. Mittnach Frères, this Pinot Blanc is appealingly restrained in the classic Alsace style. It has concentrated green, citrus fruit and ripe apple flavours, with great length. *Fields*

| | |
|---|---|
| *Price* | **€12–€15** |
| *Grape* | **Pinot Blanc** |
| *Alc/vol* | **12%** |
| *Food* | **Seafood/mussels** |
| *Drink* | **2002–3** |

## Hugel Riesling AC Alsace 98 ☆☆

Classic and delicious, true to its terroir, with lime, lemon, apple and kerosene notes and a touch of fatness and stoniness. With highish acidity, it is still very young and will improve further with time. *Grants*

| | |
|---|---|
| *Price* | **€12–€15** |
| *Grape* | **Riesling** |
| *Alc/vol* | **13.49%** |
| *Food* | **Meat/charcuterie** |
| *Drink* | **2003–6** |

## Meyer-Fonné Vieilles Vignes Pinot Blanc AC Alsace 00 ☆

Off-dry style with a floral and honeycomb nose giving a juicy impression and an exotic, lush, fruit palate with honey, melon and peach flavours. *Le Caveau*

| | |
|---|---|
| *Price* | **€12–€15** |
| *Grape* | **Pinot Blanc** |
| *Alc/vol* | **12.5%** |
| *Food* | **Quiches/Quiche Lorraine** |
| *Drink* | **2002–3** |

## Paul Buecher Réserve Personnelle Riesling AC Alsace 99

Refreshing and clean, with a fruity character. Apple, melon and peach flavours with some spice and oiliness beginning to develop. *Waterford Wine Vault*

| | |
|---|---|
| *Price* | **€12–€15** |
| *Grape* | **Riesling** |
| *Alc/vol* | **13%** |
| *Food* | **Ethnic/Thai** |
| *Drink* | **2002–3** |

## Sipp Mack Riesling Tradition AC Alsace **00** ☆☆ €

A classic and still very youthful wine with an
impressive, fleshy, peach and honey nose with
a kerosene touch and some slatey mineral
tones. The palate is wonderfully fresh with
apple and spice flavours. *Mitchells*

| | |
|---|---|
| *Price* | €12–€15 |
| *Grape* | Riesling |
| *Alc/vol* | 12% |
| *Food* | Seafood/prawns |
| *Drink* | 2002–4 |

> Just fifty vineyards on the steep slopes of the Vosges Mountains in Alsace are
> classified as **Grand Cru**. They can offer excellent value, as the jump in quality is
> not reflected proportionally in the price. For example, Rosacker and Vorbourg are
> Grands Crus. A number of producers, such as Trimbach and Hugel, have stayed
> outside the Grand Cru system. Instead, they promote their wines with their own
> names and sometimes the name of the vineyard the grapes are sourced from.

### €18–€22

## Dom. Eugène Meyer Gewurtztraminer AC Alsace **98** 🌿 ☆

Classic nose of roses, spice, lychees and melon.
Dry, fresh palate with crisp acidity and rich
flavours of peach and apricot. *Mary Pawle*

| | |
|---|---|
| *Price* | €18–€22 |
| *Grape* | Gewurtztraminer |
| *Alc/vol* | 14% |
| *Food* | Ethnic/Indian |
| *Drink* | 2002–3 |

## Sipp Mack Riesling AC Alsace Grand Cru Rosacker **00** ☆

Subtle Riesling nose with lemon and some
spice. The palate really impresses with intense,
ripe lemon, apple and honey, fresh, lively acidity and a good mineral quality. *Mitchells*

| | |
|---|---|
| *Price* | €18–€22 |
| *Grape* | Riesling |
| *Alc/vol* | 12.5% |
| *Food* | Seafood/crayfish |
| *Drink* | 2002–7 |

### €22–€25

## Dom. du Clos St Landelin Gewurztraminer AC Alsace Grand Cru Vorbourg **99** ☆☆

Golden in colour with a fresh exotic nose exuding classic aromas of lychees, roses and spice.
Although the spicy palate is on the dry side, the
rich, fleshy, ripe fruit flavours give a definite
impression of sweetness. *Mitchells*

| | |
|---|---|
| *Price* | €22–€25 |
| *Grape* | Gewurztraminer |
| *Alc/vol* | 14% |
| *Food* | Soup/French onion soup |
| *Drink* | 2002–6 |

## Dom. Schlumberger Gewurztraminer AC Alsace Grand Cru Kessler **99** ☆☆

Fascinating nose—light syrup of peach with
cloves and some spearmint. The wine really
sings on the palate with pure peach and apricot
flavours and wonderful balancing acidity giving
a full style with great freshness. *Findlaters*

| | |
|---|---|
| *Price* | €22–€25 |
| *Grape* | Gewurztraminer |
| *Alc/vol* | 13.5% |
| *Food* | Pâté/foie gras |
| *Drink* | 2002–6 |

€25–€30

### Dom. du Clos St Landelin Riesling
AC Alsace Grand Cru Vorbourg **00** ☆☆☆☆

Beautifully fresh, classic nose with apple and citrus aromas. Crisp acidity balances a great concentration of apple and lime flavours with mineral tones. Lengthy aftertaste. Will continue to improve with age. *Mitchells*

| | |
|---|---|
| *Price* | €25–€30 |
| *Grape* | Riesling |
| *Alc/vol* | 13.5% |
| *Food* | Fish/smoked salmon |
| *Drink* | 2002–7 |

### Dom. Zind Humbrecht Wintzenheim Gewurztraminer
AC Alsace **00** ☆

Perfumed nose leads to a palate full of rich, ripe fruits, spice, rose petals and Turkish Delight, all kept in check by a good level of acidity and finishing with a spicy aftertaste. *Comans*

| | |
|---|---|
| *Price* | €25–€30 |
| *Grape* | Gewurztraminer |
| *Alc/vol* | 15.5% |
| *Food* | Cheese/Munster |
| *Drink* | 2002–5 |

€35–€40

### Dom. Zind Humbrecht Wintzenheim Clos Häuserer
**Riesling** AC Alsace **00** ☆

Elegant, classic style with aromas of spice and burnt, oily, honeyed richness. The palate is fresh with crisp acidity and intense fruit—peach and apple flavours—and delicious length. *Comans*

| | |
|---|---|
| *Price* | €35–€40 |
| *Grape* | Riesling |
| *Alc/vol* | 13.5% |
| *Food* | Seafood/lobster |
| *Drink* | 2002–4 |

## Red

€25–€30

### Dom. du Clos St Landelin 'V' Pinot Noir AC Alsace **00** ☆☆

Fragrant nose of wood smoke, toffee and succulent dried fruits and a concentrated, powerful palate with red summer fruit flavours and smoky influence. A complex wine, as good as, if not better than, many Burgundies. *Mitchells*

| | |
|---|---|
| *Price* | €25–€30 |
| *Grape* | Pinot Noir |
| *Alc/vol* | 13.5% |
| *Food* | Meat/pork |
| *Drink* | 2002–3 |

# France–Bordeaux

The Bordeaux region is, in effect, a collection of very diverse wine-producing areas. North of the city of Bordeaux is the area of the Médoc and Haut-Médoc, home to the great appellations of St Estèphe, Pauillac, St Julien and Margaux, as well as Listrac and Moulis which produce some very good and interesting wines. Cabernet Sauvignon is the most important variety in this area, although lesser wines tend to have a high proportion of Merlot in the blend. East of Bordeaux and across the river are the areas of St Émilion, Pomerol, Bourg and Blaye where Merlot and Cabernet Franc are particularly important. Graves and Pessac-Léognan lie south of the city and produce much lighter but also very elegant reds and some of the best white wines of the region. A little further south are the areas where sweet wines are made including Sauternes and Barsac. Also south-east of Bordeaux is the very large area of Entre-Deux-Mers where a vast amount of basic white and red Bordeaux is made.

All of the main red and white wine producing areas in Bordeaux are represented in this year's guide. We set a top price limit of €40 so most of the very top quality that Bordeaux has to offer is automatically excluded. However, this gives scope to be very selective and we have brought you some of the best and most interesting wines for their price within each of the price categories. The whites include basic AC Bordeaux as well as wines from Graves, Pessac Léognan and Entre-Deux-Mers. In reds look out particularly for the Crus Bourgeois which can offer exceptional value for the quality level; many currently have better reputations than some of the classed growths. The classification rules are currently under review to determine which should be entitled to be included in the category. Good examples of Crus Bourgeois include Ch. Loudenne, Ch. Rollan de By, Ch. Patache d'Aux, Ch. Magnol, Ch. Chasse Spleen and Ch. Forcas Hosten.

## White

### Under €9

### Ch. La Grande Métairie AC Entre-Deux-Mers **01**

Subtle nose with honey and waxy apple aromas. Flavoursome, smooth, creamy palate with green apple and citrus flavours and good persistence. *Wines Direct*

| | |
|---|---|
| *Price* | Under €9 |
| *Alc/vol* | 12% |
| *Food* | Fish/plaice |
| *Drink* | 2002–3 |

### Ch. Peyragué AC Graves **00** ☆ €

Made from 80% Sémillon with quite a bit of oak, giving a rich buttery nose with vanilla pod and broad bean aromas. On the palate the oak is nicely married with apple and lemon flavours and some mineral elements. *Dunnes Stores*

| | |
|---|---|
| *Price* | Under €9 |
| *Grape* | Sémillon/Sauv Blanc |
| *Alc/vol* | 12% |
| *Food* | Fish/cod |
| *Drink* | 2002–3 |

> Traditionally, **white Bordeaux** is made from blends of Sémillon, Sauvignon Blanc
> and Muscadelle. Today the proportion of Sauvignon in the blend is often
> increased, sometimes to 100%, in which case this is stated on the label.

### €9–€12

### Ch. La Freynelle AC Bordeaux **00**

Stylish, with obvious pedigree. Pleasing lemon peel and citrus aromas lead on to a medley of flavours of apples, pears and citrus with refreshing acidity, all well integrated. *Searsons*

| | |
|---|---|
| Price | €9–€12 |
| Grape | Sauvignon Blanc/ Sémillon/Muscadelle |
| Alc/vol | 12% |
| Food | Poultry/chicken |
| Drink | 2002–3 |

### Ch. La Gravière AC Entre-Deux-Mers **01**

Lively golden colour and a very promising nose—fresh, grassy and youthful—fulfilled on the vibrant palate with nettle, gooseberry and citrus flavours in abundance. *McCabes*

| | |
|---|---|
| Price | €9–€12 |
| Alc/vol | 12% |
| Food | Fish/crab |
| Drink | 2002–3 |

### Mähler-Besse La Coquille AC Entre-Deux-Mers **01**

The nose is somewhat subdued but the wine really opens out to a lively palate with ripe apples, gooseberries, fennel and a touch of cardamom and almond with good citrus acidity. *TDL*

| | |
|---|---|
| Price | €9–€12 |
| Alc/vol | 12.5% |
| Food | Fish/shellfish |
| Drink | 2002–3 |

## Sirius AC Bordeaux **98**

Developed nose of Seville oranges and marmalade with a flowery touch. The oaky palate has
soft flavours of mango and pear with very good
length. *Irish Distillers*

| | |
|---|---|
| Price | €9–€12 |
| Grape | Sémillon/Sauv Blanc |
| Alc/vol | 12.5% |
| Food | Fish/tuna |
| Drink | 2002–3 |

*€12–€15*

## Ch. Timberlay AC Bordeaux **01** ☆

Fresh as a daisy with a classic Sauvignon-influ-
enced nose of asparagus, gooseberries and nettles, peppery and apple flavours and satisfying
length. *Maxxium*

| | |
|---|---|
| Price | €12–€15 |
| Grape | Sémillon/Sauv Blanc |
| Alc/vol | 12% |
| Food | Pasta/primavera |
| Drink | 2002–3 |

*€22–€25*

## L'Abeille de Fieuzal AC Pessac-Léognan **99**

Attractive, classic, complex wine. Aromas of
smoke, clove and herbs and ripe apple fruit
flavours with well-integrated toastiness.
*Findlaters*

| | |
|---|---|
| Price | €22–€25 |
| Grape | Sémillon/Sauv Blanc |
| Alc/vol | 12.5% |
| Food | Poultry/chicken |
| Drink | 2002–5 |

# Red

> The permitted grapes for **red Bordeaux blends** are Cabernet Sauvignon, Merlot,
> Cabernet Franc, Petit Verdot and Malbec and the grapes are listed accordingly.
> Wines that are predominantly Merlot are described in this book as **Merlot
> blend**; wines that are predominantly Cabernet Sauvignon are described as
> **Cabernet blend**. Wines with roughly equal proportions of each are described as
> **Cabernet/Merlot blend**. Where the blend is not known the wine is described as
> **Bordeaux blend**.

*€9–€12*

## Ch. des Gravières AC Graves **98**

Promising nose of concentrated blackcurrant
and mint leads to quite a perfumed palate of
mixed red and black currants with a touch of
spice. *Molloys*

| | |
|---|---|
| Price | €9–€12 |
| Grape | Merlot/Cab Sauv |
| Alc/vol | 12.5% |
| Food | Meat/pork |
| Drink | 2002–4 |

## Ch. Haut Pougnan AC Bordeaux Supérieur **99**

A good Bordeaux with style and concentration.
Fragrant nose of smoke, earth, blackcurrants
and leather and a tightly structured palate with
cherry and blackcurrant flavours. *McCabes*

| | |
|---|---|
| Price | €9–€12 |
| Grape | Cab/Merlot blend |
| Alc/vol | 12% |
| Food | Meat/beef burgers |
| Drink | 2002–4 |

## Ch. Nodoz AC Côtes de Bourg 99

Distinct earthy, farmyard aromas with cedar, spice, currants and plums. Rich, chewy mouth-feel with plenty of autumnal berry flavours and a good backbone of tannin. Best with meaty dishes. *Mitchells*

| | |
|---|---|
| *Price* | €9–€12 |
| *Grape* | Merlot blend |
| *Alc/vol* | 12.5% |
| *Food* | Meat/stews |
| *Drink* | 2002–3 |

## Ch. Timberlay AC Bordeaux Supérieur 99

Light and elegant with a fragrant red fruit nose and some bottle age starting to show. The palate has flavours of damsons, plums, cherries and green pepper and relaxed tannins. *Maxxium*

| | |
|---|---|
| *Price* | €9–€12 |
| *Grape* | Cab Sauv/Merlot/ Cab Franc |
| *Alc/vol* | 12.5% |
| *Food* | Meat/casseroles |
| *Drink* | 2002–3 |

## Ginestet Mascaron AC Bordeaux 99

A very decent claret in a modern, oaky style with aromas of toast, pepper and blackcurrants and a very ripe palate with smoky black fruits and a floral, perfumed edge. *Dunnes Stores*

| | |
|---|---|
| *Price* | €9–€12 |
| *Grape* | Bordeaux blend |
| *Alc/vol* | 12.5% |
| *Food* | Cheese/Camembert |
| *Drink* | 2002–4 |

## Sirius AC Bordeaux 99

Very good example of AC Bordeaux. Plummy nose with some prune and floral touches and lots of good, classic Bordeaux flavours of black-berry and mulberry and a fine, dry earthy tex-ture. *Irish Distillers*

| | |
|---|---|
| *Price* | €9–€12 |
| *Grape* | Merlot/Cab Sauv |
| *Alc/vol* | 12% |
| *Food* | Meat/roasts |
| *Drink* | 2002–3 |

### €12–€15

## Ch. Barreyre AC 1ères Côtes de Bordeaux 00 ☆

Good balance between structure and concentra-tion with fragrant, summer pudding fruit aro-mas and plenty of blackcurrant, strawberry and loganberry flavours matched by crisp acidity and firm tannins. *River Wines*

| | |
|---|---|
| *Price* | €12–€15 |
| *Grape* | Cab/Merlot blend |
| *Alc/vol* | 12.5% |
| *Food* | Meat/roasts |
| *Drink* | 2002–4 |

## Ch. Beau Rivage AC Bordeaux Supérieur 98 ☆

Ripe aromas of sweet, smoky oak, plum and cassis and very powerful smoke and plum fla-vours with spice, all underpinned with good tannic structure. Very good and made in a mod-ern style. *O'Briens*

| | |
|---|---|
| *Price* | €12–€15 |
| *Grape* | Merlot/Petit Verdot/ Cab Sauv/Cab Franc & Malbec |
| *Alc/vol* | 12.5% |
| *Food* | Poultry/chicken with garlic |
| *Drink* | 2002–4 |

### Ch. Brisson AC Côtes de Castillon 99

Herbaceous and minty nose with a spicy background. The palate is more earthy and vegetal than fruity, with good tannic grip and structure which makes it best with food. *Grants*

*Price* €12–€15
*Grape* **Bordeaux blend**
*Alc/vol* **12.5%**
*Food* **Meat/lamb**
*Drink* **2002–3**

### Ch. Brun-Despagne AC Bordeaux Supérieur 99

Very nicely balanced and elegant. Cherry nose with a hint of blackcurrant and a lovely tangy palate of ripe cherry, damson and plum flavours and some smokiness. *Le Caveau*

*Price* €12–€15
*Grape* **Merlot blend**
*Alc/vol* **12.5%**
*Food* **Cheese/Gorgonzola**
*Drink* **2002–4**

### Ch. de Camarsac AC Bordeaux 98

Rich, baked fruit nose and earthy aromas followed by black fruit flavours with a hint of pepper, firm tannins and quite a long, dry finish. *Peter Dalton*

*Price* €12–€15
*Grape* **Cabernet blend**
*Alc/vol* **12.5%**
*Food* **Meat/lamb chops**
*Drink* **2002–3**

### Ch. Durand-Laplagne AC Puisseguin St Émilion 98

A rich, plum-coloured wine with a damson and blackberry nose followed by crisp, slightly stalky black fruit flavours, damsons, cherries and blackberries, and a good bite of racy acidity. *Wines Direct*

*Price* €12–€15
*Grape* **Merlot blend**
*Alc/vol* **12.5%**
*Food* **Vegetarian/ mushroom dishes**
*Drink* **2002–3**

### Ch. Jacquinot AC Bordeaux 98 🌿

Elegant and delicate style with aromas of cherry, pepper and toffee. Softer, lighter flavoured palate though with plenty of structure, mature, earthy fruit and baked fruit pie flavours. At its best with meat dishes. *Taserra*

*Price* €12–€15
*Grape* **Bordeaux blend**
*Alc/vol* **12%**
*Food* **Meat/steak**
*Drink* **2002–3**

### Ch. Jonqueyres AC Bordeaux Supérieur 00

Subtle aromas of cherry, blackcurrant and a touch of cedar. More complexity to the palate which is layered with fruit and nice earthy characteristics, spice and leather. There are very firm tannins which should soften. *Mitchells*

*Price* €12–€15
*Grape* **Bordeaux blend**
*Alc/vol* **12.5%**
*Food* **Meat/meatballs**
*Drink* **2002–5**

> **AC Bordeaux** *is the generic appellation for white and red wines produced anywhere within the Bordeaux region. They are generally inexpensive and intended for early drinking, two to three years from the vintage. The quicker-maturing Merlot is the dominant grape in the blend.*

## Ch. La Citadelle AC Bordeaux Supérieur 99 ☆

Perfumed and evolved nose of berry fruit, candied peel and green peppers and a very good balance of green pepper and summer fruits on the palate with mellow tannins and a tangy finish. Drinking well now. All Bordeaux Supérieur should be like this. *WineKnows*

| | |
|---|---|
| Price | €12–€15 |
| Grape | Bordeaux blend |
| Alc/vol | 12.5% |
| Food | Meat/shepherd's pie |
| Drink | 2002–3 |

## Ch. La Grande Maye AC Côtes de Castillon 99 ☆

A weighty, concentrated wine, with power and class. The aromas are of warm, earthy blackcurrants and menthol with ginger and spice. The palate has tight tannins and ripe blackcurrant fruit with a resinous quality. Sunday roast material. *Findlaters*

| | |
|---|---|
| Price | €12–€15 |
| Grape | Bordeaux blend |
| Alc/vol | 12.5% |
| Food | Meat/roasts |
| Drink | 2002–4 |

## Ch. Le Chêne Cru Bourgeois AC Haut-Médoc 99

A rustic style that is best with food. Cigar box and tobacco aromas with a dry and firm tannic palate filled out with rich, dark bramble fruit and coffee flavours. *MacCormaic*

| | |
|---|---|
| Price | €12–€15 |
| Grape | Bordeaux blend |
| Alc/vol | 12.5% |
| Food | Meat/roast beef |
| Drink | 2002–3 |

## Ch. Montagne AC Côtes de Castillon 98

Mature, old style, classic Bordeaux with a ripe yet burnt blackcurrant and plum nose, good acidity and very firm tannins, nice peppery stewed fruit and a very dry finish. *Febvre*

| | |
|---|---|
| Price | €12–€15 |
| Grape | Bordeaux blend |
| Alc/vol | 12.5% |
| Food | Meat/leg of lamb |
| Drink | 2002–3 |

## Ch. Peyredoulle AC 1ères Côtes de Blaye 99 ☆

Lovely evolved nose, ripe and mature, with farmyard and dark fruit aromas. Vibrant, crunchy palate with bittersweet loganberry fruit and a hint of pepper. Very stylish with good concentration and a nice sappy finish. *Febvre*

| | |
|---|---|
| Price | €12–€15 |
| Grape | Merlot blend |
| Alc/vol | 12.5% |
| Food | Meat/steak and kidney pie |
| Drink | 2002–4 |

## Ch. St Ahon Cru Bourgeois AC Haut-Médoc 98

A ripe style with power. The aromas are quite earthy and meaty with some red fruits backed by a good fruity palate with plenty of chunky blackcurrant and plum flavours and a nice, dry classy finish. *WineOnline*

| | |
|---|---|
| Price | €12–€15 |
| Grape | Cabernet blend |
| Alc/vol | 12.5% |
| Food | Meat/stews |
| Drink | 2002–4 |

### Lafleur de Lynch AC Médoc **99** ☆

An example of New Bordeaux with a very forward nose of blackcurrant aromas. Smooth-
textured, fruity palate with plums and blackcurrants and a tangy twist of green peppers.
*Dunnes Stores*

| | |
|---|---|
| *Price* | €12–€15 |
| *Grape* | Bordeaux blend |
| *Alc/vol* | 12% |
| *Food* | Meat/beef |
| *Drink* | 2002–3 |

---

#### €15–€18

### Ch. Bertin AC Montagne-St Émilion **98**

Stylish wine with a lot to
recommend it. Soft rasp-
berry and plum aromas
and pure damson and
cherry flavours with a
lively touch of acidity.
Could be kept or drunk
happily now. *Febvre*

| | |
|---|---|
| *Price* | €15–€18 |
| *Grape* | Bordeaux blend |
| *Alc/vol* | 12.5% |
| *Food* | Meat/roasts |
| *Drink* | 2002–4 |

---

### Ch. du Raux Cru Bourgeois AC Haut-Médoc **96**

Beautifully balanced with lots to interest and
excite. Superripe and slightly earthy aromas of
raspberry and blackcurrant, fruity palate of redcurrants and vanilla tones and very good
length. *Fields*

| | |
|---|---|
| *Price* | €15–€18 |
| *Grape* | Cabernet/Merlot |
| *Alc/vol* | 12.5% |
| *Food* | Cheese/soufflé |
| *Drink* | 2002–3 |

---

### Ch. Haut Selve AC Graves **98**

Really strong cherry and liquorice on the nose
followed by generous black fruit flavours and a
sweet vanilla palate with some floral and vegetal elements. *Mitchells*

| | |
|---|---|
| *Price* | €15–€18 |
| *Grape* | Cab Sauv/Merlot |
| *Alc/vol* | 12% |
| *Food* | Meat/beef |
| *Drink* | 2002–4 |

---

### Ch. Lamothe-Cissac Cru Bourgeois AC Haut-Médoc **99**

Rich blackcurrant fruit aromas. Cedar and
tobacco flavours but tightly structured tannins
somewhat mask the ripe fruit so it would be
worth keeping for a few years longer.
*MacCormaic*

| | |
|---|---|
| *Price* | €15–€18 |
| *Grape* | Cabernet blend |
| *Alc/vol* | 12.5% |
| *Food* | Meat/lamb |
| *Drink* | 2002–5 |

---

### Ch. L'Enclos Bonis AC St Estèphe **99**

Classic style with aromas of blackcurrants and
violets and nuances of cedarwood. Dry palate
with firm tannins and hints of tar and layers of
blackberry fruit, vanilla and cedar. *Mitchells*

| | |
|---|---|
| *Price* | €15–€18 |
| *Grape* | Merlot/Cab Sauv/ |
| | Cab Franc/Petit Verdot |
| *Alc/vol* | 12.5% |
| *Food* | Meat/steak |
| *Drink* | 2002–4 |

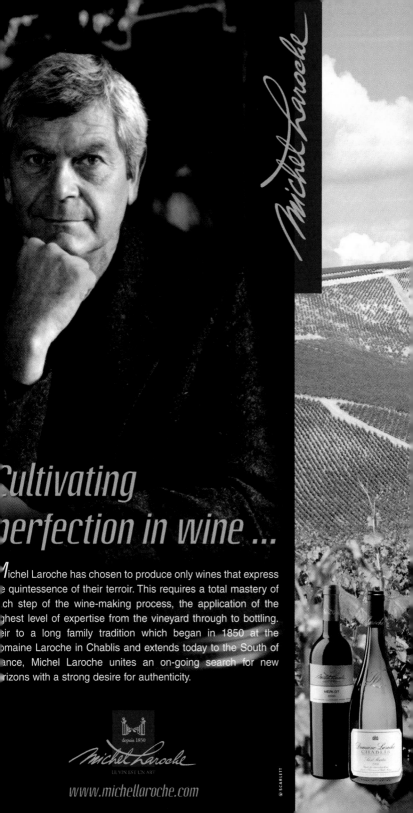

# Cultivating perfection in wine ...

Michel Laroche has chosen to produce only wines that express the quintessence of their terroir. This requires a total mastery of each step of the wine-making process, the application of the highest level of expertise from the vineyard through to bottling. Heir to a long family tradition which began in 1850 at the Domaine Laroche in Chablis and extends today to the South of France, Michel Laroche unites an on-going search for new horizons with a strong desire for authenticity.

*Michel Laroche*

depuis 1850

*Michel Laroche*

LE VIN EST UN ART

www.michellaroche.com

® SCARLETT

# A WORLD OF TASTES JUST WAITING TO BE DISCOVERED

Febvre is a family owned business,

built on a commitment to provide discerning

Irish palates with a selection of carefully chosen wines

from around the world. We bring you these wines through our

close links with grower-producers, both large and small,

who share our desire to uphold the traditions of quality

and good taste for which family owned

vineyards are renowned.

# FEBVRE

Febvre & Company Limited, Burton Hall Road,
Sandyford Industrial Estate, Dublin 18.
Tel: (01) 295 9030    Fax: (01) 295 9036    Email: info@febvre.ie

## Ch. Maine-Gazin 'Livenne' Vieilles Vignes
AC 1ères Côtes de Blaye **00** ☆

A big style with so much of everything—tannins and acidity, a burnt toffee and plum nose and a smooth palate with a core of very concentrated dark fruit and very good length. This wine deserves to be given a few more years in bottle. *Febvre*

| | |
|---|---|
| Price | €15–€18 |
| Grape | Merlot blend |
| Alc/vol | 13% |
| Food | Poultry/chicken |
| Drink | 2003–5 |

## Ch. Pichon AC Lussac St Émilion **99**

Stylish, with fragrant aromas of blackcurrant, plum and tobacco and a toasty, fruitcake palate with blackcurrant and cherry flavours. Dry on the finish. *Taserra*

| | |
|---|---|
| Price | €15–€18 |
| Grape | Bordeaux blend |
| Alc/vol | 12.5% |
| Food | Cheese/Cashel Blue |
| Drink | 2002–3 |

## Ch. Tour du Pas St Georges AC St Georges St Émilion **98**

This wine has a classic coolness which derives from the fruit and acidity. The result is an earthy, bramble fruit nose and lovely chewy fruit flavours layered with peppery spice and hints of roasted coffee. *Wines Direct*

| | |
|---|---|
| Price | €15–€18 |
| Grape | Merlot blend |
| Alc/vol | 12.5% |
| Food | Meat/lamb |
| Drink | 2002–4 |

## Cheval Noir AC St Émilion **97**

Very smooth with maturing aromas of ripe plum and undergrowth and a flavour-packed palate with layers of berry fruit, green plums, some cassis, smoky tones and truffle notes. *TDL*

| | |
|---|---|
| Price | €15–€18 |
| Grape | Bordeaux blend |
| Alc/vol | 12% |
| Food | Meat/lamb |
| Drink | 2002–3 |

### €18–€22

## Ch. Belles-Graves AC Lalande de Pomerol **99**

Elegant blackcurrant fruit and cream on the nose echoed by spicy black fruit and liquorice flavours on the palate with a smooth, concentrated finish. *Waterford Wine Vault*

| | |
|---|---|
| Price | €18–€22 |
| Grape | Merlot/Cab Franc |
| Alc/vol | 12.5% |
| Food | Meat/casseroles |
| Drink | 2002–4 |

## Ch. du Seuil AC Graves **98**

Lovely fragrant nose with some complexity giving aromas of blackcurrant, coffee, spice and pepper. Nice firm tannins on the palate balanced with blackcurrant, spice and leather flavours. *Woodford Bourne*

| | |
|---|---|
| Price | €18–€22 |
| Grape | Cabernet blend |
| Alc/vol | 12.5% |
| Food | Poultry/roast chicken |
| Drink | 2002–4 |

## Ch. Fourcas Hosten Cru Bourgeois
AC Listrac-Médoc **98** ☆☆☆

Classy, stylish wine capable of further ageing but drinking now. Big, fragrant and meaty nose with smoke and blackcurrant fruit and a smooth palate with excellent structure and good length. *O'Briens*

| | |
|---|---|
| *Price* | €18–€22 |
| *Grape* | Cab/Merlot blend |
| *Alc/vol* | 12.5% |
| *Food* | Meat/osso bucco |
| *Drink* | 2003–6 |

## Ch. Fourcas-Dumont AC Listrac-Médoc **97** ☆

Bittersweet wine with refreshing acidity and stylish rich fruits. Cigar box, leather and burnt blackcurrant and plum nose with a nice underlying richness to the smoky black fruits on the palate. Extremely pleasant wine from a lesser known appellation. *Mitchells*

| | |
|---|---|
| *Price* | €18–€22 |
| *Grape* | Merlot/Cab Sauv/ Petit Verdot |
| *Alc/vol* | 12.5% |
| *Food* | Game/pheasant |
| *Drink* | 2002–4 |

## Ch. Franc Lartigue AC St Émilion Grand Cru **98** ☆☆

A wine of power and elegance, subtly influenced by oak. Aromas are of black fruit, rubber and pepper matched with a very smooth and rich palate of spiced blackcurrants, damsons and some good, bitter chocolate.
*Waterford Wine Vault*

| | |
|---|---|
| *Price* | €18–€22 |
| *Grape* | Merlot blend |
| *Alc/vol* | 12.5% |
| *Food* | Meat/beef |
| *Drink* | 2002–4 |

## Ch. Loudenne Cru Bourgeois AC Médoc **98** ☆

Perfumed and forward cassis and spice nose with an elegant, poised, classic Médoc palate of blackcurrant flavours, nice savoury bite and good structure. *Gilbeys*

| | |
|---|---|
| *Price* | €18–€22 |
| *Grape* | Cab/Merlot blend |
| *Alc/vol* | 12.5% |
| *Food* | Cheese/soufflé |
| *Drink* | 2002–4 |

## Ch. Magnol Cru Bourgeois AC Haut-Médoc **98** ☆☆

Mature, toasty and fragrant nose with lovely, grippy blackcurrant and blackberry flavours, wood smoke and a delicious finish. Very classy and stylish. *Dillons*

| | |
|---|---|
| *Price* | €18–€22 |
| *Grape* | Merlot/Cab Sauv/ Cab Franc |
| *Alc/vol* | 12.5% |
| *Food* | Meat/veal |
| *Drink* | 2002–6 |

## Ch. Patache d'Aux Cru Bourgeois AC Médoc **98** ☆

Unmistakeably Bordeaux, this wine has the palate cleansing combination of dry tannin and crisp acidity that cries out for lamb. Ripe, evolved nose with smoke and plum and a great blackcurrant and damson flavoured palate. *Febvre*

| | |
|---|---|
| *Price* | €18–€22 |
| *Grape* | Cab Sauv/Merlot/ Cab Franc/Petit Verdot |
| *Alc/vol* | 12.5% |
| *Food* | Meat/lamb |
| *Drink* | 2002–6 |

## Ch. Tour Baladoz AC St Émilion Grand Cru 98 ☆

Elegant and classic style with a ripe black-currant and damson nose and a dry but ripe fruit palate with plum and vanilla flavours, nicely knit tannins and acidity. Could happily be drunk now or put away for further ageing. *Gilbeys*

| | |
|---|---|
| *Price* | **€18–€22** |
| *Grape* | **Merlot blend** |
| *Alc/vol* | **12.5%** |
| *Food* | **Game/partridge** |
| *Drink* | **2002-5** |

## Dom. Zédé AC Margaux 99 ☆

Still a bit young though it is quite smooth and feminine. Ripe, spicy plum and blackcurrant nose and a plum and vanilla flavoured palate with a long, persistent finish. *Le Caveau*

| | |
|---|---|
| *Price* | **€18–€22** |
| *Grape* | **Bordeaux blend** |
| *Alc/vol* | **12.5%** |
| *Food* | **Meat/steak** |
| *Drink* | **2002-5** |

### €22–€25

## Ch. Jacques Blanc Cuvée Aliénor
AC St Émilion Grand Cru 98 🌿

This wine has maturing aromas of plum and damson and a sensuous palate with a rich concentration of juicy blackcurrant and blackberry flavours, fine tannic grip and a decent length. *Mary Pawle*

| | |
|---|---|
| *Price* | **€22–€25** |
| *Grape* | **Merlot blend** |
| *Alc/vol* | **12.5%** |
| *Food* | **Poultry/duck** |
| *Drink* | **2002-4** |

## Ch. La Couronne AC St Émilion Grand Cru 99 ☆

From nose to palate this is a stylish, sleek, sexy wine, deliciously weighty with a fine classic structure. Blackberry and plum fruits in a sheen of vanilla and spice are a touch gamey and savoury. The wine will benefit from further time in bottle. *TDL*

| | |
|---|---|
| *Price* | **€22–€25** |
| *Grape* | **Merlot blend** |
| *Alc/vol* | **12.5%** |
| *Food* | **Poultry/confit** |
| *Drink* | **2002-5** |

## Ch. Rollan de By Cru Bourgeois AC Médoc 97 ☆

Classic Bordeaux drinking beautifully now. Perfumed aromas of forest fruits and pencil shavings. The palate is concentrated with chewy red and black fruits and fine woodland flavours with some herbal notes. Perfect Saturday-night-in treat. *Wines Direct*

| | |
|---|---|
| *Price* | **€22–€25** |
| *Grape* | **Merlot blend** |
| *Alc/vol* | **12.5%** |
| *Food* | **Meat/steak** |
| *Drink* | **2002-4** |

## Ch. Teyssier AC St Émilion Grand Cru 99 ☆

Stylish, perfumed nose of summer pudding, liquorice and spice and a nicely elegant and balanced palate with cherry and damson flavours and enlivening, exotic spice. *Findlaters*

| | |
|---|---|
| *Price* | **€22–€25** |
| *Grape* | **Merlot blend** |
| *Alc/vol* | **13%** |
| *Food* | **Game/pheasant** |
| *Drink* | **2002-5** |

## L'Abeille de Fieuzal AC Pessac-Léognan 99 ☆

Youthful nose with forest fruit, tobacco and vanilla aromas. A big-hitter palate with very good fruit concentration, mulberry and black cherry flavours, blessed with very firm tannins. A wine of this class needs time—patience will be rewarded. *Findlaters*

| | |
|---|---|
| Price | €22–€25 |
| Grape | Cabernet blend |
| Alc/vol | 12.5% |
| Food | Game/woodcock |
| Drink | 2003–5 |

## Ch. Liversan Cru Bourgeois AC Haut-Médoc 96

Classic dry Bordeaux with a complex undergrowth and tobacco leaf nose and chunky, mature blackcurrant flavours, smooth and earthy on the finish. It is drinking well now. *Febvre*

| | |
|---|---|
| Price | €22–€25 |
| Grape | Cab Sauv/Merlot/ Cab Franc/Petit Verdot |
| Alc/vol | 12.5% |
| Food | Game/casseroles |
| Drink | 2002–3 |

### €25–€30

## Ch. des Pèlerins AC Pomerol 99 ☆☆

The French must be a patient people as this wine needs time. It has enticing aromas of plum pie with a richly concentrated plum, smoke and roasted coffee palate and a very tannic structure. Give it at least 2 more years in the cellar. *Maxxium*

| | |
|---|---|
| Price | €25–€30 |
| Grape | Merlot blend |
| Alc/vol | 12.5% |
| Food | Meat/roast lamb |
| Drink | 2004–6 |

## Ch. Lestage Simon Cru Bourgeois AC Haut-Médoc 98

Elegantly austere due primarily to youth, this wine has aromas of redcurrants, peppers and vanilla and good flavours of blackcurrant and spice. *Terroirs*

| | |
|---|---|
| Price | €25–€30 |
| Grape | Merlot blend |
| Alc/vol | 13% |
| Food | Meat/rack of lamb |
| Drink | 2003–4 |

## Sarget de Gruaud-Larose AC St Julien 97 ☆

Attractive bramble fruit aromas promise lots and deliver on the palate. A delicious wine with firm tannins and a weight of mouth-filling, ripe, robust blackcurrant fruits. Still very young, it will continue to please for years to come. *Comans*

| | |
|---|---|
| Price | €25–€30 |
| Grape | Cabernet blend |
| Alc/vol | 12.5% |
| Food | Poultry/goose |
| Drink | 2002–7 |

### €30–€35

## Ch. Chasse-Spleen Cru Bourgeois AC Moulis-en-Médoc 98

Wonderful nose with cassis, pencil shavings, pepper and minty dark chocolate. Concentrated palate with black fruit, vanilla and a hint of leather, and firm tannins which add depth and structure. *Grants*

| | |
|---|---|
| Price | €30–€35 |
| Grape | Cabernet blend |
| Alc/vol | 12.8% |
| Food | Poultry/duck |
| Drink | 2002–5 |

## Ch. Maucaillou Cru Bourgeois AC Moulis 97 ☆☆☆

Gorgeous nose of tobacco, spice and red berries with a very concentrated and structured palate of blackcurrant, plum, nutmeg and tobacco flavours. Hugely satisfying Bordeaux to convert the most sceptical and from a vintage that is drinking well now. *Febvre*

| | |
|---|---|
| Price | **€30–€35** |
| Grape | **Bordeaux blend** |
| Alc/vol | **13%** |
| Food | **Poultry/duck** |
| Drink | **2002–4** |

### €35–€40

## Ch. Kirwan AC Margaux Grand Cru Classé 96 ☆☆

Elegance and finesse from beginning to end. Perfumed nose of luscious cassis; piercing palate with very defined blackcurrant fruit, smoky cigar box, mocha and leathery flavours. *O'Briens*

| | |
|---|---|
| Price | **€35–€40** |
| Grape | **Cabernet blend** |
| Alc/vol | **13%** |
| Food | **Meat/roasts** |
| Drink | **2002–7** |

*How to find a specified wine*
*If your local retailer does not stock a particular wine, contact the importer named in italic after the tasting note (contact details are on pages 274–279) for the name of your nearest stockist.*

# France–Burgundy

The vintages of 99 and 00 featured strongly in this year's tastings, with the 99 living up to expectations as exceptionally good, offering quality and, more importantly, consistency, while 00 was more patchy. The 00 vintage seems to steer a wider course between poor and great for both red and white wines; this is due in part to some difficult weather conditions at harvesting. The wines are not as consistently good as 99 and they may not age as well. As a result, this vintage requires a little more knowledge and a certain amount of caution on the part of the consumer. That being said, there are some very good wines from this vintage with the whites possibly being more highly regarded.

## White

### Under €9

#### Roger Roblot Blanc Prestige VdT nv

Pleasant, simple and fruity with a decent level of ripe apple flavours and reasonable length. Perfect summer drinking. *Peter Dalton*

| | |
|---|---|
| Price | **Under €9** |
| Grape | **Chardonnay** |
| Alc/vol | **11%** |
| Food | **Apéritif/picnic** |
| Drink | **2002–3** |

### €9–€12

#### Marks and Spencer Chablis AC Chablis 99

A good example of a classic style. Fresh, flinty and lively nose of lemon and green apple, crisp apple flavours with a lively acidic twist and slightly herbaceous tones, yet with a creamy, smooth texture. *Marks & Spencer*

| | |
|---|---|
| Price | **€9–€12** |
| Grape | **Chardonnay** |
| Alc/vol | **12.5%** |
| Food | **Seafood/mussels** |
| Drink | **2002–3** |

*Chablis is one of France's classic white wines, characteristically steely and fresh. Made from Chardonnay, much of its character comes from the limestone subsoil with its high content of marine fossils and chalk. AC Chablis, made from grapes grown all over the region, is flinty and minerally with green apple flavours and should be drunk about two to three years from the vintage. The best vineyards are designated Premier Cru or Grand Cru. Premier Cru wines are more intense and concentrated than AC Chablis, with pure citrus fruit flavours. Grand Cru wines are richer and fuller and may be aged for longer.*

*How to use this book*
*The wines are listed in order of country/region, colour (red or white), price band, then by name. If you can't quickly find the wine you are looking for try the index, which we have expanded for this edition. There are separate chapters for rosé, sparkling (including Champagne) and sweet wines. Since wine prices are not fixed the price bands are guidelines only. The dates suggested for when to drink the wines do not indicate their expected life but the period over which our tasters thought they would enjoy them most.*

## Pierre Ponnelle AC Chablis 00

Rich style of Chablis with tropical fruit, poached pear and citrus aromas and a smooth palate with fresh acidity and green apple, pineapple and melon flavours. Good apéritif and partner for light food. *Dunnes Stores*

| | |
|---|---|
| *Price* | €9–€12 |
| *Grape* | Chardonnay |
| *Alc/vol* | 12.5% |
| *Food* | Apéritif/salads |
| *Drink* | 2002–3 |

### €12–€15

## Chanson Père et Fils AC Chablis 00

Vegetal nose with some apple and broad bean aromas. The palate is much more classic with tart green apples, mineral tones, crisp acidity and a zesty finish. *O'Briens*

| | |
|---|---|
| *Price* | €12–€15 |
| *Grape* | Chardonnay |
| *Alc/vol* | 12.5% |
| *Food* | Pasta/seafood |
| *Drink* | 2002–3 |

## Chanson Père et Fils AC Viré-Clessé 01

Burgundy in a New World style—rich, ample and a touch tropical. There are melon and pear aromas with a hint of fudge and ripe apple flavours. *O'Briens*

| | |
|---|---|
| *Price* | €12–€15 |
| *Grape* | Chardonnay |
| *Alc/vol* | 13% |
| *Food* | Poultry/Chicken Kiev |
| *Drink* | 2002–3 |

## Dom. Laroche AC Mâcon-Lugny 01

Intense and refreshing with aromas of baked apple, melon and pear which follow through on a rounded and pleasing palate tinged with spice, cleansing acidity and a lovely, zingy after-taste. *Allied Drinks*

| | |
|---|---|
| *Price* | €12–€15 |
| *Grape* | Chardonnay |
| *Alc/vol* | 12.5% |
| *Food* | Cheese/gratins |
| *Drink* | 2002–3 |

## Dom. de la Condemine Mâcon-Péronne Le Clou AC Mâcon-Villages 00

Attractive broad nose with waxy apples and a touch of hazelnuts. Quite big in the mouth with zesty citrus, ripe apples, aniseed nuances and a slightly oily texture. *Wines Direct*

| | |
|---|---|
| *Price* | €12–€15 |
| *Grape* | Chardonnay |
| *Alc/vol* | 13% |
| *Food* | Fish/cod |
| *Drink* | 2002–3 |

## Dom. Saumaize-Michelin Les Crèches AC St Véran 00

Classy and elegant nose with walnuts, honey and some spice. Good concentration of apple and melon flavours with tangy citrus acidity, a honeyed, toasty touch and a long, lively, crisp finish. *Wines Direct*

| | |
|---|---|
| *Price* | €12–€15 |
| *Grape* | Chardonnay |
| *Alc/vol* | 13% |
| *Food* | Pasta/creamy sauces |
| *Drink* | 2002–3 |

## Dom. Séguinot-Bordet AC Chablis 00

Fresh Granny Smith nose, light, clean and crisp. Green apple flavours and a dry citrus finish. A very typical, well-made, nicely balanced Chablis. *Wines Direct*

| | |
|---|---|
| *Price* | €12–€15 |
| *Grape* | Chardonnay |
| *Alc/vol* | 12.5% |
| *Food* | Fish/sole |
| *Drink* | 2002–3 |

## Louis Latour AC Chablis 1er Cru **99**

Expressive nose with mineral and wet pebbles. Refreshingly crisp palate with broad red apples and some caramel and honey coming through on the finish. *Gilbeys*

| | |
|---|---|
| *Price* | €12–€15 |
| *Grape* | Chardonnay |
| *Alc/vol* | 13% |
| *Food* | Poultry/chicken |
| *Drink* | 2002–3 |

## Maison Champy AC Mâcon-Uchizy **00**

Flavours of crunchy green apple with spice and honey nuances, a smoky richness and mineral notes balance the fresh, crisp acidity in this appealing white which is lengthy and flavoursome. A great food match. *Allied Drinks*

| | |
|---|---|
| *Price* | €12–€15 |
| *Grape* | Chardonnay |
| *Alc/vol* | 13% |
| *Food* | Fish/hake |
| *Drink* | 2002–3 |

## Ropiteau AC Chablis **01**

Light and fresh aromas of green apples with mineral undertones. The palate is much weightier than the nose implies with ripe, baked apple and peach notes and lemony acidity. *TDL*

| | |
|---|---|
| *Price* | €12–€15 |
| *Grape* | Chardonnay |
| *Alc/vol* | 12.5% |
| *Food* | Seafood/scallops |
| *Drink* | 2002–3 |

### €15–€18

## Cuvée Jean Chartron Chardonnay Vieilles Vignes
AC Bourgogne **00**

Inviting, spicy vanilla nose. The oak is perfectly judged giving a subtle toastiness on the palate which is balanced by lemony acidity and good melon and apple flavours. *Febvre*

| | |
|---|---|
| *Price* | €15–€18 |
| *Grape* | Chardonnay |
| *Alc/vol* | 13% |
| *Food* | Poultry/chicken |
| *Drink* | 2002–3 |

## Dom. André Bonhomme AC Viré-Clessé **00**

Riper Burgundian style, with honey and flower-blossom aromas and lactic hints followed by a ripe palate with juicy apple and melon flavours, tinged with cinnamon, and gentle, balancing acidity. *Le Caveau*

| | |
|---|---|
| *Price* | €15–€18 |
| *Grape* | Chardonnay |
| *Alc/vol* | 13.5% |
| *Food* | Cheese/Cooleeney |
| *Drink* | 2002–3 |

## Dom. Daniel Dampt AC Chablis **01**

Subtle nose with apple, peach, elderflower and mineral nuances which follow through to the crisp palate with good levels of fruit and finishing on a wet pebble note. *Waterford Wine Vault*

| | |
|---|---|
| *Price* | €15–€18 |
| *Grape* | Chardonnay |
| *Alc/vol* | 12.5% |
| *Food* | Cheese/Chaource |
| *Drink* | 2002–3 |

## Dom. des Malandes AC Chablis **00**

Arresting, pronounced aromas of apple blossom and avocado. Youthful and zesty palate with intense flavours of crisp green apples in a classic Chablis style. *Searsons*

| | |
|---|---|
| *Price* | €15–€18 |
| *Grape* | Chardonnay |
| *Alc/vol* | 12.5% |
| *Food* | Seafood/mussels |
| *Drink* | 2002–4 |

## Dom. Garnier et Fils AC Chablis **99**

Bone dry and crisp with mineral, lemon and apple aromas and an apple and spice flavoured palate with fresh, citrus acidity. *Mitchells*

| | |
|---|---|
| Price | €15–€18 |
| Grape | Chardonnay |
| Alc/vol | 12.5% |
| Food | Fish/plaice |
| Drink | 2002–3 |

## Dom. Henri Naudin-Ferrand
### AC Hautes-Côtes de Beaune **99** ☆

Deliciously full-bodied classic, full of flavour, with apples, lemon juice and lemon peel together with butter and honey. *Wines Direct*

| | |
|---|---|
| Price | €15–€18 |
| Grape | Chardonnay |
| Alc/vol | 13% |
| Food | Meat/veal |
| Drink | 2002–4 |

## Dom. René Michel et ses Fils AC Viré-Clessé **98**

Superripe aromas of honey and marmalade more associated with a dessert wine. Dry, rich, spicy, concentrated palate with orange fruit. An unusual wine, not mainstream but appealing. *Searsons*

| | |
|---|---|
| Price | €15–€18 |
| Grape | Chardonnay |
| Alc/vol | 14% |
| Food | Poultry/turkey |
| Drink | 2002–3 |

## Dom. William Fèvre AC Chablis **00** ☆

Cool, clean and refreshing aromas of ripe pear. The palate is even more appealing; it is crisp but with big flavours of apple, lemon, lime and green pepper. The finish is utterly dry and refreshing. *Findlaters*

| | |
|---|---|
| Price | €15–€18 |
| Grape | Chardonnay |
| Alc/vol | 12.5% |
| Food | Fish/turbot |
| Drink | 2002–4 |

## Jaffelin AC Chablis **00**

Although quite tight and closed initially, with hints of runner beans and broad beans, this wine is concentrated and quite fruity, full of apple flavours with nervy acidity and a lively finish. *Cassidy*

| | |
|---|---|
| Price | €15–€18 |
| Grape | Chardonnay |
| Alc/vol | 12.5% |
| Food | Seafood/oysters |
| Drink | 2002–3 |

## Paul Sapin Cuvée Prestige AC St Véran **00**

Pleasant, appealing style with a cool and flinty character to the nose and aromas of fresh apples. On the palate there are concentrated melon and apple flavours with hints of tarragon. *Febvre*

| | |
|---|---|
| Price | €15–€18 |
| Grape | Chardonnay |
| Alc/vol | 13% |
| Food | Cheese/soufflé |
| Drink | 2002–3 |

### €18–€22

## Alice et Olivier de Moor Bel Air AC Chablis **00**

Unmistakeable Chablis with green apple and mineral tones on the nose and plenty of grapefruit-like acidity and Granny Smith apple flavours. Best with food. *Terroirs*

| | |
|---|---|
| Price | €18–€22 |
| Grape | Chardonnay |
| Alc/vol | 12.5% |
| Food | Seafood/oysters |
| Drink | 2002–3 |

## Denis Race AC Chablis 1er Cru Montmains **00**

Classic nose with mineral aromas merged with baked apricot and honey. Firm acidity backs the ample fruit flavours of apple, apricot and citrus with a mineral core that gives this wine great character and style. *Mitchells*

| | |
|---|---|
| *Price* | €18–€22 |
| *Grape* | Chardonnay |
| *Alc/vol* | 12.5% |
| *Food* | Seafood/scallops |
| *Drink* | 2002–5 |

## Dom. Laroche St Martin AC Chablis **00** ☆

Gorgeous nose of honey, apple and apricot with an opulent fruit palate of apple, pear and melon and fresh, mouth-watering acidity. A perfect match for fish and white meat. *Allied Drinks*

| | |
|---|---|
| *Price* | €18–€22 |
| *Grape* | Chardonnay |
| *Alc/vol* | 13% |
| *Food* | Poultry/chicken |
| *Drink* | 2002–4 |

## Dom. Robert-Denogent Macon-Solutré Clos des Bertillonnes AC Mâcon-Villages **98**

A very enjoyable, concentrated wine with character and a long finish. The nutty aromas show off the maturity of the wine as does the fruity, rich caramel palate, with its nutty, smoky undertones. *Terroirs*

| | |
|---|---|
| *Price* | €18–€22 |
| *Grape* | Chardonnay |
| *Alc/vol* | 13% |
| *Food* | Fish/hake |
| *Drink* | 2002–3 |

## La Buxynoise AC Montagny 1er Cru **99**

The 1er Cru designation for Montagny signifies the use of riper grapes. This example is very stylish, concentrated and well made. Hazelnuts and a touch of flint appear on the nose, followed by aniseed, truffle and lanolin flavours and a rich finish. *Febvre*

| | |
|---|---|
| *Price* | €18–€22 |
| *Grape* | Chardonnay |
| *Alc/vol* | 13.5% |
| *Food* | Fish/turbot |
| *Drink* | 2002–3 |

## Lucien Crochet Les Chailloux AC Pouilly-Fuissé **00**

Fresh, dry, lively style with tangerines and peaches on the nose. Rich palate with citrus, tangerine, peach and red apple flavours, good backing acidity, a deft use of spicy oak and a marvellous length of flavour. *Waterford Wine Vault*

| | |
|---|---|
| *Price* | €18–€22 |
| *Grape* | Chardonnay |
| *Alc/vol* | 13% |
| *Food* | Poultry/chicken |
| *Drink* | 2002–4 |

## Ropiteau AC Pouilly-Fuissé **00**

Beautifully constructed with a good, forward, fruity and floral nose, attractive apple flavours and a custard creaminess giving a lovely texture. *TDL*

| | |
|---|---|
| *Price* | €18–€22 |
| *Grape* | Chardonnay |
| *Alc/vol* | 13% |
| *Food* | Poultry/roast chicken |
| *Drink* | 2002–3 |

### €22–€25

## Ch. des Rontets Clos Varambon AC Pouilly-Fuissé **00** ☆

Stylish, with apple and pear fruits, floral and nutty elements. Full and ripe, tangy and minerally with a long, persistent finish. *Searsons*

| | |
|---|---|
| Price | €22–€25 |
| Grape | Chardonnay |
| Alc/vol | 13% |
| Food | Seafood/prawns |
| Drink | 2002–4 |

## Chartron et Trébuchet La Chaume AC Rully **99** ☆

Delicious, nutty, slightly spicy and certainly complex, this is a juicy fruit cocktail with limy acidity, spicy oak and lanolin and an exceptionally long finish. *Febvre*

| | |
|---|---|
| Price | €22–€25 |
| Grape | Chardonnay |
| Alc/vol | 13% |
| Food | Fish/salmon |
| Drink | 2002–3 |

### €25–€30

## Chanson Père et Fils AC Chablis 1er Cru Vaucopins **98** ☆

The nose shows complexity and some development with aromas of apples and mineral, salty and nutty nuances. The palate is very lively with apple flavours, citrus acidity and a definite smokiness with a very long finish. *O'Briens*

| | |
|---|---|
| Price | €25–€30 |
| Grape | Chardonnay |
| Alc/vol | 13% |
| Food | Fish/John Dory |
| Drink | 2002–3 |

## Dom. Valette AC Pouilly-Fuissé **99**

Big and showy with smoky new oak evident on the nose; the palate has generous honey tones with a warming tropical feel and lively citrus acidity. *Wines Direct*

| | |
|---|---|
| Price | €25–€30 |
| Grape | Chardonnay |
| Alc/vol | 13.5% |
| Food | Fish/monkfish |
| Drink | 2002–3 |

## Faiveley AC Pouilly-Fuissé **99**

Good, rich, broad nose with attractive butterscotch and lemon aromas followed by a generous, ripe palate with a slight mineral or slatey texture and lemon pie acidity. *Maxxium*

| | |
|---|---|
| Price | €25–€30 |
| Grape | Chardonnay |
| Alc/vol | 13% |
| Food | Fish/smoked salmon |
| Drink | 2002–3 |

## Vincent Girardin 'Les Murgers de Dents de Chiens' AC St Aubin 1er Cru **99** ☆

High quality, classic and complex. Smoky, toasty aromas. Creamy, smooth palate heavily influenced by oak with flavours of butterscotch and vanilla together with baked apples, honey and citrus. *Le Caveau*

| | |
|---|---|
| Price | €25–€30 |
| Grape | Chardonnay |
| Alc/vol | 13% |
| Food | Meat/pork |
| Drink | 2002–6 |

€35–€40

## Chartron et Trébuchet La Chatenière
AC St Aubin 1er Cru **99** ☆

Gorgeous, broad, nutty nose of walnuts and hazelnuts; weighty, ripe, peachy palate, with honey, caramel and cream, citrus acidity and stylish length. *Febvre*

| | |
|---|---|
| Price | €35–€40 |
| Grape | Chardonnay |
| Alc/vol | 13.5% |
| Food | Seafood/lobster |
| Drink | 2002–3 |

# Red

€9–€12

## Dom. de Fontalognier AC Régnié **01**

Very ripe, candied strawberry and pepper aromas and a refreshing red apple and vanilla palate. A light, fruity, easy-drinking style which would be good with light, spicy food.
*River Wines*

| | |
|---|---|
| Price | €9–€12 |
| Grape | Gamay |
| Alc/vol | 12.5% |
| Food | Meat/pork |
| Drink | 2002–3 |

€12–€15

## Clos de la Perrière AC Bourgogne **00**

Attractive ripe nose of red fruit jelly and a slight spiciness. The palate is full bodied with firm tannins matched with weighty fruit flavours of black cherries and plums. *O'Briens*

| | |
|---|---|
| Price | €12–€15 |
| Grape | Pinot Noir |
| Alc/vol | 12.5% |
| Food | Poultry/chicken |
| Drink | 2002–4 |

## Dom. de la Madone AC Fleurie **01**

Raspberry and redcurrant aromas and ultra-ripe strawberry flavours, cut with crisper red cherries, give a lively and refreshing style with a rich finish. *Mitchells*

| | |
|---|---|
| Price | €12–€15 |
| Grape | Gamay |
| Alc/vol | 13% |
| Food | Meat/salami |
| Drink | 2002–3 |

## Dom. Pardon AC Fleurie **01**

Light, fresh and fruity with strawberry jam aromas and a youthful, tangy, ripe strawberry and plum flavoured palate. Soft tannins make it very easy to drink. A great picnic style.
*Waterford Wine Vault*

| | |
|---|---|
| Price | €12–€15 |
| Grape | Gamay |
| Alc/vol | 13% |
| Food | Picnic/salads |
| Drink | 2002–3 |

## Faiveley AC Morgon **00**

There is a pungency to the fragrant and almost overripe nose of strawberry and cherry with a hint of soy sauce. The palate has rich cherry flavours, yet with a tangy cut of redcurrant and still that oriental tone. *Maxxium*

| | |
|---|---|
| Price | €12–€15 |
| Grape | Gamay |
| Alc/vol | 12.5% |
| Food | Poultry/duck |
| Drink | 2002–3 |

## Paul Sapin Cuvée Prestige AC Brouilly **00**

Very ripe aromas of candied cherry and raspberry and a juicy, red fruit palate of plums and spice with a good cut of refreshing acidity. *Febvre*

| | |
|---|---|
| Price | €12–€15 |
| Grape | Gamay |
| Alc/vol | 13% |
| Food | Meat/cold meats |
| Drink | 2002–3 |

## Pierre Ponnelle AC Bourgogne Côte de Nuits-Villages **97**

Classic style with a vegetal and redcurrant jelly nose. The palate is light bodied with good acidity and flavours of warm summer berries with a dusting of spice. *Dunnes Stores*

| | |
|---|---|
| Price | €12–€15 |
| Grape | Pinot Noir |
| Alc/vol | 13% |
| Food | Poultry/turkey |
| Drink | 2002–3 |

### €15–€18

## Ch. de Briante AC Brouilly **00**

Moreish style with good black cherry and earthy redcurrant aromas and a cherry-flavoured palate with a good balance between acidity and fruit. *Woodford Bourne*

| | |
|---|---|
| Price | €15–€18 |
| Grape | Gamay |
| Alc/vol | 13% |
| Food | Vegetarian/ mushroom dishes |
| Drink | 2002–3 |

## Cuvée Jean Chartron Pinot Noir Vieilles Vignes
AC Bourgogne **99**

Good-looking wine with a glistening, pinky-red colour. Fruity, earthy nose with strawberries and spice and a refined, fruity palate with summer berry flavours, particularly ripe strawberries. *Febvre*

| | |
|---|---|
| Price | €15–€18 |
| Grape | Pinot Noir |
| Alc/vol | 13% |
| Food | Cheese/Brie |
| Drink | 2002–5 |

## Dom. Arlaud Roncevie AC Bourgogne **99**

Sturdy cherry and strawberry aromas with a definite spiciness. The palate is rich and powerful with smokiness and earthy fruit, more confident in style than many Burgundies at the basic AC level. *Wicklow Wine Co.*

| | |
|---|---|
| Price | €15–€18 |
| Grape | Pinot Noir |
| Alc/vol | 12.5% |
| Food | Meat/pork |
| Drink | 2002–5 |

## Dom. Bertagna 'Les Dames Hugeuttes'
AC Bourgogne Hautes-Côtes de Nuits **99**

Fresh and elegant style with layers of smoke, cherry and strawberry on the nose and a silky-smooth palate with supple tannins, spice and lots of redcurrants. Excellent for its AC. *Waterford Wine Vault*

| | |
|---|---|
| Price | €15–€18 |
| Grape | Pinot Noir |
| Alc/vol | 13% |
| Food | Poultry/duck |
| Drink | 2002–4 |

## Dom. de Valmoissine Pinot Noir
VdP Coteaux du Verdun **99**

Appealing, easy drinking with spiciness and an earthy, farmyard character together with lots of hot, summer berry fruit. *Gilbeys*

| | |
|---|---|
| *Price* | €15–€18 |
| *Grape* | Pinot Noir |
| *Alc/vol* | 13% |
| *Food* | Meat/veal |
| *Drink* | 2002–3 |

## Dom. Jean Louis Appert AC Fleurie **01**

Attractive nose with strawberry and black pepper aromas and a good depth of fruit on the palate—ripe red cherries with some crunchy red apples. *McCabes*

| | |
|---|---|
| *Price* | €15–€18 |
| *Grape* | Gamay |
| *Alc/vol* | 13% |
| *Food* | Poultry/chicken |
| *Drink* | 2002–3 |

## Dom. Michèle et Patrice Rion Les Bois Bâtons
AC Bourgogne **00**

Rich nose of spicy dark cherries and a medicinal touch. Quite a bit of oak adds spice to a big palate of sweet summer berry flavours with a strong backbone of tannin and acidity. *Terroirs*

| | |
|---|---|
| *Price* | €15–€18 |
| *Grape* | Pinot Noir |
| *Alc/vol* | 12.5% |
| *Food* | Poultry/turkey |
| *Drink* | 2003–5 |

## Faiveley AC Brouilly **99**

This wine has quite an austere structure and would be a good foil for rich or spicy foods. Aromas are of tangy red and black currants and there are distinct black cherry, plum and liquorice flavours on the palate. *Maxxium*

| | |
|---|---|
| *Price* | €15–€18 |
| *Grape* | Gamay |
| *Alc/vol* | 12.5% |
| *Food* | Ethnic/Indian |
| *Drink* | 2002–3 |

## Jaffelin AC Hautes-Côtes de Beaune **98**

Truly classic in style with an earthy nose and a palate of spice, red cherries and strawberries, crisp acidity and firm tannins. *Cassidy*

| | |
|---|---|
| *Price* | €15–€18 |
| *Grape* | Pinot Noir |
| *Alc/vol* | 13% |
| *Food* | Meat/roast ham |
| *Drink* | 2002–5 |

## Pierre Ducret 'Clos Marolle' AC Givry 1er Cru **00**

Red fruit and earthy character; delicate strawberry and raspberry flavours come through strongly with spice. The wine's youth can be seen in its high acidity and firm tannins. *Wines Direct*

| | |
|---|---|
| *Price* | €15–€18 |
| *Grape* | Pinot Noir |
| *Alc/vol* | 13% |
| *Food* | Risotto/mushroom |
| *Drink* | 2002–4 |

### €18–€22

## Dom. Chandon de Briailles AC Savigny-lès-Beaune **99**

Fruity style with firm tannins that do not dominate the plentiful flavours of ripe red strawberries and cherries. *Wines Direct*

| | |
|---|---|
| *Price* | €18–€22 |
| *Grape* | Pinot Noir |
| *Alc/vol* | 12.5% |
| *Food* | Meat/kidneys |
| *Drink* | 2002–6 |

## J. M. Boillot AC Bourgogne 99

Earthy aromas with notes of raspberries, black cherries and spice. The fruit is somewhat masked by the tannins which demand accompanying food. *Terroirs*

| | |
|---|---|
| *Price* | €18–€22 |
| *Grape* | Pinot Noir |
| *Alc/vol* | 12.5% |
| *Food* | Game/venison |
| *Drink* | 2002–5 |

### €22–€25

## Champy Père AC Savigny-lès-Beaune 97 ☆

Supple, velvety style with mature, perfumed and forest aromas and a delicious earthiness to the palate which has layers of strawberry fruit and a hint of coffee. Tannins are very ripe and the wine is appealingly subtle. *Allied Drinks*

| | |
|---|---|
| *Price* | €22–€25 |
| *Grape* | Pinot Noir |
| *Alc/vol* | 13% |
| *Food* | Fish/mullet |
| *Drink* | 2002–4 |

## Dom. Chandon de Briailles 'Les Vergelesses'
AC Pernand-Vergelesses 1er Cru 99

A Pinot with fruit to the fore. The nose is very upfront and perfumed with ripe autumnal fruit and vegetal elements followed by a very fruity palate with strawberry and leafy flavours and wood spice. *Wines Direct*

| | |
|---|---|
| *Price* | €22–€25 |
| *Grape* | Pinot Noir |
| *Alc/vol* | 12.5% |
| *Food* | Meat/pork |
| *Drink* | 2002–4 |

## Faiveley La Framboisière AC Mercurey 99

An abundance of cherries and spice intermingle and flavour the palate. Tannins are very firm and this wine is still quite young and tight but would be just right with food. *Maxxium*

| | |
|---|---|
| *Price* | €22–€25 |
| *Grape* | Pinot Noir |
| *Alc/vol* | 12.5% |
| *Food* | Meat/ham |
| *Drink* | 2002–6 |

## Joseph Roty AC Marsannay 97 ☆

Delicious style, with a developed nose of strawberry and bonfire aromas and an elegantly balanced palate with lots of red strawberry and cherry flavours, fresh acidity and gentle, structured tannins. *Le Caveau*

| | |
|---|---|
| *Price* | €22–€25 |
| *Grape* | Pinot Noir |
| *Alc/vol* | 13% |
| *Food* | Fish/tuna |
| *Drink* | 2002–3 |

### €25–€30

## Dom. Gaston et Pierre Ravaut
AC Aloxe-Corton 1er Cru 99 ☆☆

This wine has breeding and will age really well. At the moment it has earthy and savoury aromas, with currants and Christmas pudding and an intense, very ripe and tangy palate of dried fruit, raspberries and cherries.
*Waterford Wine Vault*

| | |
|---|---|
| *Price* | €25–€30 |
| *Grape* | Pinot Noir |
| *Alc/vol* | 13% |
| *Food* | Poultry/confit of duck |
| *Drink* | 2003–7 |

## Dom. Vincent Girardin 'Les Gravières'
AC Santenay 1er Cru **99** ☆

Earthy, undergrowth aromas and concentrated red cherry and strawberry palate with oaky spiciness. Still quite young with firmness and tannins to match the multi-layered flavours, this is just starting to develop deliciously mature characteristics. *Le Caveau*

| | |
|---|---|
| Price | €25–€30 |
| Grape | Pinot Noir |
| Alc/vol | 13% |
| Food | Poultry/turkey |
| Drink | 2002–6 |

*€30–€35*

## Dom. Bouchard Père et Fils AC Beaune Marconnets **97** ☆

Elegant from start to finish, this is a rich and succulent wine with layers of ripe strawberries and bramble fruit, spice and an earthy character. *Findlaters*

| | |
|---|---|
| Price | €30–€35 |
| Grape | Pinot Noir |
| Alc/vol | 13% |
| Food | Poultry/chicken |
| Drink | 2002–4 |

## Dom. du Clos Frantin AC Gevrey-Chambertin **98** ☆

Very attractive with concentrated, ripe summer fruits and a hint of toffee, good tannins and structure. It is still young and has great potential. *Irish Distillers*

| | |
|---|---|
| Price | €30–€35 |
| Grape | Pinot Noir |
| Alc/vol | 13% |
| Food | Meat/ham |
| Drink | 2002–5 |

| The symbols | |
|---|---|
| 🍃 | *Organic* |
| € | *Exceptionally good value* |
| ☆ | *Accomplished, showing above average quality or character making it worthy of extra attention* |
| ☆☆ | *Excellent with great character, style and complexity* |
| ☆☆☆ | *Wonderful, showing terrific character and complexity, true to its origins* |
| ☆☆☆☆ | *Exceptional, with considerable complexity and classic balance. Rewards serious tasting.* |

# France–Loire

Something really good is happening in the Loire which gave us some very fine wines this year, with especially good examples of Pouilly-Fumé, Menetou-Salon and Sancerre, which are all made from Sauvignon Blanc. The Loire is home to Sauvignon Blanc and perhaps the growing popularity of this variety is a sign of our impatient times. It makes wines that are best drunk young; they are very crisp and fresh with a classic pungency and grassiness. Yet there are subtle differences between the three important adjoining areas of Sancerre, Pouilly-Fumé and Menetou-Salon, enough to provoke interest in all three and to avoid allegations of sameness.

The red grape variety Cabernet Franc has been greatly underrated but as more examples are being stocked its qualities can be better appreciated. It makes fragrant and elegant wines, not too heavy but with a seductive and mouth-watering fruitiness generally evoking flavours of raspberries. The best examples we found are from Chinon and Saumur-Champigny.

## White

### €9–€12

#### Ch. de la Ragotière Vieilles Vignes
AC Muscadet de Sèvre-et-Maine sur Lie **99**

Apple orchard nose with a very fresh palate considering the age. While crisp it has a yeasty roundness with mineral, citrus and apple flavours. Ideal accompaniment for seafood.
*Terroirs*

| | |
|---|---|
| Price | €9–€12 |
| Grape | Melon de Bourgogne |
| Alc/vol | 12% |
| Food | Seafood/shellfish |
| Drink | 2002–3 |

### €12–€15

#### Ch. d'Epiré AC Savennières **00**

Pronounced nose of lemon syrup with rich flavours of honey and lemons, a touch of mineral earthiness and a suggestion of clove spice. Savennières is a style that gets more interesting with age and this one is still very young.
*O'Briens*

| | |
|---|---|
| Price | €12–€15 |
| Grape | Chenin Blanc |
| Alc/vol | 13% |
| Food | Seafood/mussels |
| Drink | 2003–6 |

#### Dom. Doudeau-Léger AC Sancerre **00**

A light melon and citrus peel nose belies a richer, zesty green apple- and lemon-flavoured palate. It is showing some development and softening out of the fruit which counterbalances the zippiness. *Wicklow Wine Co.*

| | |
|---|---|
| Price | €12–€15 |
| Grape | Sauvignon Blanc |
| Alc/vol | 12.5% |
| Food | Salads/tomato |
| Drink | 2002–3 |

## Dom. Henry Pellé AC Menetou-Salon Morogues 01 ☆☆☆ €

Stylish and elegant with a complexity of aromas—greengage, lime, grass and mineral. The palate is classically restrained and has flavours of citrus, gooseberry and fresh grass cuttings with excellent depth and a rich mouthfeel. Super food wine. *Findlaters*

| | |
|---|---|
| Price | €12–€15 |
| Grape | Sauvignon Blanc |
| Alc/vol | 12.5% |
| Food | Fish/sole |
| Drink | 2002-3 |

### €15–€18

SHORTLIST WHITE WINE OF THE YEAR

## Chatelain AC Pouilly-Fumé 01 ☆☆☆☆ €

Delicious: possessing all the hallmarks of classic elegance with a wonderful concentration of gooseberries and citrus fruit and some richer peach and cream, undercut with terroir giving a fine mineral, stony, almost chalky, character. *Findlaters*

| | |
|---|---|
| Price | €15–€18 |
| Grape | Sauvignon Blanc |
| Alc/vol | 13% |
| Food | Cheese/goats' cheese |
| Drink | 2002-4 |

## Dom. Dominique et Janine Crochet AC Sancerre 01 ☆☆

Elegant, classic and a touch restrained with nettle and blackcurrant leaf aromas. Flavours of gooseberries, tart apples and limes. Still a little young but with all the fruit and mineral qualities needed to develop. *O'Briens*

| | |
|---|---|
| Price | €15–€18 |
| Grape | Sauvignon Blanc |
| Alc/vol | 12.5% |
| Food | Ethnic/Chinese |
| Drink | 2003-4 |

## Dom. La Croix Canat Les Blancs Gateaux
AC Sancerre **00** ☆

Delightful, vibrant lemon and grapefruit aromas matched by a complex, steely palate with flavours of citrus fruit, green grass and nettles and some fine mineral qualities. *Searsons*

| | |
|---|---|
| Price | €15–€18 |
| Grape | Sauvignon Blanc |
| Alc/vol | 12% |
| Food | Fish/skate |
| Drink | 2002–4 |

## Dom. Masson-Blondelet Villa Paulus AC Pouilly-Fumé **01**

Appealing, grassy gooseberry nose gives way to a big and very satisfying palate showing zippy gooseberry and lemon, perfumed hints and lovely length. *Wines Direct*

| | |
|---|---|
| Price | €15–€18 |
| Grape | Sauvignon Blanc |
| Alc/vol | 12.5% |
| Food | Fish/trout |
| Drink | 2002–3 |

## Fournier AC Pouilly-Fumé **98** ☆

Attractive and somewhat developed aromas of lemon and vegetal notes with a vibrant and intensely flavoured palate of citrus and gooseberry flavours. *TDL*

| | |
|---|---|
| Price | €15–€18 |
| Grape | Sauvignon Blanc |
| Alc/vol | 12.5% |
| Food | Fish/smoked salmon |
| Drink | 2002–3 |

## Fournier Vieilles Vignes AC Sancerre **00**

Very approachable as it is a tad richer than most Sancerres. Grassy and gooseberry aromas, well-judged acidity, generous lemon, apple and melon flavours and creamy and toasty elements with very good length. *TDL*

| | |
|---|---|
| Price | €15–€18 |
| Grape | Sauvignon Blanc |
| Alc/vol | 12.5% |
| Food | Starters/avocado |
| Drink | 2002–3 |

### €18–€22

## Comte Lafond AC Sancerre **00**

Elegant and crisp—just what Sancerre should be. Classic aromas of flint and stony green plums. Bone-dry palate with lovely body and plenty of lively citrus fruit, appley and grassy. *Gilbeys*

| | |
|---|---|
| Price | €18–€22 |
| Grape | Sauvignon Blanc |
| Alc/vol | 12.5% |
| Food | Cheese/goats' cheese |
| Drink | 2002–4 |

## Dom. Jean-Paul Balland AC Sancerre **00**

Light fruity and mineral aromas. Unmistakeable Sancerre, showing superb balance. Crisp and bone dry with grassiness and a weight of apple and lemon flavours. *Taserra*

| | |
|---|---|
| Price | €18–€22 |
| Grape | Sauvignon Blanc |
| Alc/vol | 12.5% |
| Food | Ethnic/Japanese |
| Drink | 2002–3 |

## Fournier La Chaudouillonne AC Sancerre **00** ☆

Vibrant and lively with aromas of gooseberry, apple and herbs. The palate reveals a perfect example of a carefully crafted Sancerre—crisp but balanced acidity and delicious, ripe flavours of apples, gooseberries and lemons. *TDL*

| | |
|---|---|
| Price | €18–€22 |
| Grape | Sauvignon Blanc |
| Alc/vol | 12.5% |
| Food | Fish/smoked salmon |
| Drink | 2002–3 |

### Pascal Jolivet AC Pouilly-Fumé **00** ☆

Excellent, fresh, lively example of a classic style with lots of ripe fruit and crisp acidity. The aromas and flavours are grassy and flinty with gooseberry and lemon fruit. *Maxxium*

| | |
|---|---|
| *Price* | €18–€22 |
| *Grape* | Sauvignon Blanc |
| *Alc/vol* | 12.5% |
| *Food* | Fish/chowder |
| *Drink* | 2002–4 |

### Pascal Jolivet AC Sancerre **00**

Fresh citrus aromas and fabulous lemon and flint flavours with some honey ripeness. This is a symphony of flavours with a rewarding, mature feel. *Maxxium*

| | |
|---|---|
| *Price* | €18–€22 |
| *Grape* | Sauvignon Blanc |
| *Alc/vol* | 12.5% |
| *Food* | Ethnic/Thai |
| *Drink* | 2002–3 |

#### €22–€25

### De Ladoucette AC Pouilly-Fumé **00** ☆

Delicious and classic. Attractive lemony-green colour with delicate, leafy aromas and intense, ripe fruit and mineral flavours. *Gilbeys*

| | |
|---|---|
| *Price* | €22–€25 |
| *Grape* | Sauvignon Blanc |
| *Alc/vol* | 12.5% |
| *Food* | Fish/sole |
| *Drink* | 2002–4 |

### Lucien Crochet Les Chailloux AC Sancerre **00**

Excellent quality, with quite a herbaceous nose of gooseberry and cut grass aromas. Light, crisp palate with fresh gooseberry, lime and green apple flavours in abundance, good length and a zippy finish. *Terroirs*

| | |
|---|---|
| *Price* | €22–€25 |
| *Grape* | Sauvignon Blanc |
| *Alc/vol* | 12.5% |
| *Food* | Fish/mullet |
| *Drink* | 2002–3 |

## Red

#### €9–€12

### Dom. de la Semellerie AC Chinon **01**

Refreshing style, still a tad young but particularly good with food. Fragrant blackcurrant nose with a tangy black cherry- and blackcurrant-flavoured palate with smoky hints. *Mitchells*

| | |
|---|---|
| *Price* | €9–€12 |
| *Grape* | Cabernet Franc |
| *Alc/vol* | 12.5% |
| *Food* | Meat/veal |
| *Drink* | 2002–4 |

### Dom. du Clos Godeaux AC Chinon **01**

Perfect hot-weather red with pure cherry, raspberry and some floral aromas and a dry, mouthwatering palate with cherry and loganberry flavours. *O'Briens*

| | |
|---|---|
| *Price* | €9–€12 |
| *Grape* | Cabernet Franc |
| *Alc/vol* | 12.5% |
| *Food* | Picnic/salads |
| *Drink* | 2002–3 |

## Dom. Duveau AC St Nicolas-de-Bourgeuil 01

The raspberry and blackcurrant nose has a rich mineral influence followed by a ripe and lively palate with red cherry and pepper flavours and good acidity. It would suit rich or spicy food. *Mitchells*

| | |
|---|---|
| Price | €9–€12 |
| Grape | Cabernet Franc |
| Alc/vol | 12.5% |
| Food | Meat/pork |
| Drink | 2002–3 |

### €12–€15

## Ch. de Targé AC Saumur-Champigny 98

Light and elegant with subtle power and very good concentration, this wine is showing good maturity. It has earthy blackcurrant aromas and a soft, mellow palate with ripe red and black-currant flavours. *Terroirs*

| | |
|---|---|
| Price | €12–€15 |
| Grape | Cabernet Franc |
| Alc/vol | 12.5% |
| Food | Fish/salmon |
| Drink | 2002–3 |

## Ch. de Varière AC Anjou-Villages Brissac 99

Very vibrant wine which would work best with food. Aromas are of cherry, pepper, and herbs, with a smoky influence, and there is a good concentration of cherry and blackcurrant flavours. *Dunnes Stores*

| | |
|---|---|
| Price | €12–€15 |
| Grape | Cabernet Franc |
| Alc/vol | 12.5% |
| Food | Poultry/turkey |
| Drink | 2002–3 |

## Dom. du Roncée Clos des Marronniers AC Chinon 99

A light and tightly structured red with mellow black and red currant aromas and quite a crisp palate with juicy cherry and raspberry flavours. *Dunnes Stores*

| | |
|---|---|
| Price | €12–€15 |
| Grape | Cabernet Franc |
| Alc/vol | 12.5% |
| Food | Fish/tuna |
| Drink | 2002–3 |

## Dom. Filliatreau AC Saumur-Champigny 00 ☆

Smooth and elegant with a blackcurrant and raspberry nose and a wild honey influence, refreshing acidity and intense crushed raspberries in the mouth. A lovely, summery wine which would be great with white meats. *Searsons*

| | |
|---|---|
| Price | €12–€15 |
| Grape | Cabernet Franc |
| Alc/vol | 12.5% |
| Food | Poultry/chicken |
| Drink | 2002–4 |

### €18–€22

## Couly-Dutheil Clos de l' Echo AC Chinon 96 ☆

Stylish yet with a lot of power. The nose has creamy and peppery blackcurrants backed up by a fruity, raspberry-flavoured palate. Perfect for roast poultry. *Le Caveau*

| | |
|---|---|
| Price | €18–€22 |
| Grape | Cabernet Franc |
| Alc/vol | 12.5% |
| Food | Poultry/duck |
| Drink | 2002–6 |

# France–Rhône

There are some outstanding Rhône wines available at the moment, especially seriously-made delicious red wines which, as a general rule, are not over-priced, and are capable of ageing. The Rhône valley enjoyed very good vintages in 98, 99 and 00 and these vintages dominated the tastings this year. While the best of the Northern Rhône wines tasted came from the 99 vintage, the 00 wines from the Southern Rhône were particularly good. But the quality is not all due to a run of good vintages. The Southern Rhône, particularly Châteauneuf-du-Pape and Gigondas, has been undergoing a rejuvenation and methods and quality have improved. Over the next few years other improving areas, such as Côtes du Luberon and Côtes du Ventoux, are likely to become more prominent.

## White

### Under €9

### **Cuvée Orélie** VdP des Coteaux de l'Ardèche **01 €**

Fresh citrus and apple blossom aromas and some peach. Fine fleshy character on the palate with good acidity and apple and peach flavours.
*Wicklow Wine Co.*

| | |
|---|---|
| *Price* | Under €9 |
| *Region* | Rhône (South) |
| *Grape* | Chardonnay/ Sauvignon Blanc |
| *Alc/vol* | 12% |
| *Food* | Pasta/seafood |
| *Drink* | 2002–3 |

### €9–€12

> **White Côtes du Rhône** *is usually made from a blend of white grapes—Clairette, Roussanne and Bourboulenc, although it may also be made from other grapes, for example Viognier.*

### **Ch. de Ruth** AC Côtes du Rhône **99**

A very different and welcome style with an appealing, complex nose, combining floral and fruit aromas with hints of honey. The refreshing blend gives a full mouthfeel and a layered fruit palate with baked apple, pear, peach and melon.
*Dillons*

| | |
|---|---|
| *Price* | €9–€12 |
| *Region* | Rhône (South) |
| *Grape* | Clairette/Roussanne/ Bourboulenc |
| *Alc/vol* | 13% |
| *Food* | Poultry/chicken |
| *Drink* | 2002–3 |

### **Dom. des Anges** AC Côtes du Ventoux **00**

Very pleasant, fresh, crisp wine with layers of fruit, floral and wood spice aromas. The blend of grapes gives complexity and a subtle mix of caramelised banana, pear and apple flavours.
*O'Briens*

| | |
|---|---|
| *Price* | €9–€12 |
| *Region* | Rhône (South) |
| *Grape* | Marsanne/Roussanne/ Bourboulenc/ Grenache blanc |
| *Alc/vol* | 13.5% |
| *Food* | Salads/Nicoise |
| *Drink* | 2002–3 |

## La Vieille Ferme AC Côtes du Lubéron 00

Multi-dimensional wine. The nose has lots of aromas but is predominantly grapey with apricots. Myriad flavours of apples, apricots and a touch of green grass cuttings. *Allied Drinks*

| | |
|---|---|
| Price | €9–€12 |
| Region | Rhône (South) |
| Grape | Grenache Blanc/ Roussanne/Ugni Blanc |
| Alc/vol | 12% |
| Food | Fish/salmon |
| Drink | 2002–3 |

### €12–€15

## Guigal AC Côtes du Rhône 00

Spicy and floral nose followed by a ripe, fruity palate with pineapple and pear flavours, pepper and spice. The Viognier character really comes through. *Barry & Fitzwilliam*

| | |
|---|---|
| Price | €12–€15 |
| Region | Rhône (South) |
| Grape | Roussanne/Clairette/ Viognier/Bourboulenc Grenache Blanc |
| Alc/vol | 13% |
| Food | Vegetarian/ratatouille |
| Drink | 2002–3 |

### €15–€18

## Dom. Grand Veneur Blanc de Viognier
AC Côtes du Rhône 99

Pungent and spicy aromas on the nose are followed by a pleasant mouthful of spicy vanilla essence with ripe pineapple and lychee flavours and crisp acidity. *Mitchells*

| | |
|---|---|
| Price | €15–€18 |
| Region | Rhône (South) |
| Grape | Viognier |
| Alc/vol | 13% |
| Food | Seafood/crab |
| Drink | 2002–3 |

### €18–€22

## Ch. de Bastet AC Côtes du Rhône 99 🌿

Attractive apple blossom and honeysuckle nose. The palate has a good weight of ripe apples, peaches, nutty almonds and floral tones, held together with lemony acidity. *Mary Pawle*

| | |
|---|---|
| Price | €18–€22 |
| Region | Rhône (South) |
| Grape | Viognier |
| Alc/vol | 12.5% |
| Food | Seafood/swordfish |
| Drink | 2002–3 |

## Ch. du Trignon AC Côtes du Rhône 00

Excellent example of Viognier giving a very appealing nose of honeycomb, spice, sweet peach and pineapple. The palate is equally big with flavours of peach and mango, vanilla pod and honey. *River Wines*

| | |
|---|---|
| Price | €18–€22 |
| Region | Rhône (South) |
| Grape | Viognier |
| Alc/vol | 14% |
| Food | Fish/turbot |
| Drink | 2002–3 |

€30–€35

## Cuilleron Gaillard Villard AC Condrieu **00** ☆☆

Classic, very concentrated but with elegance. The nose shows complexity with a variety of fruity, vegetal and woody aromas. Flavours are quite full bodied—tropical fruit matched with spice—and backed with good acidity, with a long finish. *Searsons*

| | |
|---|---|
| *Price* | €30–€35 |
| *Region* | Rhône (North) |
| *Grape* | Viognier |
| *Alc/vol* | 14% |
| *Food* | Seafood/lobster |
| *Drink* | 2002–3 |

# Red

Under €9

## Côtes du Rhône des Papes AC Côtes du Rhône **01 €**

Warm and spicy blackberry and raspberry aromas with a soft, rounded, mellow palate of ripe currant and berry fruit. Easy drinking with nice concentration. *Oddbins*

| | |
|---|---|
| *Price* | Under €9 |
| *Region* | Rhône (South) |
| *Grape* | Rhône blend |
| *Alc/vol* | 12.5% |
| *Food* | Pizza/pasta |
| *Drink* | 2002–3 |

## Les Vignerons Ardèchois Cuvée Prestige Merlot
VdP des Coteaux de l'Ardèche **00**

Pleasant and well-made wine with nice fruit levels. Intense aromas of plums and red berries are followed by flavours of plums, damsons and black cherries. *Wicklow Wine Co.*

| | |
|---|---|
| *Price* | Under €9 |
| *Region* | Rhône (South) |
| *Grape* | Merlot |
| *Alc/vol* | 12.5% |
| *Food* | Pasta/Bolognese |
| *Drink* | 2002–3 |

€9–€12

## Cave de Rasteau Réserve AC Côtes du Rhône **00**

Rustic, warming style with plum, cherry and warm spice aromas and a nice plum- and cherry-flavoured palate with good structure. *Peter Dalton*

| | |
|---|---|
| *Price* | €9–€12 |
| *Region* | Rhône (South) |
| *Grape* | Grenache/Cinsault/ Syrah/Mourvèdre |
| *Alc/vol* | 13.5% |
| *Food* | Meat/beef burgers |
| *Drink* | 2002–3 |

## Ch. de Bastet AC Côtes du Rhône **01** 🌿

A fresh, light style, 80% Grenache to 20% Syrah, with a slightly green herbaceous nose of redcurrants and raspberries which is mirrored on the palate. Firm tannins suggest this wine needs food. *Mary Pawle*

| | |
|---|---|
| *Price* | €9–€12 |
| *Region* | Rhône (South) |
| *Grape* | Grenache/Syrah |
| *Alc/vol* | 13% |
| *Food* | Meat/cold meats |
| *Drink* | 2002–3 |

# Peter A. Dalton Food & Wine

Importers of Fine Wines, Champagnes and
Extra Virgin Olive Oils, Olive Pâtés & Pesto

Château Roubaud, Costières de Nîmes
*Celebrating the fourth generation
producing wine. Winner of the Mâcon
Silver Medal for their 2000 Rosé.*

*Côtes du Rhône:* Cave de Rasteau,
Carte Réserve, Village, Beulière

Colavita Olive Oils from
Campobasso, Italy
*Kosher approved, only 100 per
cent Italian olives used*

Roger Roblot
*Silver medals and Guide
Hachette recommended*

Domain St. George
*Award-winning wines with a difference, newly arrived from California*

L. Dumont Champagne
*Watch out for this new arrival for the discerning Irish consumer*

Nostros
*from Chile*

Phone (01) 295-4945  Fax (01) 295-4945
Mobile 087-263-9665  Fax 087-263-96657
Email padwines@indigo.ie
Visit our range and links at www.daltonwines.com

## Ch. de Ruth AC Côtes du Rhône 99 ☆ €

Lots of regional character makes this a rustic wine with cloves, spice and pepper, really ripe fruit, nicely structured with a chewy length. A very good example. *Dillons*

| | |
|---|---|
| *Price* | €9–€12 |
| *Region* | Rhône (South) |
| *Grape* | Grenache/Cinsault/ Syrah/Mourvèdre |
| *Alc/vol* | 13.5% |
| *Food* | Pasta/arrabiata |
| *Drink* | 2002–3 |

> *Côtes du Rhône-Villages wines require lower yields from the vineyard and stipulate a minimum of 12.5% alcohol for reds, compared to higher yields and an 11% minimum for basic **Côtes du Rhône** wines. Villages red wines must contain a maximum of 65% Grenache and a minimum of 25% Syrah, Cinsault and/or Mourvèdre, which are seen as 'improver' grapes. No such restrictions apply to basic Côtes du Rhône reds.*

## Dom. Didier Charavin Rasteau AC Côtes du Rhône-Villages 00

Restrained aromas of redcurrants, plums, blackcurrants and spice and a ripe, dark fruit compote palate with peppery notes. An attractive wine, elegant and stylish. *Wines Direct*

| | |
|---|---|
| *Price* | €9–€12 |
| *Region* | Rhône (South) |
| *Grape* | Rhône blend |
| *Alc/vol* | 13.5% |
| *Food* | Meat/barbecue |
| *Drink* | 2002–3 |

## La Vieille Ferme AC Côtes du Ventoux 00

Classically made with a sweet fruit nose of strawberry jam and cherry and a supple palate with good red berry fruit and pepperiness. *Allied Drinks*

| | |
|---|---|
| *Price* | €9–€12 |
| *Region* | Rhône (South) |
| *Grape* | Grenache/Syrah/ Mourvèdre/Cinsault |
| *Alc/vol* | 12.5% |
| *Food* | Meat/pork |
| *Drink* | 2002–3 |

## Vidal-Fleury AC Côtes du Rhône 99

Good, complex nose of ripe fruits with an earthy, vegetal edge and a slight touch of rubber. Medium to full bodied on the palate with cherry and plum flavours and a pleasant, rustic aftertaste. *Irish Distillers*

| | |
|---|---|
| *Price* | €9–€12 |
| *Region* | Rhône (South) |
| *Grape* | Grenache/Cinsault/ Syrah/Mourvèdre |
| *Alc/vol* | 12.5% |
| *Food* | Meat/roasts |
| *Drink* | 2002–3 |

### €12–€15

## Alain Jaume AC Vacqueyras 00 ☆

Savoury and blackberry aromas with pure blackberries, pepper and spice on the palate and a touch of runner bean flavours underpinned by a firm tannic structure. Archetypal Vacqueyras. *Mitchells*

| | |
|---|---|
| *Price* | €12–€15 |
| *Region* | Rhône (South) |
| *Grape* | Grenache/Syrah/ Mourvèdre |
| *Alc/vol* | 13.5% |
| *Food* | Meat/veal |
| *Drink* | 2002–4 |

## Cave de Rasteau AC Côtes du Rhône-Villages **99**

Mature, and drinking perfectly now, with earthy, dark fruit aromas and rich, stewed fruit flavours of plum and damson. *Peter Dalton*

| | |
|---|---|
| Price | €12–€15 |
| Region | Rhône (South) |
| Grape | Grenache/Cinsault/ Syrah/Mourvèdre |
| Alc/vol | 14% |
| Food | Meat/casseroles |
| Drink | 2002–3 |

## Chapoutier Les Meysonniers AC Crozes-Hermitage **98**

Complex nose which is more vegetal than fruity. There are good, earthy blackcurrant flavours on the palate, still firm, structured tannins and a very long, satisfying, savoury length. *Grants*

| | |
|---|---|
| Price | €12–€15 |
| Region | Rhône (North) |
| Grape | Syrah (75% min.) |
| Alc/vol | 12.5% |
| Food | Poultry/turkey |
| Drink | 2002–4 |

## Ch. du Trignon Sablet AC Côtes du Rhône-Villages **99**

Lots of character. Roast beef nose with violets, spice and berry fruit and a warm, ripe palate with elegant length and good structure. *River Wines*

| | |
|---|---|
| Price | €12–€15 |
| Region | Rhône (South) |
| Grape | Rhône blend |
| Alc/vol | 13.5% |
| Food | Meat/stews |
| Drink | 2002–3 |

## Dom. de la Renjarde AC Côtes du Rhône-Villages **98**

Classic and representative of the style. Still lively and nicely knit with cherry and red berry fruit and good, spicy pepper. *Fields*

| | |
|---|---|
| Price | €12–€15 |
| Region | Rhône (South) |
| Grape | Rhône blend |
| Alc/vol | 14% |
| Food | Meat/liver |
| Drink | 2002–3 |

## Dom. Martin Rasteau AC Côtes du Rhône-Villages **98**

This blend of 70% Grenache and 30% Syrah produces a strong, earthy, almost meaty, nose with a mellowing, full-bodied palate, good black fruit and leather flavours and firm tannins. *Wicklow Wine Co.*

| | |
|---|---|
| Price | €12–€15 |
| Region | Rhône (South) |
| Grape | Grenache/Syrah |
| Alc/vol | 13.5% |
| Food | Meat/lamb |
| Drink | 2002–3 |

## Guigal AC Côtes du Rhône **98**

A wine with very agreeable and attractive fruit. Although quite a light style, it has a very good length of flavour which is particularly savoury and peppery. *Barry & Fitzwilliam*

| | |
|---|---|
| Price | €12–€15 |
| Region | Rhône (South) |
| Grape | Grenache/Syrah/ Mourvèdre |
| Alc/vol | 13% |
| Food | Meat/salami |
| Drink | 2002–3 |

## Jaboulet Les Jalets AC Crozes-Hermitage **99** ☆

Elegant and smooth. Fruity, spicy nose of plum, damson and stewed apple; plummy palate with clove spice and resinous oak. *Gilbeys*

| | |
|---|---|
| *Price* | €12–€15 |
| *Region* | Rhône (North) |
| *Grape* | Syrah (75% min.) |
| *Alc/vol* | 13% |
| *Food* | Game/rabbit |
| *Drink* | 2002–4 |

## Jaboulet Les Jalets AC Crozes-Hermitage **00**

Toasty, intriguingly smoky and earthy nose backed up by quite a tangy palate with plenty of raspberry, damson and mint flavours. *Gilbeys*

| | |
|---|---|
| *Price* | €12–€15 |
| *Region* | Rhône (North) |
| *Grape* | Syrah (75% min.) |
| *Alc/vol* | 13% |
| *Food* | Poultry/turkey |
| *Drink* | 2002–3 |

## Louis Bernard Grande Réserve AC Côtes du Ventoux **99**

Equal proportions of Grenache and Syrah produce a wine with a super colour and lots of white pepper and violets on the nose. The fruit is quite ripe and fleshy with hints of strawberry jam, currants, spice and vanilla. *O'Briens*

| | |
|---|---|
| *Price* | €12–€15 |
| *Region* | Rhône (South) |
| *Grape* | Grenache/Syrah |
| *Alc/vol* | 13.5% |
| *Food* | Meat/pork |
| *Drink* | 2002–3 |

## Perrin Réserve AC Côtes du Rhône **99**

Very refreshing style but with good concentration of flavour. Burnt, spicy plum and cherry aromas are followed by a stewed plum- and damson-flavoured palate. *Allied Drinks*

| | |
|---|---|
| *Price* | €12–€15 |
| *Region* | Rhône (South) |
| *Grape* | Grenache/Cinsault/ Syrah/Mourvèdre |
| *Alc/vol* | 13% |
| *Food* | Meat/steak |
| *Drink* | 2002–3 |

### €15–€18

## Alain Jaume AC St Joseph **00**

00 was a lighter vintage and this is coming through in the light berry fruit aromas of plum and red apple and the raspberry and peppery palate. *Mitchells*

| | |
|---|---|
| *Price* | €15–€18 |
| *Region* | Rhône (North) |
| *Grape* | Syrah (90% min.) |
| *Alc/vol* | 13% |
| *Food* | Meat/ham |
| *Drink* | 2002–3 |

> **St Joseph** is the second-largest AC in the northern Rhône. Up to 10% of the white grape Marsanne may be added to Syrah at the fermentation stage to soften and add perfume to the wine.

## Guigal AC Crozes-Hermitage 99

A big style of Crozes-Hermitage with a nose of fruitcake, tobacco and earthy notes. It has a warm mouthfeel with a big extraction of bramble fruit flavours. High in tannins, it is made for keeping. *Barry & Fitzwilliam*

| | |
|---|---|
| *Price* | **€15–€18** |
| *Region* | **Rhône (North)** |
| *Grape* | **Syrah (75% min)** |
| *Alc/vol* | **12.5%** |
| *Food* | **Meat/beef** |
| *Drink* | **2003–6** |

## Laurus AC Crozes-Hermitage 97

Strong vegetal nose with a touch of spice. Intense palate of black fruit which is wonderfully perfumed and spicy. A wine with more finesse than blockbuster power. *Dillons*

| | |
|---|---|
| *Price* | **€15–€18** |
| *Region* | **Rhône (North)** |
| *Grape* | **Syrah (75% min.)** |
| *Alc/vol* | **12.5%** |
| *Food* | **Poultry/duck** |
| *Drink* | **2002–4** |

## Louis Bernard Grande Réserve AC Côtes du Rhône 99

Australian-style fruitiness. Upfront, inky nose of plums and spice with a rich, fruity plum and spicy palate, nicely rounded out with a touch of vanilla. *O'Briens*

| | |
|---|---|
| *Price* | **€15–€18** |
| *Region* | **Rhône (South)** |
| *Grape* | **Grenache/Syrah** |
| *Alc/vol* | **13.5%** |
| *Food* | **Meat/lamb** |
| *Drink* | **2002–3** |

### €18–€22

## Ch. de St Cosme AC Gigondas 99 ☆

A Gigondas with extra ripeness and complexity. Lovely nose with cherries, dark chocolate and herbs, a warm fruit and currant palate with a twist of vanilla and caramel and a lingering finish. *Findlaters*

| | |
|---|---|
| *Price* | **€18–€22** |
| *Region* | **Rhône (South)** |
| *Grape* | **Grenache/Syrah/ Cinsault** |
| *Alc/vol* | **14%** |
| *Food* | **Meat/lamb** |
| *Drink* | **2002–4** |

> Up to thirteen grape varieties are permitted in the **Châteauneuf-du-Pape** blend (some of them white). The style is full bodied and high in alcohol, 12.5% being the minimum volume permitted.

## Ch. Gigognan Vigne du Dauphin AC Châteauneuf-du-Pape 98

Rustic and a little warm, with lots of good ripe fruit, hot pepper, toasted nuts, tar and liquorice with a superb, pleasing length of flavour. *Taserra*

| | |
|---|---|
| *Price* | **€18–€22** |
| *Region* | **Rhône (South)** |
| *Grape* | **Châteauneuf varieties** |
| *Alc/vol* | **13.5%** |
| *Food* | **Poultry/coq au vin** |
| *Drink* | **2002–4** |

### Dom. de Nalys AC Châteauneuf-du-Pape **00** ☆

Aromas are laden with eastern spices, blackcurrants and cedarwood. The palate has chocolate and spice with red berry flavours and still very firm tannins but a good fruity finish. *TDL*

| | |
|---|---|
| *Price* | **€18–€22** |
| *Region* | **Rhône (South)** |
| *Grape* | **Châteauneuf varieties** |
| *Alc/vol* | **14%** |
| *Food* | **Game/venison** |
| *Drink* | **2003–5** |

### Dom. des Senechaux AC Châteauneuf-du-Pape **99** ☆

A wine that should win friends. A very good example of the style with cherry and berry fruit underlayered with herbs and mint, and classic pepper and spice. *River Wines*

| | |
|---|---|
| *Price* | **€18–€22** |
| *Region* | **Rhône (South)** |
| *Grape* | **Châteauneuf varieties** |
| *Alc/vol* | **14%** |
| *Food* | **Poultry/goose** |
| *Drink* | **2002–3** |

### Dom. Grand Veneur AC Châteauneuf-du-Pape **99** ☆

Attractive, elegant nose of mixed black fruit jam and cigar box with unexpected fruity delights on the palate—plum, blackberry, damson, blackcurrant—a veritable black fruit cocktail with a peppery edge. Long, lingering finish. *Mitchells*

| | |
|---|---|
| *Price* | **€18–€22** |
| *Region* | **Rhône (South)** |
| *Grape* | **Châteauneuf varieties** |
| *Alc/vol* | **14%** |
| *Food* | **Poultry/chicken** |
| *Drink* | **2002–5** |

### Dom. Jerôme Quiot Les Combes d'Arnevel
AC Châteauneuf-du-Pape **00** ☆

Big, beefy nose with some cherry tart aromas and a smooth, fruity palate showing a rich complexity of flavours—earthy blackberries, cherries, spice and pepper. *Febvre*

| | |
|---|---|
| *Price* | **€18–€22** |
| *Region* | **Rhône (South)** |
| *Grape* | **Grenache/Syrah/ Cinsault/Counoise** |
| *Alc/vol* | **13.5%** |
| *Food* | **Meat/roasts** |
| *Drink* | **2003–5** |

### Dom. Les Goubert AC Gigondas **97**

Some development is beginning to show in the very earthy and leathery aromas and the complex, elegant palate with quite subtle raspberry and blackberry flavours and just a touch of spice. *Terroirs*

| | |
|---|---|
| *Price* | **€18–€22** |
| *Region* | **Rhône (South)** |
| *Grape* | **Grenache/Syrah/ Mourvèdre** |
| *Alc/vol* | **13.5%** |
| *Food* | **Game/casseroles** |
| *Drink* | **2002–3** |

### Dom. St Gayan AC Gigondas **98**

Fantastic ripe nose with rustic charm, vegetal and spicy. The tannins are quite firm but there is lots of damson fruit to match a pervading, spicy pepperiness. *Searsons*

| | |
|---|---|
| *Price* | **€18–€22** |
| *Region* | **Rhône (South)** |
| *Grape* | **Grenache/Syrah/ Mourvèdre** |
| *Alc/vol* | **14%** |
| *Food* | **Meat/steak** |
| *Drink* | **2002–4** |

## Gabriel Meffre Laurus AC Gigondas 99

Intense nose of fruit, spice and a touch of earth-iness. Very supple with velvety rich fruit and spice, it is soft yet chunky and has excellent length. *Dillons*

| | |
|---|---|
| Price | €18–€22 |
| Region | Rhône (South) |
| Grape | Grenache/Syrah/ Mourvèdre |
| Alc/vol | 13.5% |
| Food | Poultry/duck |
| Drink | 2002–4 |

## Jaboulet Dom. de Thalabert AC Crozes-Hermitage 99 ☆

Classic, pungent Syrah with signature earthy and smoky bacon aromas and a full-bodied juicy, spicy palate with raspberries, vanilla and crunchy plums. *Gilbeys/Oddbins*

| | |
|---|---|
| Price | €18–€22 |
| Region | Rhône (North) |
| Grape | Syrah (75% min.) |
| Alc/vol | 13% |
| Food | Meat/spicy sausages |
| Drink | 2002–4 |

## Jaboulet Le Grand Pompée AC St Joseph 99

Rich, deep colour. Ripe nose of black fruits, herbs and meaty aromas followed by pepper and blackcurrant flavours on a young and tan-nic palate which should soften with time. *Gilbeys*

| | |
|---|---|
| Price | €18–€22 |
| Region | Rhône (North) |
| Grape | Syrah (90% min.) |
| Alc/vol | 13% |
| Food | Meat/beef |
| Drink | 2003–4 |

## Louis Bernard AC Châteauneuf-du-Pape 98

This wine is made in a classic style and for the long haul. The aromas are quite meaty and beefy as is the very savoury palate although there is rich red berry fruit there too. *O'Briens*

| | |
|---|---|
| Price | €18–€22 |
| Region | Rhône (South) |
| Grape | Châteauneuf varieties |
| Alc/vol | 13.5% |
| Food | Meat/beef |
| Drink | 2002–5 |

### €22–€25

## Clos de Cuminaille AC St Joseph 99 ☆☆

The nose is good enough to eat, with vanilla pod, crème brulée, chocolate and lots of black fruit compote, and so is the fruity and peppery palate. Still marked with gripping tannins and good acidity, this can only get better. *Terroirs*

| | |
|---|---|
| Price | €22–€25 |
| Region | Rhône (North) |
| Grape | Syrah (90% min.) |
| Alc/vol | 12.5% |
| Food | Meat/beef |
| Drink | 2002–5 |

## Gabriel Meffre Laurus AC Châteauneuf-du-Pape 98

Quite a big, complex nose with vegetal, spicy and floral hints echoed in the rich, warm fruit on the palate, with spice and earthiness. *Dillons*

| | |
|---|---|
| Price | €22–€25 |
| Region | Rhône (South) |
| Grape | Grenache/Syrah/ Mourvèdre |
| Alc/vol | 13.5% |
| Food | Meat/stews |
| Drink | 2002–4 |

€25–€30

## **Ch. Fortia** AC Châteauneuf-du-Pape **98**

Distinctive and very tasty, with quite a floral nose of rose petals, lots of black fruit and spicy flavours and an intense, pleasant finish. *Taserra*

| | |
|---|---|
| Price | €25–€30 |
| Region | Rhône (South) |
| Grape | Châteauneuf varieties |
| Alc/vol | 14% |
| Food | Game/venison |
| Drink | 2002–4 |

## **Dom. de la Roquette** AC Châteauneuf-du-Pape **98**

A firm structure underpins the rustic berry fruit and spice to produce a wine of character in a traditional style. *Findlaters*

| | |
|---|---|
| Price | €25–€30 |
| Region | Rhône (South) |
| Grape | Châteauneuf varieties |
| Alc/vol | 14% |
| Food | Meat/pork |
| Drink | 2002–4 |

## **Jaboulet Les Cèdres** AC Châteauneuf-du-Pape **00**

Herbaceous, green bean touch together with ripe damson, plum, blackcurrant and cherry aromas and flavours. Very fruit-driven, almost New-World style, with noticeable but ripe tannins. *Gilbeys*

| | |
|---|---|
| Price | €25–€30 |
| Region | Rhône (South) |
| Grape | Châteauneuf varieties |
| Alc/vol | 14% |
| Food | Poultry/goose |
| Drink | 2002–3 |

## **Perrin Les Sinards** AC Châteauneuf-du-Pape **99**

Classic in style, with a nose of rosemary, spice and black plums. The palate is full bodied with lots of ripe, juicy black fruits, mellow notes of leather and tobacco and very good length and finish. *Allied Drinks*

| | |
|---|---|
| Price | €25–€30 |
| Region | Rhône (South) |
| Grape | Châteauneuf varieties |
| Alc/vol | 13.5% |
| Food | Game/pheasant |
| Drink | 2002–3 |

€30–€35

## **Vidal-Fleury** AC Côte Rôtie **98**

Wonderfully intense nose revealing some development and smokiness. The palate is rich with earthy overtones, pepper, stewed berries and spice. Although the tannins are still softening, it can be enjoyed now but patience will reward. *Irish Distillers*

| | |
|---|---|
| Price | €30–€35 |
| Region | Rhône (North) |
| Grape | Syrah (80% min.) |
| Alc/vol | 13% |
| Food | Meat/pork |
| Drink | 2002–4 |

# Hot off the
# Wine Press ...
# A New Look
# for Vina MontGras

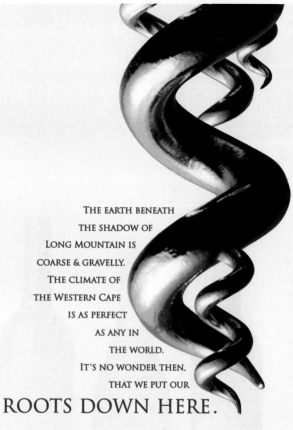

THE EARTH BENEATH
THE SHADOW OF
LONG MOUNTAIN IS
COARSE & GRAVELLY.
THE CLIMATE OF
THE WESTERN CAPE
IS AS PERFECT
AS ANY IN
THE WORLD.
IT'S NO WONDER THEN,
THAT WE PUT OUR
ROOTS DOWN HERE.

THE WINEMAKER'S PARADISE
-LONG MOUNTAIN-
BORN IN SOUTH AFRICA

# France–South

The vast areas of Languedoc and Roussillon produce excellent, reasonably priced wines, very drinkable and fruity, all showing a sunny and warm regional character. The region has been modernising its winemaking but has kept its character producing wines with ripe fruit, good structure, balanced use of oak, integrated tannins and decent acidity. The Vins de Pays d'Oc were diverse in style, coming from a very general appellation which allows for a wide choice of grape. Regional typicity and character were most clearly expressed in the wines from specific ACs, particularly the reds from Minervois, St Chinian, Costières de Nimes and Corbières. The Minervois reds tend to be smooth with quite an intense, perfumed, herbal and spicy character. The red Corbières were a tad more rustic and robust with a warmer and baked fruit character. St Chinian reds were quite full and juicy with ripe fruit whereas the reds from Costières de Nimes had lots of heat and spice and the whites were fragrant with quite lush fruit.

## White

### Under €9

#### Didier Picot Sauvignon Blanc VdP d'Oc **01**

Inviting aromas of pineapple and peach fruit follow through to the palate with crisp acidity which cuts through the ripeness giving a nicely balanced, fruity wine. *MacCormaic*

| | |
|---|---|
| Price | Under €9 |
| Region | Languedoc-Roussillon |
| Grape | Sauvignon Blanc |
| Alc/vol | 12.5% |
| Food | Ethnic/Thai |
| Drink | 2002–3 |

#### Foxwood Bruno's Block Chardonnay VdP d'Oc **00**

Fresh, brisk, light-bodied style with lemon, lime and apple flavours married with crisp acidity. *Wines Direct*

| | |
|---|---|
| Price | Under €9 |
| Region | Languedoc-Roussillon |
| Grape | Chardonnay |
| Alc/vol | 13% |
| Food | Seafood/mussels |
| Drink | 2002–3 |

#### Laurent Miquel Chardonnay Viognier VdP d'Oc **01 €**

Attractive, rich style. Aromas of peach with floral tones are matched by a ripe palate of tropical fruit and apple, pear and citrus flavours. *Dunnes Stores*

| | |
|---|---|
| Price | Under €9 |
| Region | Languedoc-Roussillon |
| Grape | Chardonnay/Viognier |
| Alc/vol | 13% |
| Food | Poultry/chicken |
| Drink | 2002–3 |

#### Michel Laroche South of France Terret VdP d'Oc **01 €**

Vibrant, refreshing summery combination of flavours—ripe apples, pears and cream, vanilla and butter. An example of how France can compete with New World wines. *Allied Drinks*

| | |
|---|---|
| Price | Under €9 |
| Region | Languedoc-Roussillon |
| Grape | Terret |
| Alc/vol | 12.5% |
| Food | Fish/tuna |
| Drink | 2002–4 |

## Tesco Viognier VdP d'Oc 00

Dry, with rich flavours of peach and melon, pepper and spice and some classic Viognier floral touches—so rich that the acidity is hardly noticeable. Serve well chilled. *Tesco*

| | |
|---|---|
| Price | Under €9 |
| Region | Languedoc-Roussillon |
| Grape | Viognier |
| Alc/vol | 12.5% |
| Food | Seafood/fish |
| Drink | 2002–3 |

## Virginie Chardonnay VdP d'Oc 01 €

Well-constructed, appealing style with just a touch of complexity. Aromatic, smoky vanilla nose with rich, fleshy tropical fruits followed by an oaky and toasty palate with good, peachy fruit character and a warm, spicy finish. *Oddbins*

| | |
|---|---|
| Price | Under €9 |
| Region | Languedoc-Roussillon |
| Grape | Chardonnay |
| Alc/vol | 13.5% |
| Food | Fish/cod |
| Drink | 2002–3 |

## Virginie Viognier VdP d'Oc 01 €

Crisp, thirst-quenching style with the classically floral and perfumed attributes of Viognier—peach and apricot aromas and pear and lemon flavours. *Oddbins*

| | |
|---|---|
| Price | Under €9 |
| Region | Languedoc-Roussillon |
| Grape | Viognier |
| Alc/vol | 12.5% |
| Food | Fish/crab cakes |
| Drink | 2002–3 |

### €9–€12

## Ch. Roubaud Cuvée Prestige AC Costières de Nîmes 00

Wonderful combination of fruit and acidity. Nose of rose petals and fleshy peaches. Peaches and cream on first tasting yet there is also a definite impression of green apples. *Peter Dalton*

| | |
|---|---|
| Price | €9–€12 |
| Region | Languedoc-Roussillon |
| Grape | Southern French varieties |
| Alc/vol | 13% |
| Food | Indian/curries |
| Drink | 2002–3 |

## Dom. de Poussan le Haut Chardonnay VdP d'Oc 00

Pronounced aromas and flavours make this a wine of wide appeal. Lots of ripe, tropical fruit flavours of pineapple and melon with equal proportions of spices. *Mitchells*

| | |
|---|---|
| Price | €9–€12 |
| Region | Languedoc-Roussillon |
| Grape | Chardonnay |
| Alc/vol | 13.5% |
| Food | Pasta/seafood |
| Drink | 2002–3 |

## Dom. Luc Lapeyre Nuit Blanche VdP d'Oc 00

Pungent nose of blackcurrant leaf, pea pod and grass which follows on the gooseberry, fennel and herbal palate with nicely balanced acidity giving a fresh, crisp finish. *Wines Direct*

| | |
|---|---|
| Price | €9–€12 |
| Region | Languedoc-Roussillon |
| Grape | Chardonnay/ Viognier/Muscat |
| Alc/vol | 13.5% |
| Food | Fish/plaice |
| Drink | 2002–3 |

## Dom. St Hilaire Chardonnay VdP d'Oc 00

Understated aromas hint at apples, lemon peel and butter. Stylish, vibrant, mineral richness on the palate with green apple and gooseberry jam flavours. *Wines Direct*

| | |
|---|---|
| Price | €9–€12 |
| Region | Languedoc-Roussillon |
| Grape | Chardonnay |
| Alc/vol | 13% |
| Food | Poultry/chicken |
| Drink | 2002–3 |

## Laurent Miquel Viognier VdP d'Oc 01

Lively, zesty style with aromas of apples and limes, crisp citrus acidity and a full weight of apple and pineapple flavours with a good, concentrated, zippy finish. *Dunnes Stores*

| | |
|---|---|
| Price | €9–€12 |
| Region | Languedoc-Roussillon |
| Grape | Viognier |
| Alc/vol | 13.5% |
| Food | Fish/fish stew |
| Drink | 2002–3 |

## Mas des Bressades Cuvée Tradition AC Costières de Nîmes 00

Almost sweet mango aromas on the nose; spicy cinnamon flavours dominate the palate, plus lychees and honey, beautifully held together with crisp, fresh acidity. *Bubble Brothers*

| | |
|---|---|
| Price | €9–€12 |
| Region | Languedoc-Roussillon |
| Grape | Southern French varieties |
| Alc/vol | 13% |
| Food | Seafood/shellfish |
| Drink | 2002–3 |

## Michel Laroche South of France Chardonnay VdP d'Oc 01

Fresh and fruity with aromas of red apples and honeysuckle. Very attractive palate with crisp acidity balanced with ripe, honeyed citrus fruit. *Allied Drinks*

| | |
|---|---|
| Price | €9–€12 |
| Region | Languedoc-Roussillon |
| Grape | Chardonnay |
| Alc/vol | 13.5% |
| Food | Fish/salmon |
| Drink | 2002–3 |

### €12–€15

## Dom. de Brau Chardonnay VdP d'Oc 00 🌿

Rich, upfront aromas of pineapple with hints of cloves and honey give way to a very fresh palate bursting with tropical and lime flavours. *On the Case*

| | |
|---|---|
| Price | €12–€15 |
| Region | Languedoc-Roussillon |
| Grape | Chardonnay |
| Alc/vol | 13% |
| Food | Starters/salads |
| Drink | 2002–3 |

# Red

*Under €9*

## Bushman VdP d'Oc **99**

Easy, everyday drinking. Cool and chunky with aromas of cherry, raspberry and plum and a good concentration of raspberry and blackcurrant flavours, with a rustic, earthy finish. Good with meats and cheese. *WineOnline*

| | |
|---|---|
| *Price* | Under €9 |
| *Region* | Languedoc-Roussillon |
| *Grape* | Cabernet Sauvignon/ Merlot/Syrah |
| *Alc/vol* | 13% |
| *Food* | Meat/beef |
| *Drink* | 2002–3 |

## Ch. Salauze AC Minervois **99 €**

Robust and earthy with dense stewed plums and damsons and underlying dark chocolate tones with slightly tarry, liquorice flavours. *O'Briens*

| | |
|---|---|
| *Price* | Under €9 |
| *Region* | Languedoc-Roussillon |
| *Grape* | Carignan/Syrah/ Grenache |
| *Alc/vol* | 13.5% |
| *Food* | Poultry/chicken |
| *Drink* | 2002–3 |

## Didier Picot Cabernet Sauvignon VdP d'Oc **99 €**

A good party wine. Strong nose of blackcurrant, raspberry, fudge and spice and an excellent weight of rich blackcurrant and cedarwood flavours, a smooth and creamy texture and a long, spicy finish. *MacCormaic*

| | |
|---|---|
| *Price* | Under €9 |
| *Region* | Languedoc-Roussillon |
| *Grape* | Cabernet Sauvignon |
| *Alc/vol* | 12.5% |
| *Food* | Meat/beef |
| *Drink* | 2002–3 |

## Dom. de Cauvy AC Faugères **00**

A wine for blackberry lovers. The slightly earthy and rustic nose of blackberry and blackcurrant is followed by a pure fruit palate with firm tannins. A very good example of this appellation. *Mitchells*

| | |
|---|---|
| *Price* | Under €9 |
| *Region* | Languedoc-Roussillon |
| *Grape* | Carignan/Grenache/ Cinsault/Syrah/ Mourvèdre |
| *Alc/vol* | 13.5% |
| *Food* | Meat/roasts |
| *Drink* | 2002–3 |

## Dom. Vignelaure Cabernet Sauvignon
VdP des Coteaux du Verdun **00**

Pleasant, subtle redcurrant and red berry nose with fragrant tones and ripe but noticeable tannins matching the blackberry and bramble fruit flavours. *Dunnes Stores*

| | |
|---|---|
| *Price* | Under €9 |
| *Region* | Languedoc-Roussillon |
| *Grape* | Cabernet Sauvignon |
| *Alc/vol* | 12.5% |
| *Food* | Meat/stews |
| *Drink* | 2002–3 |

## Hugues le Juste Syrah VdP d'Oc **99**

Interesting peppery, spicy aromas with a meaty richness. The palate is still quite fruity with blackberries and raisins plus smoky and green herbal influences. Drinking well now. *McCabes*

| | |
|---|---|
| *Price* | Under €9 |
| *Region* | Languedoc-Roussillon |
| *Grape* | Syrah |
| *Alc/vol* | 12.5% |
| *Food* | Meat/barbecue |
| *Drink* | 2002–3 |

## Laurent Miquel Cabernet Syrah VdP d'Oc **01 €**

Fruity and appealing with a good weight of blackcurrant and red berry flavours, firm tannins and a spicy, peppery punch that lasts well. *Dunnes Stores*

| | |
|---|---|
| *Price* | Under €9 |
| *Region* | Languedoc-Roussillon |
| *Grape* | Cab Sauv/Syrah |
| *Alc/vol* | 13% |
| *Food* | Meat/barbecue |
| *Drink* | 2002–3 |

## Laurent Miquel Syrah VdP d'Oc **01**

Gutsy style with plenty of heat; aromas of blackberry jam and cassis with a palate of black fruit, olives and slightly smoky flavours. For meaty food or takeaways. *Dunnes Stores*

| | |
|---|---|
| *Price* | Under €9 |
| *Region* | Languedoc-Roussillon |
| *Grape* | Syrah |
| *Alc/vol* | 13% |
| *Food* | Meat/lamb |
| *Drink* | 2002–3 |

## Michel Laroche South of France Grenache VdP d'Oc **00**

Subtle, fruity nose, perfumed with rosemary. Dry, firm, fairly light-bodied palate with good red fruit, pepper and leather flavours. *Allied Drinks*

| | |
|---|---|
| *Price* | Under €9 |
| *Region* | Languedoc-Roussillon |
| *Grape* | Grenache |
| *Alc/vol* | 13% |
| *Food* | Seafood/squid |
| *Drink* | 2002–3 |

## Virginie Syrah VdP Catalan **00 €**

Nicely constructed and classy with an inviting nose of plum, blackcurrant and vanilla and a rounded, ripe black fruit palate with a lovely creamy influence. *Oddbins*

| | |
|---|---|
| *Price* | Under €9 |
| *Region* | Languedoc-Roussillon |
| *Grape* | Syrah |
| *Alc/vol* | 12.5% |
| *Food* | Cheese/Cheddar |
| *Drink* | 2002–3 |

### €9–€12

## Bergerie de l'Hortus Pic St Loup Classique
## AC Coteaux du Languedoc **00**

Ripe cherries on the nose. Deeply concentrated and fruity palate of cherry and blackcurrant flavours with a touch of earthiness and noticeably good length. *Wines Direct*

| | |
|---|---|
| *Price* | €9–€12 |
| *Region* | Languedoc-Roussillon |
| *Grape* | Syrah/Grenache/ Mourvèdre |
| *Alc/vol* | 12.5% |
| *Food* | Poultry/turkey |
| *Drink* | 2002–3 |

## Ch. de Campuget AC Costières de Nîmes **00**

Generous style with big, juicy fruit character. Peppery plums on the nose are followed by concentrated plum jam and blackberry flavours and some mint. *River Wines*

| | |
|---|---|
| *Price* | €9–€12 |
| *Region* | Languedoc-Roussillon |
| *Grape* | Southern French varieties |
| *Alc/vol* | 13% |
| *Food* | Meat/sausages |
| *Drink* | 2002–3 |

## Ch. de Caraguilhes AC Corbières **00**

Wonderfully rustic style with a nose reminiscent of burning turf or sweet pipe tobacco. Plenty of hot sun flavours, mixed fruit jam and baked fruit. *O'Briens*

| | |
|---|---|
| *Price* | €9–€12 |
| *Region* | Languedoc-Roussillon |
| *Grape* | Carignan/Grenache/ Syrah |
| *Alc/vol* | 12% |
| *Food* | Pasta/Bolognese |
| *Drink* | 2002–3 |

## Ch. d'Or et de Gueules AC Costières de Nîmes **98** ☆ **€**

Heat and sunshine in a bottle. Warm liquorice tones, plums, prunes and wild strawberries together with some spicy wood and floral notes and lemony acidity. *River Wines*

| | |
|---|---|
| *Price* | €9–€12 |
| *Region* | Languedoc-Roussillon |
| *Grape* | Southern French varieties |
| *Alc/vol* | 13% |
| *Food* | Meat/pork |
| *Drink* | 2002–3 |

> *AC regulations stipulate the **grape varieties** that may be used in each of the regional appellations. Mourvèdre, Syrah, Grenache, Carignan and Cinsault may be used for AC Corbières, Costières de Nimes, Coteaux du Languedoc, Faugères and Minervois and Syrah, Grenache, Mourvèdre, Lladoner, Pelut, Carignan and Cinsault may be used for St Chinian. Depending on the appellation, minimum and maximum proportions of the grape varieties used in the blend may be laid down.*

## Ch. Etienne des Lauzes AC St Chinian **99**

Attractive, rustic, plummy nose with a full-flavoured, concentrated palate of blackberry and blackcurrant and a dash of pepper. *Mitchells*

| | |
|---|---|
| *Price* | €9–€12 |
| *Region* | Languedoc-Roussillon |
| *Grape* | Carignan/Grenache/ Cinsault/Syrah |
| *Alc/vol* | 12.5% |
| *Food* | Pizza/pasta |
| *Drink* | 2002–3 |

## Ch. Maris AC Minervois **99**

Attractive and concentrated but also refreshing. The nose is full of ripe cherries, smoke and spice, followed by a soft cherry palate with some richer flavours of blackcurrants and plums. *Oddbins*

| | |
|---|---|
| *Price* | €9–€12 |
| *Region* | Languedoc-Roussillon |
| *Grape* | Syrah/Grenache/ Carignan |
| *Alc/vol* | 14% |
| *Food* | Meat/pork |
| *Drink* | 2002–3 |

### Ch. Roubaud AC Costières de Nîmes 99

This is a soft, ripe, tangy style for drinking now. The aromas and flavours are of blackcurrant, vanilla and plum with a slightly charred or earthy influence. *Peter Dalton*

| | |
|---|---|
| *Price* | €9–€12 |
| *Region* | Languedoc-Roussillon |
| *Grape* | Southern French varieties |
| *Alc/vol* | 12.5% |
| *Food* | Meat/stews |
| *Drink* | 2002–3 |

### Comté de Mérinville AC Minervois 97 ☆☆ €

Mature, intense, herbal and liquorice nose follows through on the palate together with dark fruit flavours of blackcurrant and blackberry and vanilla spice. *Bubble Brothers*

| | |
|---|---|
| *Price* | €9–€12 |
| *Region* | Languedoc-Roussillon |
| *Grape* | Mainly Syrah |
| *Alc/vol* | 12% |
| *Food* | Meat/kebabs |
| *Drink* | 2002–3 |

SHORTLIST BEST VALUE RED

### Cuvée de l'Arjolle VdP des Côtes de Thongue 00

Equal proportions of Cabernet Sauvignon and Merlot offer quite an understated though pure blackcurrant nose and a very ripe, concentrated palate with blackcurrant and redcurrant flavours peppered with spice. *Mitchells*

| | |
|---|---|
| *Price* | €9–€12 |
| *Region* | Languedoc-Roussillon |
| *Grape* | Cab Sauv/Merlot |
| *Alc/vol* | 13% |
| *Food* | Meat/ribs |
| *Drink* | 2002–3 |

### Didier Picot Dom. Haut St Georges AC Corbières 99

Robust and rich with a firm structure. Aromas are of blackcurrant and blackberry with toffee and coffee elements followed by earthy and spicy flavours, baked plum and red berry fruit. *MacCormaic*

| | |
|---|---|
| *Price* | €9–€12 |
| *Region* | Languedoc-Roussillon |
| *Grape* | Syrah/Mourvèdre/ Carignan/Grenache |
| *Alc/vol* | 13% |
| *Food* | Meat/lamb |
| *Drink* | 2002–4 |

### Dom. Borie de Maurel Esprit d'Automne AC Minervois 00

Very satisfying style, rich yet rustic and spicy, with a super nose of morello cherry, plum and raspberry and a crisp cherry, plum and black pepper palate. *Oddbins*

| | |
|---|---|
| *Price* | €9–€12 |
| *Region* | Languedoc-Roussillon |
| *Grape* | Southern French varieties |
| *Alc/vol* | 13% |
| *Food* | Meat/pork |
| *Drink* | 2002–3 |

### Dom. Cazelles-Verdier AC Minervois 00

Firm, structured but extremely approachable with a peppery black fruit nose and a fleshy, fruity palate of plums, black cherries and damsons dusted with vanilla and pepper. *Mitchells*

| | |
|---|---|
| *Price* | €9–€12 |
| *Region* | Languedoc-Roussillon |
| *Grape* | Carignan/Grenache/ Syrah |
| *Alc/vol* | 13% |
| *Food* | Meat/leg of lamb |
| *Drink* | 2002–3 |

## Dom. de Pujol Vieilles Vignes AC Minervois **98**

An honest wine with a sound weight of sweet, black fruit aromas and flavours of blackcurrants and red peppers. With a firm tannic structure, it would be best with food. *WineOnline*

| | |
|---|---|
| *Price* | €9–€12 |
| *Region* | Languedoc-Roussillon |
| *Grape* | Mourvèdre/Syrah/ Grenache |
| *Alc/vol* | 13% |
| *Food* | Meat/lamb |
| *Drink* | 2002-3 |

## Dom. des Guirlandes Merlot VdP d'Oc **00**

Excellent, everyday wine with attractive dark berry fruits and green pepper on the nose and almost overripe fleshy plum and vegetal flavours on the palate. *Mitchells*

| | |
|---|---|
| *Price* | €9–€12 |
| *Region* | Languedoc-Roussillon |
| *Grape* | Merlot |
| *Alc/vol* | 13% |
| *Food* | Meat/lamb chops |
| *Drink* | 2002-3 |

## Dom. du Trillol AC Corbières **99**

Gorgeous nose has some complexity with sun-soaked plums and raisins and a touch of hot rubberiness followed by a good, chewy, mixed black fruit palate. *Mitchells*

| | |
|---|---|
| *Price* | €9–€12 |
| *Region* | Languedoc-Roussillon |
| *Grape* | Grenache/Syrah/ Carignan |
| *Alc/vol* | 13.5% |
| *Food* | Vegetarian/casseroles |
| *Drink* | 2002-3 |

## Dom. Laporte Ruscino VdP Catalan **00**

This very well-made wine is drinking well now, particularly with red meat, but has the tannins and fruit structure to go further. It has blackcurrant and ripe raspberry and leathery aromas and a plum- and liquorice-flavoured palate. *Oddbins*

| | |
|---|---|
| *Price* | €9–€12 |
| *Region* | Languedoc-Roussillon |
| *Grape* | Merlot/Syrah/ Mourvèdre/Cab Sauv |
| *Alc/vol* | 13% |
| *Food* | Meat/roasts |
| *Drink* | 2002-4 |

## Gaillard VdP des Collines Rhodaniennes **00**

Nice levels of complexity are expressed in this spicy and toasty wine with dark, ripe fruit aromas and a smoky and peppery palate with good tannic structure. *Terroirs*

| | |
|---|---|
| *Price* | €9–€12 |
| *Region* | Languedoc-Roussillon |
| *Grape* | Syrah |
| *Alc/vol* | 12% |
| *Food* | Meat/stews |
| *Drink* | 2002-3 |

## L'Amourier AC Minervois **99**

Interesting range of aromas and flavours. The nose has spice and soft fruits plus some vegetal and herbal elements showing signs of development. The palate is quite floral and fruity with ripe flavours of cassis and black jam. *Wines Direct*

| | |
|---|---|
| *Price* | €9–€12 |
| *Region* | Languedoc-Roussillon |
| *Grape* | Syrah/Mourvèdre/ Carignan |
| *Alc/vol* | 13% |
| *Food* | Meat/pork |
| *Drink* | 2002-3 |

## Laurent Miquel Nord-Sud Syrah VdP d'Oc **00**

Attractive nose perfumed with lilies and lavender; quite a savoury palate with red and black fruit and smoky bacon flavours. *Dunnes Stores*

| | |
|---|---|
| Price | €9–€12 |
| Region | Languedoc-Roussillon |
| Grape | Syrah |
| Alc/vol | 13.5% |
| Food | Poultry/duck |
| Drink | 2002–3 |

## Les Maîtres Vignerons de Tautavel
AC Côtes du Roussillon Villages Tautavel **98** ☆ €

Big and beefy style with a wealth of blackberries, blueberries and blackcurrants and nuances of dried, raisined fruit in a spicy, vibrant palate with heat, cinnamon and cloves. *O'Briens*

| | |
|---|---|
| Price | €9–€12 |
| Region | Languedoc-Roussillon |
| Grape | Grenache/Syrah |
| Alc/vol | 13.5% |
| Food | Meat/barbecue |
| Drink | 2002–3 |

## Michel Laroche South of France Merlot VdP d'Oc **00**

Soft, plummy Merlot with damson and raisin aromas and a very balanced, fruity palate with plums, red berries and a touch of vanilla. *Allied Drinks*

| | |
|---|---|
| Price | €9–€12 |
| Region | Languedoc-Roussillon |
| Grape | Merlot |
| Alc/vol | 13.5% |
| Food | Poultry/chicken |
| Drink | 2002–3 |

### €12–€15

## Ch. Camplazens L'Hermitage VdP d'Oc **99** ☆

A mellow wine with an underlying richness and good structure. It has creamy, smoky and tangy blackcurrant aromas with ripe blackcurrants on the smoky palate. *Oddbins*

| | |
|---|---|
| Price | €12–€15 |
| Region | Languedoc-Roussillon |
| Grape | Cab Sauv/Merlot/ Grenache/Syrah/ Carignan |
| Alc/vol | 12% |
| Food | Vegetarian/gratins |
| Drink | 2002–4 |

## Ch. de Brau Cuvée Exquise AC Cabardès **01** 🌿

Inky and toasty nose with fennel seed aromas followed by a palate of cassis, vanilla and fudge with slight medicinal touches. Still very young, it would benefit from some extra time to integrate further. *On the Case*

| | |
|---|---|
| Price | €12–€15 |
| Region | Languedoc-Roussillon |
| Grape | Merlot/Grenache/ Cabernet/Syrah |
| Alc/vol | 13% |
| Food | Meat/casseroles |
| Drink | 2003–4 |

## Ch. de Ribaute Cuvée François le Noir AC Corbières **99**

A versatile and cheering wine. While the tannins are still firmish it would be perfect with food, for a mid-week supper. The aromas are of blackcurrant, tobacco, spice and medicinal notes followed by a pure, concentrated plum, damson and black cherry palate. *Mitchells*

| | |
|---|---|
| Price | €12–€15 |
| Region | Languedoc-Roussillon |
| Grape | Mourvèdre/Grenache |
| Alc/vol | 13% |
| Food | Pasta/lasagne |
| Drink | 2002–3 |

## Ch. Gléon Montanié Cuvée Gaston Bonnes AC Corbières **98**

Concentrated fruity nose with just a hint of rubber on the edge. The palate is equally weighty and full bodied with ripe black fruits and a smooth, rounded mouthfeel. *WineKnows*

| | |
|---|---|
| *Price* | €12–€15 |
| *Region* | Languedoc-Roussillon |
| *Grape* | Carignan/Grenache/ Cinsault |
| *Alc/vol* | 12% |
| *Food* | Meat/chilli con carne |
| *Drink* | 2002–4 |

## Ch. Grès St Paul AC Coteaux du Languedoc **99**

A subtle wine, lightly fragrant, with plums and mixed red fruits, spicy tones and a smooth and nicely structured fruity palate. *Searsons*

| | |
|---|---|
| *Price* | €12–€15 |
| *Region* | Languedoc-Roussillon |
| *Grape* | Grenache/Cinsault/ Mourvèdre/Syrah |
| *Alc/vol* | 13% |
| *Food* | Meat/lamb |
| *Drink* | 2002–3 |

## Ch. St Auriol AC Corbières **98**

Mature, perfumed nose of fruits of the forest, quite floral, herbal and minty. Elegant and feminine palate with blackberry and raspberry and queen of puddings flavours. *Searsons*

| | |
|---|---|
| *Price* | €12–€15 |
| *Region* | Languedoc-Roussillon |
| *Grape* | Syrah/Grenache |
| *Alc/vol* | 12.5% |
| *Food* | Meat/meatballs |
| *Drink* | 2002–3 |

## Dom. Cazal-Viel Syrah VdP d'Oc **00**

This wine has quite a rustic and charming character and would be perfect with food. Dark and inky in colour, with spicy fruit aromas, vanilla and caramel. The palate is laden with spicy damsons and blackberries. *Papillon*

| | |
|---|---|
| *Price* | €12–€15 |
| *Region* | Languedoc-Roussillon |
| *Grape* | Syrah |
| *Alc/vol* | 13% |
| *Food* | Pasta/tomato sauces |
| *Drink* | 2002–3 |

## Dom. Gardiès AC Côtes du Roussillon Villages Tautavel **99**

Hot climate, ripe, fruity nose with floral touches and a pronounced use of oak. The palate has a velvety texture and a very good weight of black fruit and spice. *Wines Direct*

| | |
|---|---|
| *Price* | €12–€15 |
| *Region* | Languedoc-Roussillon |
| *Grape* | Syrah/Mourvèdre/ Grenache |
| *Alc/vol* | 13.5% |
| *Food* | Pasta/arrabiata |
| *Drink* | 2002–3 |

### €15–€18

## Ch. de Mérinville AC Minervois **99** ☆

A near perfect nose, rich and warm with a luscious mix of plums, blackcurrants, damsons and herbs, gives way to a mix of flavours of all these fruits plus cherry and spice and a chocolatey texture. *Bubble Brothers*

| | |
|---|---|
| *Price* | €15–€18 |
| *Region* | Languedoc-Roussillon |
| *Grape* | Southern French varieties, Syrah based |
| *Alc/vol* | 13% |
| *Food* | Poultry/confit |
| *Drink* | 2002–3 |

## Ch. Mas Neuf Cuvée Compostelle AC Costières de Nîmes 00

Rustic style with a baked fruit nose, perfumed with spice, and a wild fruit palate of damsons, sloes and blackberries, rich and robust with very good length on the finish. Try it with Asian food. *Febvre*

| | |
|---|---|
| Price | €15–€18 |
| Region | Languedoc-Roussillon |
| Grape | Syrah/Mourvèdre/ Grenache |
| Alc/vol | 13% |
| Food | Ethnic/Indian |
| Drink | 2002–3 |

## Ch. Tour Boisée 'À Marie Claude' AC Minervois 99 ☆

A big and fruity wine with structure and complexity behind it. Aromas of cassis and spice, robust and forward palate with violet and new leather flavours. *Terroirs*

| | |
|---|---|
| Price | €15–€18 |
| Region | Languedoc-Roussillon |
| Grape | Southern French varieties |
| Alc/vol | 13.8% |
| Food | Meat/pork |
| Drink | 2002–5 |

## Dom le Cazal Le Pas de Zarat AC Minervois 99

Just what one expects from the South of France. Dark fruit and slightly tannic style with a quirky, complex nose of damsons, blackberries, pepper and perfumed floral aromas and a dark, blackberry- and cherry-flavoured palate. *Mitchells*

| | |
|---|---|
| Price | €15–€18 |
| Region | Languedoc-Roussillon |
| Grape | Carignan/Grenache/ Syrah |
| Alc/vol | 12.5% |
| Food | Meat/lamb |
| Drink | 2003–4 |

## Dom. de Bellevue Grand Délicatesse AC Corbières 99

A rustic style with noticeable tannins demanding food—a hearty stew, perhaps—with a nose of plums and blackcurrants following through in the mouth. *Gilbeys*

| | |
|---|---|
| Price | €15–€18 |
| Region | Languedoc-Roussillon |
| Grape | Southern French varieties |
| Alc/vol | 13% |
| Food | Meat/stews |
| Drink | 2002–3 |

## Dom. Luc Lapeyre Les Clots AC Minervois 99

Distinctive aromas of black cherry, pepper and herbs with an intense mouthful of flavours— blackcurrant cordial and chocolate. Such a youthful wine with dry tannins and very crisp acidity would be best with food or held for a few years longer. *Wines Direct*

| | |
|---|---|
| Price | €15–€18 |
| Region | Languedoc-Roussillon |
| Grape | Southern French varieties |
| Alc/vol | 13.5% |
| Food | Meat/cassoulet |
| Drink | 2003–4 |

## Dom. Rimbert Le Mas au Schiste AC St Chinian 00

A French reply to New World competition, this wine is concentrated and juicy with flavours of blackcurrant pastilles and blackberries, ripe cherry and fennel and a dash of pepper with caramel and rich chocolate tones. *Bubble Brothers*

| | |
|---|---|
| Price | €15–€18 |
| Region | Languedoc-Roussillon |
| Grape | Southern French varieties |
| Alc/vol | 14% |
| Food | Meat/lamb stew |
| Drink | 2002–3 |

## Laurent Miquel Bardou AC St Chinian **00** ☆

Charmingly fruity wine with wonderful added savoury elements of black olives and nuts. Tasty palate with blackberry flavours, further earthy complexity and slightly rustic character.
*Dunnes Stores*

| | |
|---|---|
| *Price* | €15–€18 |
| *Region* | Languedoc-Roussillon |
| *Grape* | Syrah |
| *Alc/vol* | 13.5% |
| *Food* | Poultry/turkey |
| *Drink* | 2002–3 |

## Laurent Miquel Saga Pegot AC Faugères **00**

Big hearty wine, with peppery black aromas and a rich and fruity palate with blackcurrant purée, rubber and spice, gentle oaky vanilla and a persistent, long finish. *Dunnes Stores*

| | |
|---|---|
| *Price* | €15–€18 |
| *Region* | Languedoc-Roussillon |
| *Grape* | Syrah |
| *Alc/vol* | 13.5% |
| *Food* | Meat/casseroles |
| *Drink* | 2002–3 |

## Merlot de l'Arjolle Synthèse VdP des Côtes de Thongue **00**

Dense plum, damson and blackberry nose is echoed in the mouth. Firm tannins and a decent length round off a well-made, ripe, fruity wine. Good with a hearty stew or barbecued steak. *Mitchells*

| | |
|---|---|
| *Price* | €15–€18 |
| *Region* | Languedoc-Roussillon |
| *Grape* | Merlot |
| *Alc/vol* | 13% |
| *Food* | Meat/steak |
| *Drink* | 2002–3 |

### €22–€25

## Ch. Dalmeran AC Les Baux de Provence **98**

Interesting and beautifully smooth blend giving a complex, baked fruit nose and a delicious palate with ripe tannins and juicy, summer pudding fruit and vanilla flavours.
*Wicklow Wine Co.*

| | |
|---|---|
| *Price* | €22–€25 |
| *Region* | Provence |
| *Grape* | Grenache/Cab Sauv/ Syrah |
| *Alc/vol* | 13.5% |
| *Food* | Meat/roasts |
| *Drink* | 2002–4 |

---

**How to use this book**
*The wines are listed in order of country/region, colour (red or white), price band, then by name. If you can't quickly find the wine you are looking for try the index, which we have expanded for this edition. There are separate chapters for rosé, sparkling (including Champagne) and sweet wines. Since wine prices are not fixed the price bands are guidelines only. The dates suggested for when to drink the wines do not indicate their expected life but the period over which our tasters thought they would enjoy them most.*

# France–South West

This year we have included a separate section on south-west France, reflecting the growing number of wines available from this area which includes the sub-regions of Bergerac, Cahors, Gascony and Madiran. Bergerac, one of the best sub-regions, uses the same grape varieties as neighbouring Bordeaux to produce wines that compare favourably with good Bordeaux. It contributed two starred wines this year, a red and a white. Madiran and Cahors use different red grape varieties, Malbec and Tannat, to produce much firmer and more tannic wines. The white wines from Gascony and Jurancon are particularly fresh and interesting. Made from lesser known varieties such as Ugni Blanc, Grenache Blanc, Colombard and Gros Manseng, they offer taste sensations that are just a little bit different.

## White

*Under €9*

### **Ch. Pique-Sègue** AC Montravel **00**

Light, crisp and fresh, not unlike lemon juice seasoning, with aromas of baked apple and spice and flavours of melon, apple and citrus with a slight pineapple twist. *Comans*

| | |
|---|---|
| Price | **Under €9** |
| Grape | **Sémillon/Sauv Blanc** |
| Alc/vol | **12%** |
| Food | **Fish/sole** |
| Drink | **2002–3** |

### **Dom. Beraut Cuvée Harmonie** VdP des Côtes de Gasgogne **01**

Rich in ripe pineapple and citrus flavours with zippy acidity balancing quite a weighty fruit cocktail palate. Small proportions of Ugni Blanc and Gros Manseng are also included in the blend. *Mitchells*

| | |
|---|---|
| Price | **Under €9** |
| Grape | **Chardonnay/ Colombard/Sauv Blanc** |
| Alc/vol | **12%** |
| Food | **Starters/salads** |
| Drink | **2002–3** |

### **Dom. de Joy** VdP des Côtes de Gascogne **01 €**

Very good, classic example from this region with pungent citrus aromas and a palate which has a creamy ripeness together with lively acidity, lime juice and lemon trifle flavours. *Oddbins*

| | |
|---|---|
| Price | **Under €9** |
| Grape | **Colombard/Ugni Blanc/Gros Manseng** |
| Alc/vol | **12%** |
| Food | **Fish/plaice** |
| Drink | **2002–3** |

### **Dom. du Tariquet** VdP des Côtes de Gascogne **01**

Zesty and fresh style. Lemon and grassy aromas lead to a cleansing, crisp palate with citrus, spice, stewed apples and green-tinged flavours. *River Wines*

| | |
|---|---|
| Price | **Under €9** |
| Grape | **Ugni Blanc/ Colombard** |
| Alc/vol | **11.5%** |
| Food | **Fish/trout** |
| Drink | **2002–3** |

€9–€12

## Ch. Court-les-Mûts AC Bergerac Sec **00** ☆☆ €

Exotic, appealing aromas of mango and citrus with an oaky impression. The palate is mouth-filling and spicy with rich dried apricot, fig and grapefruit flavours. *Wicklow Wine Co.*

| | |
|---|---|
| *Price* | €9–€12 |
| *Grape* | Sémillon/Sauv Blanc/ Muscadelle |
| *Alc/vol* | 12% |
| *Food* | Fish/creamy sauces |
| *Drink* | 2002–3 |

## Ch. Jolys AC Jurançon Sec **00**

An unusual style with white pepper and mandarin aromas and flavours of orange and mild clove; very smooth in texture and nicely rounded. *Wines Direct*

| | |
|---|---|
| *Price* | €9–€12 |
| *Grape* | Gros Manseng/ Petit Manseng/Courbu |
| *Alc/vol* | 13% |
| *Food* | Seafood/shellfish |
| *Drink* | 2002–3 |

## Grain Sauvage AC Jurançon Sec **00**

Lovely impression from the fragrant orange and peach nose to the crisp but juicy palate, full of flavours of apricot, peach and nectarine. *Searsons*

| | |
|---|---|
| *Price* | €9–€12 |
| *Grape* | Gros Manseng |
| *Alc/vol* | 13% |
| *Food* | Cheese/fondue |
| *Drink* | 2002–3 |

## La Gascogne VdP des Côtes de Gascogne **00**

Something different and delicious. Gros Manseng is a warm, slightly honey-flavoured grape from the South of France. Blended here with Sauvignon Blanc it makes a fine, crisp, apple-, pear- and citrus-flavoured wine. *Le Caveau*

| | |
|---|---|
| *Price* | €9–€12 |
| *Grape* | Gros Manseng/ Sauvignon Blanc |
| *Alc/vol* | 12% |
| *Food* | Starters/avocado |
| *Drink* | 2002–3 |

€15–€18

## L'Inspiration des Miaudoux AC Bergerac Sec **00**

Very expressive with rich stewed apple aromas and a soft, fruity palate. Tinned fruit salad flavour—peaches and apricots—good, clean acidity and a tasty, full finish. *WineKnows*

| | |
|---|---|
| *Price* | €15–€18 |
| *Grape* | Sémillon/Sauv Blanc/ Muscadelle |
| *Alc/vol* | 13% |
| *Food* | Poultry/chicken |
| *Drink* | 2002–3 |

# Red

## Dom. de Pellehaut VdP des Côtes de Gascogne 00

Very approachable, picnic-style wine with a dark fruit and somewhat medicinal nose and a solid core of damson and black cherry fruits on the palate. *Mitchells*

| | |
|---|---|
| *Price* | Under €9 |
| *Grape* | Merlot/Tannat |
| *Alc/vol* | 12% |
| *Food* | Picnic/barbecue |
| *Drink* | 2002–3 |

## Ch. Court-les-Mûts AC Côtes de Bergerac 98

Made in a Bordeaux style but with more guts and an earthy touch, this is a very attractive food wine, ideal for roasts. Aromas are of soft, ripe plums and cherries. Great concentration of black fruit and spice on the palate with a nice cut of acidity. *Wicklow Wine Co.*

| | |
|---|---|
| *Price* | €9–€12 |
| *Grape* | Merlot/Cab Franc/ Cab Sauv/Malbec |
| *Alc/vol* | 12% |
| *Food* | Meat/roasts |
| *Drink* | 2002–4 |

## Dom. du Pech AC Buzet 97

Well-made, slightly rustic Bordeaux lookalike with an earthy nose and smoky cedar tones with spice and mixed fruit flavours of juicy plums, redcurrants, raspberries and black-berries. *River Wines*

| | |
|---|---|
| *Price* | €9–€12 |
| *Grape* | Merlot/Cab Sauv/ Cabernet Franc |
| *Alc/vol* | 12.5% |
| *Food* | Meat/beef |
| *Drink* | 2002–3 |

## Ch. de Biran AC Pécharmant 98

Bordeaux style at Southern France prices. Elegant, restrained blackcurrant and raspberry flavours with a classic earthiness. *River Wines*

| | |
|---|---|
| *Price* | €12–€15 |
| *Grape* | Cab Sauv/Cab Franc/ Merlot/Malbec |
| *Alc/vol* | 12.5% |
| *Food* | Meat/lamb |
| *Drink* | 2002–3 |

## Ch. Miaudoux AC Bergerac 99

Modern style. A lovely smoky nose with plummy aromas is followed by a cassis-flavoured palate with spicy vanilla oak and a closed, tannic finish. Gets better the longer it is opened—try decanting and drinking with food. *WineKnows*

| | |
|---|---|
| *Price* | €12–€15 |
| *Grape* | Merlot/Cab Franc/ Cab Sauvignon |
| *Alc/vol* | 12% |
| *Food* | Poultry/chicken |
| *Drink* | 2002–4 |

€15–€18

## Ch. Bouscassé AC Madiran 95

Intense, vegetal, savoury and mature nose with an austere palate due to big tannins and a long, dry finish. Flavours of bitter chocolate, leather, plum and damson and quite a lot of dried fruits. *Le Caveau*

| | |
|---|---|
| *Price* | €15–€18 |
| *Grape* | Tannat |
| *Alc/vol* | 12.5% |
| *Food* | Meat/stews |
| *Drink* | 2002–4 |

## Ch. du Cèdre Le Prestige AC Cahors 99

Really lovely nose, rich with currants, cherries and some floral perfume. The palate, still buried beneath a massive tannic structure, has a cherry bitterness with blackcurrant sweetness and some fig and vanilla flavours. *Le Caveau*

| | |
|---|---|
| *Price* | €15–€18 |
| *Grape* | Malbec/Merlot/ Tannat/Jurançon Noir |
| *Alc/vol* | 13% |
| *Food* | Meat/lamb |
| *Drink* | 2003–7 |

## L'Inspiration des Miaudoux AC Bergerac 00 ☆☆

Spicy and fruity, though still young and tannic, with a nose that has cherry and plum and burnt aromas and a palate with oodles of sweet blackcurrant fruit and new, toasty oak. *WineKnows*

| | |
|---|---|
| *Price* | €15–€18 |
| *Grape* | Merlot |
| *Alc/vol* | 12.5% |
| *Food* | Meat/beef |
| *Drink* | 2003–5 |

| The symbols | |
|---|---|
| ⩔ | *Organic* |
| € | *Exceptionally good value* |
| ☆ | *Accomplished, showing above average quality or character making it worthy of extra attention* |
| ☆☆ | *Excellent with great character, style and complexity* |
| ☆☆☆ | *Wonderful, showing terrific character and complexity, true to its origins* |
| ☆☆☆☆ | *Exceptional, with considerable complexity and classic balance. Rewards serious tasting.* |

# Germany

Most of the white wines from Germany recommended this year are made from Riesling. This grape has become very fashionable with more and more examples appearing from all over the world, not only from the traditional heartlands of Germany and Alsace but also from Australia, New Zealand and the USA. While Rieslings from the New World and Alsace tend to be dry, German Rieslings may be dry, medium-dry, or sweet. (See the panel on page 174 for an explanation of the often confusing German wine labelling terms.) Given the exceptional quality of German Rieslings, it is very appropriate that the White Wine of the Year should be awarded to the Carl Erhard Riesling Auslese Trocken. Although dry, or trocken, this is an immensely rich, luscious wine.

A number of different regions are represented this year with a large number of wines coming from the Pfalz which is one of the more exciting and dynamic areas. Some of the best Rieslings, however, come from the Rheingau, the Mosel-Saar-Ruwer and the Nahe which lies between these two areas.

## White

### Under €9

### Bend in the River Dry Riesling QbA 00

Lime, apple and hedgerow aromas. Citrus flavours to the fore on the palate though with a slight floral element. Youthful, with good length and a lingering fruit finish. *Findlaters*

| | |
|---|---|
| *Price* | Under €9 |
| *Region* | Pfalz |
| *Grape* | Riesling |
| *Alc/vol* | 11.5% |
| *Food* | Ethnic/Japanese |
| *Drink* | 2002–4 |

### Lingenfelder Bird Label Riesling QbA 01

Delicate and light floral nose. Very refreshing with ripe apple flavours and a wonderful, crisp, lemony tanginess. *Oddbins*

| | |
|---|---|
| *Price* | Under €9 |
| *Region* | Pfalz |
| *Grape* | Riesling |
| *Alc/vol* | 11% |
| *Food* | Cheese/feta |
| *Drink* | 2002–3 |

### Schmitt Söhne Riesling QbA 00

Light and easy style. Apple aromas, and a crisp, dry palate with apple and lime flavours and just a little peach and honey. *Dunnes Stores*

| | |
|---|---|
| *Price* | Under €9 |
| *Region* | Pfalz |
| *Grape* | Riesling |
| *Alc/vol* | 11% |
| *Food* | Ethnic/Thai |
| *Drink* | 2002–3 |

## €9–€12

### Anheuser Kreuznacher Narrenkappe Grauburgunder Kabinett Trocken QmP 00

Impressive, rich orange colour with a full, grapey and honey-scented nose. Not at all sweet but very fresh and clean with good acidity and flavours of limes, honey and spice.
*The Wine Seller*

| | |
|---|---|
| Price | €9–€12 |
| Region | Nahe |
| Grape | Grauburgunder (Pinot Gris) |
| Alc/vol | 11% |
| Food | Meat/pork |
| Drink | 2002–5 |

---

**German wine labelling terms**
*QbA (Qualitätswein bestimmter Anbaugebiete) means 'quality wine from a specified region'. Regions of importance in Germany include Mosel-Saar-Ruwer, Rheingau, Rheinhessen, Nahe and Pfalz. QbA wines may be made trocken or halbtrocken.* **Trocken** *means dry,* **halb-trocken** *means medium-dry, although these wines may have better balance than a more austere trocken wine. The terms* **Kabinett, Spatlese, Auslese, Beerenauslese, Eiswein** *and* **Trockenbeerenauslese** *indicate an ascending order of sugar or sweetness in the grapes used to make the wine. The first three may be made in a dry style, whereas the last three are always made in a sweet style.*

---

### Anheuser Kreuznacher St Martin Weissburgunder Kabinett Halbtrocken QmP 00

Honey and nougat nose followed by a nicely spicy palate with a good concentration of lemon, stewed apple and pear flavours.
*The Wine Seller*

| | |
|---|---|
| Price | €9–€12 |
| Region | Nahe |
| Grape | Weissburgunder (Pinot Blanc) |
| Alc/vol | 10.5% |
| Food | Pasta/pesto |
| Drink | 2002–4 |

---

### Carl Ehrhard Rüdesheimer Riesling Trocken QbA 00

Refreshingly cool and green with flavours of apples, gooseberries and limes. Acidity is very crisp and the overall impression is of austerity which would work best with food. *Karwig Wines*

| | |
|---|---|
| Price | €9–€12 |
| Region | Rheingau |
| Grape | Riesling |
| Alc/vol | 12% |
| Food | Fish/plaice |
| Drink | 2002–4 |

---

### Edition Deinhimer Falkenberg Riesling Spätlese Trocken QmP 00

Traditional style with a fragrant floral nose, peach and rice pudding aromas, mouth-watering acidity and crisp apple and citrus flavours.
*The Wine Seller*

| | |
|---|---|
| Price | €9–€12 |
| Region | Rheinhessen |
| Grape | Riesling |
| Alc/vol | 11% |
| Food | Fish/smoked |
| Drink | 2002–3 |

## Edition Niersteiner Bildstock Riesling Spätlese Halbtrocken QmP **99**

Clean, oily and lemony at the same time, the spicy palate hangs together well although the nose is less conventional being quite floral, powdered and perfumed. *The Wine Seller*

| | |
|---|---|
| *Price* | €9–€12 |
| *Region* | Rheinhessen |
| *Grape* | Riesling |
| *Alc/vol* | 10.5% |
| *Food* | Fish/smoked salmon |
| *Drink* | 2002–3 |

## Guldentaler Hipperich Riesling Spätlese Trocken QmP **00**

A food-friendly style. Mineral, apple and marshmallow on the nose with a bone-dry palate of Granny Smith apple and mineral flavours and very crisp acidity. *The Wine Seller*

| | |
|---|---|
| *Price* | €9–€12 |
| *Region* | Nahe |
| *Grape* | Riesling |
| *Alc/vol* | 11% |
| *Food* | Ethnic/Chinese |
| *Drink* | 2002–3 |

## Villa Anheuser Riesling Trocken QbA **00**

Very fresh style, light and tangy, with lime and lemon flavours and good, green, crunchy bite and acidity. *The Wine Seller*

| | |
|---|---|
| *Price* | €9–€12 |
| *Region* | Nahe |
| *Grape* | Riesling |
| *Alc/vol* | 12% |
| *Food* | Vegetarian/cous-cous |
| *Drink* | 2002–3 |

*175*

### €12–€15

## Edition Kauzenberg Riesling Kabinett Trocken QmP 00

Classic style with citrus and some oily and
peachy aromas, cleansing apple and melon flavours and a lengthy, fruity aftertaste.
*The Wine Seller*

| | |
|---|---|
| *Price* | **€12–€15** |
| *Region* | **Nahe** |
| *Grape* | **Riesling** |
| *Alc/vol* | **10.5%** |
| *Food* | **Meat/ham** |
| *Drink* | **2002–3** |

## Louis Guntrum Niersteiner Rehbach Riesling Spätlese QmP 99

Green apple and lime nose with a touch of
oiliness and spice and a mouth-watering juicy
palate with apple and lime flavours and lemony
acidity. *Waterford Wine Vault*

| | |
|---|---|
| *Price* | **€12–€15** |
| *Region* | **Rheinhessen** |
| *Grape* | **Riesling** |
| *Alc/vol* | **10%** |
| *Food* | **Cheese/fondue** |
| *Drink* | **2002–3** |

## Reichsgraf von Kesselstatt Riesling Qualitätswein 00

The perfumed nose is a touch tropical with
mango, peach and some lemon zest. Easy, fresh,
sweetish palate with great flavours of nectarines
and quince. *Searsons*

| | |
|---|---|
| *Price* | **€12–€15** |
| *Region* | **Mosel-Saar-Ruwer** |
| *Grape* | **Riesling** |
| *Alc/vol* | **9.5%** |
| *Food* | **Ethnic/Asian** |
| *Drink* | **2002–3** |

## Weingut Schumacher Riesling Kabinett QmP 99

Distinctive and very pro-
nounced aromas of oil
drum and diesel. This
comes through on the
palate as a hint of oiliness
on what is otherwise a
fresh, lean, green, lemon
and apple style with crisp acidity. *Mitchells*

WEINGUT SCHUMACHER
HERXHEIM AM BERG

| | |
|---|---|
| *Price* | **€12–€15** |
| *Region* | **Pfalz** |
| *Grape* | **Riesling** |
| *Alc/vol* | **11.5%** |
| *Food* | **Starters/salads** |
| *Drink* | **2002–4** |

### €15–€18

## Weingut Schumacher Riesling Spätlese Trocken QmP 99 ☆

A classic, fruity and floral nose with characteristic oiliness is followed by a refreshingly dry
palate with fresh citrus acidity and flavours of
ripe red apples and herbs. *Mitchells*

| | |
|---|---|
| *Price* | **€15–€18** |
| *Region* | **Pfalz** |
| *Grape* | **Riesling** |
| *Alc/vol* | **13%** |
| *Food* | **Seafood/crab** |
| *Drink* | **2002–4** |

€18–€22

## Winkler Jesuitgarten Riesling Spätlese Trocken QmP 00 ☆

Nice example of good Riesling with crunchy, green apple fruitiness balanced by mouth-watering, zesty, lemony acidity, some peach, honey and floral tones and a very appealing, clean, fresh finish. *Waterford Wine Vault*

| | |
|---|---|
| *Price* | **€18–€22** |
| *Region* | **Rheingau** |
| *Grape* | **Riesling** |
| *Alc/vol* | **12%** |
| *Food* | **Fish/sole** |
| *Drink* | **2002–4** |

€25–€30

## Carl Ehrhard Riesling Auslese Trocken QmP 99 ☆☆☆☆

Delicious, benchmark German Riesling, in a highly complex, big style with excellent length. Flavours of peach, mango, ripe apples, honey, lime and some leafiness with crispish acidity, perfect balance and lingering, classic Riesling finish. *Karwig Wines*

| | |
|---|---|
| *Price* | **€25–€30** |
| *Region* | **Rheingau** |
| *Grape* | **Riesling** |
| *Alc/vol* | **14%** |
| *Food* | **Poultry/duck** |
| *Drink* | **2002–5** |

**WHITE WINE OF THE YEAR**

# Red

€12–€15

## Louis Guntrum Dornfelder Rotwein Trocken QbA 99

Aromas of autumnal berries and blackcurrants. Very flavoursome with plenty of delicious, juicy red and black fruit on the palate, cassis and a tantalising hint of exotic spice.
*Waterford Wine Vault*

| | |
|---|---|
| *Price* | **€12–€15** |
| *Region* | **Rheinhessen** |
| *Grape* | **Dornfelder** |
| *Alc/vol* | **11.5%** |
| *Food* | **Meat/beef** |
| *Drink* | **2002–3** |

## Mandeler Rosengarten Dornfelder Rotwein Trocken QbA 00

In a world of blockbuster reds this makes a pleasant change. It is light and dry with an earthy blackcurrant nose and a soft, juicy, red berry and redcurrant jelly palate. *The Wine Seller*

| | |
|---|---|
| *Price* | **€12–€15** |
| *Region* | **Nahe** |
| *Grape* | **Dornfelder** |
| *Alc/vol* | **11.5%** |
| *Food* | **Meat/ham** |
| *Drink* | **2002–3** |

# Greece

When, as happens every now and then, we get bored with the usual run of Cabernet and Chardonnay, Greece offers an interesting alternative, with its delicious red and white wines made from indigenous grapes, as well as some classic varietals, such as the very good Syrah we recommend this year. If you are looking for a taste of Greece, try Dunnes Stores or Oddbins—both have good selections of Greek wines.

## White

### Under €9

### Mount Athos 00

Very pleasant drinking. Fresh, spritzy and fruity with flavours of apples and citrus fruit.
*Dunnes Stores*

| | |
|---|---|
| *Price* | **Under €9** |
| *Region* | **Agioritikos** |
| *Grape* | **Assyrtiko-Athiri** |
| *Alc/vol* | **12%** |
| *Food* | **Fish/fried fish** |
| *Drink* | **2002–3** |

### Xerolithia 01

Quite spritzy with lovely grapey aromas and a light, dry palate with ripe pear flavours and crisp, lemony acidity. *Oddbins*

| | |
|---|---|
| *Price* | **Under €9** |
| *Region* | **Crete** |
| *Alc/vol* | **12%** |
| *Food* | **Vegetarian/hummus** |
| *Drink* | **2002–3** |

## Red

### Under €9

### Achaia Clauss Peloponnesiakos Pelopas Topikos Oenos 98

Light and fruity aromas with a hint of green pepper. More intense on the palate with supple blackcurrant flavours. *Taserra*

| | |
|---|---|
| *Price* | **Under €9** |
| *Region* | **Peloponnese** |
| *Grape* | **Cabernet Sauvignon/ Aghiorghitiko** |
| *Alc/vol* | **12%** |
| *Food* | **Meat/kebabs** |
| *Drink* | **2002–3** |

### Boutari Naoussa 98

Earthy, rustic style with a cherry and rubbery nose and subtle raspberry flavours with a touch of tangerine. A wine that needs food.
*Irish Distillers*

| | |
|---|---|
| *Price* | **Under €9** |
| *Region* | **Naoussa** |
| *Grape* | **Xynomavro** |
| *Alc/vol* | **11.5%** |
| *Food* | **Salads/Greek** |
| *Drink* | **2002–3** |

## Mirambelo 99  €

Full-bodied winter warmer with a developed nose of spice, leather and fennel and delicious flavours of damson, mulberry, liquorice, tar and dark coffee. Perfect with lamb casserole or spicy meatballs. *Oddbins*

| | |
|---|---|
| *Price* | Under €9 |
| *Region* | Peza |
| *Grape* | Kotsifali/Mandilari |
| *Alc/vol* | 12.5% |
| *Food* | Meat/casseroles |
| *Drink* | 2002–4 |

### €9–€12

## Boutari Aghiorgitiko 99

Old World style with a mature, vegetal, black-berry nose, raspberry, cherry and strawberry fla-vours and a firm, tannic grip. *Irish Distillers*

| | |
|---|---|
| *Price* | €9–€12 |
| *Region* | Nemea |
| *Grape* | Aghiorghitiko |
| *Alc/vol* | 12% |
| *Food* | Fish/salmon |
| *Drink* | 2002–3 |

## Notios 01

Very moreish style with appealing aromas of cranberry and heather with a generous, full-bodied, silky texture and luscious berry fruits, vanilla, cedarwood and cinnamon flavours. *Oddbins*

| | |
|---|---|
| *Price* | €9–€12 |
| *Region* | Peloponnese |
| *Grape* | Aghiorghitiko |
| *Alc/vol* | 13% |
| *Food* | Meat/moussaka |
| *Drink* | 2002–4 |

## Tsantalis Rapsani Epilegmenos Reserve 96

Concentrated, juicy blackcurrants and black-berries with peppery spice and hints of choco-late on both nose and palate. Good party wine. *Dunnes Stores*

| | |
|---|---|
| *Price* | €9–€12 |
| *Region* | Rapsani |
| *Grape* | Xynomavro/Stavroto/ Krassato |
| *Alc/vol* | 12.5% |
| *Food* | Meat/lamb chops |
| *Drink* | 2002–3 |

### €15–€18

## Dom. Gerovassiliou Syrah 00

A Syrah with plenty of Greek sunshine. Aromas of plum jam, smoke and black olives and a ripe, sweet, damson palate with liquorice, rich cinna-mon and vanilla spice. *Oddbins*

| | |
|---|---|
| *Price* | €15–€18 |
| *Region* | Epanomi |
| *Grape* | Syrah |
| *Alc/vol* | 13.5% |
| *Food* | Meat/lamb |
| *Drink* | 2002–4 |

# Hungary

Although there is a lot happening in the wine making regions of Hungary we are not yet seeing the results of this in Ireland. In this short chapter we recommend two excellent white wines, one made from Irsai Olivér, which can make spicy and citrus flavoured wines, the other from Furmint, made in a dry style. Furmint and another variety, Hárslevelu, are used to produce Tokaji, one of the greatest sweet wines of the world (see pages 270–273).

## White

### Under €9

### Chapel Hill Irsai Olivér Minoségi Bor 99  €

Interesting, very defined style, reminiscent of an Alsace Pinot Gris. Full of spicy aromas, heady, petal scents and on the palate a mixture of citrus and gooseberry flavours. *Barry & Fitzwilliam*

| | |
|---|---|
| *Price* | Under €9 |
| *Region* | Balaton |
| *Grape* | Irsai Olivér |
| *Alc/vol* | 11.5% |
| *Food* | Pasta/tomato sauces |
| *Drink* | 2002–3 |

### €12–€15

### Tokaji Furmint Mandolas 98

Dramatic wine, extraordinarily intense and complex with lots of power and character. Layers of fruit, quince and kiwi and other interesting flavours—toast, oak and earth, with honey, anise and horseradish. *Searsons*

| | |
|---|---|
| *Price* | €12–€15 |
| *Region* | Tokaj |
| *Grape* | Furmint |
| *Alc/vol* | 12% |
| *Food* | Poultry/chicken |
| *Drink* | 2002–5 |

| The symbols | |
|---|---|
| 🌿 | *Organic* |
| € | *Exceptionally good value* |
| ☆ | *Accomplished, showing above average quality or character making it worthy of extra attention* |
| ☆☆ | *Excellent with great character, style and complexity* |
| ☆☆☆ | *Wonderful, showing terrific character and complexity, true to its origins* |
| ☆☆☆☆ | *Exceptional, with considerable complexity and classic balance. Rewards serious tasting.* |

# Italy

As in previous years, Italian wines, both white and red, performed extremely well in the tastings. It was the reds, however, that really stood out, winning many stars. The Red Wine of the Year is a fantastic Barbera from the producer Enzo Boglietti in Piedmont. Italy also produced the Best Value Red Wine of the Year, Archidamo from Puglia, made from the Primitivo grape. Traditional indigenous grape varieties predominate, producing classic and original wines reflecting their Italian identity. While all of the major regions are represented in the guide from Veneto, Friuli, Alto-Adige, Piedmont and Lombardy in the north to Tuscany, Abruzzo, Marche, and Umbria in the centre, right down to Puglia, Campania and Sicily in the south, some deserve to be singled out: Puglia for producing such full-flavoured and well-priced reds; Piedmont for some very elegant and classic wines, although at a price; Veneto for some excellent Merlot and very serious Valpolicella and Amarone; Tuscany for uniquely identifiable wines over a wide price range.

## White

Under €9

### **Sartori** DOC Soave **01** 🌿

Fresh and lively with an attractive nose of lime, lemon and apple blossom and a crisp but rounded palate with pear, lemon and apple flavours. For summer heat waves. *Dunnes Stores*

| | |
|---|---|
| *Price* | **Under €9** |
| *Region* | **Veneto** |
| *Grape* | **Garganega/Trebbiano** |
| *Alc/vol* | **11.5%** |
| *Food* | **Fish/barbecue** |
| *Drink* | **2002–3** |

### **Straccali Garbino** VdT

Light, fruity nose; excellent crisp, green apple flavours and a subtle texture. Serve well chilled for a very refreshing glass. *Molloys*

| | |
|---|---|
| *Price* | **Under €9** |
| *Alc/vol* | **11.5%** |
| *Food* | **Apéritif/olives** |
| *Drink* | **2002–3** |

### **Tesco** DOC Frascati Superiore **01**

A crisp and fruity Frascati with fresh, zesty lemon peel, pear and green apple flavours and good length. A super summery apéritif. *Tesco*

| | |
|---|---|
| *Price* | **Under €9** |
| *Region* | **Latium** |
| *Grape* | **Malvasia/Trebbiano** |
| *Alc/vol* | **12%** |
| *Food* | **Apéritif/antipasti** |
| *Drink* | **2002** |

*€9–€12*

## Alasia Dry Muscat VdT **01**

A really pleasing, distinctive wine with slightly different flavours. Intense floral, grapey and herbal nose with a matching palate of flavours and crisp acidity giving great freshness.
*Findlaters*

| | |
|---|---|
| *Price* | €9–€12 |
| *Region* | Piedmont |
| *Grape* | Muscat |
| *Alc/vol* | 12% |
| *Food* | Chinese/spring rolls |
| *Drink* | 2002–3 |

## Casa alla Terra DOCG Vernaccia di San Gimignano **01**

Easy style, particularly suited to the outdoors. Very fresh, almost green, with apple, lemon and grapefruit flavours. *Select Wines*

| | |
|---|---|
| *Price* | €9–€12 |
| *Region* | Tuscany |
| *Grape* | Vernaccia |
| *Alc/vol* | 12.5% |
| *Food* | Picnic/antipasti |
| *Drink* | 2002–3 |

## di Lenardo TOH ! DOC Friuli Grave **01**

Ripe lemon and pear nose and ample spicy flavours of fresh melon, ripe apples and oranges.
*Michael's Wines*

| | |
|---|---|
| *Price* | €9–€12 |
| *Region* | Friuli-Venezia Giulia |
| *Grape* | Tocai Friulano |
| *Alc/vol* | 13% |
| *Food* | Poultry/turkey |
| *Drink* | 2002–3 |

## Grigio Luna Pinot Grigio DOC Valdadige **01**

Classic Italian white with lively aromas of fresh limes and a dry, strawlike palate with appetising apple flavours. Best with food. *TDL*

| | |
|---|---|
| *Price* | €9–€12 |
| *Region* | Trentino-Alto Adige |
| *Grape* | Pinot Grigio |
| *Alc/vol* | 12% |
| *Food* | Pasta/ravioli |
| *Drink* | 2002–3 |

## Sagramoso DOC Soave Superiore **00**

Light bodied with melon and grapey aromas and fruity flavours of lemon and apple with some bready tones and a very good finish.
*Woodford Bourne*

| | |
|---|---|
| *Price* | €9–€12 |
| *Region* | Veneto |
| *Grape* | Garganega |
| *Alc/vol* | 12% |
| *Food* | Fish/haddock |
| *Drink* | 2002–3 |

*Classico* on an Italian wine label indicates that the wine's source is the heartland of the original centre of a DOC quality region, making the most typical styles of wine.

## Terlan Pinot Bianco DOC Alto Adige Terlano Classico **01** ☆ €

With a light, fresh, grassy nose, this wine really comes into its own on the palate which has lovely balance and flavours of apple, peach, toast and stony, mineral qualities.
*Michael's Wines*

| | |
|---|---|
| *Price* | €9–€12 |
| *Region* | Trentino-Alto Adige |
| *Grape* | Pinot Bianco |
| *Alc/vol* | 13% |
| *Food* | Pasta/vongole |
| *Drink* | 2002–3 |

## Zenato San Benedetto DOC Lugana **01**

Attractive and classically Italian, full of limes, lemons, apples and peppery spice. It is also a little smoky and creamy with a lovely, long length. *Searsons*

| | |
|---|---|
| Price | €9–€12 |
| Region | Lombardy |
| Grape | Trebbiano di Lugana |
| Alc/vol | 13% |
| Food | Fish/brill |
| Drink | 2002–3 |

### €12–€15

## Broglia La Meirana DOCG Gavi di Gavi **01** ☆

This wine's ripeness is balanced with crispness. The aromas of steely, crisp apples are also perfumed with peach and apricot skins. The palate is tightly knit with ginger and lemon flavours and some riper, red apple elements. *Wines Direct*

| | |
|---|---|
| Price | €12–€15 |
| Region | Piedmont |
| Grape | Cortese |
| Alc/vol | 12% |
| Food | Pasta/creamy sauces |
| Drink | 2002–3 |

## Camillona DOC Monferrato Blanco **00**

Very attractive nose with citrus fruits and spice. Pear- and apple-flavoured palate with lemony acidity make for a smooth, subtle, nicely integrated wine. *Findlaters*

| | |
|---|---|
| Price | €12–€15 |
| Region | Piedmont |
| Grape | Sauvignon Blanc |
| Alc/vol | 13% |
| Food | Meat/veal |
| Drink | 2002–3 |

183

## Cesani DOCG Vernaccia di San Gimignano 00

Light style of white, with green and lemon aromas and a palate of apple and pineapple flavours with a biting, crisp greenness. *Searsons*

| | |
|---|---|
| *Price* | €12–€15 |
| *Region* | Tuscany |
| *Grape* | Vernaccia |
| *Alc/vol* | 12.5% |
| *Food* | Fish/fish stew |
| *Drink* | 2002–3 |

## Danzante Pinot Grigio IGT delle Venezie 01 ☆

Charming nose, very fresh and fruity with aromas of apple and peapod. Concentrated flavours of apples and limes, with perfect balancing acidity. *Allied Drinks*

| | |
|---|---|
| *Price* | €12–€15 |
| *Region* | Friuli-Venezia Giulia |
| *Grape* | Pinot Grigio |
| *Alc/vol* | 12% |
| *Food* | Fish/sole |
| *Drink* | 2002–3 |

## Le Rime IGT Toscana 01

Lovely summer choice, attractive, fresh and fruity with grapey and floral aromas, crisp acidity and a zesty palate with apple and citrus flavours. *Febvre*

| | |
|---|---|
| *Price* | €12–€15 |
| *Region* | Tuscany |
| *Grape* | Chardonnay/Pinot Grigio |
| *Alc/vol* | 12% |
| *Food* | Soup/borscht |
| *Drink* | 2002–3 |

## Regaleali Bianco IGT Sicilia 01

Nice apricot fruit aromas with a light and very pleasant, refreshing palate of good acidity balanced with melon and apple flavours. *Select Wines*

| | |
|---|---|
| *Price* | €12–€15 |
| *Region* | Sicily |
| *Grape* | Inzolia/Cataratto/Varieta Tasca |
| *Alc/vol* | 12% |
| *Food* | Apéritif/salads |
| *Drink* | 2002–3 |

## Terlan Pinot Grigio DOC Alto Adige Pinot Grigio 01 ☆

Subtle and restrained with quite a bit of elegance. Citrus and biscuit aromas are echoed on the palate which has shortbread and lemon peel flavours. *Michael's Wines*

| | |
|---|---|
| *Price* | €12–€15 |
| *Region* | Trentino-Alto Adige |
| *Grape* | Pinot Grigio |
| *Alc/vol* | 13% |
| *Food* | Chinese/Szechuan |
| *Drink* | 2002–3 |

## Villa Canlungo Collavini Pinot Grigio DOC Collio 01

Lemony nose with an abundance of citrus, apple and melon flavours. There is also an oiliness or richness which is balanced by very refreshing acidity. *Woodford Bourne*

| | |
|---|---|
| *Price* | €12–€15 |
| *Region* | Friuli-Venezia Giulia |
| *Grape* | Pinot Grigio |
| *Alc/vol* | 12.5% |
| *Food* | Pasta/carbonara |
| *Drink* | 2002–3 |

## Walter Filiputti Pinot Grigio IGT Venezia Giulia **01**

Attractive, summery style with aromas of freshly-cut grass, apple and pineapple and a very fresh, crisp palate with lemon and apple flavours.
*Wines Direct*

| | |
|---|---|
| Price | €12–€15 |
| Region | Friuli-Venezia Giulia |
| Grape | Pinot Grigio |
| Alc/vol | 12.5% |
| Food | Pasta/creamy sauces |
| Drink | 2002–3 |

---

### €15–€18

## Cesani Sanice DOCG Vernaccia di San Gimignano **00**

Quite an unusual wine with an intense nose of honey, nuts, and figs showing oak ageing. The rich palate has pepper and caramel as well as lemon and apple flavours and a lemony finish.
*Searsons*

| | |
|---|---|
| Price | €15–€18 |
| Region | Tuscany |
| Grape | Vernaccia |
| Alc/vol | 14% |
| Food | Fish/bouillabaisse |
| Drink | 2002–3 |

---

## di Lenardo Father's Eyes IGT Venezia Giulia **01**

Completely different style of white from Italy with New World oakiness in evidence. Perfumed with aromas of melon, fig and coconut, it has a full-bodied palate with plenty of ripe fruit to balance the woody spiciness.
*Michael's Wines*

| | |
|---|---|
| Price | €15–€18 |
| Region | Friuli-Venezia Giulia |
| Grape | Tocai Friulano/Riesling |
| Alc/vol | 13% |
| Food | Ethnic/Chinese |
| Drink | 2002–3 |

---

## Eisacktaler Gewürztraminer della Valle Isarco DOC Alto Adige **01**

This may not be Alsace but it has the classic Gewürztraminer flavours of lychees and rose petals. It is in a cool style with good crispness.
*Select Wines*

| | |
|---|---|
| Price | €15–€18 |
| Region | Trentino-Alto Adige |
| Grape | Gewürztraminer |
| Alc/vol | 13% |
| Food | Vegetarian/peppers |
| Drink | 2002–3 |

---

## Kettmeir Pinot Grigio DOC Alto Adige Südtirol **01** ☆

A dry wine, powerfully flavoured with really sweet apple and pear flavours and a wonderful spiciness giving a richness which is beautifully balanced by crisp acidity. *Select Wines*

| | |
|---|---|
| Price | €15–€18 |
| Region | Trentino-Alto Adige |
| Grape | Pinot Grigio |
| Alc/vol | 12.5% |
| Food | Salads/rocket |
| Drink | 2002–4 |

---

## Michele Chiarlo DOCG Gavi **01**

Agreeable, fruity wine with quite intense apricot and peach flavours edged with spices giving a big, rich, rounded feel in the mouth. *Taserra*

| | |
|---|---|
| Price | €15–€18 |
| Region | Piedmont |
| Grape | Cortese |
| Alc/vol | 12% |
| Food | Seafood/prawns |
| Drink | 2002–3 |

€18–€22

## San Angelo Pinot Grigio IGT Toscana **00**

Attractive, well-made Pinot Grigio with apple tart and cinnamon aromas and a very ripe, apple- and pineapple-flavoured, creamy palate. Good food wine. *Febvre*

| | |
|---|---|
| Price | €18–€22 |
| Region | Tuscany |
| Grape | Pinot Grigio |
| Alc/vol | 12.5% |
| Food | Pasta/carbonara |
| Drink | 2002–3 |

€25–€30

## Ascheri Montalupa di Bra VdT **99**

A Viognier that could be mistaken for Condrieu, with its honeyed fruit fragrance and a palate which is nicely rounded and very peachy and spicy. It would be interesting to give this wine further time to see how it develops. *Findlaters*

| | |
|---|---|
| Price | €25–€30 |
| Region | Piedmont |
| Grape | Viognier |
| Alc/vol | 13% |
| Food | Fish/trout |
| Drink | 2002–3 |

# Red

Under €9

## Arbos Primitivo IGT Puglia **00**

Pleasant, smoky nose with dried fig aromas. On the palate it has a juicy, fruity character with flavours of blackcurrants and plums and a hot, spicy finish. *Dunnes Stores*

| | |
|---|---|
| Price | Under €9 |
| Region | Puglia |
| Grape | Primitivo |
| Alc/vol | 13.5% |
| Food | Meat/salami |
| Drink | 2002–3 |

## Arcano DOCG Chianti Colli Senesi **00** 🌿

Fragrant nose of soft black fruit with earthy tones. The palate is muscular with firm tannins and slight stalkiness but matched with intense berry flavours. A wine to complement food. *Dunnes Stores*

| | |
|---|---|
| Price | Under €9 |
| Region | Tuscany |
| Grape | Sangiovese/Canaiolo |
| Alc/vol | 13% |
| Food | Pasta/meat sauce |
| Drink | 2002–3 |

## Fantini DOC Salice Salentino **00 €**

Summery nose of strawberries and an intensely pleasing palate with good depth of plum and raspberry flavours with a seductive, bitter cherry twist to the finish. Well made, of typical Italian character. *Molloys*

| | |
|---|---|
| Price | Under €9 |
| Region | Puglia |
| Grape | Mainly Negroamaro |
| Alc/vol | 13% |
| Food | Meat/stews |
| Drink | 2002–3 |

> **Montepulciano** is both a grape and a town. The Montepulciano grape is one of Italy's finest-quality grapes, grown mainly in Abruzzo. The town of Montepulciano is in Tuscany, south of Siena. Vino Nobile di Montepulciano is made from Sangiovese.

## Fantini **Montelpulciano** DOC Montepulciano d'Abruzzo **00**

Concentrated, typically Italian wine with black-currant and cherry aromas and dark cherry and red berry flavours with wood and spice and a decent, lengthy finish. *Molloys*

| | |
|---|---|
| Price | Under €9 |
| Region | Abruzzo |
| Grape | Montepulciano |
| Alc/vol | 12.5% |
| Food | Vegetarian/gratins |
| Drink | 2002–3 |

## Fantini **Primitivo** IGT Puglia **00**

Inviting, warm nose, vegetal and earthy, with aromas of truffle and raisin, matched by a dark palate of fig and raisin and somewhat bitter mushroom flavours. *Molloys*

| | |
|---|---|
| Price | Under €9 |
| Region | Puglia |
| Grape | Primitivo |
| Alc/vol | 12.5% |
| Food | Meat/barbecue |
| Drink | 2002–3 |

## Fantini **Sangiovese** IGT Sangiovese Daunia **00**

Pleasantly savoury and herbal notes on the nose and a rich blackberry character translate into a nicely structured and balanced wine with a bitter cherry edge and red fruit flavours. *Molloys*

| | |
|---|---|
| Price | Under €9 |
| Grape | Sangiovese |
| Alc/vol | 13% |
| Food | Pizza/pasta |
| Drink | 2002–3 |

## Incanto **Fabiano Pinot Nero** IGT Provincia di Pavia **99**

The nose is scented with soft summer fruits and plums with a nice creamy edge. This is matched by a palate of concentrated strawberry flavours with vanilla spice. Lovely to drink on its own or with food. *WineOnline*

| | |
|---|---|
| Price | Under €9 |
| Region | Lombardy |
| Grape | Pinot Nero |
| Alc/vol | 12.5% |
| Food | Meat/cold meats |
| Drink | 2002–3 |

## **Rocca** IGT Rosso Salento **98 €**

Big, beefy, almost port-style with a powerful nose of raisin, tar and warm black fruit. The palate is complex and concentrated with mature raisins, plums and prunes, fleshed out with a luscious, long finish. *O'Briens*

| | |
|---|---|
| Price | Under €9 |
| Region | Puglia |
| Grape | Negroamaro/ Malvasia Nera |
| Alc/vol | 13% |
| Food | Meat/goulash |
| Drink | 2002–3 |

## Straccali Tramontano VdT

An everyday drinking wine of nice proportions with a vanilla, bitter cherry and stewed fruit character. Very pleasant drinking on its own or with food. *Molloys*

| | |
|---|---|
| Price | Under €9 |
| Region | Tuscany |
| Alc/vol | 12.5% |
| Food | Starters/antipasti |
| Drink | 2002–3 |

---

€9–€12

## 35th Parallel Nero d'Avola IGT Sicilia 00

Rich, meaty, hearty style with plenty of guts, full and spicy with plummy fruit, anise and a slightly medicinal edge for added interest. *Gleeson*

| | |
|---|---|
| Price | €9–€12 |
| Region | Sicily |
| Grape | Nero d'Avola |
| Alc/vol | 13.5% |
| Food | Meat/pork |
| Drink | 2002–4 |

## 35th Parallel Primitivo DOC Primitivo di Manduria 00

A very big and generous wine, amazingly concentrated, port-like in its depth and warmth, with chocolate and plum pudding flavours. *Gleeson*

| | |
|---|---|
| Price | €9–€12 |
| Region | Puglia |
| Grape | Primitivo |
| Alc/vol | 14% |
| Food | Meat/hamburgers |
| Drink | 2002–5 |

## Archidamo DOC Primitivo di Manduria 00 ☆☆ €

BEST VALUE RED WINE OF THE YEAR

Smooth and wonderfully warming vanilla, chocolate and liquorice aromas. Smoky, dark chocolate palate oozing cherry and red berry flavours, with a concentrated texture and a lengthy finish. *O'Briens*

| | |
|---|---|
| Price | €9–€12 |
| Region | Puglia |
| Grape | Primitivo |
| Alc/vol | 14% |
| Food | Pasta/arrabiata |
| Drink | 2002–3 |

## Bolla DOC Valpolicella Classico 00

Medium bodied but full of juicy cherry aromas and flavours. Concentrated red berry flavours on the palate with a lively acidic and tannic structure. *Dillons*

| | |
|---|---|
| Price | €9–€12 |
| Region | Veneto |
| Grape | Corvina/Rondinella/ Molinara |
| Alc/vol | 12.5% |
| Food | Pizza/pasta |
| Drink | 2002–3 |

## Cataldi Madonna DOC Montepulciano d'Abruzzo 00

Intense ripe blueberry and blackberry aromas are echoed by a substantial weight of fruit and warm, spicy, earthy tones on the palate. Tannins match the fruit and the wine has a fantastically long finish. *Michael's Wines*

| | |
|---|---|
| Price | €9–€12 |
| Region | Abruzzo |
| Grape | Montepulciano |
| Alc/vol | 13% |
| Food | Meat/stews |
| Drink | 2002–4 |

## di Lenardo Refosco DOC Friuli Grave 01

A very cheerful and sunny wine with upfront, fruity aromas of raspberry, strawberry and cherry. Lively, juicy palate with ripe flavours of summer fruit and a creamy vanilla character. *Michael's Wines*

| | |
|---|---|
| Price | €9–€12 |
| Region | Friuli-Venezia Giulia |
| Grape | Refosco |
| Alc/vol | 12.5% |
| Food | Pasta/spicy sauces |
| Drink | 2002–3 |

## Marchesi de' Frescobaldi Rèmole IGT Toscana 00

Delightful, crisp and chewy wine, with very fine cherry and blackberry flavours, an enticing peppery streak and a hint of coffee. *Allied Drinks*

| | |
|---|---|
| Price | €9–€12 |
| Region | Tuscany |
| Grape | Sangiovese/Cab Sauv |
| Alc/vol | 12.5% |
| Food | Pasta/tomato sauces |
| Drink | 2002–4 |

## MezzoGiorno Nero d'Avola IGT Sicilia 00

A general pleaser and very typically Italian with a juicy and concentrated, bittersweet cherry character and some good vegetal tones. *Woodford Bourne*

| | |
|---|---|
| Price | €9–€12 |
| Region | Sicily |
| Grape | Nero d'Avola |
| Alc/vol | 13% |
| Food | Meat/casseroles |
| Drink | 2002–3 |

> *Riserva* on a label means that the wine has been aged in cask and/or bottle and has a higher alcoholic strength.

## Millesimato Riserva DOC Teroldego Rotaliano 99 ☘ ☆☆ €

Seductive and smoky with aromas of black cherries and creamy strawberries. The palate has a mix of bittersweet red berry fruits integrated with vanilla creaminess and crisp, lively acidity giving a classic style. *Mitchells*

| | |
|---|---|
| Price | €9–€12 |
| Region | Trentino-Alto Adige |
| Grape | Teroldego |
| Alc/vol | 12.5% |
| Food | Meat/lamb |
| Drink | 2002–4 |

## Scàranto Rosso DOC Colli Euganei 98

Gorgeous, dark, smoky fruit nose. Mouth-filling richness with cherry cake, strong espresso coffee and liquorice flavours and a tantalising, long finish. *Oddbins*

| | |
|---|---|
| Price | €9–€12 |
| Region | Veneto |
| Alc/vol | 13% |
| Food | Meat/beef |
| Drink | 2002–4 |

## Tormaresca IGT Puglia 99 ☆☆ €

A stylish wine with great flair, bursting with flavours of sweet cherry, baked plums, raisins and spice. It is also a touch tarry and earthy with appealing tannic grip but the ripeness dominates. *Grants*

| | |
|---|---|
| Price | €9–€12 |
| Region | Puglia |
| Grape | Aglianico/Cab Sauv |
| Alc/vol | 12.5% |
| Food | Meat/shepherd's pie |
| Drink | 2002–4 |

## Trulli Primitivo IGT Salento 99

Very approachable wine with a nice weight and depth of flavour. Black fruit and plum cake on the nose and flavours of blackberry, cherry and spice. *Cassidy*

| | |
|---|---|
| *Price* | €9–€12 |
| *Region* | Puglia |
| *Grape* | Primitivo |
| *Alc/vol* | 13% |
| *Food* | Meat/barbecue |
| *Drink* | 2002–4 |

### €12–€15

## Allegrini DOC Valpolicella Classico 00

Classic Valpolicella aromas of raspberry and red berries and a good, bitter cherry twist. There is also a touch of stalkiness and greenness which adds to the impression of freshness. *Fields*

| | |
|---|---|
| *Price* | €12–€15 |
| *Region* | Veneto |
| *Grape* | Corvina/Rondinella/ Molinara |
| *Alc/vol* | 12.5% |
| *Food* | Vegetarian/ mushroom dishes |
| *Drink* | 2002–3 |

## Anticaia Riserva VQPRD Salice Salentino 98 ☆

Big, generous wine with aromas of red cherry and ripe raspberry, burning rubber and a hot tarriness. Rich and creamy caramel and milk chocolate palate with black fruit and spicy flavours. Cries out for some chorizo or penne arrabiata. *WineKnows*

| | |
|---|---|
| *Price* | €12–€15 |
| *Region* | Puglia |
| *Grape* | Mainly Negroamaro |
| *Alc/vol* | 13.5% |
| *Food* | Pasta/arrabiata |
| *Drink* | 2002–4 |

## Barbera Rive DOC Barbera d'Asti 00 ☆

Complex and concentrated, this is a wine to be savoured as it yields its flavours slowly. Aromas of plum and damson, with a nice burnt influence and touch of cinnamon are matched by rich, savoury flavours, dark cherry and espresso. *Findlaters*

| | |
|---|---|
| *Price* | €12–€15 |
| *Region* | Piedmont |
| *Grape* | Barbera |
| *Alc/vol* | 14.5% |
| *Food* | Risotto/mushroom |
| *Drink* | 2002–5 |

## Berengarium DOC Barbera d'Asti Superiore 99

Fragrant nose with plum and mushroom. Generous palate of chocolate mousse, marinated black cherries and a touch of sweet dried fruits. With good balance and integrated tannins, it finishes on a warm, spicy note. *Nectar Wines*

| | |
|---|---|
| *Price* | €12–€15 |
| *Region* | Piedmont |
| *Grape* | Barbera |
| *Alc/vol* | 13.5% |
| *Food* | Meat/lamb |
| *Drink* | 2002–4 |

## Bironi de Brolio 1141 DOCG Chianti Classico 99

Supple and mature with good concentration and a rich, elegant dimension. The palate is very tangy with ripe black fruits, plums and cherries and a satisfying, long finish. *Cassidy*

| | |
|---|---|
| *Price* | €12–€15 |
| *Region* | Tuscany |
| *Grape* | Mainly Sangiovese |
| *Alc/vol* | 13.5% |
| *Food* | Pasta/Bolognese |
| *Drink* | 2002–4 |

## Brusco dei Barbi IGT Toscana 99

This is a fine, soothing, savoury style. The nose is evolved and smoky with mushrooms and vegetal elements. The palate has a touch of sweet, ripe fruit but is predominately savoury and chewy with a charming, gentle rusticity. *Select Wines*

| | |
|---|---|
| Price | €12–€15 |
| Region | Tuscany |
| Grape | Sangiovese |
| Alc/vol | 13% |
| Food | Pizza/Quattro Stagioni |
| Drink | 2002–3 |

## Casa Emma DOCG Chianti Classico 99

Subtle, classy and nicely constructed wine. The fragrant and savoury nose with raspberry, herb, spice and smoke aromas is followed by a feminine and refined palate with ripe raspberry and pepper flavours. *Wines Direct*

| | |
|---|---|
| Price | €12–€15 |
| Region | Tuscany |
| Grape | Mainly Sangiovese |
| Alc/vol | 13% |
| Food | Poultry/chicken |
| Drink | 2002–4 |

## Cascina Pallerino di Bono Bricco della Saluta DOC Barbera d'Alba 00

Pleasant, easy drinking, showing good regional character with savoury and herbal notes, stewed blackcurrant and cherry flavours and some light touches of vanilla. *Wines Direct*

| | |
|---|---|
| Price | €12–€15 |
| Region | Piedmont |
| Grape | Barbera |
| Alc/vol | 13% |
| Food | Pasta/Bolognese |
| Drink | 2002–3 |

## Cesari Mara Vino di Ripasso DOC Valpolicella Classico Superiore 98

Intriguing, beefy nose with stewed tea and forest fruit aromas. Amazingly full-bodied palate with meaty tones, spice and sweet berries. Perfect with lasagne or meaty sauces. *TDL*

| | |
|---|---|
| Price | €12–€15 |
| Region | Veneto |
| Grape | Corvina/Rondinella |
| Alc/vol | 13% |
| Food | Pasta/lasagne |
| Drink | 2002–3 |

## Col di Sasso Sangiovese & Cabernet Sauvignon IGT Toscana 00 ☆☆

Superripe and forward nose of blackcurrant and blueberry pie, cinnamon and mint. The palate is beautifully balanced and extremely rich with raisined fruit, prunes, damson, and kirsch. Definitely a food wine. *Febvre*

| | |
|---|---|
| Price | €12–€15 |
| Region | Tuscany |
| Grape | Sangiovese/Cab Sauv |
| Alc/vol | 12.5% |
| Food | Meat/beef |
| Drink | 2002–5 |

## Colle Secco Rubino DOC Montepulciano d'Abruzzo 98 ☆☆ €

Fantastically juicy wine with an inviting, warm and rich nose of earthy, spicy clove and chocolate aromas. Luscious, ripe blackberry palate with great concentration, spicy tones and supple tannins. *Febvre*

| | |
|---|---|
| Price | €12–€15 |
| Region | Abruzzo |
| Grape | Montepulciano |
| Alc/vol | 13.5% |
| Food | Meat/hamburgers |
| Drink | 2002–4 |

## Corte Sant'Alda DOC Valpolicella 98

A very fruity wine with plenty of life left. Acidity and tannins, though high, are well balanced by the juicy flavours of blackberry and raisins with liquorice, chocolate and cassis and a slightly nutty finish. *Terroirs*

| | |
|---|---|
| *Price* | €12–€15 |
| *Region* | Veneto |
| *Grape* | Corvina/Rondinella/ Molinara |
| *Alc/vol* | % |
| *Food* | Meat/bresaola |
| *Drink* | 2002–3 |

## Danzante Merlot IGT delle Venezie 00 ☆

Stylish and seductive, the nose is scented with herbal elements. The palate is soft and supple with flavours of warm blackberry compote and spice. *Allied Drinks*

| | |
|---|---|
| *Price* | €12–€15 |
| *Region* | Friuli-Venezia Giulia |
| *Grape* | Merlot |
| *Alc/vol* | 13.5% |
| *Food* | Meat/lamb |
| *Drink* | 2002–4 |

## Danzante Sangiovese IGT delle Marche 98

Fresh and fragrant with aromas of black cherries and raspberries, this is a lovely crisp and stylish wine with a mix of fruit flavours—plum, cranberry and a hint of raisin. Perfectly suited to Italian-style cuisine. *Allied Drinks*

| | |
|---|---|
| *Price* | €12–€15 |
| *Region* | Marche |
| *Grape* | Sangiovese |
| *Alc/vol* | 12.5% |
| *Food* | Starters/antipasti |
| *Drink* | 2002–3 |

## Genius Loci Sangiovese IGT Toscana 99

A concentrated, big nose gives way to earthy tones and autumnal berry fruit with a bitter cherry twist in the finish. Made for food. *Dunnes Stores*

| | |
|---|---|
| *Price* | €12–€15 |
| *Region* | Tuscany |
| *Grape* | Sangiovese |
| *Alc/vol* | 12.5% |
| *Food* | Vegetarian/peppers |
| *Drink* | 2002–3 |

## Musella DOC Valpolicella Superiore 98

Nice example of Valpolicella with its fragrant raspberry nose and restrained, stony cherry and damson palate with lemony acidity and a crisp finish. *Oddbins*

| | |
|---|---|
| *Price* | €12–€15 |
| *Region* | Veneto |
| *Grape* | Corvina/Rondinella/ Molinara |
| *Alc/vol* | 13% |
| *Food* | Meat/sausages |
| *Drink* | 2002–3 |

## Panizzari DOC San Colombano Riserva 98

Quite a mellow wine, ideal with hearty food. On the nose there is a rustic, truffle touch with soft berries, plums and cherry stones. The palate has a nice creamy influence with hints of chocolate and coffee. *Select Wines*

| | |
|---|---|
| *Price* | €12–€15 |
| *Region* | Lombardy |
| *Grape* | Barbera/Bonarda |
| *Alc/vol* | 12.5% |
| *Food* | Pasta/lasagne |
| *Drink* | 2002–3 |

## Poliziano DOC Rosso di Montepulciano 00 ☆☆

A nose to wow with smoky black fruit, fig and date aromas. Concentrated palate flavoured with espresso, mocha, chocolate mousse, leather and cinnamon. Acidity and tannins are high but the fruit can handle it. *WineKnows*

| | |
|---|---|
| *Price* | €12–€15 |
| *Region* | Tuscany |
| *Grape* | Mainly Sangiovese |
| *Alc/vol* | 13.5% |
| *Food* | Meat/steak |
| *Drink* | 2002–6 |

## Prunotto DOC Barbera d'Alba 99 ☆

A terrific wine, the ripeness together with classic Italian acidity give a lovely biting concentration. Plenty of dark plum and cherry flavours, burnt, smoky elements, and raisins with hints of liquorice and dark chocolate. *Grants*

| | |
|---|---|
| *Price* | €12–€15 |
| *Region* | Piedmont |
| *Grape* | Barbera |
| *Alc/vol* | 13% |
| *Food* | Meat/salami |
| *Drink* | 2002–3 |

## Regaleali Rosso IGT Sicilia 99 ☆

A richly concentrated, spicy wine with toffee apple and caramel tones intermingled with baked fruit cake and deep brambly flavours.
*Select Wines*

| | |
|---|---|
| *Price* | €12–€15 |
| *Region* | Sicily |
| *Grape* | Nero d'Avola/ Perricone |
| *Alc/vol* | 13% |
| *Food* | Meat/casseroles |
| *Drink* | 2002–4 |

## San Lorenzo de Luca IGT Rosso dell'Umbria 99

Complex, rich nose with baked fruit character. Generous and robust palate of juicy cherries, blackberries, sweet raisins and prunes. Youthful tannins dominate the fruit at present, so best to decant or let the wine age for a year or two. *O'Briens*

| | |
|---|---|
| *Price* | €12–€15 |
| *Region* | Umbria |
| *Alc/vol* | 13.5% |
| *Food* | Meat/pork |
| *Drink* | 2002–4 |

## Santa Margherita Versato IGT Veneto Merlot 99

Gorgeous sweet fruits to the fore, plums and blackberries, with peppery and spicy elements and an earthy touch, well structured with a good backbone of tannin. *Select Wines*

| | |
|---|---|
| *Price* | €12–€15 |
| *Region* | Veneto |
| *Grape* | Merlot |
| *Alc/vol* | 12.5% |
| *Food* | Meat/steak |
| *Drink* | 2002–4 |

## Solyss IGT Rosso Salento 01 ☆

Rich, warm nose with chocolate and raisin aromas opens out to a big palate packed with juicy blackberries. Soft and satiny, smooth and easy drinking, with a long, fruity finish.
*Michael's Wines*

| | |
|---|---|
| *Price* | €12–€15 |
| *Region* | Puglia |
| *Grape* | Negroamaro/ Primitivo |
| *Alc/vol* | 14.5% |
| *Food* | Cheese/Parmesan |
| *Drink* | 2002–4 |

## Taurino Notorpanaro IGT Salento Rosso **97**

Vegetal and spicy notes on the nose and a full, robust palate with concentrated blackcurrant jelly flavour. *Woodford Bourne*

| | |
|---|---|
| *Price* | €12–€15 |
| *Region* | Puglia |
| *Grape* | Negroamaro/ Malvasia Nera |
| *Alc/vol* | 14.5% |
| *Food* | Vegetarian/ratatouille |
| *Drink* | 2002–3 |

---

€15–€18

## Cerasuolo di Vittoria DOC Sicilia **99** ☆

Raspberry, stewed prune and lemon nose is followed by a very rich, intense, dried fruit palate of prunes, plums and damsons, with chocolate tones, liquorice and a long, spicy finish. *WineKnows*

| | |
|---|---|
| *Price* | €15–€18 |
| *Region* | Sicily |
| *Grape* | Nero d'Avola/ Frappato di Vittoria |
| *Alc/vol* | 13% |
| *Food* | Meat/moussaka |
| *Drink* | 2002–3 |

## Enzo Boglietti DOC Dolcetto d'Alba **00**

Delightful style, distinctively Italian, warm and juicy with bramble fruit and cherry flavours and a classic bitter twist. *WineKnows*

| | |
|---|---|
| *Price* | €15–€18 |
| *Region* | Piedmont |
| *Grape* | Dolcetto |
| *Alc/vol* | 13% |
| *Food* | Cheese/fondue |
| *Drink* | 2002–3 |

## Falesco IGT Umbria Merlot **00**

Not typically Merlot, yet typically Italian. Apple and blackberry tart aromas with some vegetal tones. Spicy palate with plum, cherry and smoky tobacco flavours, high acidity and firm tannins—quite complex as a result. *O'Briens*

| | |
|---|---|
| *Price* | €15–€18 |
| *Region* | Umbria |
| *Grape* | Merlot |
| *Alc/vol* | 12.5% |
| *Food* | Poultry/chicken wings |
| *Drink* | 2002–3 |

## La Gavina Cabernet Sauvignon IGT Toscana **98** ☆

Lovely aromas of spicy blackcurrants and liquorice. Intense, fruity and minty palate with some spicy touches and a good, tannic backbone. *Dunnes Stores*

| | |
|---|---|
| *Price* | €15–€18 |
| *Region* | Tuscany |
| *Grape* | Cabernet Sauvignon |
| *Alc/vol* | 13% |
| *Food* | Meat/lamb chops |
| *Drink* | 2002–4 |

## Lamole di Lamole DOCG Chianti Classico **99**

Refreshing, fruity style with ample stony cherry and damson fruit, hints of smoke and pepper and a pleasant, chewy finish. *Select Wines*

| | |
|---|---|
| *Price* | €15–€18 |
| *Region* | Tuscany |
| *Grape* | Mainly Sangiovese |
| *Alc/vol* | 12.5% |
| *Food* | Meat/pork |
| *Drink* | 2002–3 |

## Leone de Castris Vino Rosso Riserva
DOC Salice Salentino **98**

| | |
|---|---|
Spicy punch from start to finish. A big wine with baked plums, raisins and black cherries—a particularly good winter-food wine. *Select Wines*

| | |
|---|---|
| Price | €15–€18 |
| Region | Puglia |
| Grape | Negroamaro/ Malvasia Nera |
| Alc/vol | 13.5% |
| Food | Vegetarian/aubergine |
| Drink | 2002–4 |

## Madonna di Como Marchesi di Barolo
DOC Dolcetto d'Alba **01**

Ripe yet tangy, youthful style due to very good, crisp, lemony acidity. Flavours are of mulberries, blackcurrant pastilles, raspberries and white pepper. *Select Wines*

| | |
|---|---|
| Price | €15–€18 |
| Region | Piedmont |
| Grape | Dolcetto |
| Alc/vol | 13.5% |
| Food | Pizza/pasta |
| Drink | 2002–3 |

## Marchesi di Barolo Ruvei DOC Barbera d'Alba **00** ☆☆☆ €

A rich delight, beautifully concentrated with oodles of ripe fruit, white pepper and liquorice. Lots of flavours to be savoured with black cherries, damsons, mulberries, raspberries and mineral and coffee elements. *Select Wines*

| | |
|---|---|
| Price | €15–€18 |
| Region | Piedmont |
| Grape | Barbera |
| Alc/vol | 13.5% |
| Food | Pasta/lasagne |
| Drink | 2002–5 |

## Mazer Inferno DOC Valtellina Superiore **97** ☆

Beautifully developed wine with truffle and wild mushroom aromas and a very refined, maturing palate, delicate and feminine, with savoury and fruity cherry flavours. *Findlaters*

| | |
|---|---|
| Price | €15–€18 |
| Region | Lombardy |
| Grape | Nebbiolo |
| Alc/vol | 13.5% |
| Food | Meat/lamb |
| Drink | 2002–3 |

## Montegradella Santá Sofiá
DOC Valpolicella Classico Superiore **97**

Very elegant with layers and layers of depth and concentration. There is a generous dose of nutmeg and mixed spice in this wine together with sweet, stewed fruit flavours. *Select Wines*

| | |
|---|---|
| Price | €15–€18 |
| Region | Veneto |
| Grape | Corvina/Rondinella/ Molinara |
| Alc/vol | 12.5% |
| Food | Vegetarian/roasted vegetables |
| Drink | 2002–4 |

## Santo Stefano Vino di Ripasso IGT Rosso del Veronese **98**

Made in quite a rustic style, with crisp acidity and firm tannins, this wine needs food to match. It has an interesting nose of vegetal and leafy aromas and a tightly packed spice and berry palate *Febvre*

| | |
|---|---|
| Price | €15–€18 |
| Region | Veneto |
| Grape | Corvina/Rondinella/ Molinara |
| Alc/vol | 13.5% |
| Food | Meat/cassoulet |
| Drink | 2002–3 |

## Tommasi Ripasso DOC Valpolicella Classico Superiore **98** ☆

Soft and plumply seductive style with lots of raisin and plum flavours together with some floral, perfumed notes and classic, nutmeg spiciness. *Cassidy*

| | |
|---|---|
| *Price* | €15–€18 |
| *Region* | Veneto |
| *Grape* | Corvina/Rondinella/Molinara |
| *Alc/vol* | 13% |
| *Food* | Fish/tuna |
| *Drink* | 2002–4 |

## Villa Antinori Riserva DOCG Chianti Classico **98**

This wine hits all the right notes with its typically Italian palate of cherries, stewed plums, chocolate and mocha, with a lovely, crisp, bitter, herbal and cherry finish. *Grants*

| | |
|---|---|
| *Price* | €15–€18 |
| *Region* | Tuscany |
| *Grape* | Mainly Sangiovese |
| *Alc/vol* | 13% |
| *Food* | Pasta/tomato sauces |
| *Drink* | 2002–5 |

## Vistarenni Vigneto Assolo DOCG Chianti Classico **97** ☆

Very smooth due to an abundance of fruit balanced with a classic grip of lemon peel acidity. Flavours of juicy, ripe cherry and raspberry are persistent and concentrated. *Select Wines*

| | |
|---|---|
| *Price* | €15–€18 |
| *Region* | Tuscany |
| *Grape* | Mainly Sangiovese |
| *Alc/vol* | 12.5% |
| *Food* | Poultry/duck |
| *Drink* | 2002–4 |

## Zenato Ripassa DOC Valpolicella Superiore **99** ☆☆

This wine has fantastic concentration. Really fruity and vibrant, it offers serious depths of flavours—blackberry, plum, chocolate, spice and vanilla. *Searsons*

| | |
|---|---|
| *Price* | €15–€18 |
| *Region* | Veneto |
| *Grape* | Corvina/Rondinella/Molinara |
| *Alc/vol* | 13% |
| *Food* | Meat/ham |
| *Drink* | 2002–4 |

### €18–€22

## Il Baciale DOC Monferrato Rosso **00**

'Il Baciale' means 'the matchmaker' and this is an unusual mix of grapes producing a wine with a slightly stalky nose and intense, earthy, black fruit flavours with aniseed nuances. It has a firm tannic structure and a delicious, savoury finish. *Fields*

| | |
|---|---|
| *Price* | €18–€22 |
| *Region* | Piedmont |
| *Grape* | Barbera/Pinot Noir |
| *Alc/vol* | 13% |
| *Food* | Meat/lamb |
| *Drink* | 2002–3 |

## La Corte Negroamaro IGT Salento **00** ☆☆☆

Deep and opaque in colour with smoked bacon, Bovril, crushed blackberry and raisined sweetness on the nose. Big, generous palate of juicy blackberries, plums and cherries. Very youthful, it will continue to give enjoyment as it develops. *Michael's Wines*

| | |
|---|---|
| *Price* | €18–€22 |
| *Region* | Puglia |
| *Grape* | Negroamaro |
| *Alc/vol* | 15% |
| *Food* | Game/venison |
| *Drink* | 2003–6 |

## La Corte Zinfandel IGT Tarantino 99 ☆☆

Great colour and an intense, earthy and raisined, dried fruit nose. Rich cherry and blackberry flavours, spicy and chocolatey. With crisp acidity and firm tannins, this is a wine of unmistakeable quality made for the long haul. *Michael's Wines*

| | |
|---|---|
| Price | €18–€22 |
| Region | Puglia |
| Grape | Zinfandel |
| Alc/vol | 15% |
| Food | Meat/beef stroganoff |
| Drink | 2002–6 |

## Lamole di Lamole Barrique DOCG Chianti Classico 99

Sumptuous and smooth with juicy flavours of ripe black cherry and plum sprinkled with warm cake spice, and touches of leather and liquorice. It will continue to get better. *Select Wines*

| | |
|---|---|
| Price | €18–€22 |
| Region | Tuscany |
| Grape | Mainly Sangiovese |
| Alc/vol | 12.5% |
| Food | Meat/cassoulet |
| Drink | 2002–5 |

## Monteregio Riserva DOC Massa Maritima 97

Characterful nose with warm, spicy tones mingling with bitter chocolate, dried fruits and liquorice. Juicy and spicy fruit palate with a velvety texture in spite of firm tannins. *Dunnes Stores*

| | |
|---|---|
| Price | €18–€22 |
| Region | Tuscany |
| Alc/vol | 13.5% |
| Food | Meat/veal |
| Drink | 2002–3 |

## Nipozzano DOCG Chianti Rufina 98

Reserved style which is still quite tannic and would be great with food. Fragrant blackcurrant aromas with a hint of toffee with a palate of plums and cherries, bitter dark chocolate and a touch of leather. *Allied Drinks*

| | |
|---|---|
| Price | €18–€22 |
| Region | Tuscany |
| Grape | Mainly Sangiovese |
| Alc/vol | 12.5% |
| Food | Meat/steak |
| Drink | 2002–5 |

## Rocca Guicciarda Riserva DOCG Chianti Classico 98 ☆☆

Mature style with a complex flavour. The nose is pungently concentrated with succulent raisins, sultanas and candied peel. Very smooth palate with a great weight of fruit—figs, damsons and loganberries—and still quite a bit of tannic grip. *Cassidy*

| | |
|---|---|
| Price | €18–€22 |
| Region | Tuscany |
| Grape | Mainly Sangiovese |
| Alc/vol | 13% |
| Food | Meat/pork |
| Drink | 2002–5 |

## Toar IGT Rosso del Veronese 97

Very flavoursome and quite savoury with medicinal and herbal notes bound together with blackberry and cherry flavours. *Grants*

| | |
|---|---|
| Price | €18–€22 |
| Region | Veneto |
| Grape | Corvina/ Rondinella/ Oseleta |
| Alc/vol | 12.5% |
| Food | Game/casseroles |
| Drink | 2002–4 |

## Enzo Boglietti Nebbiolo DOC Langhe 00

Dense berry fruit, rich, warm and generous. With very high acidity and firm tannins at present, this wine should be accompanied by food or given a little extra time in bottle for the acidity and tannins to settle. *WineKnows*

| | |
|---|---|
| Price | €22–€25 |
| Region | Piedmont |
| Grape | Nebbiolo |
| Alc/vol | 14% |
| Food | Poultry/goose |
| Drink | 2002–3 |

## Marchesi di Barolo Le Lune DOCG Barolo 96 ☆☆☆

A very distinguished, rich nose with a developed bouquet of dried fruit, prunes and fennel. Mouth-watering palate, robust yet elegant, with spicy, raisined fruit. *Dunnes Stores*

| | |
|---|---|
| Price | €22–€25 |
| Region | Piedmont |
| Grape | Nebbiolo |
| Alc/vol | 13.5% |
| Food | Poultry/confit of duck |
| Drink | 2002–3 |

## Poliziano DOC Vino Nobile di Montepulciano 99 ☆

Complex and elegant, with a divine nose of black cherry, vanilla and nutmeg. Intensely flavoured palate with dark plums and cherries, raisins, chocolate and aniseed. Very youthful, with gripping tannins, it will smooth out further with time. *WineKnows*

| | |
|---|---|
| Price | €22–€25 |
| Region | Tuscany |
| Grape | Mainly Sangiovese |
| Alc/vol | 13.5% |
| Food | Game/quail |
| Drink | 2002–7 |

## Valdipiatta DOCG Vino Nobile di Montepulciano 98 ☆☆

Fragrant, ripe, enticing perfume of blackcurrants, plums and a little tar. Very elegant palate, full of ripeness and flavour, ripe plums, cranberries, roasted coffee, chocolate and liquorice, and a chewy, smoky twist. *Select Wines*

| | |
|---|---|
| Price | €22–€25 |
| Region | Tuscany |
| Grape | Mainly Sangiovese |
| Alc/vol | 13.5% |
| Food | Game/quail |
| Drink | 2002–4 |

## Carpineto Riserva DOCG Chianti Classico 97 ☆☆

A brooding and smouldering wine from a great vintage. Mellow and slightly nutty nose with sultana, prune, morello cherry, cake spice and mocha aromas. The texture is smooth, soft and dark with smoky leather, coffee bean and black cherry flavours. *Taserra*

| | |
|---|---|
| Price | €25–€30 |
| Region | Tuscany |
| Grape | Mainly Sangiovese |
| Alc/vol | 13% |
| Food | Game/pigeon |
| Drink | 2002–5 |

## Carpineto Riserva DOCG Vino Nobile di Montepulciano 97 ☆

Stylish, with power and elegance, big structure and lots of character. Flavours of dark mulberry, fig and chocolate-coated cherries, rich espresso and smoky leather. It has time to go. *Taserra*

| | |
|---|---|
| Price | €25–€30 |
| Region | Tuscany |
| Grape | Sangiovese/Canaiolo |
| Alc/vol | 13% |
| Food | Pasta/truffles |
| Drink | 2002–5 |

## Cataldi Madonna Tonì DOC Montepulciano d'Abruzzo 98

Rich on the nose with fennel and smoky aromas. Sweet fruitcake on the palate makes for a full and generous style. *Michael's Wines*

| | |
|---|---|
| *Price* | €25–€30 |
| *Region* | Abruzzo |
| *Grape* | Montepulciano |
| *Alc/vol* | 14% |
| *Food* | Meat/beef |
| *Drink* | 2002–5 |

## Cesari Il Bosco
### DOC Amarone della Valpolicella Classico 97 ☆☆☆

Great nose with scents of violets and blackberries. Very full-bodied, rich palate with intense black fruit and chocolate flavours with peppery spice. The flavour goes on and on and has a slightly minty feel. *TDL*

| | |
|---|---|
| *Price* | €25–€30 |
| *Region* | Veneto |
| *Grape* | Corvina/Rondinella/ Molinara |
| *Alc/vol* | 14.5% |
| *Food* | Meat/casseroles |
| *Drink* | 2002–5 |

*SHORTLIST RED WINE OF THE YEAR*

## Donna Lisa Riserva DOC Salice Salentino 97 ☆

A substantial wine with very spicy, hot baked fruit and some earthiness. It is not at all overpowering and really expresses the quality and purity of the fruit. *Select Wines*

| | |
|---|---|
| *Price* | €25–€30 |
| *Region* | Puglia |
| *Grape* | Negroamaro/ Malvasia Nera |
| *Alc/vol* | 13.5% |
| *Food* | Meat/ribs |
| *Drink* | 2002–5 |

## Luenzo IGT Toscano 99 ☆

Gorgeous nose full of concentrated, juicy fruit with pepper and spice, earthy tones and rich cassis aromas. Equally luscious palate with juicy, ripe blackcurrants and creamy, chocolatey texture and flavours. *Searsons*

| | |
|---|---|
| *Price* | €25–€30 |
| *Region* | Tuscany |
| *Grape* | Sangiovese |
| *Alc/vol* | 14% |
| *Food* | Meat/roasts |
| *Drink* | 2002–3 |

## Michele Chiarlo Valle del Sole
### DOC Barbera d'Asti Superiore 96

Like many Italian wines this would be best with food. The finely balanced palate has rich, smoky nuances, flavours of red currants and summer red fruits and mouth-watering acidity making it quite zesty and tangy. *Taserra*

| | |
|---|---|
| *Price* | €25–€30 |
| *Region* | Piedmont |
| *Grape* | Barbera |
| *Alc/vol* | 13% |
| *Food* | Meat/veal |
| *Drink* | 2002–3 |

### €30–€35

## Castello Vicchiomaggio La Prima Riserva
### DOCG Chianti Classico 97

The nose is showing some development with spicy, cigar box aromas. The palate is equally spicy with blackberry and herb flavours and sustaining, firm tannins. *Febvre*

| | |
|---|---|
| *Price* | €30–€35 |
| *Region* | Tuscany |
| *Grape* | Mainly Sangiovese |
| *Alc/vol* | 13% |
| *Food* | Meat/roasts |
| *Drink* | 2002–5 |

## Enzo Boglietti Roscaleto DOC Barbera d'Alba 99 ☆☆☆☆

Brilliant deep ruby in colour with chocolate, bitter cherry and rich, raisiny aromas. The seductively rich and spicy palate is vibrant and packed with dense berry fruit and plum flavours, with a memorable length.
*WineKnows*

| | |
|---|---|
| Price | €30–€35 |
| Region | Piedmont |
| Grape | Barbera |
| Alc/vol | 14.5% |
| Food | Meat/lamb |
| Drink | 2002–5 |

## Radici Mastroberardino DOCG Taurasi 97

Gamey and spicy tones on the nose follow through to a big palate of baked black fruit, anise, vanilla, meaty and herbaceous flavours. Delicious but not for the faint hearted.
*Select Wines*

| | |
|---|---|
| Price | €30–€35 |
| Region | Campania |
| Grape | Aglianico |
| Alc/vol | 13% |
| Food | Game/rabbit |
| Drink | 2002–6 |

## Zenato DOC Amarone della Valpolicella Classico 98 ☆☆

Very expressive with layers and layers of wonderful flavours of plums, raisins and spicy, sweet berry compote. Big and generous, quite fleshy and obviously high in alcohol, it is powerful but not overpowering. *Searsons*

| | |
|---|---|
| Price | €30–€35 |
| Region | Veneto |
| Grape | Corvina/Rondinella/ Molinara |
| Alc/vol | 14.5% |
| Food | Game/pheasant |
| Drink | 2002–6 |

### €35–€40

## Boscaini Marano DOC Amarone della Valpolicella Classico 97

Very ripe nose of stewed and spiced fruits follows through to an equally complex and intense palate of autumnal berry and pepper flavours. With excellent body and weight, the wine would be fantastic with food and should be decanted. *Febvre*

| | |
|---|---|
| Price | €35–€40 |
| Region | Veneto |
| Grape | Corvina/Rondinella/ Molinara |
| Alc/vol | 15% |
| Food | Meat/beef |
| Drink | 2002–3 |

## Countacc! DOC Monferrato 95 ☆☆☆

Deliciously perfumed with violets and strawberries and some savoury elements. Very impressive and memorable palate, rich and smooth with ripe plums and cherries, blackcurrant leaves and a rich finish. *Taserra*

| | |
|---|---|
| Price | €35–€40 |
| Region | Piedmont |
| Grape | Barbera/Nebbiolo/ Cabernet Sauvignon |
| Alc/vol | 13.5% |
| Food | Poultry/duck |
| Drink | 2002–6 |

# Lebanon

Ch. Musar has long been an ambassador for Lebanese wines and continues to produce serious wines. However, it is exciting to see some new names appearing in Ireland, such as the well-regarded Dom. Wardy Perle du Château; other names to look out for include Massaya, Ch. Ksara and Ch. Kefraya.

## White

€15–€18

### Dom. Wardy Perle du Château 00

An exciting wine that has won a number of international awards. Lemon toffee on the nose. The palate doesn't disappoint with layers of buttered citrus fruit and a pleasant finish. *Gleeson*

| | |
|---|---|
| *Price* | **€15–€18** |
| *Region* | **Bekaa Valley** |
| *Grape* | **Chardonnay** |
| *Alc/vol* | **13%** |
| *Food* | **Fish/salmon** |
| *Drink* | **2002–3** |

## Red

€12–€15

### Hochar Père et Fils 98

Made by Ch. Musar, this is a lighter style of red wine which sees no oak and is bottle-aged for 2–3 years before release. Raspberry jam and earthy aromas are followed by ripe blackberries, leather and dried fruit flavours. *Grants*

| | |
|---|---|
| *Price* | **€12–€15** |
| *Region* | **Bekaa Valley** |
| *Grape* | **Cab Sauv/Cinsault** |
| *Alc/vol* | **13.5%** |
| *Food* | **Meat/salami** |
| *Drink* | **2002–3** |

€15–€18

### Dom. Wardy Ch. Les Cèdres 98

Slightly unusual but all the more welcome for that. Wonderful depth of red fruits and a red apple and redcurrant character. Soft and generous palate with spicy, earthy tones, good acidity and softening tannins. *Gleeson*

| | |
|---|---|
| *Price* | **€15–€18** |
| *Region* | **Bekaa Valley** |
| *Grape* | **Blend of varieties** |
| *Alc/vol* | **12%** |
| *Food* | **Meat/pork** |
| *Drink* | **2002–3** |

€18–€22

### Ch. Musar 96 ☆

A lighter more refined vintage having an interesting nose of tangerines and blackcurrants, showing definite maturity, with a slight farmyard aroma more associated with Pinot Noir. Flavours are of spiced oranges, redcurrants and a hint of tobacco. *Grants*

| | |
|---|---|
| *Price* | **€18–€22** |
| *Region* | **Bekaa Valley** |
| *Grape* | **Cab Sauv/Cinsault/ Syrah** |
| *Alc/vol* | **13%** |
| *Food* | **Meat/lamb** |
| *Drink* | **2002–3** |

# New Zealand

Sauvignon Blanc and Pinot Noir are the most widely produced varietal wines in New Zealand and not surprisingly it is examples of these that dominate our recommendations this year. New Zealand Sauvignons tend to be pungent and upfront on the nose, with more obvious fruitiness and alcohol, than Sancerre or Pouilly Fumé from the Loire. Some excellent wines are also being produced with other white varieties, notably Chardonnay and Riesling. The common feature we detected in Pinot Noir from New Zealand is an elegance which is not dissimilar to good French Burgundy. Merlot and Cabernet blends tended to be powerful and we were most impressed with a tremendously peppery Syrah from Babich.

## White

### Under €9

### Tesco New Zealand Dry White Wine NV

All the right notes—crisp and fresh, with a pungent, grassy nose and light, attractive flavours of lime, lemon, gooseberry and blackcurrant leaf. *Tesco*

| | |
|---|---|
| *Price* | Under €9 |
| *Alc/vol* | 11.5% |
| *Food* | Chinese/Thai |
| *Drink* | 2002–3 |

### €12–€15

### Berry's Own Selection Nelson Sauvignon Blanc 01

Appealing gooseberry, citrus and flinty aromas and a sublime, sweet and sour palate of pineapple and lemon with a herbaceous character. *Fields*

| | |
|---|---|
| *Price* | €12–€15 |
| *Region* | South Island |
| *Grape* | Sauvignon Blanc |
| *Alc/vol* | 13% |
| *Food* | Pasta/tomato sauces |
| *Drink* | 2002–3 |

### Huia Sauvignon Blanc 01 ☆

Benchmark New Zealand Sauvignon with classic aromas of grass cuttings, nettles and a mineral quality. The palate is weighty with tangy grapefruit, gooseberries and electrifying, crisp acidity which makes it all the more vivacious. *Searsons*

| | |
|---|---|
| *Price* | €12–€15 |
| *Region* | Marlborough |
| *Grape* | Sauvignon Blanc |
| *Alc/vol* | 13% |
| *Food* | Cheese/goats' cheese |
| *Drink* | 2002–3 |

### Montana Vineyard Selection Reserve Sauvignon Blanc 01 ☆

A lovely, zingy, racy style. Upfront aromas are of asparagus, peas and pineapple. The palate is packed with rich, ripe, exotic flavours—passion fruit, mango and green pineapple. *Grants*

| | |
|---|---|
| *Price* | €12–€15 |
| *Region* | Marlborough |
| *Grape* | Sauvignon Blanc |
| *Alc/vol* | 13.5% |
| *Food* | Seafood/crab cakes |
| *Drink* | 2002–4 |

## The Crossings Sauvignon Blanc 01

Lean and green style of Sauvignon Blanc, bone dry with crisp acidity. Delightful, classic aromas of asparagus and abundant flavours of lime, green fruit and grapefruit. *Cassidy*

| | |
|---|---|
| *Price* | €12–€15 |
| *Region* | Marlborough |
| *Grape* | Sauvignon Blanc |
| *Alc/vol* | 13.5% |
| *Food* | Apéritif/salads |
| *Drink* | 2002–3 |

## Villa Maria Private Bin Riesling 01 ☆☆

Accomplished, appealing, fresh style with an aromatic nose showing good herbal and mineral elements. The palate is appley, green and peppery with a great balance of fruit and acidity—the hallmark of an excellent Riesling. *Allied Drinks*

| | |
|---|---|
| *Price* | €12–€15 |
| *Region* | Marlborough |
| *Grape* | Riesling |
| *Alc/vol* | 12.5% |
| *Food* | Seafood/squid |
| *Drink* | 2002–4 |

## Wairau River Sauvignon Blanc 01 ☆

Luscious and lively with exotic aromas of pineapple and paw paw and a concentrated, bone-dry palate packed with citrus and peapod flavours. *TDL*

| | |
|---|---|
| *Price* | €12–€15 |
| *Region* | Marlborough |
| *Grape* | Sauvignon Blanc |
| *Alc/vol* | 13% |
| *Food* | Meat/black pudding |
| *Drink* | 2002–4 |

## Wither Hills Chardonnay 99 ☆

Rich aromas of sweet fruit, vanilla and hints of honey. Flavoursome and generous palate with honeyed, tropical fruit flavours and oaky vanilla giving a weighty feel and texture. *Oddbins*

| | |
|---|---|
| *Price* | €12–€15 |
| *Region* | Marlborough |
| *Grape* | Chardonnay |
| *Alc/vol* | 13.5% |
| *Food* | Fish/smoked salmon |
| *Drink* | 2002–3 |

## Wither Hills Sauvignon Blanc 01

Fruity, opulent and refreshing, this has gooseberry and apple aromas and flavours of lemon trifle, ripe pineapple and passion fruit. It leaves a lovely, tingling feeling that says 'more, please'. *Comans*

| | |
|---|---|
| *Price* | €12–€15 |
| *Region* | Marlborough |
| *Grape* | Sauvignon Blanc |
| *Alc/vol* | 13% |
| *Food* | Vegetables/asparagus |
| *Drink* | 2002–3 |

### €15–€18

## Babich Winemaker's Reserve Sauvignon Blanc 01

A gentler, smoky style of Sauvignon Blanc from New Zealand. Lemon sherbet acidity gives a nice, zingy twist but this is balanced against plenty of tropical fruit and peapod flavours. *Gleeson*

| | |
|---|---|
| *Price* | €15–€18 |
| *Region* | Marlborough |
| *Grape* | Sauvignon Blanc |
| *Alc/vol* | 13.5% |
| *Food* | Cheese/goats' cheese |
| *Drink* | 2002–3 |

## Grove Mill Sauvignon Blanc 01 ☆☆☆

Fabulous fruit character with fresh, lively acidity. The aromas are perfumed with honeysuckle and crêpe suzette and the ripe, textured palate has cream and melon flavours, perfect structure, balance and concentration. A really delicious wine. *Woodford Bourne*

| | |
|---|---|
| Price | €15–€18 |
| Region | Marlborough |
| Grape | Sauvignon Blanc |
| Alc/vol | 13.5% |
| Food | Fish/mullet |
| Drink | 2002–5 |

## Huia Pinot Gris 01 ☆☆

Gorgeous, flavoursome, classy style, spicy with abundant fruit—apples and pears, peach and lime—lemony acidity and a wonderful, lengthy finish. *Searsons*

| | |
|---|---|
| Price | €15–€18 |
| Region | Marlborough |
| Grape | Pinot Gris |
| Alc/vol | 14% |
| Food | Quiches/Quiche Lorraine |
| Drink | 2002–4 |

## Lawson's Dry Hills Riesling 99

Excellent, steely style with plenty of ripe apple fruit, gripping limy acidity and very good length. *Febvre*

| | |
|---|---|
| Price | €15–€18 |
| Region | Marlborough |
| Grape | Riesling |
| Alc/vol | 13% |
| Food | Vegetarian/avocado |
| Drink | 2003–4 |

## Tohu Sauvignon Blanc 01

Grassy, nettle and floral aromas abound in a light, gently fruity wine with all the crisp citrus, asparagus and vegetal flavours you would expect in such a classic style.
*Waterford Wine Vault*

| | |
|---|---|
| Price | €15–€18 |
| Region | Marlborough |
| Grape | Sauvignon Blanc |
| Alc/vol | 13% |
| Food | Cheese/goats' cheese |
| Drink | 2002–3 |

## Waipara Hills Sauvignon Blanc 01

Good example of a nicely styled Sauvignon with strong nettle and asparagus scents on the nose and quite a full-flavoured palate with vegetal, gooseberry and green fruit flavours. Crisp and refreshing. *Koala Wines*

| | |
|---|---|
| Price | €15–€18 |
| Region | Marlborough |
| Grape | Sauvignon Blanc |
| Alc/vol | 13% |
| Food | Seafood/clams |
| Drink | 2002–3 |

### €18–€22

## Felton Road Dry Riesling 01 ☆

Bright and zesty with a very smooth texture and attractive, refined palate. Flavours of citrus peel, lemon, lime, mineral and leafy herbs and just a touch of honey. *Fields*

| | |
|---|---|
| Price | €18–€22 |
| Region | Central Otago |
| Grape | Riesling |
| Alc/vol | 10% |
| Food | Fish/gravlax |
| Drink | 2002–5 |

## Goldwater Dog Point Sauvignon Blanc 01

A lighter style of New Zealand Sauvignon offering lots of fresh, zippy gooseberry and lime zest with a distinctive smokiness and nettley, green flavours. *Taserra*

| | |
|---|---|
| *Price* | €18–€22 |
| *Region* | Marlborough |
| *Grape* | Sauvignon Blanc |
| *Alc/vol* | 14% |
| *Food* | Seafood/crab |
| *Drink* | 2002–3 |

## Hunter's Sauvignon Blanc 01 ☆

Swirl the glass to get wonderful green aromas of mange tout and pineapple. This is a delicious, fresh, frisky wine with lots of ripe, juicy citrus and crisp apple flavours. *Gilbeys*

| | |
|---|---|
| *Price* | €18–€22 |
| *Region* | Marlborough |
| *Grape* | Sauvignon Blanc |
| *Alc/vol* | 13% |
| *Food* | Fish/Thai |
| *Drink* | 2002–4 |

## Waimarie Gimblett Road Chardonnay 99 ☆

Impressive and terribly elegant. The nose has aromas of pineapple and vanilla fudge and the palate has fresh pineapple flavours with good acidity and a lingering, crisp citrus finish. *Fields*

| | |
|---|---|
| *Price* | €18–€22 |
| *Region* | Central Otago |
| *Grape* | Chardonnay |
| *Alc/vol* | 13.5% |
| *Food* | Seafood/scallops |
| *Drink* | 2002–3 |

# Red

### €12–€15

## Babich Winemakers Reserve Syrah 99 ☆☆

The really peppery nose with plenty of clove and white pepper is matched by an equally peppery palate with big and rich black fruit and fennel flavours. *Gleeson*

| | |
|---|---|
| *Price* | €12–€15 |
| *Region* | Hawkes Bay |
| *Grape* | Syrah |
| *Alc/vol* | 13% |
| *Food* | Meat/bacon |
| *Drink* | 2002–5 |

### €15–€18

## Babich Winemaker's Reserve Pinot Noir 99

Perfumed nose with floral aromas and some medicinal and liquorice elements. The palate is light bodied and lightly fruity with hints of cherries and redcurrants and good persistence of flavour. *Gleeson*

| | |
|---|---|
| *Price* | €15–€18 |
| *Region* | Marlborough |
| *Grape* | Pinot Noir |
| *Alc/vol* | 12% |
| *Food* | Meat/pork |
| *Drink* | 2002–3 |

## Hunter's Pinot Noir 99

Oozing charm and flavour this is a light but ripe Pinot Noir with strawberries, spice and pleasant, soft tannins. *Gilbeys*

| | |
|---|---|
| *Price* | €15–€18 |
| *Region* | Marlborough |
| *Grape* | Pinot Noir |
| *Alc/vol* | 13.5% |
| *Food* | Poultry/duck |
| *Drink* | 2002–4 |

## Montana Reserve Pinot Noir 99

Delicately perfumed aromas of earth, red berries
and chocolate with flavours of ripe strawberries
in a very good Pinot which will hold up well for
a number of years. *Grants*

| | |
|---|---|
| *Price* | €15–€18 |
| *Region* | Marlborough |
| *Grape* | Pinot Noir |
| *Alc/vol* | 13.5% |
| *Food* | Poultry/chicken |
| *Drink* | 2002–3 |

## Villa Maria Private Bin Cabernet Sauvignon Merlot 99

Attractive and elegant, light style with a stalky,
red berry nose and richer raspberry and redcurrant fruit on the palate with good ripe tannins. *Allied Drinks*

| | |
|---|---|
| *Price* | €15–€18 |
| *Region* | Hawkes Bay |
| *Grape* | Cab Sauv/Merlot |
| *Alc/vol* | 12.5% |
| *Food* | Poultry/goose |
| *Drink* | 2002–3 |

### €18–€22

## Lawson's Dry Hills Pinot Noir 01

The youth of this wine shows in its high level
of ripe, spicy black cherry fruits and firm tannins. Quite a full, powerful style with an earthy,
smoky and spicy character. *Febvre*

| | |
|---|---|
| *Price* | €18–€22 |
| *Region* | Marlborough |
| *Grape* | Pinot Noir |
| *Alc/vol* | 13.5% |
| *Food* | Fish/tuna |
| *Drink* | 2003–5 |

### €25–€30

## Cloudy Bay Pinot Noir 99 ☆

Big nose with aromas of ripe cherries, black
forest gâteau, jam, spice and earthiness. Equally
big and fruity palate with dark cherry and spice,
layers of complexity—clearly evolving nicely.
*Findlaters*

| | |
|---|---|
| *Price* | €25–€30 |
| *Region* | Marlborough |
| *Grape* | Pinot Noir |
| *Alc/vol* | 13.5% |
| *Food* | Game/pheasant |
| *Drink* | 2002–4 |

### €30–€35

## Esk Valley Merlot/Cabernet Sauvignon 99 ☆☆

Pronounced cassis and green pepper nose is
followed by an amazing intensity of chewy flavours, predominately mint and blackcurrants.
This generous wine is also quite peppery, spicy
and punchy. *Findlaters*

| | |
|---|---|
| *Price* | €30–€35 |
| *Region* | Hawkes Bay |
| *Grape* | Merlot/Cab Sauv |
| *Alc/vol* | 13.5% |
| *Food* | Meat/steak |
| *Drink* | 2002–4 |

# Portugal

Anyone with an interest in wine who has travelled to Portugal will enthuse about the fantastic range of wines available there. We have tried to reflect this richness in the guide and the number of Portuguese wines listed this year has greatly increased. They are made from a mix of classic and indigenous grape varieties and hail from the major regions from north to south. Many are from top class estates, including Duas Quintas, Esporão, Palha-Canas and Luis Pato.

Unfortunately, it has to be admitted that Portuguese wines are poorly represented in Ireland. The majority of outlets don't stock any wines from Portugal and even in the more adventurous shops, with the express intention of selling interesting wine, it is hard to find more than a handful of Portuguese labels. This is a shame. Portugal represents a great opportunity to importers and wine sellers and it would be good to see more rising to the challenge.

## White

### Under €9

#### Caves Bonifácio VdM Branco **nv**

Golden hues with a ripe mature floral bouquet. Crisp acidity on the palate with very mature, nutty flavours of pecans, walnuts, hazelnuts and toffee apples. A distinctive style, best suited to food. *Peter Dalton*

| | |
|---|---|
| Price | Under €9 |
| Region | Ribatejo |
| Alc/vol | 12.5% |
| Food | Fish/salmon |
| Drink | 2002–3 |

### €9–€12

#### Quinta de Azevedo DOC Vinho Verde **01**

Textbook Vinho Verde at its best. Vibrant, youthful, fresh nose of kiwi, gooseberry and sweet pea flowers. Crunchy green apple and asparagus flavours. Refreshing, crisp acidity and a delicious spritz bring the fruit to life. *Febvre*

| | |
|---|---|
| Price | €9–€12 |
| Region | Vinho Verde |
| Grape | Loureiro/Pederna |
| Alc/vol | 10% |
| Food | Fish/salads |
| Drink | 2002–3 |

## Red

### Under €9

#### Almargem VQPRD Palmela **96**

Very fruity wine with a nose of ripe strawberries and pepper and a richer palate of cassis and blackberries with soft tannins. *WineOnline*

| | |
|---|---|
| Price | Under €9 |
| Region | Palmela |
| Grape | Castelão Frâncès/ Periquita |
| Alc/vol | 12.5% |
| Food | Fish/tuna |
| Drink | 2002–3 |

## Caves Bonifácio VdM Tinto **nv**

A rustic and chewy wine with individuality. Concentrated nose of blackberries and plums and an earthy, stewed fruit palate with rosemary and thyme. *Peter Dalton*

| | |
|---|---|
| *Price* | Under €9 |
| *Alc/vol* | 12% |
| *Food* | Poultry/chicken |
| *Drink* | On purchase |

## JP Barrel Selection Red Wine VR Terras do Sado **96 €**

A wine of very fine character, oozing flavour. Layers of ripe blackberry and plum flavours, with hints of spice and chocolate and appealing ripe tannins. Drinking well now. *Tesco*

| | |
|---|---|
| *Price* | Under €9 |
| *Region* | Terras do Sado |
| *Grape* | Periquita |
| *Alc/vol* | 13% |
| *Food* | Meat/pork |
| *Drink* | 2002–3 |

## Terra das Fragas DOC Douro **96**

Strawberry and blackberry nose with earthy touches and a surprising, juicy mouthful of concentrated, ripe black fruit, strawberry and chocolate flavours with a spicy aftertaste. *WineOnline*

| | |
|---|---|
| *Price* | Under €9 |
| *Region* | Douro |
| *Grape* | Touriga Nacional/ Tinta Roriz |
| *Alc/vol* | 12% |
| *Food* | Poultry/chicken |
| *Drink* | 2002–3 |

### €9–€12

## Cardeal Reserva DOC Dão **98**

An example of just how fruity Dão wines can be. Intense fruit—blackcurrant, damson, cherry and strawberry—on both nose and palate. *WineOnline*

| | |
|---|---|
| *Price* | €9–€12 |
| *Region* | Dão |
| *Grape* | Touriga Nacional blend |
| *Alc/vol* | 12% |
| *Food* | Meat/stews |
| *Drink* | 2002–3 |

## Duque de Viseu DOC Dão **99**

Subtle but complex nose with layers of bramble fruits and vegetal and spice tones. Appetising burst of ripe raspberry and cherry flavours with a subtle wood influence giving balance and creaminess and some mellow tobacco tones. *Febvre*

| | |
|---|---|
| *Price* | €9–€12 |
| *Region* | Dão |
| *Grape* | Touriga Nacional/ Tinta Roriz/ Alfrocheiro/Jaen |
| *Alc/vol* | 12.5% |
| *Food* | Meat/lamb |
| *Drink* | 2002–4 |

## José da Sousa VR Alentejo **96**

Mature nose of dried fruits and leather with a palate of redcurrant, cherry, prune and spice flavours. Impressive winemaking from Portugal showing the elegance and complexity of native varieties. *Gilbeys*

| | |
|---|---|
| *Price* | €9–€12 |
| *Region* | Alentejo |
| *Grape* | Trincadeira/ Aragonês/Bastardo |
| *Alc/vol* | 12.5% |
| *Food* | Meat/lamb |
| *Drink* | 2002–3 |

## Primum  99

A food-friendly, everyday wine with strong aromas of raspberries, cashew nuts and dates and a smoky, red fruit palate with lemon peel crispness. *Gilbeys*

| | |
|---|---|
| *Price* | €9–€12 |
| *Region* | Estremadura |
| *Grape* | Touriga Nacional/ Touriga Franca/ Tinto Cão |
| *Food* | Meat/ham |
| *Drink* | 2002–3 |

## Quinta d'Almergem Garrafeira DOC Ribatejo **96**

Upfront, black fruit nose and an equally fruity, well-balanced palate with blackberry, plum and blackcurrant flavours and an almost tea-like character. *WineOnline*

| | |
|---|---|
| *Price* | €9–€12 |
| *Region* | Ribatejo |
| *Grape* | Periquita blend |
| *Alc/vol* | 12.5% |
| *Food* | Meat/barbecue |
| *Drink* | 2002–3 |

## Quinta de Pancas Cabernet Sauvignon VR Estremadura **97**

Perfumed nose of plum, pepper and herbal aromas with a redcurrant, dried fruit, smoky and leathery palate. Slightly rustic but holding its age well. *Terroirs*

| | |
|---|---|
| *Price* | €9–€12 |
| *Region* | Estremadura |
| *Grape* | Cabernet Sauvignon |
| *Alc/vol* | 12% |
| *Food* | Meat/pork |
| *Drink* | 2002–3 |

## Quinta do Crasto DOC Douro **00**

Heated and concentrated black fruit nose with quite a mellow palate of black cherry and blackcurrant flavours and some floral elements. *Oddbins*

| | |
|---|---|
| *Price* | €9–€12 |
| *Region* | Douro |
| *Grape* | Tinta Roriz/Tinta Barroca/Tinta Francesca |
| *Alc/vol* | 13.5% |
| *Food* | Meat/beef |
| *Drink* | 2002–5 |

### €12–€15

## Duas Quintas DOC Douro **99**

Subtle, elegant aromas of strawberry and raspberry. Tannins are fully ripe and the flavours are of blackberry and plum with a spicy, slightly rustic and earthy character. *Searsons*

| | |
|---|---|
| *Price* | €12–€15 |
| *Region* | Douro |
| *Grape* | Tinta Roriz/ Touriga Nacional |
| *Alc/vol* | 12% |
| *Food* | Meat/roasts |
| *Drink* | 2002–4 |

## Luis Pato DOC Barraida **98** ☆

Big wine of character with an unusual nose of blackcurrants and boiled ham and an intense, delicious mouthful of blackcurrant and spice and a meaty and savoury palate. *Karwig Wines*

| | |
|---|---|
| *Price* | €12–€15 |
| *Region* | Bairrada |
| *Grape* | Baga |
| *Alc/vol* | 13% |
| *Food* | Meat/veal |
| *Drink* | 2002–5 |

## Palha-Canas VR Estremadura **00**

Made in a modern style with great colour, good structure and oodles of black, juicy fruits. The kind of wine that might tempt lovers of Australian wine back to Europe. *Searsons*

| | |
|---|---|
| Price | €12–€15 |
| Region | Estremadura |
| Grape | Periquita/Camarate/ Touriga Nacional |
| Alc/vol | 13% |
| Food | Meat/pork |
| Drink | 2002–4 |

## Quinta do Cachão DOC Douro **99**

A very fine, youthful wine. Quite port-like without the added alcohol, it hints at port aromas with rich damsons and tobacco while on the palate it has very ripe plum, blackcurrant and smoky spices *Karwig Wines*

| | |
|---|---|
| Price | €12–€15 |
| Region | Douro |
| Grape | Tinta Barocca |
| Alc/vol | 14% |
| Food | Meat/beef |
| Drink | 2002–3 |

### €15–€18

## Esporão Reserva DOC Alentejo **99**

Fruit- and spice-driven aromas and flavours of intense cassis, vanilla and elderflower. Beautifully crafted and balanced, the wine is drinking well now but it would be worth keeping some bottles for future pleasure. *Karwig Wines*

| | |
|---|---|
| Price | €15–€18 |
| Region | Alentejo |
| Grape | Trincadaira/Aragonês/ Cabernet Sauvignon |
| Alc/vol | 13.5% |
| Food | Meat/lamb |
| Drink | 2002–4 |

---

*How to use this book*
*The wines are listed in order of country/region, colour (red or white), price band, then by name. If you can't quickly find the wine you are looking for try the index, which we have expanded for this edition. There are separate chapters for rosé, sparkling (including Champagne) and sweet wines. Since wine prices are not fixed the price bands are guidelines only. The dates suggested for when to drink the wines do not indicate their expected life but the period over which our tasters thought they would enjoy them most.*

# Romania

Romania hasn't really capitalised on its popularity of the early 90s when Romanian wines made from Pinot Noir and other international varieties, e.g. Chardonnay, Cabernet Sauvignon and Merlot, first became readily available. While they were inexpensive and occasionally very good, the quality varied. As a general rule, Romanian wines at lower prices are best consumed when young and very old vintages should be approached with caution.

## Red

### Under €9

#### Rovit Winery Special Reserve Cabernet Sauvignon 98

Easy drinking in a light, soft and fruity style with red currants, cherries and hints of spice. *Barry & Fitzwilliam*

| | |
|---|---|
| Price | Under €9 |
| Region | Dealul Mare |
| Grape | Cabernet Sauvignon |
| Alc/vol | 12.5% |
| Food | Cheese/Cheddar |
| Drink | 2002–3 |

### €9–€12

#### Sahateni Vineyards Reserve Merlot 98

Quite a juicy wine with a sweet caramel, strawberry nose and light raspberry and strawberry flavours. *Barry & Fitzwilliam*

| | |
|---|---|
| Price | €9–€12 |
| Region | Dealul Mare |
| Grape | Merlot |
| Alc/vol | 13% |
| Food | Meat/sausages |
| Drink | 2002–3 |

| The symbols | |
|---|---|
| ❧ | *Organic* |
| € | *Exceptionally good value* |
| ☆ | *Accomplished, showing above average quality or character making it worthy of extra attention* |
| ☆☆ | *Excellent with great character, style and complexity* |
| ☆☆☆ | *Wonderful, showing terrific character and complexity, true to its origins* |
| ☆☆☆☆ | *Exceptional, with considerable complexity and classic balance. Rewards serious tasting.* |

# South Africa

South Africa's share of the wine market in Ireland is growing and currently stands at about 8 per cent, just ahead of Italy. The wines available here represent a good cross section, from budget wines to more expensive, prestige estate blends, the top names in their field, too many to mention but well represented in the guide.

This year, South Africa provided the Best Value White Wine of the Year—Clos Malverne Sauvignon Blanc 02 (see page 214). Sauvignon Blanc covers around 5 per cent of the vineyard area in South Africa; the examples from Stellenbosch and Elgin are particularly good and have been improving for some time. Vivid and crisp, with distinctive green flavours of nettles, gooseberries and asparagus, their style falls somewhere between Sauvignons from the Loire in the Old World and hot climate examples from Australia and California. Chardonnays are made in a range of styles and rank with the best that the New World has to offer. The red blends are most impressive, offering complexity and interest, for example the star wines of Kanonkop, Rust en Vrede and Warwick. The single red varietals are also very good, Cabernet Sauvignon, Merlot and Shiraz all make their mark as do some very good examples of Pinotage.

## White

### Under €9

### Bellingham Sauvignon Blanc 01 €

Aromas suggest a good concentration of tropical fruits but a much more biting palate emerges with crisp, zingy acidity and mouth-watering freshness from lots of lemon juice, pineapple, gooseberry and green apple flavours. The finish is peppery. *Cassidy*

| | |
|---|---|
| *Price* | **Under €9** |
| *Region* | **Coastal Region** |
| *Grape* | **Sauvignon Blanc** |
| *Alc/vol* | **13.5%** |
| *Food* | **Vegetarian/tomato dishes** |
| *Drink* | **2002–3** |

> **Coastal Region** *is a term indicating that the grapes have been sourced from one or more of a number of regions—it includes Swartland, Tulbagh, Paarl and Stellenbosch and the wards of Constantia and Durbanville.*

### Flagstone Noon Gun White 01

The lightly fruity nose has a stony character which is followed by a warming and smooth palate of ripe apple with hints of spice. *Oddbins*

| | |
|---|---|
| *Price* | **Under €9** |
| *Region* | **Coastal Region** |
| *Grape* | **Sauvignon Blanc/ Chardonnay/Chenin Blanc/Riesling** |
| *Alc/vol* | **13.5%** |
| *Food* | **Seafood/prawns** |
| *Drink* | **2002–3** |

## Kleinrivier Chardonnay 00 €

Attractive, elegant style. Beguiling nose of apricot and honey aromas and a very fresh palate with lemon and lime flavours. *Molloys*

| | |
|---|---|
| *Price* | Under €9 |
| *Region* | Western Cape |
| *Grape* | Chardonnay |
| *Alc/vol* | 13.5% |
| *Food* | Indian/curries |
| *Drink* | 2002–3 |

The **Western Cape** covers a vast area and includes all the main wine-producing regions in South Africa.

## KWV Chenin Blanc 01

Distinctive and different with a fresh, green, grassy nose and a very zesty palate with restrained, light apple and pear flavours. Crisp acidity demands food, maybe pork with apple or sage. *TDL*

| | |
|---|---|
| *Price* | Under €9 |
| *Region* | Western Cape |
| *Grape* | Chenin Blanc |
| *Alc/vol* | 12.5% |
| *Food* | Meat/pork |
| *Drink* | 2002–3 |

## Scholtzenhof Petit Chenin 01

Very pleasant, spicy nose with quite an array of fruit flavours ranging from apple to pear to pineapple. Easy going, light and fruity with good spice definition. *Oddbins*

| | |
|---|---|
| *Price* | Under €9 |
| *Region* | Stellenbosch |
| *Grape* | Chenin Blanc |
| *Alc/vol* | 13.5% |
| *Food* | Chinese/spring rolls |
| *Drink* | 2002–3 |

## Vaughan Johnson's Good Everyday Cape White nv

Simple and uncomplicated but well made, light and subtle in style with green apple aromas and flavours and refreshing acidity. *Papillon*

| | |
|---|---|
| *Price* | Under €9 |
| *Region* | Western Cape |
| *Grape* | Blend of four grapes |
| *Alc/vol* | 12.5% |
| *Food* | Vegetables/roasted |
| *Drink* | 2002–3 |

### €9–€12

## Backsberg Estate Chenin Blanc 01

Quite an intense and herbal nose with a lemon sorbet- and pear-flavoured palate. A very pleasant wine, nicely balanced with good acidity and good fruit flavours. *Papillon*

| | |
|---|---|
| *Price* | €9–€12 |
| *Region* | Paarl |
| *Grape* | Chenin Blanc |
| *Alc/vol* | 13% |
| *Food* | Seafood/squid |
| *Drink* | 2002–3 |

## Blue White Chenin Blanc 98

Rich yellow colour with honey aromas and a really big, dryish palate full of honey, baked apple and lemon flavours with butter and vanilla. Very distinctive and probably best with rich food—pork, monkfish or veal.
*Barry & Fitzwilliam*

| | |
|---|---|
| *Price* | €9–€12 |
| *Region* | Stellenbosch |
| *Grape* | Chenin Blanc |
| *Alc/vol* | 14% |
| *Food* | Meat/pork |
| *Drink* | 2002–3 |

## Clos Malverne Sauvignon Blanc 02 ☆☆☆ €

Wonderfully intense, layered bouquet displaying nettles, cut grass and tropical fruit. Explosive palate with classic flavours of green fruit, blackcurrant leaf and nettles and lusher pineapple and mango. Great texture and superb length. *Dunnes Stores*

| | |
|---|---|
| *Price* | €9–€12 |
| *Region* | Stellenbosch |
| *Grape* | Sauvignon Blanc |
| *Alc/vol* | 13.3% |
| *Food* | Cheese/goats' cheese |
| *Drink* | 2002–3 |

## Delheim Sauvignon Blanc 01 ☆ €

Interesting, minerally nose with hints of asparagus, gooseberry and fresh, grassy tones. Packed with ripe citrus flavours and tropical fruit. This is a vibrant, juicy and lively style which would work well with simple, fresh dishes. *O'Briens*

| | |
|---|---|
| *Price* | €9–€12 |
| *Region* | Stellenbosch |
| *Grape* | Sauvignon Blanc |
| *Alc/vol* | 13.5% |
| *Food* | Seafood/prawns |
| *Drink* | 2002–3 |

## Kleine Zalze Unwooded Chardonnay 99

Quite a deep-coloured wine with a hot-climate character and ripeness. Flavours of ripe peach, melon, pineapple and herbs, nice structure and good acidity. *Papillon*

| | |
|---|---|
| *Price* | €9–€12 |
| *Region* | Stellenbosch |
| *Grape* | Chardonnay |
| *Alc/vol* | 13% |
| *Food* | Poultry/smoked chicken |
| *Drink* | 2002–3 |

## Paul Cluver Weisser Riesling 01

Appetising, green and crisp style with nettle and vegetal aromas, lively, lemony acidity and flavours of lime, grapefruit and green apple. *Findlaters*

| | |
|---|---|
| *Price* | €9–€12 |
| *Region* | Elgin |
| *Grape* | Riesling |
| *Alc/vol* | 13% |
| *Food* | Meat/bacon |
| *Drink* | 2002–3 |

## Robert's Rock Chenin Blanc Chardonnay 01

Attractive, fruity style with aromas of peach, honeysuckle and Golden Delicious apples. Beautifully balanced palate with flavours of honey, pear and tangerine. Pleasing to a range of tastes—a good party wine. *TDL*

| | |
|---|---|
| *Price* | €9–€12 |
| *Region* | Western Cape |
| *Grape* | Chenin Blanc/ Chardonnay |
| *Alc/vol* | 13% |
| *Food* | Apéritif/starters |
| *Drink* | 2002–3 |

## Simonsig Estate Chardonnay 98

Nice intensity of honeyed fruits with a forward oakiness on the nose and a delightfully luscious palate of pineapple in syrup, banana, toffee and a rich butteriness. *Comans*

| | |
|---|---|
| *Price* | €9–€12 |
| *Region* | Stellenbosch |
| *Grape* | Chardonnay |
| *Alc/vol* | 13% |
| *Food* | Vegetarian/leeks |
| *Drink* | 2002–3 |

## Spier Chardonnay 00

Pronounced aromas of tropical fruits and warm vanilla. The concentration carries through in the mouth with ripe pineapples, apples and limes, crisp, zingy acidity and a good finish. *Allied Drinks*

| | |
|---|---|
| Price | €9–€12 |
| Region | Western Cape |
| Grape | Chardonnay |
| Alc/vol | 13% |
| Food | Fish/cod |
| Drink | 2002–3 |

## Villiera Chenin Blanc 01

Weighty nose with ripe pear and tangerine aromas. The palate shows full flavours of sweet ripe fruit, baked apples, apricots and melon with a luscious, oily mouthfeel. *Grants*

| | |
|---|---|
| Price | €9–€12 |
| Region | Paarl |
| Grape | Chenin Blanc |
| Alc/vol | 14.5% |
| Food | Meat/veal |
| Drink | 2002–3 |

## Zalse Chardonnay 01

Appealing, versatile style, good for a dinner party or apéritif. Crisp and fruity with apple, lime and lemon flavours balanced by fresh acidity. *MacCormaic*

| | |
|---|---|
| Price | €9–€12 |
| Region | Stellenbosch |
| Grape | Chardonnay |
| Alc/vol | 14% |
| Food | Apéritif/starters |
| Drink | 2002–3 |

### €12–€15

## Durbanville Hills Chardonnay 00

Fresh and green on the nose—lemon, lime and mineral. The palate is a ripe fruit cocktail with a warming and smooth texture. *Febvre*

| | |
|---|---|
| Price | €12–€15 |
| Region | Durbanville |
| Grape | Chardonnay |
| Alc/vol | 14% |
| Food | Fish/monkfish |
| Drink | 2002–3 |

## Jordan Sauvignon Blanc 97

Golden in colour and showing maturity. Caramel on the nose together with herbs, green salad and stony aromas and a spicy and herb-flavoured palate. Interesting to taste a Sauvignon of this age. *Maxxium*

| | |
|---|---|
| Price | €12–€15 |
| Region | Stellenbosch |
| Grape | Sauvignon Blanc |
| Alc/vol | 13% |
| Food | Fish/hake |
| Drink | 2002–3 |

## Neil Ellis Groenekloof Sauvignon Blanc 01

Sauvignon Blanc in a lively style with an extremely pungent nose of mange tout and asparagus. The palate has ripe citrus flavours of lemon, lime and grapefruit and some spiciness. *Findlaters*

| | |
|---|---|
| Price | €12–€15 |
| Region | Darling Hills |
| Grape | Sauvignon Blanc |
| Alc/vol | 13.5% |
| Food | Fish/mackerel |
| Drink | 2002–3 |

## Paul Cluver Chardonnay 01 ☆

Rich, concentrated and toasty aromas precede a fruit-packed palate bursting with ripe pineapple and buttery, lemon pancake flavours. *Findlaters*

| | |
|---|---|
| *Price* | €12–€15 |
| *Region* | Elgin |
| *Grape* | Chardonnay |
| *Alc/vol* | 13.5% |
| *Food* | Fish/haddock |
| *Drink* | 2002–3 |

## Paul Cluver Sauvignon Blanc 01

Very appealing nose, soft yet layered with black-currant leaf and tropical fruit. Rounded palate with crisp acidity and nettle, gooseberry and lime flavours. Stylishly made. *Findlaters*

| | |
|---|---|
| *Price* | €12–€15 |
| *Region* | Elgin |
| *Grape* | Sauvignon Blanc |
| *Alc/vol* | 13.5% |
| *Food* | Indian/Tandoori |
| *Drink* | 2002–3 |

### €15–€18

## Groot Constantia Sauvignon Blanc 01

Very fresh with some spritz on pouring. The attractively fragrant nose has lemon, goose-berry and herbaceous aromas. There is mineral on the palate with some sherbet, zesty lemon acidity and gooseberry and melon flavours. *Irish Distillers*

| | |
|---|---|
| *Price* | €15–€18 |
| *Region* | Constantia |
| *Grape* | Sauvignon Blanc |
| *Alc/vol* | 14% |
| *Food* | Fish/halibut |
| *Drink* | 2002–3 |

## Jordan Chardonnay 96 ☆

Great power and concentration on the nose with rich, fleshy fruits and buttery and hazelnut notes. Flavours are fruity, vegetal and spicy with a long, lingering finish. Still drinking beautifully and has further to go. *Maxxium*

| | |
|---|---|
| *Price* | €15–€18 |
| *Region* | Stellenbosch |
| *Grape* | Chardonnay |
| *Alc/vol* | 13% |
| *Food* | Poultry/turkey |
| *Drink* | 2002–3 |

## Plaisir de Merle Chardonnay 99

Broad, ample aromas of cinnamon and melon with evident but agreeable oaking. On the palate there is more lively citrus fruit offset by spicy oak and a big finish. *Dillons*

| | |
|---|---|
| *Price* | €15–€18 |
| *Region* | Paarl |
| *Grape* | Chardonnay |
| *Alc/vol* | 13% |
| *Food* | Poultry/chicken |
| *Drink* | 2002–3 |

## Waterford Sauvignon Blanc 01

A slightly off-dry character is balanced by crispness and excellent fruit intensity. Assertive herbaceous aromas followed by nettle, gooseberry and green pepper flavours. *Fields*

| | |
|---|---|
| *Price* | €15–€18 |
| *Region* | Stellenbosch |
| *Grape* | Sauvignon Blanc |
| *Alc/vol* | 13.5% |
| *Food* | Vegetarian/asparagus |
| *Drink* | 2002–4 |

€18–€22

## Oude Weltevreden Chardonnay 00

A big wine but nicely balanced with toasty and fruity melon aromas on the nose. It has enticing, rich pear and peach flavours on the palate with lively acidity to keep it in check. *Taserra*

| | |
|---|---|
| *Price* | **€18–€22** |
| *Region* | **Robertson** |
| *Grape* | **Chardonnay** |
| *Alc/vol* | **13.5%** |
| *Food* | **Meat/black pudding** |
| *Drink* | **2002–3** |

# Red

Under €9

## Hutton Ridge Cabernet Sauvignon 00

Blackcurrant, mint and herb nose. Very defined blackcurrant flavours with some vegetal touches and big, assertive tannins. Particularly good finish and decent length. *Barry & Fitzwilliam*

| | |
|---|---|
| *Price* | **Under €9** |
| *Region* | **Swartland** |
| *Grape* | **Cabernet Sauvignon** |
| *Alc/vol* | **13.5%** |
| *Food* | **Meat/frankfurters** |
| *Drink* | **2002–3** |

## Hutton Ridge Cinsault 00

Generous baked fruit and spice aromas. A ripe, fruity palate with some earthiness and soft tannins make this a good, easy-drinking, party-style wine. *Barry & Fitzwilliam*

| | |
|---|---|
| *Price* | **Under €9** |
| *Region* | **Coastal Region** |
| *Grape* | **Cinsault/Ruby Cabernet** |
| *Alc/vol* | **12%** |
| *Food* | **Meat/cold meats** |
| *Drink* | **2002–3** |

## Hutton Ridge Merlot 00

Cheerful colour with sweet damson and plum aromas. Warm and rustic palate with solid fruit concentration, plummy and spicy, with a good bite of tannin which cries out for some red meat. *Barry & Fitzwilliam*

| | |
|---|---|
| *Price* | **Under €9** |
| *Region* | **Western Cape** |
| *Grape* | **Merlot** |
| *Alc/vol* | **14.5%** |
| *Food* | **Meat/beef** |
| *Drink* | **2002–3** |

## Hutton Ridge Pinotage 00 ☆ €

Hearty wine for winter dishes. Appealing aromas of stewed plums, rhubarb and sweet spices and a very concentrated, sweet, minty and fruity palate with hints of dark chocolate and fairly big tannins. *Barry & Fitzwilliam*

| | |
|---|---|
| *Price* | **Under €9** |
| *Region* | **Swartland** |
| *Grape* | **Pinotage** |
| *Alc/vol* | **14%** |
| *Food* | **Meat/casseroles** |
| *Drink* | **2002–3** |

## Hutton Ridge Shiraz 00 ☆ €

Big and very fruity. The nose is laden with spices and the palate is equally rich and concentrated with juicy blackberries, mint and white pepper. Softening tannins and a long finish add to the appeal. *Barry & Fitzwilliam*

| | |
|---|---|
| *Price* | **Under €9** |
| *Region* | **Swartland** |
| *Grape* | **Shiraz** |
| *Alc/vol* | **14.5%** |
| *Food* | **Meat/ribs** |
| *Drink* | **2002–3** |

## Kleinrivier Cabernet Sauvignon Merlot 00

Soft fruity nose is followed by a dry, earthy, Old World-style palate with a punchy blackcurrant flavour. *Molloys*

| | |
|---|---|
| *Price* | Under €9 |
| *Region* | Stellenbosch |
| *Grape* | Cab Sauv/Merlot |
| *Alc/vol* | 13.5% |
| *Food* | Indian/dhal |
| *Drink* | 2002–3 |

## Kleinrivier Pinotage Merlot 00

Pleasant, juicy fruit character with a nice core of blackberry and plum flavours and some leathery and vegetal effects. No real tannins, ready to go and very drinkable. *Molloys*

| | |
|---|---|
| *Price* | Under €9 |
| *Region* | Western Cape |
| *Grape* | Pinotage/Merlot |
| *Alc/vol* | 12.5% |
| *Food* | Meat/barbecue |
| *Drink* | 2002–3 |

## Long Mountain Merlot Shiraz 00 €

A very satisfying wine. Sweet, spicy vanilla combined with plenty of ripe cherries and plums, and good chewy tannins. *Irish Distillers*

| | |
|---|---|
| *Price* | Under €9 |
| *Region* | Western Cape |
| *Grape* | Merlot/Shiraz |
| *Alc/vol* | 13% |
| *Food* | Meat/stews |
| *Drink* | 2002–3 |

## Long Mountain Pinotage 00

Alluring, warm, spicy, leathery nose with plenty of sweet plum aromas. Fleshy, soft fruit and floral flavours are complemented by refreshing acidity. *Irish Distillers*

| | |
|---|---|
| *Price* | Under €9 |
| *Region* | Western Cape |
| *Grape* | Pinotage |
| *Alc/vol* | 13% |
| *Food* | Vegetarian/bean dishes |
| *Drink* | 2002–3 |

## Oude Kaap Cabernet Sauvignon Merlot 01

Very typical South African character and well made. Blackberry jam nose and ripe blackcurrant flavours on the palate, slightly earthy with very good bite. *Dunnes Stores*

| | |
|---|---|
| *Price* | Under €9 |
| *Region* | Western Cape |
| *Grape* | Cab Sauv/Merlot |
| *Alc/vol* | 13.5% |
| *Food* | Meat/barbecue |
| *Drink* | 2002–3 |

## Vaughan Johnson's Good Everyday Cape Red nv €

An unusual and pleasing style of wine with pronounced, creamy, ripe bramble fruits on the nose and a good weight of juicy blackcurrant and damson flavours with an earthy touch. *Papillon*

| | |
|---|---|
| *Price* | Under €9 |
| *Region* | Western Cape |
| *Grape* | Mainly Tinta Barocca |
| *Alc/vol* | 14% |
| *Food* | Meat/pork |
| *Drink* | 2002–3 |

## Bellingham Classic Cabernet Merlot 01

Particularly charming and classy nose, broad, ample and leafy with autumnal fruit and a nicely judged oaky dimension. Good palate with blackcurrant flavours, firm tannins and a dry finish. *Cassidy*

| | |
|---|---|
| Price | €9–€12 |
| Region | Western Cape |
| Grape | Cab Sauv/Merlot |
| Alc/vol | 13.5% |
| Food | Meat/hamburgers |
| Drink | 2002–3 |

## Clos Malverne Pinotage 00

Firm plum, cassis and floral aromas and good, rich fruit flavours with strong tannins and a dry, medicinal finish. Great with food. *Dunnes Stores*

| | |
|---|---|
| Price | €9–€12 |
| Region | Stellenbosch |
| Grape | Pinotage |
| Alc/vol | 14% |
| Food | Meat/stews |
| Drink | 2002–3 |

## Clos Malverne Reserve Pinotage 00

This wine has a solid core of ripe blackcurrant flavours with plum and mulberry, pine cones and vanilla pod nuances. It is also slightly earthy with a nice, dry, tannic finish. *Dunnes Stores*

| | |
|---|---|
| Price | €9–€12 |
| Region | Stellenbosch |
| Grape | Pinotage |
| Alc/vol | 14% |
| Food | Meat/chilli con carne |
| Drink | 2002–3 |

## Kleinrivier Pinotage 00

Powerful, substantial style which is quite rustic and earthy but with good, ripe blackberry and plum skin flavours, pine bark and a medicinal touch. *Molloys*

| | |
|---|---|
| Price | €9–€12 |
| Region | Stellenbosch |
| Grape | Pinotage |
| Alc/vol | 14% |
| Food | Meat/barbecue |
| Drink | 2002–3 |

## KWV Cabernet Sauvignon 99

Showing good bottle development and mellowness, this wine has leathery aromas with blackcurrants, rosehips, pepper and bramble fruit flavours. *TDL*

| | |
|---|---|
| Price | €9–€12 |
| Region | Western Cape |
| Grape | Cabernet Sauvignon |
| Alc/vol | 12.5% |
| Food | Meat/stews |
| Drink | 2002–3 |

## Spier Cabernet Sauvignon 00

Very well balanced with firm tannins and concentrated, ripe, spicy blackcurrant flavours. *Allied Drinks*

| | |
|---|---|
| Price | €9–€12 |
| Region | Western Cape |
| Grape | Cabernet Sauvignon |
| Alc/vol | 13% |
| Food | Meat/ham |
| Drink | 2002–3 |

## Spier Pinotage 00

Subtle aromas and flavours of summer fruits with sweeter blackberries, some new oak showing (pine-kernels) and a dry finish. *Allied Drinks*

| | |
|---|---|
| *Price* | €9–€12 |
| *Region* | Western Cape |
| *Grape* | Pinotage |
| *Alc/vol* | 12.5% |
| *Food* | Meat/barbecue |
| *Drink* | 2002–3 |

## Vaughan Johnson's Sunday Best nv

A very honest and easy style that would suit a summer barbecue. It has sweet, ripe fruits and a touch of smokiness on the nose and an abundance of juicy fruit flavours with leather and smoky, charred touches. *Papillon*

| | |
|---|---|
| *Price* | €9–€12 |
| *Region* | Western Cape |
| *Grape* | Merlot/Shiraz |
| *Alc/vol* | 13% |
| *Food* | Meat/barbecue |
| *Drink* | 2002–3 |

### €12–€15

## Backsberg Estate Merlot 00

Sun-baked fruit and wood shavings on the nose are followed by creamy vanilla and deep berry fruit flavours on the palate, wrapped up in a smooth, velvety texture. *Papillon*

| | |
|---|---|
| *Price* | €12–€15 |
| *Region* | Paarl |
| *Grape* | Merlot |
| *Alc/vol* | 13% |
| *Food* | Meat/liver |
| *Drink* | 2002–3 |

## Clos Malverne Auret Cabernet Sauvignon Pinotage 99

Very appealing and just a little bit different, this wine has aromas of spice and mulberries and a soft, fruity palate with hints of violets and tomato sauce. *Dunnes Stores*

| | |
|---|---|
| *Price* | €12–€15 |
| *Region* | Stellenbosch |
| *Grape* | Cab Sauv/Pinotage/ Merlot |
| *Alc/vol* | 13.5% |
| *Food* | Pasta/meaty sauces |
| *Drink* | 2002–3 |

## Fleur du Cap Cabernet Sauvignon 97 ☆

Stylish, maturing nose with a wealth of aromas—plums, spice, tomatoes, prunes and currants. There are still plenty of juicy blackcurrants and cherries on the palate with fairly soft tannins. *Febvre*

| | |
|---|---|
| *Price* | €12–€15 |
| *Region* | Coastal Region |
| *Grape* | Cabernet Sauvignon |
| *Alc/vol* | 13.5% |
| *Food* | Meat/roasts |
| *Drink* | 2002–3 |

## Graham Beck Cabernet Sauvignon 97 ☆

Ripe and elegant blackberry nose, quite enticing and fragrant. The palate is very smooth with quite a bit of complexity, fruity, spicy and floral with some vegetal elements. Still tannic but developing nicely. *Cassidy*

| | |
|---|---|
| *Price* | €12–€15 |
| *Region* | Robertson |
| *Grape* | Cabernet Sauvignon |
| *Alc/vol* | 13% |
| *Food* | Vegetarian/peppers |
| *Drink* | 2002–3 |

## Kadette Kanonkop Estate Wine 99 ☆☆

Elegant, velvety and outgoing, the nose is attractive and earthy with blackcurrant and spiced plum aromas. The palate is packed with layers of damsons, black cherries, blackcurrant and smoky cedarwood. *Waterford Wine Vault*

| | |
|---|---|
| *Price* | €12–€15 |
| *Region* | Stellenbosch |
| *Grape* | Merlot/Cab Sauv/ Pinotage/Ruby Cab |
| *Alc/vol* | 13% |
| *Food* | Vegetarian/stuffed aubergines |
| *Drink* | 2002–4 |

## Knorhoek Pinotage 00

The nose exudes heat with leather, medicinal and pine needle aromas. The palate is smoky, spicy and earthy with huge tannins backed up by a big, juicy mouthful of berries and bramble flavours. *MacCormaic*

| | |
|---|---|
| *Price* | €12–€15 |
| *Region* | Stellenbosch |
| *Grape* | Pinotage |
| *Alc/vol* | 14% |
| *Food* | Meat/roasts |
| *Drink* | 2002–3 |

## Laborie Estate Cabernet Sauvignon 00

Baked fruits and figs on the nose with a coolness and freshness. The palate offers chewy tannins but very easy drinking with decent flavours of cassis, blackberries and herbs. *TDL*

| | |
|---|---|
| *Price* | €12–€15 |
| *Region* | Paarl |
| *Grape* | Cabernet Sauvignon |
| *Alc/vol* | 13.5% |
| *Food* | Cheese/Cheddar |
| *Drink* | 2002–3 |

## L'Avenir Cabernet Sauvignon 98

Super-ripe aromas of blackcurrants, laden with vanilla, spice and mincemeat which follow through on the palate which is rich, dark and tannic with flavours of cassis and liquorice. *Dunnes Stores*

| | |
|---|---|
| *Price* | €12–€15 |
| *Region* | Stellenbosch |
| *Grape* | Cabernet Sauvignon |
| *Alc/vol* | 13.5% |
| *Food* | Meat/shepherd's pie |
| *Drink* | 2002–3 |

## Le Riche Cabernet Sauvignon 99 ☆

Beautifully balanced, sensual wine with an intensity of ripe, summer berry aromas. The creamy and smoky palate is filled with bramble berry flavours and integrated with oaky vanilla. *Comans*

| | |
|---|---|
| *Price* | €12–€15 |
| *Region* | Stellenbosch |
| *Grape* | Cabernet Sauvignon |
| *Alc/vol* | 12.5% |
| *Food* | Poultry/goose |
| *Drink* | 2002–5 |

## Simonsig Estate Shiraz 99

A showy, upfront wine which will catch your attention. Very ripe blueberry and plum flavours with spiced fruit and eucalyptus; it is also slightly earthy and vegetal. *Comans*

| | |
|---|---|
| *Price* | €12–€15 |
| *Region* | Stellenbosch |
| *Grape* | Shiraz |
| *Alc/vol* | 13.5% |
| *Food* | Meat/barbecue |
| *Drink* | 2002–3 |

## Villiera Cru Monro Cabernet Sauvignon Merlot 98

Stylish and well constructed blend. Plenty of ripe black berry fruit, vanilla essence flavours and gutsy tannins with the Merlot providing the essential juiciness and accessibility. *Grants*

| | |
|---|---|
| *Price* | €12–€15 |
| *Region* | Paarl |
| *Grape* | Cab Sauv/Merlot |
| *Alc/vol* | 13.5% |
| *Food* | Meat/stews |
| *Drink* | 2002–3 |

---

### €15–€18

## Cathedral Cellar Pinotage 96

Lush and powerful with a touch of class. Very ripe cassis and spicy nose with rich overripe, almost jammy, fruit on the palate, overlaid with spicy new oak. *TDL*

| | |
|---|---|
| *Price* | €15–€18 |
| *Region* | Coastal Region |
| *Grape* | Pinotage |
| *Alc/vol* | 13% |
| *Food* | Meat/spicy dishes |
| *Drink* | 2002–3 |

## De Leuwen Jagt Pinotage 01

This wine has a massive and somewhat rustic character. It is opaque with deeply medicinal and mineral notes and lots of baked black-currants together with smoke, spice and tar. *The Wine Seller*

| | |
|---|---|
| *Price* | €15–€18 |
| *Region* | Paarl |
| *Grape* | Pinotage |
| *Food* | Meat/ribs |
| *Drink* | 2002–3 |

## Excelsior Cabernet Sauvignon 01

Fragrant and ripe, fruity nose of blackcurrant jam with oodles of fruit in a velvety-textured palate with a lasting finish. *The Wine Seller*

| | |
|---|---|
| *Price* | €15–€18 |
| *Region* | Robertson |
| *Grape* | Cabernet Sauvignon |
| *Alc/vol* | 14% |
| *Food* | Meat/lamb chops |
| *Drink* | 2002–3 |

## Groot Constantia Pinotage 00

Sweet, smoky, earthy, fruity nose with lots of plum aromas. This is a full and concentrated style, fat but also quite chewy with good tannic grip, stewed fruit and cherry flavours with text-book medicinal touches and an inky-rich finish. *Irish Distillers*

| | |
|---|---|
| *Price* | €15–€18 |
| *Region* | Constantia |
| *Grape* | Pinotage |
| *Alc/vol* | 13.5% |
| *Food* | Meat/stews |
| *Drink* | 2002–4 |

## Knorhoek Cabernet Sauvignon 00

This wine has an intense character. It has huge concentration of ripe blackcurrants with medic-inal and coffee bean aromas, well-structured tannins, plum pudding and spicy blackcurrant flavours with some cedarwood and tobacco. *MacCormaic*

| | |
|---|---|
| *Price* | €15–€18 |
| *Region* | Stellenbosch |
| *Grape* | Cabernet Sauvignon |
| *Alc/vol* | 14% |
| *Food* | Meat/steak |
| *Drink* | 2002–3 |

## Landskroon Shiraz 00

Well-made, mellow, Old World style with spicy red fruit aromas and coffee notes. Juicy and fruity with ripe black plum fruit and spice and mocha on the palate. An absolute pleasure. *Waterford Wine Vault*

| | |
|---|---|
| *Price* | €15–€18 |
| *Region* | Paarl |
| *Grape* | Shiraz |
| *Alc/vol* | 13.5% |
| *Food* | Meat/cassoulet |
| *Drink* | 2002–3 |

## Lanzerac Merlot 98

Mature nose showing ripe berry fruit, vegetal and farmyard aromas. Decent weight of black-currant fruitiness on the palate with mellow tobacco and cigar box flavours. *Gleeson*

| | |
|---|---|
| *Price* | €15–€18 |
| *Region* | Stellenbosch |
| *Grape* | Merlot |
| *Alc/vol* | 12% |
| *Food* | Pasta/tomato sauces |
| *Drink* | 2002–3 |

## Lanzerac Pinotage 98 ☆☆

Perfumed aromas of apple, blackcurrant and elderflower. This follows through to a wonder-ful palate with silky-textured, ripe red fruit, hints of vanilla and dark chocolate and a bitter cherry twist, all underpinned with firm tannins. *Gleeson*

| | |
|---|---|
| *Price* | €15–€18 |
| *Region* | Stellenbosch |
| *Grape* | Pinotage |
| *Alc/vol* | 14% |
| *Food* | Meat/kebabs |
| *Drink* | 2002–3 |

## Paul Cluver Cabernet Sauvignon 98 ☆

Beautifully developed with blackcurrants on the nose and palate together with undertones of mint and vanilla. This wine has plenty of life left and would be a good choice for a special dinner. *Findlaters*

| | |
|---|---|
| *Price* | €15–€18 |
| *Region* | Elgin |
| *Grape* | Cabernet Sauvignon |
| *Alc/vol* | 13.5% |
| *Food* | Meat/lamb |
| *Drink* | 2002–4 |

## Paul Cluver Pinot Noir 00 ☆

Lovely New World Pinot Noir. Aromas of mashed strawberries, smoke, spice and some classic farmyard elements. The palate is quite ripe with strawberry and vanilla flavours, and some green pepper, adding up to a very moreish style. *Findlaters*

| | |
|---|---|
| *Price* | €15–€18 |
| *Region* | Elgin |
| *Grape* | Pinot Noir |
| *Alc/vol* | 13% |
| *Food* | Meat/roasts |
| *Drink* | 2002–3 |

## Plaisir de Merle Cabernet Sauvignon 99

Gentle aromas, ripe if not overly expressive. The palate shows ripe yet taut blackcurrant and cherry flavours,  firm tannins and a dry woodiness. It will benefit from decanting or with more time in bottle. *Dillons*

| | |
|---|---|
| *Price* | €15–€18 |
| *Region* | Paarl |
| *Grape* | Cabernet Sauvignon |
| *Alc/vol* | 13.5% |
| *Food* | Meat/steak |
| *Drink* | 2002–3 |

## Rust en Vrede Shiraz 98 ☆

Extremely vibrant nose of ripe and rich black fruits, floral and spicy. The palate is all about fruit with blackberry, cherry, some spice, mint and liquorice. *O'Briens*

| | |
|---|---|
| Price | €15–€18 |
| Region | Stellenbosch |
| Grape | Shiraz |
| Alc/vol | 13% |
| Food | Meat/goulash |
| Drink | 2002–3 |

## Wildekrans Pinotage 00 ☆

Very definitely Pinotage—brambly, floral, crunchy, herbaceous and medicinal. This is a huge wine, rich on all fronts, tannic, bruising and spicy. *Barry & Fitzwilliam*

| | |
|---|---|
| Price | €15–€18 |
| Region | Walker Bay |
| Grape | Pinotage |
| Alc/vol | 14% |
| Food | Meat/steak |
| Drink | 2002–3 |

### €18–€22

## Simonsig Estate Tiara 97

Ripe blackcurrant and mint nose, which takes a while to open out. Sturdy palate with firm tannins and mature blackcurrant and vegetal flavours which have depth and concentration. *Comans*

| | |
|---|---|
| Price | €18–€22 |
| Region | Stellenbosch |
| Grape | Cab Sauv/Merlot/ |
| | Cab Franc/Petit Verdot |
| Alc/vol | 13% |
| Food | Meat/roasts |
| Drink | 2002–3 |

### €22–€25

## Le Riche Reserve Cabernet Sauvignon 00 ☆☆

Gorgeous wine with complexity and panache, rich, ripe and robust. Blackcurrant, strawberry and oaky vanilla aromas. Abundant blackcurrant, vanilla and cigar box flavours and an excellent creamy, spicy finish. *Comans*

| | |
|---|---|
| Price | €22–€25 |
| Region | Stellenbosch |
| Grape | Cabernet Sauvignon |
| Alc/vol | 13.5% |
| Food | Meat/bacon |
| Drink | 2002–6 |

## Warwick Estate Trilogy 97 ☆☆

A classic. Made in an Old World style, this wine is wonderfully complex with an aged nose of berries, mint and herbal aromas. The palate is rich, oaky and firm with flavours of cedar, spice, mint and bramble fruits. *Searsons*

| | |
|---|---|
| Price | €22–€25 |
| Region | Stellenbosch |
| Grape | Cab Sauv/Merlot/ |
| | Cab Franc |
| Alc/vol | 12.5% |
| Food | Game/game pie |
| Drink | 2002–3 |

## Waterford Cabernet Sauvignon 98

Sturdy, fruity wine with a great mix of flavours—ripe blackcurrants, blackberries, spice, and mint—supported by nicely firm tannins. *Fields*

| | |
|---|---|
| Price | €22–€25 |
| Region | Stellenbosch |
| Grape | Cabernet Sauvignon |
| Alc/vol | 13.5% |
| Food | Meat/beef |
| Drink | 2002–4 |

## €25–€30

### Kanonkop Estate Pinotage 00 ☆

Delightfully rustic nose with red fruits, leafy and earthy but ripe. Still very tannic on the palate but with great warmth and spice, meaty with black fruit flavours. Great elegance on the length. *Findlaters*

| | |
|---|---|
| Price | €25–€30 |
| Region | Stellenbosch |
| Grape | Pinotage |
| Alc/vol | 13.5% |
| Food | Meat/pork |
| Drink | 2002–3 |

### Rust en Vrede Estate Wine 98 ☆ ☆

Very stylish with lovely balance and complexity, elegant, smooth and enveloping. A classic, in a Bordeaux style, with an oaky, taut and obviously blackcurrant nose, a little tarry. Flavours are of very intense cassis and almost sweet bramble fruits. *O'Briens*

| | |
|---|---|
| Price | €25–€30 |
| Region | Stellenbosch |
| Grape | Cabernet Sauvignon/ Shiraz/Merlot |
| Alc/vol | 13% |
| Food | Meat/steak |
| Drink | 2002–3 |

## €30–€35

### Kanonkop Paul Sauer Wine 98 ☆ ☆ ☆

Pronounced, classic aromas of blackcurrant and fresh mint. Super palate with intensity and complexity and a weight of red berry and bramble fruits, spice, mint and vanilla, all beautifully integrated to make an outstanding wine of great character. *Findlaters*

| | |
|---|---|
| Price | €30–€35 |
| Region | Stellenbosch |
| Grape | Cab Sauv/Merlot/ Cab Franc |
| Alc/vol | 13.5% |
| Food | Game/pheasant |
| Drink | 2002–3 |

# Spain

Spain's white wines have not had a high reputation in the past but this is changing. Leading the way to higher quality is the region of Rueda, using the fashionable Sauvignon Blanc grape, either on its own or in conjunction with Verdejo, to produce excellent, crisp, fresh and lemony wines. Six very good value Rueda white wines are recommended this year, with four of them receiving stars. There were also some very good wines made from Chardonnay and Albariño.

Most of the really interesting Spanish reds tasted this year were from the northerly areas of Rioja, Navarra, Ribera del Duero and Priorat, and Penedès in Catalonia. Each region uses similar grape varieties, principally Tempranillo or Garnacha with some being permitted to add Cabernet Sauvignon, Merlot or Syrah. Certain trends are common to each region, the most important being the move to fruitier and more experimental styles of wine and away from extended oak ageing. As the style and quality of Spanish red wines have risen so too have the prices and as a result Spain is not the bargain hunter's paradise that it once was. However, it is still not overpriced and continues to offer high quality for fair prices.

## White

### Under €9

### Blanco Flor DO Utiel-Requena **01**

Aromas of waxy red apple skins. Light-bodied style with very crisp acidity and red apple flavours which would be delicious partnered with food. *IberExpo*

| | |
|---|---|
| *Price* | Under €9 |
| *Region* | Valencia |
| *Grape* | Viura/Chardonnay |
| *Alc/vol* | 12% |
| *Food* | Seafood/squid |
| *Drink* | 2002–3 |

### Con Class Sauvignon Blanc DO Rueda **01** ☆ €

Intense, green, grassy, herbaceous nose is echoed in the appealing palate which has crisp, citrus acidity and robust, ripe apple and gooseberry mingling with herbaceous and asparagus flavours. *Oddbins*

| | |
|---|---|
| *Price* | Under €9 |
| *Region* | Castilla-León |
| *Grape* | Sauvignon Blanc |
| *Alc/vol* | 12.5% |
| *Food* | Cheese/goats' cheese |
| *Drink* | 2002–3 |

### Herencia Remondo Viura DOC Rioja

Apple, toast and golden syrup aromas. The palate has crisp citrus acidity with layers of apples baked with vanilla and nuts and a delicious, savoury length. *IberExpo*

| | |
|---|---|
| *Price* | Under €9 |
| *Region* | Rioja |
| *Grape* | Viura |
| *Alc/vol* | 12% |
| *Food* | Soup/gazpacho |
| *Drink* | 2002–3 |

## Viña Cascarela Sauvignon Blanc DO Rueda **00** ☆☆☆ €

Fresh, lively nose with green, grassy, gooseberry and asparagus aromas. The palate is
wonderfully concentrated with fresh green
fruit and apple flavours and a persistent
length. *WineOnline*

| | |
|---|---|
| Price | Under €9 |
| Region | Castilla-León |
| Grape | Sauvignon Blanc |
| Alc/vol | 12.5% |
| Food | Starters/avocado |
| Drink | 2002–3 |

### €9–€12

## Basa Blanco DO Rueda **01**

Pungent nose of grass, citrus and almonds. The
palate is rich and flavoursome with lemon and
ripe apple flavours. It would be particularly
good with seafood. *Approach Trade*

| | |
|---|---|
| Price | €9–€12 |
| Region | Castilla-León |
| Grape | Verdejo/Sauv Blanc |
| Alc/vol | 12.5% |
| Food | Seafood/crab |
| Drink | 2002–3 |

## Can Vendrell de la Codina Chardonnay Xarel-lo
DO Penedès **01** 🍃

Fresh aromas of apples and lemons give way to
a light, crisp and beautifully integrated palate
with an abundance of fresh flavours—lemons,
limes, grapefruit, apples and asparagus—with a
satisfying finish. *Mary Pawle*

| | |
|---|---|
| Price | €9–€12 |
| Region | Catalonia |
| Grape | Chardonnay/Xarel-lo |
| Alc/vol | 11% |
| Food | Pasta/pesto |
| Drink | 2002–3 |

## Castillo de Chiva DO Valencia **nv**

Very inviting, floral, perfumed nose of honeysuckle and rosewater and a wonderfully crisp
palate with good fruity tones and green apple
flavours. *Bubble Brothers*

| | |
|---|---|
| Price | €9–€12 |
| Region | Valencia |
| Grape | Moscatel |
| Alc/vol | 12% |
| Food | Chinese/spring rolls |
| Drink | 2002–3 |

## Con Class Vendimia Excepcional DO Rueda **01** ☆ €

Striking green and grassy nose reminiscent of
spring. The palate has very clean and refreshing
flavours of fresh grapefruit, lemon and a just a
touch of pine kernels. *Searsons*

| | |
|---|---|
| Price | €9–€12 |
| Region | Castilla-León |
| Grape | Verdejo/Sauv Blanc |
| Alc/vol | 12.5% |
| Food | Ethnic/Thai |
| Drink | 2002–3 |

## Mantel Blanco Verdejo Sauvignon Blanc
DO Rueda **01** ☆☆ €

Classic Sauvignon aromas of gooseberry and cut
grass with heaps of gooseberry, Granny Smith
apple and citrus flavours and zesty, high acidity.
*Approach Trade*

| | |
|---|---|
| Price | €9–€12 |
| Region | Castilla-León |
| Grape | Verdejo/Sauv Blanc |
| Alc/vol | 12.5% |
| Food | Fish/mackerel |
| Drink | 2002–3 |

### Marqués de Alella Classico DO Alella **00**

Aromas are quite subtle, smelling faintly of apples and blossom but wow! the palate is super fresh and zesty with apples and citrus, some spice and honey, all very appealing. *Searsons*

| | |
|---|---|
| *Price* | €9–€12 |
| *Region* | Catalonia |
| *Grape* | Pansa Blanca |
| *Alc/vol* | 11.5% |
| *Food* | Seafood/Fish |
| *Drink* | 2002–3 |

### Marqués de Riscal Sauvignon DO Rueda **01**

Pungent nose of ripe melons but also nettles and lemons. The palate has citrus acidity and is full of melon flavours with spicy elements. *Findlaters*

| | |
|---|---|
| *Price* | €9–€12 |
| *Region* | Castilla-León |
| *Grape* | Sauvignon Blanc |
| *Alc/vol* | 12.5% |
| *Food* | Vegetarian/tomato salad |
| *Drink* | 2002–3 |

### Monopole DOC Rioja **00**

A wine in a very traditional style that everyone should try. Aromas of honey, figs and herbs. The palate is equally distinctive and a touch floral and spicy. *Findlaters*

| | |
|---|---|
| *Price* | €9–€12 |
| *Region* | Rioja |
| *Grape* | Viura/Malvasia/ Garnacha Blanca |
| *Alc/vol* | 12.5% |
| *Food* | Meat/ham |
| *Drink* | 2002–3 |

## Torres Viña Sol DO Penedès **01**

Refreshing, summery drinking. Light nose of melon and citrus fruits backed up by a palate with a pleasant, light, mouthfeel, balanced acidity and citrus and pear flavours.
*Woodford Bourne*

| | |
|---|---|
| *Price* | €9–€12 |
| *Region* | Catalonia |
| *Grape* | Parellada |
| *Alc/vol* | 11.5% |
| *Food* | Picnic/salads |
| *Drink* | 2002–3 |

### €12–€15

## Abadia San Campio Albariño DO Rías Baixas **01**

Pleasant and refreshing aromas of lemon and baked apple. Nutty, savoury palate with apple, grapefruit and lemon flavours—delicious, complex and layered. Would suit full-flavoured, white meat dishes. *IberExpo*

| | |
|---|---|
| *Price* | €12–€15 |
| *Region* | Galicia |
| *Grape* | Albariño |
| *Alc/vol* | 12% |
| *Food* | Poultry/chicken |
| *Drink* | 2002–4 |

## Martín Códax Albariño DO Rías Baixas **01**

An excellent Albariño with a honeyed and citrus nose and a very ripe palate with apples, limes and tangerines. Acidity is very fresh and zingy but does not overpower the ripe fruit.
*Approach Trade*

| | |
|---|---|
| *Price* | €12–€15 |
| *Region* | Galicia |
| *Grape* | Albariño |
| *Alc/vol* | 12% |
| *Food* | Fish/anchovies |
| *Drink* | 2002–3 |

## Terras Gauda O Rosal DO Rías Baixas **01**

Very distinctive lemon and pineapple aromas give way to a full and firm palate of baked apple and oak flavours with noticeable ripeness and a rounded, savoury finish. *IberExpo*

| | |
|---|---|
| *Price* | €12–€15 |
| *Region* | Galicia |
| *Grape* | Mainly Albariño |
| *Alc/vol* | 12% |
| *Food* | Seafood/squid |
| *Drink* | 2002–3 |

### €15–€18

## Enate Chardonnay 2-3-4 DO Somontano **00** ☆

Excellent quality with a good nose of pineapple and butterscotch and a rich, full, rounded palate flavoured with baked apple, nuts, toast and honey. Well-balanced, with citrus acidity and a subtle use of oak complementing the ripe fruit.
*Febvre*

| | |
|---|---|
| *Price* | €15–€18 |
| *Region* | Aragón |
| *Grape* | Chardonnay |
| *Alc/vol* | 13% |
| *Food* | Fish/bream |
| *Drink* | 2002–3 |

### Guitian Godello DO Valdeorras **00**

A bone-dry style—a very good apéritif. The nose is vegetal and floral, with green plum aromas, and the palate is crisp with lemon and tangerine flavours. *Approach Trade*

| | |
|---|---|
| *Price* | €15–€18 |
| *Region* | Galicia |
| *Grape* | Godello |
| *Alc/vol* | 12% |
| *Food* | Apéritif/tapas |
| *Drink* | 2002–3 |

### Viña Lidon Chardonnay DO Utiel-Requena **01** 🍃

Interesting, smoky nose with slight floral hints. Finesse on the palate with pepper and mango flavours and tangy acidity. *IberExpo*

| | |
|---|---|
| *Price* | €15–€18 |
| *Region* | Valencia |
| *Grape* | Chardonnay |
| *Alc/vol* | 12% |
| *Food* | Fish/haddock |
| *Drink* | 2002–3 |

€18–€22

### Torres Fransola DO Penedès **00** ☆

Very stylish and accomplished. Opulent, scented, green and grassy nose. The palate is very fresh and juicy with limy acidity, green apple and pea flavours and a citrus-zest aftertaste.
*Woodford Bourne*

| | |
|---|---|
| *Price* | €18–€22 |
| *Region* | Catalonia |
| *Grape* | Sauv Blanc/Parellada |
| *Alc/vol* | 13.5% |
| *Food* | Fish/hake |
| *Drink* | 2002–3 |

> Red **Riojas** are made from Tempranillo, Garnacha, Mazuelo and Graciano (and
> sometimes Cabernet Sauvignon) and are traditionally aged in wooden barrels,
> giving creamy, soft wines with strawberry and vanilla aromas from the oak
> barrels. Whites are made from Viura, Malvasia Riojana and Garnacha Blanca
> grapes. Traditional-style whites are dark in colour, oak aged and creamy; newer-
> style white Riojas are crisp and fresh.

# Red

## Under €9

### **Agramont Crianza** DO Navarra **98** ☆☆ **€**

Delicious wine with concentrated bramble
fruit aromas and an excellent weight of sweet,
ripe blackcurrant and vanilla flavours. Drinking well now, full of character and with very
good length. *Dunnes Stores*

| | |
|---|---|
| Price | Under €9 |
| Region | Navarra |
| Grape | Tempranillo/Cab Sauv |
| Alc/vol | 13% |
| Food | Poultry/chicken |
| Drink | 2002–4 |

SHORTLIST BEST VALUE RED WINE

### **Albada** DO Calatayud **00**

Rustic, earthy style with a big heart, full of ripe,
sweet, baked black fruit, spice, pepper and some
cigar box flavours and a dry, earthy finish of
good length. *Dunnes Stores*

| | |
|---|---|
| Price | Under €9 |
| Region | Aragón |
| Grape | Garnacha |
| Alc/vol | 14% |
| Food | Meat/kebabs |
| Drink | 2002–3 |

### **Entari** DOC Rioja **nv**

Fruity nose with some peppery aromas. Pleasant, fruity mouthfeel with cherry flavours and a
touch of earthiness with a background of spice.
Best with food. *IberExpo*

| | |
|---|---|
| Price | Under €9 |
| Region | Rioja |
| Grape | Tempranillo |
| Alc/vol | 12% |
| Food | Meat/grills |
| Drink | 2002–3 |

### **Ercavio Tempranillo Roble** DO La Mancha **00**

Spicy and fruity from start to finish. Quite a
characterful nose of fig, mint and eucalyptus
followed by a robust, tannic palate with abundant spicy, earthy strawberries and a touch of
dark coffee. *O'Briens*

| | |
|---|---|
| Price | Under €9 |
| Region | Castilla-La Mancha |
| Grape | Tempranillo |
| Alc/vol | 13.5% |
| Food | Vegetarian/ mushroom dishes |
| Drink | 2002–4 |

### **La Vendimia** DOC Rioja **01**

This wine has a deeply earthy character with
floral and blackcurrant aromas and a good,
fruity palate with morello cherry and some mellow tobacco flavours. *IberExpo*

| | |
|---|---|
| Price | Under €9 |
| Region | Rioja |
| Grape | Tempranillo |
| Alc/vol | 13% |
| Food | Meat/sausages |
| Drink | 2002–4 |

### Valdemoya Crianza VdT **97**

Good intensity on the nose and palate with very mellow tobacco and vanilla and a rich depth of blackcurrant flavours with some spice. *WineOnline*

| | |
|---|---|
| *Price* | Under €9 |
| *Region* | Castilla-León |
| *Grape* | Tempranillo/Cab Sauv |
| *Alc/vol* | 13% |
| *Food* | Eggs/tortilla |
| *Drink* | 2002–3 |

### Vega Ibor Crianza DO Valdepeñas **98**

Big and chunky style with chocolate and blackcurrant aromas and flavours, cooling acidity and a ripe but firm finish. *Approach Trade*

| | |
|---|---|
| *Price* | Under €9 |
| *Region* | Castilla-La Mancha |
| *Grape* | Tempranillo |
| *Alc/vol* | 13% |
| *Food* | Vegetarian/bean casserole |
| *Drink* | 2002–3 |

*€9–€12*

### A. L. Monastrell DO Alicante **00**

Very pleasant, characterful style with a perfumed and inky nose and dark blackcurrant flavours with earthy tones and a dry finish. Match with hearty food. *Approach Trade*

| | |
|---|---|
| *Price* | €9–€12 |
| *Region* | Valencia |
| *Grape* | Monastrell |
| *Alc/vol* | 14% |
| *Food* | Meat/ribs |
| *Drink* | 2002–3 |

### Alma Garnacha DO Navarra **00**

A gentle and fruity style with a fragrant, red berry jam nose. Smooth-textured palate with strawberry and cherry flavours, perfumed with floral violet hints and blessed with gentle supporting tannins. *Approach Trade*

| | |
|---|---|
| *Price* | €9–€12 |
| *Region* | Navarra |
| *Grape* | Garnacha |
| *Alc/vol* | 12.5% |
| *Food* | Pizza/pepperoni |
| *Drink* | 2002–3 |

### Campobarro Oak Aged DO Ribera del Guadiana **01**

This wine has very good weight and concentration with a blackcurrant nose and very fruity blackcurrant flavours. The tannins are very firm and it would be best decanted and served with food. *Bubble Brothers*

| | |
|---|---|
| *Price* | €9–€12 |
| *Region* | Extremadura |
| *Grape* | Tempranillo |
| *Alc/vol* | 12.5% |
| *Food* | Meat/roasts |
| *Drink* | 2003–4 |

### Castaño Hécula DO Yecla **00**

Lovely nose with cherry and vanilla aromas. The palate has rich cherry flavours and is also quite rustic and earthy in style with very firm, youthful tannins. Drink with food or wait for the tannins to soften. *Karwig Wines*

| | |
|---|---|
| *Price* | €9–€12 |
| *Region* | Murcia |
| *Grape* | Monastrell |
| *Alc/vol* | 14% |
| *Food* | Vegetarian/cous-cous |
| *Drink* | 2003–4 |

## Castelar Crianza DO Ribera del Guidiana 98

Big and showy nose with clove spice, bundles of berries and a touch of green pepper. Generous palate, ranging from ripe fruit flavours to very earthy, almost compost-like elements with tobacco tones. *Approach Trade*

| | |
|---|---|
| *Price* | €9–€12 |
| *Region* | Extremadura |
| *Grape* | Tempranillo |
| *Alc/vol* | 13% |
| *Food* | Meat/barbecue |
| *Drink* | 2002–4 |

## Chivite Gran Feudo Crianza DO Navarra 99

Well-made, balanced style with power. The aromas are of ripe blackcurrant and spice with a floral undertone. The palate has flavours of dark cherry and plum with some spicy and vegetal elements. *TDL*

| | |
|---|---|
| *Price* | €9–€12 |
| *Region* | Navarra |
| *Grape* | Tempranillo/ Garnacha/Cab Sauv |
| *Alc/vol* | 12.5% |
| *Food* | Vegetarian/peppers |
| *Drink* | 2002–4 |

## Iglesia Vieja Crianza DO Yecla 97

Robust style with lots of charm and a deep, earthy character. Mature and developed with baked fruit, vanilla and cigar box flavours, peppery and vegetal with a good, long finish. *Approach Trade*

| | |
|---|---|
| *Price* | €9–€12 |
| *Region* | Murcia |
| *Grape* | Monastrell |
| *Alc/vol* | 13% |
| *Food* | Meat/pork |
| *Drink* | 2002–5 |

## Marqués de Aragon Old Vine Garnacha DO Calatayud 00

Quite a charmer with a good weight of plum and damson flavours, leathery and spicy, with warming vanilla and chocolate. *Searsons*

| | |
|---|---|
| *Price* | €9–€12 |
| *Region* | Aragón |
| *Grape* | Garnacha |
| *Alc/vol* | 13.5% |
| *Food* | Vegetarian/cous-cous |
| *Drink* | 2002–3 |

## Marqués de Valcarlos Crianza DO Navarra 97

The delicate nose has a smoky, toasty and cherry character. Nice maturity is showing well on the palate with integrated tannins and acidity and delicate wood flavours together with blackcurrant, plum and vanilla. *Gilbeys*

| | |
|---|---|
| *Price* | €9–€12 |
| *Region* | Navarra |
| *Grape* | Tempranillo/Cab Sauv |
| *Alc/vol* | 12.5% |
| *Food* | Meat/beef |
| *Drink* | 2002–3 |

## Montecillo Crianza DOC Rioja **97**

Pronounced aromas of figs, prunes, tar, chocolate and spice. Dry on the palate, with firm tannins, and a huge weight of rich dark fruit, savoury, meaty flavours and very good length. *Dillons*

| | |
|---|---|
| *Price* | €9–€12 |
| *Region* | Rioja |
| *Grape* | Rioja varieties |
| *Alc/vol* | 13% |
| *Food* | Meat/stews |
| *Drink* | 2002–3 |

## Montesierra Crianza DO Somontano **98**

Attractive, fruity nose with damsons, blackcurrants, pepper and mulled wine spice. The palate has the same delicious, ripe fruit profile with smokiness and spicy length. *Dunnes Stores*

| | |
|---|---|
| *Price* | €9–€12 |
| *Region* | Aragón |
| *Grape* | Tempranillo/ Cab Sauv/Moristel |
| *Alc/vol* | 13% |
| *Food* | Meat/steak |
| *Drink* | 2002–4 |

## Palacio de la Vega Merlot Crianza DO Navarra **98**

Soft and ripe style with stewed red fruit aromas, floral and vegetal touches. The palate is very spicy and tasty with baked plum flavours and gentle tannins making for very easy drinking. *Irish Distillers*

| | |
|---|---|
| *Price* | €9–€12 |
| *Region* | Navarra |
| *Grape* | Merlot |
| *Alc/vol* | 13.5% |
| *Food* | Fish/tuna |
| *Drink* | 2002–3 |

## Petit Caus DO Penedès **98**

Classy and spicy nose with cassis and vanilla aromas. The palate is quite concentrated with plum and blackcurrant flavours.Try decanting the wine to open up its flavours as it is a little closed and very tannic. *Approach Trade*

| | |
|---|---|
| *Price* | €9–€12 |
| *Region* | Catalonia |
| *Grape* | Merlot/Cab Sauv/ Cabernet Franc/ Tempranillo/ Monastrell |
| *Alc/vol* | 12.5% |
| *Food* | Meat/kebabs |
| *Drink* | 2003–4 |

## Riscal Tempranillo VdT Castilla León **00**

A chewy style with a vibrant, youthful and fruity nose and a distinguished palate with dry tannins, flavours of blackberry, leafy undergrowth and dark chocolate, and a bitter cherry finish. *Findlaters*

| | |
|---|---|
| *Price* | €9–€12 |
| *Region* | Castilla-León |
| *Grape* | Tempranillo |
| *Alc/vol* | 13% |
| *Food* | Meat/beef burgers |
| *Drink* | 2002–3 |

## Señorío de los Llanos Gran Reserva DO Valdepeñas **94**

A wine that has developed subtlety and complexity over the years but is still very fresh. It has appealing aromas of red fruits and a delicious and elegant palate with strawberries, blackberries and sweet vanilla. *Dillons*

| | |
|---|---|
| *Price* | €9–€12 |
| *Region* | Castilla-La Mancha |
| *Grape* | Tempranillo |
| *Alc/vol* | 12.5% |
| *Food* | Meat/meatballs |
| *Drink* | 2002–3 |

## Tesco Spanish Tempranillo DO La Mancha **99**

Upfront, fruity wine bursting with lovely, ripe flavours of blackcurrants and blackberries with some creamy, spicy tones and good, firm tannins. *Tesco*

| | |
|---|---|
| *Price* | €9–€12 |
| *Region* | Castilla-La Mancha |
| *Grape* | Tempranillo |
| *Alc/vol* | 12.5% |
| *Food* | Meat/lamb |
| *Drink* | 2002–3 |

## Vega Esteban Tempranillo DO Ribera del Guadiana **00**

Quite a concentrated nose of blackcurrant, vegetal and spicy aromas. There follows a very dry palate with firm tannins, crisp acidity and green pepper flavours making food a must.
*Nectar Wines*

| | |
|---|---|
| *Price* | €9–€12 |
| *Region* | Extremadura |
| *Grape* | Tempranillo |
| *Alc/vol* | 13% |
| *Food* | Meat/smoked ham |
| *Drink* | 2002–3 |

## Vega Estebàn Tempranillo Crianza
DO Ribera del Guadiana **98**

Big and full nose with aromas of Christmas pudding and cigar box. Rich palate with gutsy tannins, ripe black fruits, some earthiness and a good, long finish. *Nectar Wines*

| | |
|---|---|
| *Price* | €9–€12 |
| *Region* | Extremadura |
| *Grape* | Tempranillo |
| *Alc/vol* | 13% |
| *Food* | Meat/Serrano ham |
| *Drink* | 2002–4 |

## Vega Sauco DO Toro **99**

Plenty of plum and tobacco aromas bode well and are mirrored on the fruity palate which also has good, firm tannins. *Approach Trade*

| | |
|---|---|
| *Price* | €9–€12 |
| *Region* | Castilla-León |
| *Grape* | Tempranillo |
| *Alc/vol* | 13.5% |
| *Food* | Meat/grilled |
| *Drink* | 2003–4 |

## Viña 105 DO Cigales **00**

The intriguing medicinal nose with rubber and leather aromas is spicy, vegetal and earthy. There is lovely, soft, sweet raspberry fruit on the palate with supporting acidity and decent length. *Approach Trade*

| | |
|---|---|
| *Price* | €9–€12 |
| *Region* | Castilla-León |
| *Grape* | Tempranillo/Garnacha |
| *Alc/vol* | 13% |
| *Food* | Meat/barbecue |
| *Drink* | 2002–3 |

## Viña Hermosa Crianza DOC Rioja **98**

A light and tasty Rioja with sweet raspberries, cassis and spicy oak, no noticeable tannins and a stylish finish. *Approach Trade*

| | |
|---|---|
| *Price* | €9–€12 |
| *Region* | Rioja |
| *Grape* | Rioja varieties |
| *Alc/vol* | 12.5% |
| *Food* | Poultry/chicken |
| *Drink* | 2002–3 |

## Viña Mater Tempranillo Reserva DO Terra Alta 96

A very mature wine with medicinal and farm-yard aromas. The fruit is still there on the palate but it is in a rustic and baked style with spice and liquorice. *Approach Trade*

| | |
|---|---|
| *Price* | €9–€12 |
| *Region* | Catalonia |
| *Grape* | Tempranillo |
| *Alc/vol* | 12.5% |
| *Food* | Meat/hamburgers |
| *Drink* | 2002–3 |

---

### €12–€15

## Abadia Retuerta Rívola VdM de Castilla y León 99 ☆☆ €

Rich and beautifully made with smoky and fresh blackcurrant aromas and a dramatic palate of blackcurrant, coffee, spice and earthy flavours. Each mouthful brings added complexity and the richness continues to a delicious, fruity finish with tremendous length. *O'Briens*

| | |
|---|---|
| *Price* | €12–€15 |
| *Region* | Castilla-León |
| *Grape* | Tempranillo/Cab Sauv |
| *Alc/vol* | 13% |
| *Food* | Meat/lamb |
| *Drink* | 2002–5 |

## Albet i Noya Lignum DO Penedès 99 🌿

Baked and earthy nose with spice, raisin and stewed fruit hints. Spicy palate with abundant berry fruit character, gentle tannins and judicious oak. A well-structured, flavoursome wine with a long finish. *Mary Pawle*

| | |
|---|---|
| *Price* | €12–€15 |
| *Region* | Catalonia |
| *Grape* | Garnacha/Cariñena/ Cabernet Sauvignon |
| *Alc/vol* | 13% |
| *Food* | Poultry/chicken |
| *Drink* | 2002–3 |

## Beronia Tempranillo DOC Rioja 99

Exactly what Rioja is all about: oodles of strawberry, raspberry and smoky vanilla on the nose, followed by smooth, velvety, mouth-watering flavours—red berries, chocolate, spice and wood. *Barry & Fitzwilliam*

| | |
|---|---|
| *Price* | €12–€15 |
| *Region* | Rioja |
| *Grape* | Tempranillo |
| *Alc/vol* | 13% |
| *Food* | Meat/cold meats |
| *Drink* | 2002–4 |

## Bodegas Emilio Moro Finca Resalso DO Ribera del Duero 99

A 'Euro Shiraz' style, quite youthful and fiery with broad, spicy plum and sea shell aromas and very good plum and blackcurrant flavours. *Approach Trade*

| | |
|---|---|
| *Price* | €12–€15 |
| *Region* | Castilla-León |
| *Grape* | Tempranillo |
| *Alc/vol* | 13% |
| *Food* | Meat/lamb |
| *Drink* | 2002–3 |

## Campo Viejo Reserva DOC Rioja 96

Sweet red berries to the fore here, backed up by mature tannins and a balanced, woody character. Other flavours include cloves, raisins and dark chocolate. Smooth and very pleasant on the finish. *Cassidy*

| | |
|---|---|
| *Price* | €12–€15 |
| *Region* | Rioja |
| *Grape* | Rioja varieties |
| *Alc/vol* | 12.5% |
| *Food* | Meat/grilled |
| *Drink* | 2002–3 |

## Carchelo Syrah DO Jumilla **98**

You could be forgiven for thinking that this is an Australian Shiraz with its upfront fruit flavours and ripe tannins—blackberries together with leather, spice and pepperiness. *Searsons*

| | |
|---|---|
| *Price* | €12–€15 |
| *Region* | Murcia |
| *Grape* | Syrah |
| *Alc/vol* | 13% |
| *Food* | Meat/salami |
| *Drink* | 2002–4 |

## Casa Castillo Monastrell DO Jumilla **99**

A lovely, big, juicy wine with rich aromas of cassis and violets, bags of ripe fruit flavours and a pleasant touch of rusticity on the palate. *Approach Trade*

| | |
|---|---|
| *Price* | €12–€15 |
| *Region* | Murcia |
| *Grape* | Monastrell/Syrah |
| *Alc/vol* | 13.5% |
| *Food* | Meat/pork |
| *Drink* | 2002–3 |

## Castell del Remei Gotim Bru DO Costers del Segre **99**

Promising nose with warm, woody tones, bitter chocolate and spice. Sweet blackberries and liquorice on the palate, firm tannins and refreshing acidity and a flavoursome, persistent finish. *Searsons*

| | |
|---|---|
| *Price* | €12–€15 |
| *Region* | Catalonia |
| *Grape* | Tempranillo/Merlot/ Cabernet Sauvignon |
| *Alc/vol* | 12.5% |
| *Food* | Risotto/mushroom |
| *Drink* | 2002–3 |

## Guelbenzu Azul VdM Ribera de Queiles **99** ☆

Super, robust style with great structure and concentration, full of generous blackcurrants, minty, spicy and a touch meaty, with a smooth texture. *Searsons*

| | |
|---|---|
| *Price* | €12–€15 |
| *Region* | Navarra |
| *Grape* | Tempranillo/ Cab Sauv/Merlot |
| *Alc/vol* | 13% |
| *Food* | Meat/pork |
| *Drink* | 2002–5 |

## Jarrero DOC Rioja **99**

Rich, fruity and spicy nose will draw you in. Very pure and fruit-driven palate of blackcurrant and blackberry flavours with firm but supporting tannins. *Approach Trade*

| | |
|---|---|
| *Price* | €12–€15 |
| *Region* | Rioja |
| *Grape* | Rioja varieties |
| *Alc/vol* | 12.5% |
| *Food* | Poultry/duck |
| *Drink* | 2002–3 |

## L'Agnet DO Priorat **99**

Very ripe with a baked fruit nose and a big baked, peppery palate with saturated black fruit and port-like qualities. *Approach Trade*

| | |
|---|---|
| *Price* | €12–€15 |
| *Region* | Catalonia |
| *Grape* | Cariñena/Garnacha |
| *Alc/vol* | 13.8% |
| *Food* | Meat/beef |
| *Drink* | 2002–3 |

## **Marqués de Murrieta Coleccion 2100 Tempranillo**
DOC Rioja **00**

Ample nose with vegetal and morello cherry aromas. The palate is rich with quite a bit of character and depth, black fruit flavours and firm tannins. *Gilbeys*

| | |
|---|---|
| Price | €12–€15 |
| Region | Rioja |
| Grape | Tempranillo |
| Alc/vol | 12.5% |
| Food | Meat/beef |
| Drink | 2002–4 |

## **Martinez Bermell Merlot** DO Utiel-Requena **01**

Substantial and powerful wine, with intense hot plum and cassis aromas and a fruity and spicy palate tasting of soft, ripe plums and blackcurrants. *IberExpo*

| | |
|---|---|
| Price | €12–€15 |
| Region | Valencia |
| Grape | Merlot |
| Alc/vol | 12% |
| Food | Meat/sausages |
| Drink | 2002–4 |

## **Muga Reserva** DOC Rioja **97** ☆

Classic strawberry and tobacco aromas follow through on the palate which has soft tannins and ripe, gentle, red fruit flavours. Quite spicy and smoky with a super, long finish. *Comans*

| | |
|---|---|
| Price | €12–€15 |
| Region | Rioja |
| Grape | Tempranillo/Garnacha/ Mazuelo/Graciano |
| Alc/vol | 13% |
| Food | Poultry/chicken |
| Drink | 2002–4 |

## **Osca Crianza** DO Somontano **99**

Heady, perfumed, hothouse nose, burnt and earthy. Beautifully made with a taste of the earth and sun and an oaky, smoky and brambly palate with personality. *Approach Trade*

| | |
|---|---|
| Price | €12–€15 |
| Region | Aragón |
| Grape | Tempranillo/Cab Sauv |
| Alc/vol | 13% |
| Food | Meat/roasts |
| Drink | 2002–4 |

## **Osoti** DOC Rioja **00** 🍂

Appealing aromas of juicy strawberries and vanilla. Delicious, exuberant flavours of raspberries, plums and cherries and a touch of aniseed. Oak is subtle, tannins are ripe, and with the balancing acidity the result is a well-constructed, rounded wine. *Mary Pawle*

| | |
|---|---|
| Price | €12–€15 |
| Region | Rioja |
| Grape | Tempranillo/Mazuelo/ Buscando |
| Alc/vol | 13.5% |
| Food | Meat/barbecue |
| Drink | 2002–3 |

## **Palacio de Muruzabal Cosecha Particular**
DO Navarra **97** ☆

A wine with balance and the complexity that comes from a little age. Spicy baked fruit aromas plus a ripe blackberry palate blended with pepper and spice. *Approach Trade*

| | |
|---|---|
| Price | €12–€15 |
| Region | Navarra |
| Grape | Cab Sauv/Merlot/ Tempranillo |
| Alc/vol | 13% |
| Food | Meat/ribs |
| Drink | 2002–4 |

## Raïmat Cabernet Sauvignon DO Costers del Segre 97 ☆

Very stylish wine with inviting aromas of smoke, liquorice and prunes and generous flavours of blackcurrant, plum and oaky vanilla, combined with gentle tannins.The result is a balanced, developed red with a fruity aftertaste that goes on and on. *Grants*

| | |
|---|---|
| Price | €12–€15 |
| Region | Catalonia |
| Grape | Cab Sauv/Merlot |
| Alc/vol | 13% |
| Food | Meat/lamb chops |
| Drink | 2002–3 |

## Torres Atrium Merlot 00

A Merlot which provides lots of interest. Lovely aromas of plum skin, blackberry, herbs and creamy chocolate tones are followed by lots of ripe, plummy flavours teased out with green pepper and herbal layers. *Woodford Bourne*

| | |
|---|---|
| Price | €12–€15 |
| Region | Catalonia |
| Grape | Merlot |
| Alc/vol | 13.5% |
| Food | Meat/casseroles |
| Drink | 2002–4 |

## Vega Sauco Crianza DO Toro 97

This is an extremely tannic and dry wine with a lovely fruit pie nose and very concentrated, blackcurrant-flavoured palate. *Approach Trade*

| | |
|---|---|
| Price | €12–€15 |
| Region | Castilla-León |
| Grape | Tempranillo |
| Alc/vol | 13.5% |
| Food | Meat/steak |
| Drink | 2002–3 |

### €15–€18

## Abando Crianza DOC Rioja 99

Stylish Rioja with a rich nose of vanilla, raspberry and cigar smokiness. Tasty raspberry and pepper on the palate mingle with vanilla oak giving a warm, baked fruit character.
*Approach Trade*

| | |
|---|---|
| Price | €15–€18 |
| Region | Rioja |
| Grape | Tempranillo |
| Alc/vol | 12.5% |
| Food | Poultry/duck |
| Drink | 2003–5 |

## Bagordi Crianza DOC Rioja 98 ☘ ☆

Some developed aromas of spicy, baked fruit, leather and tar with tobacco. The palate is a mouth-watering experience of soft, ripe berry fruit, integrated tannins, big muscular body and great length, weight and balance. *Searsons*

| | |
|---|---|
| Price | €15–€18 |
| Region | Rioja |
| Grape | Tempranillo/Garnacha |
| Alc/vol | 13.5% |
| Food | Meat/frankfurters |
| Drink | 2002–5 |

## Balbas Crianza DO Ribera del Duero 98 ☆

Perfectly balanced and layered this is an ideal fireside or winter wine. Warming peppery spice, Christmas cake fruit, lots of raisins and figs, vanilla and some cigar box.
*Waterford Wine Vault*

| | |
|---|---|
| Price | €15–€18 |
| Region | Castilla-León |
| Grape | Tempranillo |
| Alc/vol | 13% |
| Food | Meat/roasts |
| Drink | 2002–5 |

### Gago DO Toro 99

Big and powerful style with concentrated, cassis-flavoured fruit, peppery spice and green tannins. This wine is youthful and will benefit from more time. *Approach Trade*

| | |
|---|---|
| *Price* | €15–€18 |
| *Region* | Castilla-León |
| *Grape* | Tempranillo |
| *Alc/vol* | 13.5% |
| *Food* | Meat/beef |
| *Drink* | 2002–3 |

### Lanzaga DOC Rioja 99

Very attractive and intense cherry aromas, and a spicy, chunky, baked fruit palate. Still youthful and a touch fiery, it would be perfect for barbecued or grilled meat *Approach Trade*

| | |
|---|---|
| *Price* | €15–€18 |
| *Region* | Rioja |
| *Grape* | Rioja varieties |
| *Alc/vol* | 13.5% |
| *Food* | Meat/barbecue |
| *Drink* | 2003–5 |

### Montecillo Gran Reserva DOC Rioja 85 ☆

The age says it all—this is a mature wine with a serious, smooth, vegetal, spicy and caramelised character. Flavours are of stewed plums, rhubarb, prunes, and the palate is also gamey and earthy with soft tannins and good acidity holding it all together. *Dillons*

| | |
|---|---|
| *Price* | €15–€18 |
| *Region* | Rioja |
| *Grape* | Rioja varieties |
| *Alc/vol* | 12.5% |
| *Food* | Meat/lamb |
| *Drink* | 2002–3 |

### Sierra Cantabria Reserva DOC Rioja 96 ☆

Plummy nose with some toffee and caramel aromas. Soft, ripe red fruits on the palate with oaky flavours. Rustic and earthy with quite firm tannins and an excellent, spicy length. *O'Briens*

| | |
|---|---|
| *Price* | €15–€18 |
| *Region* | Rioja |
| *Grape* | Tempranillo |
| *Alc/vol* | 13% |
| *Food* | Meat/kebabs |
| *Drink* | 2002–4 |

### Viña Salceda Reserva DOC Rioja 96

Beautifully balanced and very fresh with pronounced aromas of black fruit and spice and a warm mouthfeel with a persistent length of richly spiced blackcurrant flavours. *TDL*

| | |
|---|---|
| *Price* | €15–€18 |
| *Region* | Rioja |
| *Grape* | Tempranillo/Graciano/ Mazuelo |
| *Alc/vol* | 13% |
| *Food* | Ethnic/Asian |
| *Drink* | 2002–4 |

*€18–€22*

### Albet i Noya Collecció Cabernet Sauvignon
DO Penedès 99 🌿

Vibrant, ripe, modern style, very concentrated and rich in black fruit flavours. It is also spicy and savoury with a lengthy, fruity finish. *Mary Pawle*

| | |
|---|---|
| *Price* | €18–€22 |
| *Region* | Catalonia |
| *Grape* | Cabernet Sauvignon |
| *Alc/vol* | 14% |
| *Food* | Meat/stews |
| *Drink* | 2002–4 |

## Albet i Noya Collecció Syrah DO Penedès **99** 🌿 ☆

Rhône-like nose of spice, meat, plum, smoke and truffle. Gorgeous, spicy palate full of juicy fruit, cassis and blueberry, firm tannins and lots of body and an appealing, lengthy finish.
*Mary Pawle*

| | |
|---|---|
| *Price* | €18–€22 |
| *Region* | Catalonia |
| *Grape* | Syrah |
| *Alc/vol* | 13.5% |
| *Food* | Poultry/goose |
| *Drink* | 2002–4 |

## Albet i Noya Collecció Tempranillo DO Penedès **98** 🌿 ☆

Chocolate and spice and all things nice on the nose. Abundant plum and blackberry flavours in a big and robust, but smooth and elegant, palate with firm tannins and good texture.
*Mary Pawle*

| | |
|---|---|
| *Price* | €18–€22 |
| *Region* | Catalonia |
| *Grape* | Tempranillo |
| *Alc/vol* | 13.5% |
| *Food* | Poultry/lamb |
| *Drink* | 2002–5 |

## Arzuaga Crianza DO Ribera del Duero **98** ☆

Classic, confident style with an opulent perfumed nose. It has all the right elements—meaty, earthy and spicy with ripe dark berry fruit and plum flavours wrapped around warm, toasty oak. *Searsons*

| | |
|---|---|
| *Price* | €18–€22 |
| *Region* | Castilla-León |
| *Grape* | Tempranillo/Cab Sauv |
| *Alc/vol* | 13.5% |
| *Food* | Meat/roasts |
| *Drink* | 2002–4 |

## Condado de Haza DO Ribera del Duero **99**

Big and meaty, this is a full and weighty blockbuster with a firm tannic structure. Intense nose of juicy dark fruits and oak. Very tasty palate with hugely concentrated blackcurrant flavours. *Searsons*

| | |
|---|---|
| *Price* | €18–€22 |
| *Region* | Castilla-León |
| *Grape* | Tempranillo |
| *Alc/vol* | 13% |
| *Food* | Meat/casseroles |
| *Drink* | 2002–6 |

## El Vínculo DO La Mancha **99**

Made by the legendary Alejandro Fernández of Pesquera. Quite a luscious wine with a terrific nose of strawberry tart, vanilla and crème brulée and a creamy, soft red fruit palate with a sexy, smooth mouthfeel and toffee and caramel flavours. *Oddbins*

| | |
|---|---|
| *Price* | €18–€22 |
| *Region* | Castilla-La Mancha |
| *Grape* | Tempranillo |
| *Alc/vol* | 13% |
| *Food* | Meat/chorizo |
| *Drink* | 2002–3 |

## Emilio Moro Crianza DO Ribera del Duero **98**

Wonderfully rich on the nose with tobacco, blackcurrant and creamy aromas. Mature damsons on the palate with good acidity and excellent length; gets better with each mouthful.
*Approach Trade*

| | |
|---|---|
| *Price* | €18–€22 |
| *Region* | Castilla-León |
| *Grape* | Tempranillo |
| *Alc/vol* | 13% |
| *Food* | Meat/lamb |
| *Drink* | 2002–3 |

## Guelbenzu Evo DO Navarra **98**

Cassis, chocolate, spice, blackcurrants, mint
and subtle oaky flavours make for a beautifully
silky and soft-textured style and a warm, generous finish. *Searsons*

| | |
|---|---|
| *Price* | €18–€22 |
| *Region* | Navarra |
| *Grape* | Cabernet Sauvignon/ Tempranillo/Merlot |
| *Alc/vol* | 13.5% |
| *Food* | Poultry/chicken with rice |
| *Drink* | 2002–4 |

## Igneus DO Priorat **00** 🌿

Aromas of pepper, spice and blueberries. Youthful and a little shy on the palate, displaying a
green tannic edge which is dominating the fruit
at present and needs time to evolve as it is
clearly a wine with potential. *Mary Pawle*

| | |
|---|---|
| *Price* | €18–€22 |
| *Region* | Catalonia |
| *Grape* | Garnacha/Cariñena/ Cabernet Sauvignon |
| *Alc/vol* | 14% |
| *Food* | Meat/stews |
| *Drink* | 2003–6 |

## La Xarmada Crianza DO Conca de Barberà **99** ☆

'Intensity' sums up this wine. It has a layered.
baked fruit nose and a robust palate but with a
luscious, smooth, velvety mouthfeel with ripe
figs and blackberries, warm smokiness, earthiness and spice. *Approach Trade*

| | |
|---|---|
| *Price* | €18–€22 |
| *Region* | Catalonia |
| *Grape* | Syrah/Cab Sauv/ Merlot |
| *Alc/vol* | 13.5% |
| *Food* | Vegetarian/casseroles |
| *Drink* | 2002–5 |

## Les Terrasses DO Priorat **99** ☆

Powerful and substantial wine with big fruit
extraction, firm tannins and an excellent intensity of spiced raisin and blackcurrant flavour.
*Approach Trade*

| | |
|---|---|
| *Price* | €18–€22 |
| *Region* | Catalonia |
| *Grape* | Garnacha/Cariñena/ Cabernet Sauvignon |
| *Alc/vol* | 13.5% |
| *Food* | Meat/shepherd's pie |
| *Drink* | 2002–4 |

## Marqués de Cáceres Gran Reserva DOC Rioja **90** ☆

Mature, developed nose of farmyard, fig, prune
and raisin (Christmas cake mix) repeated in the
smooth, muti-layered, appealing palate with
excellent fruit, oak and tobacco flavours. *Grants*

| | |
|---|---|
| *Price* | €18–€22 |
| *Region* | Rioja |
| *Grape* | Rioja varieties |
| *Alc/vol* | 13% |
| *Food* | Meat/roast pork |
| *Drink* | 2002–3 |

## Montecillo Gran Reserva DOC Rioja **94** ☆

The nose is rich, full and complex and offers
raisin-like fruit, cigar box/tobacco aromas and
pure vanilla pod. The full-bodied palate has
maturing red fruit flavours. *Dillons*

| | |
|---|---|
| *Price* | €18–€22 |
| *Region* | Rioja |
| *Grape* | Tempranillo |
| *Alc/vol* | 13% |
| *Food* | Poultry/chicken |
| *Drink* | 2002–5 |

## Pesquera Tinto DO Ribera del Duero 99

Tantalising fruity nose to this wine which is beautifully restrained on tasting, with firm tannins but still yielding, ripe black fruits. A big wine with great concentration and complexity. *Searsons*

| | |
|---|---|
| *Price* | €18–€22 |
| *Region* | Castilla-León |
| *Grape* | Tempranillo |
| *Alc/vol* | 13% |
| *Food* | Poultry/duck |
| *Drink* | 2002–3 |

## Remelluri DOC Rioja 98 ☆

This wine has class, finesse and complexity with deliciously ripe and mature red fruits, a soft and sexy texture and some spice and savoury elements. *Approach Trade*

| | |
|---|---|
| *Price* | €18–€22 |
| *Region* | Rioja |
| *Grape* | Tempranillo |
| *Alc/vol* | 13% |
| *Food* | Meat/pork |
| *Drink* | 2002–3 |

## Valderiz DO Ribera del Duero 98

Initially quite closed, this wine needs to be decanted and allowed to open up. It will then reveal creamy vanilla and dark fruit aromas and an elegant and balanced palate with intense blackcurrant and tobacco flavours. *Approach Trade*

| | |
|---|---|
| *Price* | €18–€22 |
| *Region* | Castilla-León |
| *Grape* | Tempranillo |
| *Alc/vol* | 13.5% |
| *Food* | Meat/lamb |
| *Drink* | 2002–4 |

### €22–€25

## Albet i Noya Núria DO Penedès 99 🌿 ☆

Intense aromas of truffle and earth. Plenty of fruit and spice on the palate but firm, gripping tannins. A youthful wine with great potential, it will become a great wine with a little more maturity. *Mary Pawle*

| | |
|---|---|
| *Price* | €22–€25 |
| *Region* | Catalonia |
| *Grape* | Merlot/Petite Syrah/ Caladoc |
| *Alc/vol* | 13.5% |
| *Food* | Meat/roasts |
| *Drink* | 2003–6 |

## Casa Castillo Las Gravas DO Jumilla 98

Interesting aromas of clove, plum and some medicinal touches and a similarly intriguing palate with very big tannins and flavours of Christmas pudding, allspice, prunes, nuts and plums. *Approach Trade*

| | |
|---|---|
| *Price* | €22–€25 |
| *Region* | Murcia |
| *Grape* | Monastrell/Cab Sauv |
| *Alc/vol* | 14.5% |
| *Food* | Meat/beef |
| *Drink* | 2002–4 |

## Gran Caus DO Penedès 95 ☆

Excellent: ripe, soft and mature, with barnyard and savoury aromas and a concentrated palate with flavours of tobacco, spice and leather and overall subtlety and length. *Approach Trade*

| | |
|---|---|
| *Price* | €22–€25 |
| *Region* | Catalonia |
| *Grape* | Merlot/Cab Sauv/ Cab Franc |
| *Alc/vol* | 13% |
| *Food* | Meat/lamb |
| *Drink* | 2002–3 |

€25–€30

## Descendentes de J. Palacios DO Bierzo **00**

Big nose with a vegetal background. Ripe, full-bodied, fruity palate with raspberry and banana and flowery elements. Perfect for bistro-style food. *Approach Trade*

| | |
|---|---|
| *Price* | €25–€30 |
| *Region* | Castilla-León |
| *Grape* | Mencia |
| *Alc/vol* | 13.5% |
| *Food* | Meat/cassoulet |
| *Drink* | 2002–3 |

## Mauro VdT **99**

This wine has a very rich nose, fruity, floral and spicy with a preponderance of blackcurrant aromas and a soft, ripe, fruity and extremely spicy palate. *Approach Trade*

| | |
|---|---|
| *Price* | €25–€30 |
| *Region* | Castilla-León |
| *Grape* | Tempranillo |
| *Alc/vol* | 13.5% |
| *Food* | Game/pheasant |
| *Drink* | 2002–4 |

## Palacio de Muruzabal Reserva DO Navarra **94**

Classically elegant with development showing in aromas and flavours of coffee, leather and spice with still very good black and red fruit character. *Approach Trade*

| | |
|---|---|
| *Price* | €25–€30 |
| *Region* | Navarra |
| *Grape* | Cab Sauv/Merlot/ Tempranillo |
| *Alc/vol* | 13% |
| *Food* | Poultry/duck |
| *Drink* | 2002–3 |

€30–€35

## Faustino de Autor Reserva DOC Rioja **94**

Big and concentrated fruitcake nose of spice, damson and plum. Oaky, vanilla overtones to the palate which has good overall balance and lots of baked fruit and some leathery flavours from maturity. *Gilbeys*

| | |
|---|---|
| *Price* | €30–€35 |
| *Region* | Rioja |
| *Grape* | Rioja varieties |
| *Alc/vol* | 13% |
| *Food* | Meat/lamb chops |
| *Drink* | 2002–5 |

## Malleolus DO Ribera del Duero **98** ☆

Big, black, fruity flavours to the fore with a powerful dose of cassis and some spicy and savoury elements starting to emerge. This wine is still youthful with lots of life ahead. *Approach Trade*

| | |
|---|---|
| *Price* | €30–€35 |
| *Region* | Castilla-León |
| *Grape* | Tempranillo |
| *Alc/vol* | 14% |
| *Food* | Meat/lamb |
| *Drink* | 2002–6 |

## Prado Enea Gran Reserva DOC Rioja **94** ☆

Great example of Gran Reserva showing perfect development in its mature aromas of figs, vanilla, spice and leather. Finely balanced palate, fruity with fig, raisin and prune flavours and spicy complexity, with great length and persistent flavour. *Comans*

| | |
|---|---|
| *Price* | €30–€35 |
| *Region* | Rioja |
| *Grape* | Tempranillo/Garnacha/ Mazuelo/Graciano |
| *Alc/vol* | 13.5% |
| *Food* | Poultry/turkey |
| *Drink* | 2002–4 |

# USA

We were very impressed with the US wines submitted this year, mainly from California but also from Washington State. There were some particularly interesting red blends of Shiraz and Zinfandel. The majority of red varietals were either Zinfandel or Cabernet Sauvignon with some examples of Shiraz, Merlot and Pinot Noir. The white wines, which included some excellent Chardonnays and an unusual Riesling from Washington State, Eroica Ch. Ste Michelle, were also very good. Some producers stood out for their interesting and very well-made wines, some at very reasonable prices: Geyser Peak and its sister winery Canyon Road, Bonterra, with its organic wines and Ernest and Juio Gallo for their Sonoma Selections.

## White

### Under €9

### Nathanson Creek Chardonnay 99

Red apple nose with citrus notes and a mineral, stony influence. Quite a delicate palate with citrus flavours and tropical undertones with nice weight complemented by a persistent, refreshing finish. *Barry & Fitzwilliam*

| | |
|---|---|
| Price | Under €9 |
| Region | California |
| Grape | Chardonnay |
| Alc/vol | 13% |
| Food | Fish/turbot |
| Drink | 2002–3 |

### Tesco West Coast Chardonnay 00

Lots of oak gives buttered apple and caramel aromas. The fleshy, tropical fruit palate has toasty and buttery tones. *Tesco*

| | |
|---|---|
| Price | Under €9 |
| Region | California |
| Grape | Chardonnay |
| Alc/vol | 13.5% |
| Food | Fish/salmon |
| Drink | 2002–3 |

### €9–€12

### Canyon Road Chardonnay 99 ☆☆ €

Delicious, smoky, spicy and vanilla aromas on the nose. Rich palate with layers of sun-ripened tropical fruits, oily, toasty and buttery with great body and a long, fruity finish. *Maxxium*

| | |
|---|---|
| Price | €9–€12 |
| Region | California |
| Grape | Chardonnay |
| Alc/vol | 13.5% |
| Food | Poultry/duck |
| Drink | 2002–4 |

### Fetzer Chardonnay Viognier 00

Lovely, light, fruity nose with apricot and peach aromas. More concentrated palate with generous levels of ripe apricots and peaches and a warm, pleasant finish. *Dillons*

| | |
|---|---|
| Price | €9–€12 |
| Region | California |
| Grape | Chardonnay/Viognier |
| Alc/vol | 13.5% |
| Food | Fish/fish pie |
| Drink | 2002–3 |

## Talus Chardonnay 00

Quite a ripe, almost Burgundian, opulent style with good structure and finesse. Smoky and peachy aromas and orchard fruit flavours with a hint of fresh herbs. *Barry & Fitzwilliam*

| | |
|---|---|
| *Price* | €9–€12 |
| *Region* | California |
| *Grape* | Chardonnay |
| *Alc/vol* | 13% |
| *Food* | Fish/salmon |
| *Drink* | 2002–4 |

### €12–€15

## Beringer Appellation Collection Fumé Blanc 00

Intense, grassy, green bouquet with a hint of oak. Very distinctive herbal and black pepper flavours at first with citrus following. A big, spicy, earthy wine—highly distinctive, courageous winemaking. *Allied Drinks*

| | |
|---|---|
| *Price* | €12–€15 |
| *Region* | Napa Valley, California |
| *Grape* | Sauvignon Blanc |
| *Alc/vol* | 13.5% |
| *Food* | Ethnic/Indian |
| *Drink* | 2002–3 |

## Fetzer Viognier 99

Inviting perfumed and floral aromas with generous flavours of peaches and pears and an intriguing touch of smokiness. *Dillons*

| | |
|---|---|
| *Price* | €12–€15 |
| *Region* | North Coast, California |
| *Grape* | Viognier |
| *Alc/vol* | 13.5% |
| *Food* | Poultry/chicken |
| *Drink* | 2002–3 |

## Stratford Chardonnay 99

Quite tangy with lemon and apple sherbet. The fruit is ripe but not heavy, with predominately citrus and lemon zest flavours. Well made and easy drinking. *Barry & Fitzwilliam*

| | |
|---|---|
| *Price* | €12–€15 |
| *Region* | California |
| *Grape* | Chardonnay |
| *Alc/vol* | 13% |
| *Food* | Fish/sole |
| *Drink* | 2002–3 |

## Clos du Bois Chardonnay 00

Benchmark Californian Chardonnay in a crisp style with delicate flavours of apple and citrus fruits, hints of spice and lovely warmth. Showing some smoky elements and complexity. *Grants*

| | |
|---|---|
| *Price* | €12–€15 |
| *Region* | Sonoma County, California |
| *Grape* | Chardonnay |
| *Alc/vol* | 13.5% |
| *Food* | Fish/monkfish |
| *Drink* | 2002–3 |

## Columbia Crest Chardonnay 00

Full-on oaky nose of vanilla, toast and smoke with tropical fruit and butterscotch. Full-bodied, matching palate of ripe apple, toffee, caramel and oaky vanilla sweetness. *Comans*

| | |
|---|---|
| *Price* | €12–€15 |
| *Region* | Columbia Valley, Washington State |
| *Grape* | Chardonnay |
| *Alc/vol* | 13.5% |
| *Food* | Poultry/garilc chicken |
| *Drink* | 2002–3 |

€15–€18

## Geyser Peak Chardonnay 97

For those who like heavy, oaked whites. This is a generous wine with a big nose of ripe, oily, luscious pineapple and a hint of toffee, and a seriously tropical and honeyed palate. *Maxxium*

| | |
|---|---|
| *Price* | **€15–€18** |
| *Region* | **California** |
| *Grape* | **Chardonnay** |
| *Alc/vol* | **13.5%** |
| *Food* | **Poultry/turkey** |
| *Drink* | **2002–3** |

€18–€22

## Murphy-Goode Barrel-Fermented Chardonnay 99

The initial impression on the nose is of butterscotch with some lemon and lime aromas. Very full palate with warm fruits, oily, rich, spicy hints and crisp acidity. *Wines Direct*

| | |
|---|---|
| *Price* | **€18–€22** |
| *Region* | **Sonoma County, California** |
| *Grape* | **Chardonnay** |
| *Alc/vol* | **13.5%** |
| *Food* | **Fish/barbecue** |
| *Drink* | **2002–4** |

€22–€25

## Benziger Fumé Blanc 00 ☆

Quality and breeding are obvious with ripe citrus and exotic, luscious fruit, greengage, pineapple and lime blossom, an exciting smokiness and a richly concentrated structure. *Febvre*

| | |
|---|---|
| *Price* | **€22–€25** |
| *Region* | **Sonoma County, California** |
| *Grape* | **Sauvignon Blanc** |
| *Alc/vol* | **13.5%** |
| *Food* | **Fish/trout** |
| *Drink* | **2002–4** |

€25–€30

## Ernest and Julio Gallo Laguna Ranch Chardonnay 99

Inviting, smoky bacon nose with an intensely rich, fruity palate, sumptuous, creamy, lemon meringue, ripe melons, tangerines and toasty oak which allows the fruit to show through. *Irish Distillers*

| | |
|---|---|
| *Price* | **€25–€30** |
| *Region* | **Sonoma County, California** |
| *Grape* | **Chardonnay** |
| *Alc/vol* | **14.5%** |
| *Food* | **Fish/chowder** |
| *Drink* | **2002–4** |

## Eroica Ch. Ste Michelle Riesling 01 ☆

Beautifully-made Riesling—fruity and lively with fresh lime and lemon aromas. The citrus and apple flavours are equally zesty, with tingling, mouth-watering acidity. *Comans*

| | |
|---|---|
| *Price* | **€25–€30** |
| *Region* | **Columbia Valley, Washington State** |
| *Grape* | **Riesling** |
| *Alc/vol* | **12%** |
| *Food* | **Meat/honey-roast ham** |
| *Drink* | **2002–4** |

# Red

*Under €9*

## Nathanson Creek Cabernet Sauvignon 98

Good. easy, midweek-drinking style, with juicy, blackcurrant pie and jam, mulberries and vanilla. Balanced, with a good finish.
*Barry & Fitzwilliam*

| | |
|---|---|
| *Price* | **Under €9** |
| *Region* | **California** |
| *Grape* | **Cabernet Sauvignon** |
| *Alc/vol* | **12%** |
| *Food* | **Cheese/Cheshire** |
| *Drink* | **2002–3** |

## Vendange Cabernet Sauvignon 98 €

Good, mature wine in a classic mode. Restrained blackcurrant nose with hints of pepper. Nice touch of complexity to the palate with nuances of undergrowth and chocolate.
*Barry & Fitzwilliam*

| | |
|---|---|
| *Price* | **Under €9** |
| *Region* | **California** |
| *Grape* | **Cabernet Sauvignon** |
| *Alc/vol* | **13%** |
| *Food* | **Vegetarian/peppers** |
| *Drink* | **2002–3** |

*€9–€12*

## Canyon Road Cabernet Sauvignon 00

Ripe, creamy nose with sweet damsons, plums, currants and spicy oak hints. Soft and silky-textured, though with a backbone of tannin, the palate has persistent flavours of black fruits, spice and anise. *Maxxium*

| | |
|---|---|
| *Price* | **€9–€12** |
| *Region* | **Alexander Valley, California** |
| *Grape* | **Cabernet Sauvignon** |
| *Alc/vol* | **13.5%** |
| *Food* | **Ethnic/Chinese** |
| *Drink* | **2002–5** |

## Fetzer Zinfandel Shiraz 00

Gutsy, with slightly stewed damsons and plums and peppery spice, this is nicely warmed with California sunshine. *Dillons*

| | |
|---|---|
| *Price* | **€9–€12** |
| *Region* | **California** |
| *Grape* | **Zinfandel/Shiraz** |
| *Alc/vol* | **14%** |
| *Food* | **Meat/hamburgers** |
| *Drink* | **2002–3** |

## Pepperwood Grove Zinfandel 99

A strong combination of fruit and spice, packing a punch of plum, fig, damson and mulberry flavours laced with cinnamon and nutmeg.
*Gleeson*

| | |
|---|---|
| *Price* | **€9–€12** |
| *Region* | **California** |
| *Grape* | **Zinfandel** |
| *Alc/vol* | **13.5%** |
| *Food* | **Poultry/duck** |
| *Drink* | **2002–4** |

## Talus Cabernet Sauvignon 98 ☆ €

Made in a classic style with fine balance. Generous, smooth palate with good tannic grip and delicious, ripe redcurrant and blackcurrant flavours leading to a good, clinching length.
*Barry & Fitzwilliam*

| | |
|---|---|
| *Price* | €9–€12 |
| *Region* | California |
| *Grape* | Cabernet Sauvignon |
| *Alc/vol* | 13% |
| *Food* | Meat/lamb |
| *Drink* | 2002–4 |

### €12–€15

## Beringer Appellation Collection Zinfandel 99

Well made Zin, full bodied, with a rich, creamy, spicy oak nose with raspberry and cherry aromas. It packs quite a punch on the palate with lots of fruitcake, chewy, spicy and earthy, maturing flavours. *Allied Drinks*

| | |
|---|---|
| *Price* | €12–€15 |
| *Region* | California |
| *Grape* | Zinfandel |
| *Alc/vol* | 13.5% |
| *Food* | Meat/barbecue |
| *Drink* | 2002–3 |

## Canyon Road Merlot 99

A big and powerful winter warmer, supple and seductive from beginning to end with very ripe plummy fruits, raisins, cherries, prunes and spice, reminiscent of Christmas cake. *Maxxium*

| | |
|---|---|
| *Price* | €12–€15 |
| *Region* | California |
| *Grape* | Merlot |
| *Alc/vol* | 13.5% |
| *Food* | Meat/grills |
| *Drink* | 2002–3 |

## CK Vineyards Wildwood Canyon Syrah 99

Substantial, almost exotic, wine. Ample concentration of ripe plum fruits with liquorice, pepper and star anise. *Findlaters*

| | |
|---|---|
| *Price* | €12–€15 |
| *Region* | California |
| *Grape* | Syrah |
| *Alc/vol* | 14% |
| *Food* | Meat/stews |
| *Drink* | 2002–4 |

## CK Vineyards Wildwood Canyon Zinfandel 00

Big style wine with aromas of sweet loganberry and blackberry and a palate which is big on pepper and spice with layers of dried fruit, raisins and figs. *Findlaters*

| | |
|---|---|
| *Price* | €12–€15 |
| *Region* | California |
| *Grape* | Zinfandel |
| *Alc/vol* | 14% |
| *Food* | Meat/dishes with soy |
| *Drink* | 2003–4 |

## Ernest & Julio Gallo Sonoma Selection Pinot Noir 99 ☆

Quite seductive and pleasant impression from the concentrated nose of vanilla and summer fruits. The palate measures up—dry and spicy with ripe, dark cherry flavours. *Irish Distillers*

| | |
|---|---|
| *Price* | €12–€15 |
| *Region* | California |
| *Grape* | Pinot Noir |
| *Alc/vol* | 14% |
| *Food* | Fish/tuna |
| *Drink* | 2002–5 |

## Ernest & Julio Gallo Sonoma Selection Zinfandel 97 ☆

Rich, herb-infused raspberry, cherry and plum aromas. Weighty, lush palate with sweet and generous fruit, soft, well-hidden tannins and a flowery finish. *Irish Distillers*

| | |
|---|---|
| *Price* | €12–€15 |
| *Region* | Sonoma County, California |
| *Grape* | Zinfandel |
| *Alc/vol* | 14.5% |
| *Food* | Meat/steak |
| *Drink* | 2002–3 |

## Fetzer Eagle Peak Merlot 99

Soft, plummy fruits characterise this Merlot. It has lovely ripeness and a very attractive oak and spice influence plus a warm, fleshy finish.
*Dillons*

| | |
|---|---|
| *Price* | €12–€15 |
| *Region* | California |
| *Grape* | Merlot |
| *Alc/vol* | 13.5% |
| *Food* | Meat/shepherd's pie |
| *Drink* | 2002–4 |

## Fetzer Valley Oaks Zinfandel 99

Packed with flavour and spice with lots of concentrated, ripe, stewed plums and cranberries and a strong mineral heart. *Dillons*

| | |
|---|---|
| *Price* | €12–€15 |
| *Region* | California |
| *Grape* | Zinfandel |
| *Alc/vol* | 13.5% |
| *Food* | Poultry/turkey |
| *Drink* | 2002–4 |

## Kendall-Jackson Collage Zinfandel Shiraz 98

The Californian recipe of Zin and Syrah works well here giving lots of ripe, juicy fruits and a fine, spicy, soft palate. Very smooth, balanced and accomplished. *Cassidy*

| | |
|---|---|
| *Price* | €12–€15 |
| *Region* | California |
| *Grape* | Zinfandel/Shiraz |
| *Alc/vol* | 13.5% |
| *Food* | Meat/lamb |
| *Drink* | 2002–3 |

## Live Oak Road Zinfandel 00 ☆

Complex. smoky nose with fruit of the forest aromas and a very full-bodied, soft and elegant palate, rich and creamy, with oriental spices, sweet raspberry and cherry and ripe tannins. *Marks & Spencer*

| | |
|---|---|
| *Price* | €12–€15 |
| *Region* | California |
| *Grape* | Zinfandel |
| *Alc/vol* | 14.5% |
| *Food* | Meat/roasts |
| *Drink* | 2002–4 |

## Pepperwood Grove Pinot Noir 99 ☆

Seductive nose with cherry fruit, spice, nuts and coffee hints, this is a benchmark US Pinot. It has good structure and is full bodied and fruity with layers of toasted spice, blackberries, anise and cherries on an elegant yet powerful palate. *Gleeson*

| | |
|---|---|
| *Price* | €12–€15 |
| *Region* | California |
| *Grape* | Pinot Noir |
| *Alc/vol* | 13% |
| *Food* | Fish/salmon |
| *Drink* | 2002–5 |

## Bonterra Cabernet Sauvignon 98 🍷 ☆

Stylish and structured, in the mode of good Bordeaux, this is great winemaking. Elegant and classic with a rich concentration of black-currants, cigar box and tobacco leaf. *Dillons*

| | |
|---|---|
| Price | €12–€15 |
| Region | North Coast, California |
| Grape | Cabernet Sauvignon |
| Alc/vol | 13% |
| Food | Poultry/goose |
| Drink | 2002–4 |

## Bonterra Zinfandel 99 🍷 ☆

This weighty Zin really delivers. Big, bold and chewy, it has luscious, ripe raspberry and cran-berry aromas on the nose and a delicious weight of sweet fruit flavours, vanilla pod, mocha, coffee and liquorice. *Dillons*

| | |
|---|---|
| Price | €12–€15 |
| Region | Mendocino, California |
| Grape | Zinfandel |
| Alc/vol | 14% |
| Food | Game/pheasant |
| Drink | 2002–3 |

## Columbia Crest Merlot 99

A wine to chew on, very concentrated and best with food. It has a wealth of aromas—cherry, plum, green pepper, mint, spice and earthiness. The palate is equally flavoursome with lots of baked black fruit, prunes and spice. *Comans*

| | |
|---|---|
| Price | €12–€15 |
| Region | Columbia Valley, Washington State |
| Grape | Merlot |
| Alc/vol | 13.5% |
| Food | Meat/liver |
| Drink | 2002–5 |

## Clos du Bois Pinot Noir 99

Accessible New World Pinot Noir with soft, easy tannins, raspberry, overripe strawberry and cherry flavours and just a touch of vegetal leaf-iness with hints of spice. *Grants*

| | |
|---|---|
| Price | €12–€15 |
| Region | Sonoma County, California |
| Grape | Pinot Noir |
| Alc/vol | 12.8% |
| Food | Meat/ham |
| Drink | 2002–3 |

### €15–€18

## Francis Coppola Presents Rosso 00

Ripe berry, vanilla and spicy nose with lots of soft raspberry, strawberry, cherry and black-currant flavours, and a nice touch of defining stalkiness. *Woodford Bourne*

| | |
|---|---|
| Price | €15–€18 |
| Region | California |
| Grape | Zinfandel/Syrah/ Cabernet/Sangiovese |
| Alc/vol | 13.5% |
| Food | Meat/casseroles |
| Drink | 2002–3 |

## €18–€22

### Geyser Peak Cabernet Sauvignon 97 ☆☆

Restrained and elegant nose with aromas of
fruit of the forest, cold tea and cigar box. The
palate has ripe cassis, layers of flavour and a
concentrated heart. It's a Paul McGrath—a wine
to ooh and aah over. *Maxxium*

| | |
|---|---|
| *Price* | **€18–€22** |
| *Region* | **Sonoma County, California** |
| *Grape* | **Cabernet Sauvignon** |
| *Alc/vol* | **13.5%** |
| *Food* | **Meat/steak** |
| *Drink* | **2002–4** |

### Geyser Peak Shiraz 96 ☆

Great depth of colour despite its age, with damson, leather and liquorice aromas, a touch
herbal or medicinal. The flavours are a melange
of sun-dried tomatoes and black olives, pepper
and blackcurrant. Great concentration and a
strong finish *Maxxium*

| | |
|---|---|
| *Price* | **€18–€22** |
| *Region* | **Sonoma County, California** |
| *Grape* | **Shiraz** |
| *Alc/vol* | **13.5%** |
| *Food* | **Meat/pork** |
| *Drink* | **2002–4** |

### Kendall-Jackson Vintner's Reserve Cabernet Sauvignon 97 ☆

Big, strong wine, very ripe with smooth black
fruit, blackcurrant leaf, tobacco and espresso
coffee nose. Intense, rich, laid-back palate with
luscious fruit and a smoky, almost roasted, character, and a fine, memorable finish. *Cassidy*

| | |
|---|---|
| *Price* | **€18–€22** |
| *Region* | **California** |
| *Grape* | **Cabernet Sauvignon** |
| *Alc/vol* | **13.5%** |
| *Food* | **Meat/beef** |
| *Drink* | **2002–5** |

### Ravenswood Vintners Blend Zinfandel 99

A big, full-bodied Zin, with more aged aromas
and more pronounced tannins than most
examples. Aromas are of spice, earth, sweet
cherry and raspberry and the palate is full of
sweet, silky, warm black fruit.
*Woodford Bourne*

| | |
|---|---|
| *Price* | **€18–€22** |
| *Region* | **Napa Valley, California** |
| *Grape* | **Zinfandel** |
| *Alc/vol* | **13.5%** |
| *Food* | **Meat/steak** |
| *Drink* | **2002–4** |

## €22–€25

### Robert Mondavi Coastal Cabernet Sauvignon 98

A serious wine with an intense nose of cassis
and pencil shavings with some herbaceous
characteristics. Quite chewy fruit on the palate
with firm, dry tannins, violet and floral flavours
as well as blackcurrants. *Febvre*

| | |
|---|---|
| *Price* | **€22–€25** |
| *Region* | **California** |
| *Grape* | **Cabernet Sauvignon** |
| *Alc/vol* | **13.5%** |
| *Food* | **Meat/beef** |
| *Drink* | **2002–4** |

## €30–€35

### Benziger Zinfandel 98

Excellent complexity with aromas of spice, pepper, mint and cherry and a good, juicy mouthful of cherry, plum pudding and raspberry flavours mixed with spicy oak, good tannins and overall balance. *Febvre*

| | |
|---|---|
| *Price* | €30–€35 |
| *Region* | Sonoma County, California |
| *Grape* | Zinfandel/Cab Sauv/ Syrah/Petite Sirah |
| *Alc/vol* | 14.5% |
| *Food* | Poultry/duck |
| *Drink* | 2002–5 |

### Francis Coppola Diamond Series Merlot 99

Spicy, rustic and a touch earthy with intense mulled plum aromas. The palate is very ripe and plummy with Christmas cake flavours, liquorice, spice and creamy oak. *Woodford Bourne*

| | |
|---|---|
| *Price* | €30–€35 |
| *Region* | California |
| *Grape* | Merlot |
| *Alc/vol* | 13.5% |
| *Food* | Meat/roasts |
| *Drink* | 2002–4 |

## €35–€40

### Francis Coppola Diamond Series Zinfandel 99 ☆

An intense nose of cherries spiced with cloves and cinnamon is matched by a warm and spicy palate with mellow tannins and flavours of herbs, cherries and raspberries. *Woodford Bourne*

| | |
|---|---|
| *Price* | €35–€40 |
| *Region* | California |
| *Grape* | Zinfandel |
| *Alc/vol* | 13.5% |
| *Food* | Meat/lamb |
| *Drink* | 2002–4 |

### Geyser Peak Reserve Cabernet Sauvignon 96 ☆☆☆

Elegant, with classic finesse, ample cassis, cigar box and smoky aromas and flavours. Tannins are still firm. This is one to brood and ponder over and savour slowly; it will continue to improve. *Maxxium*

| | |
|---|---|
| *Price* | €35–€40 |
| *Region* | Alexander Valley California |
| *Grape* | Cabernet Sauvignon |
| *Alc/vol* | 13.5% |
| *Food* | Meat/lamb |
| *Drink* | 2002–6 |

SHORTLIST RED WINE OF THE YEAR

# Rosé

Most rosés are made in the same way as red wines. However, the grape juice, or must, is run off the skins after a shorter time so that less colour is absorbed by the wine. The colour depends on the grapes used, and the amount of time their skins are left in contact with the must, and can vary dramatically from producer to producer and region to region. In some cases, rosés are as full bodied as red wines but with white wine type acidity. This is perhaps why they are such a good choice for warmer weather and outdoor dining.

## Under €9

### Dom. de Pellehaut VdP des Côtes de Gascogne 01

A foodie style of rosé with quite a stewed red fruit nose and a juicy and crisp palate with strawberry fruitiness, pepper and earthy spiciness. *Mitchells*

| | |
|---|---|
| Price | Under €9 |
| Country | France–South West |
| Grape | Merlot/Tannat |
| Alc/vol | 12% |
| Food | Salad/Niçoise |
| Drink | 2002–3 |

### Dom. Vignelaure 01

Very pale and delicate in colour for a rosé, this has a candied and fragrant, floral scented nose with a light, silky texture and cherry and raspberry flavours. *Dunnes Stores*

| | |
|---|---|
| Price | Under €9 |
| Country | France–South |
| Grape | Cab Sauv/Syrah |
| Alc/vol | 12% |
| Food | Meat/salami |
| Drink | 2002–3 |

### Gran Feudo DO Navarra 01

Crisp, fresh, zingy rosé perfect for summer drinking. It has an attractive salmon colour and crisp red apple, raspberry and strawberry flavours. Serve with a platter of Serrano ham for a perfect summer picnic. *TDL*

| | |
|---|---|
| Price | Under €9 |
| Country | Spain |
| Grape | Garnacha |
| Alc/vol | 12.5% |
| Food | Picnic/salads |
| Drink | 2002–3 |

### Marqués de Cáceres DOC Rioja 00

A wine that looks as good as it tastes with a most attractive, rosy-pink colour. Aromas of strawberries, raspberries and red cherries, and a dry, fruity palate with hints of pepper and grapefruit peel. *Grants*

| | |
|---|---|
| Price | Under €9 |
| Country | Spain |
| Grape | Garnacha |
| Alc/vol | 13% |
| Food | Fish/tuna |
| Drink | 2002–3 |

### Mount Hurtle Grenache Rosé 01

A pretty and refreshing summer drink, just a touch off-dry, with rosehip and raspberry aromas and fuller flavours of squashed cherries and raspberries with a sprinkle of white pepper. *Comans*

| | |
|---|---|
| Price | Under €9 |
| Country | Australia |
| Grape | Grenache |
| Alc/vol | 14% |
| Food | Risotto/seafood |
| Drink | 2002–3 |

## Nathanson Creek White Zinfandel 99

A sweeter style with a fair amount of residual sugar. Coral pink in colour, fruity, with rose petal and boiled sweet flavours.
*Barry & Fitzwilliam*

| | |
|---|---|
| Price | Under €9 |
| Country | USA, California |
| Grape | Zinfandel |
| Alc/vol | 11% |
| Food | Fish/smoked salmon |
| Drink | 2002–3 |

## Viña Carmina DO Utiel-Requena 01

The nose suggests a relatively sweet wine with very ripe strawberry aromas but the palate is dry and has good crisp acidity overlaying flavours of strawberries. *IberExpo*

| | |
|---|---|
| Price | Under €9 |
| Country | Spain |
| Alc/vol | 12.5% |
| Food | Fish/salmon |
| Drink | 2002–3 |

### €9–€12

## Alma DO Navarra 00

A most appealing candyfloss pink with deliciously vibrant wild berry and floral aromas and a soft red fruit character of strawberries and raspberries with a smoky, pink grapefruit edge and fine, crisp length. *Approach Trade*

| | |
|---|---|
| Price | €9–€12 |
| Country | Spain |
| Grape | Garnacha |
| Alc/vol | 12.5% |
| Food | Fish/trout |
| Drink | 2002–3 |

## Ch. Lacroix Merlot Saignée Rosé AC Bordeaux Rosé 00

Really delicious strawberry and rich smoky aromas are followed by a generous helping of red fruit pie flavours and strawberry and vanilla ice-cream. This has lots of character and would be great with salmon or sea trout. *Findlaters*

| | |
|---|---|
| Price | €9–€12 |
| Country | France–Bordeaux |
| Grape | Merlot |
| Alc/vol | 12.5% |
| Food | Fish/salmon |
| Drink | 2002–3 |

## Ch. Miaudoux AC Bergerac Rosé 01

Light pink in colour with red cherry and loganberry aromas and a good, juicy, red fruit palate with pink peppercorns. Crisp acidity adds to the overall impression of elegance and balance.
*WineKnows*

| | |
|---|---|
| Price | €9–€12 |
| Country | France–South West |
| Grape | Cab Sauv/Merlot |
| Alc/vol | 12% |
| Food | Vegetarian/cous-cous |
| Drink | 2002–3 |

## Miguel Torres Cabernet Sauvignon Rosé 01 ☆ €

A full style, rich in colour, with quite complex aromas of herbs, tomato skins and red berry jam. The palate is very fruity with flavours of raspberry and strawberry and a creamy texture.
*Woodford Bourne*

| | |
|---|---|
| Price | €9–€12 |
| Country | Chile |
| Grape | Cabernet Sauvignon |
| Alc/vol | 13.5% |
| Food | Poultry/chicken |
| Drink | 2002–3 |

€12–€15

## Guigal AC Côtes du Rhône 00

Delightful floral aromas of rosehip and geranium with quite a chewy, tart loganberry palate and a twist of citrus peel making the wine crisp and flavoursome. *Barry & Fitzwilliam*

| | |
|---|---|
| *Price* | **€12–€15** |
| *Country* | **France–Rhône** |
| *Grape* | **Grenache/Cinsault/ Carignan/Mourvèdre** |
| *Alc/vol* | **13%** |
| *Food* | **Pizza/seafood** |
| *Drink* | **2002–3** |

€15–€18

## Enate Rosado Cabernet Sauvignon DO Somontano 00

Attractive, rosy, pink colour with light cassis aromas and lots of good, juicy, summer fruit flavours of morello cherry and raspberry. Strikingly crisp, lemony acidity makes this a very fresh style. *Febvre*

| | |
|---|---|
| *Price* | **€15–€18** |
| *Country* | **Spain** |
| *Grape* | **Cabernet Sauvignon** |
| *Alc/vol* | **13%** |
| *Food* | **Fish/sardines** |
| *Drink* | **2002–3** |

## Gran Caus Rosado DO Penedès 99

Pure, deep colour for a rosé, almost like a very light red. Lots of blackcurrant and plum aromas and mixed berry jam and plum compote flavours with a touch of caramel. With such a big heart and rich flavours this rosé could work well with pasta sauces. *Approach Trade*

| | |
|---|---|
| *Price* | **€15–€18** |
| *Country* | **Spain** |
| *Grape* | **Merlot** |
| *Alc/vol* | **13%** |
| *Food* | **Pasta/seafood** |
| *Drink* | **2002–3** |

| The symbols | |
|---|---|
| ⚘ | *Organic* |
| € | *Exceptionally good value* |
| ☆ | *Accomplished, showing above average quality or character making it worthy of extra attention* |
| ☆☆ | *Excellent with great character, style and complexity* |
| ☆☆☆ | *Wonderful, showing terrific character and complexity, true to its origins* |
| ☆☆☆☆ | *Exceptional, with considerable complexity and classic balance. Rewards serious tasting.* |

# Sparkling

While vintage and prestige cuvées are perhaps the most impressive and most expensive of Champagnes, the most important are the non-vintage (nv) blends which dominated the tastings this year. An nv Champagne blend may include up to three different grape varieties, selected from a number of vineyard areas, and most importantly includes wines from a number of different years. The art of blending gives each Champagne house a unique style, which can be recreated each year to ensure a consistency of style and continuity of taste. Many of the best nvs are household names. However, label snobbery does a great injustice to the increasing number of lesser known Champagnes now available. At more modest prices these are well worth seeking out.

A growing number of sparkling wines are now available that are good alternatives to Champagne and at a lower price tag. Overall, the most interesting sparkling wines this year were either French or Australian. Sparkling wines are produced in nearly all of France's wine regions, outside Champagne. Known as crémants they are made by the same traditional method as Champagne although they may be aged for shorter periods and different grape varieties are used. The Sparkling Wine of the Year is from Australia—Green Point Brut 97, made in collaboration with the Champagne house Dom. Chandon, marrying the best that Australia and France have to offer.

## Champagne

### €18–€22

#### Comte L. de Ferande Brut nv ☆☆ €

Seductive and appealing with aromas of almond biscuits, baked apples and lemon zest. The palate has a classic elegance with crisp acidity and a full mousse with lingering, delicate, sweet, red fruit flavours. *Dunnes Stores*

| | |
|---|---|
| Price | €18–€22 |
| Region | France–Champagne |
| Grape | Champagne varieties |
| Alc/vol | 12% |
| Food | Apéritif/smoked fish |
| Drink | On purchase |

*SHORTLIST SPARKLING WINE OF THE YEAR*

### €22–€25

#### Henri Harlin Brut nv

Quite intense nose of rich, fermenting apples with oily and nutty hints. Crisp and firm palate, big and lemony with crunchy apples and rhubarb flavours. *Oddbins*

| | |
|---|---|
| Price | €22–€25 |
| Region | France–Champagne |
| Grape | Pinot Noir, Chardonnay, Pinot Meunier |
| Alc/vol | 12% |
| Food | Apéritif/shrimps |
| Drink | 2002–3 |

### €25–€30

## Bernard Depoivre Brut nv ☆☆

Wonderfully balanced, complex and classy. Yeasty and underlying citrus fruit aromas, subtle yet rich fruit on the palate showing peaches and raspberries and a cool, acidic structure. *Bubble Brothers*

| | |
|---|---|
| Price | €25–€30 |
| Region | France–Champagne |
| Grape | Champagne varieties |
| Alc/vol | 12% |
| Food | Apéritif/crab |
| Drink | 2002–3 |

## J. Dumangin Fils Carte d'Or 1er Cru Brut nv

Summery style with good fruit quality. The nose is fragrant with apple blossom aromas. The palate has crisp apple flavours and an apple skin finish. *River Wines*

| | |
|---|---|
| Price | €25–€30 |
| Region | France–Champagne |
| Grape | Chardonnay/Pinot Noir/Pinot Meunier |
| Alc/vol | 12% |
| Food | Apéritif/Indian |
| Drink | On purchase |

## J. M. Gobillard Grande Réserve Brut nv ☆

Golden orange in colour, this has an ample yeasty and toasty nose of brioche, nuts and toffee apple. Full and long-lasting mousse with yeasty and orange peel flavours. *Le Caveau*

| | |
|---|---|
| Price | €25–€30 |
| Region | France–Champagne |
| Grape | Chardonnay/Pinot Noir/Pinot Meunier |
| Alc/vol | 12% |
| Food | Apéritif/smoked chicken |
| Drink | On purchase |

### €30–€35

## Canard-Duchêne Brut nv

Very lively and vibrant with crunchy fresh apple. The palate is particularly biscuity and yeasty with a warm, cinnamon toastiness and good, persistent length and mousse. *TDL*

| | |
|---|---|
| Price | €30–€35 |
| Region | France–Champagne |
| Grape | Pinot Noir |
| Alc/vol | 12% |
| Food | Apéritif/tapenade |
| Drink | On purchase |

> The recommendation to drink **on purchase** has been given for most non-vintage (nv) Champagnes, which are generally ready to drink on release. In practice, nv Champagne is usually drunk shortly after purchase.

## Delbeck Heritage Brut nv

Excellent apéritif style—light and lemony with cheerful bubbles. The palate has fresh, crisp acidity and delicious flavours of apple and lemon. *Mitchells*

| | |
|---|---|
| Price | €30–€35 |
| Region | France–Champagne |
| Grape | Pinot Noir/Chardonnay |
| Alc/vol | 12% |
| Food | Apéritif/oysters |
| Drink | On purchase |

## Heidsieck Monopole Blue Top Brut nv

The nose is light and elegant with floral and honeyed aromas. This is followed by a seductive palate with flavours of mango, kiwi, lemon and apple with a hint of cinnamon. *Cassidy*

| | |
|---|---|
| *Price* | €30–€35 |
| *Region* | France–Champagne |
| *Grape* | Pinot Noir/ Chardonnay |
| *Alc/vol* | 12% |
| *Food* | Apéritif/raspberries |
| *Drink* | 2002–3 |

> **Champagne styles: Extra Dry** is actually an off-dry style. **Brut** is drier. **Extra Brut** or **Brut Nature** are even drier styles.

## J. Charpentier Prestige Brut nv

Extremely stylish, the nose is quite intense with aromas of strawberry, cherry and red apple. There is a good, rich, weight of chunky red fruit and a touch of brioche on the palate with a lasting, moussy finish. *Wines Direct*

| | |
|---|---|
| *Price* | €30–€35 |
| *Region* | France–Champagne |
| *Grape* | Pinot Noir/ Chardonnay/ Pinot Meunier |
| *Alc/vol* | 12% |
| *Food* | Apéritif/Chinese |
| *Drink* | On purchase |

## L. Dumont Brut nv

Pleasant and appealing, this Champagne has aromas of lemon zest, almond, grapefruit and apple skins, elegant bubbles and a lively palate of biscuit and pear flavours with cleansing acidity. *Peter Dalton*

| | |
|---|---|
| *Price* | €30–€35 |
| *Region* | France–Champagne |
| *Grape* | Champagne varieties |
| *Alc/vol* | 12% |
| *Food* | Apéritif/shellfish |
| *Drink* | On purchase |

### €35–€40

## Charles Heidsieck Réserve Brut mis en cave 97 nv

Appealing, softer style of sparkler, not bone dry. Aromas of honey, biscuit and a burnt toastiness with a touch of sticky bun or baklava on the palate, which is also quite lemony. *Maxxium*

| | |
|---|---|
| *Price* | €35–€40 |
| *Region* | France–Champagne |
| *Grape* | Chardonnay/ Pinot Noir/ Pinot Meunier |
| *Alc/vol* | 12% |
| *Food* | Apéritif/Chinese |
| *Drink* | On purchase |

## Joseph Perrier Cuvée Royale Brut nv

Ample nose with apple and melon aromas, followed by a zesty and full palate with crisp, lemony acidity and flavours of apple, citrus fruit and brioche and a creamy-textured mousse. *Comans*

| | |
|---|---|
| *Price* | €35–€40 |
| *Region* | France–Champagne |
| *Grape* | Chardonnay/ Pinot Noir/ Pinot Meunier |
| *Alc/vol* | 12% |
| *Food* | Apéritif/Thai |
| *Drink* | 2002–3 |

## Louis Roederer Premier Brut nv ☆

Substantial nose with apple, yeast and floral aromas. Very appealing, elegant palate with balance, nutty and yeasty, with apple and citrus fruits. This is an nv that could age well. *Searsons*

| | |
|---|---|
| Price | €35–€40 |
| Region | France–Champagne |
| Grape | Chardonnay/Pinot Noir/Pinot Meunier |
| Alc/vol | 12% |
| Food | Apéritif/salads |
| Drink | 2002–4 |

## Nicolas Feuillatte Réserve Particulière Brut nv

Good, classic, stylish example with yeasty notes and a palate with flavours of toast, nuts, lemon and soft, ripe, green fruit plus a crisp zesty finish. *Febvre*

| | |
|---|---|
| Price | €35–€40 |
| Region | France–Champagne |
| Grape | Chardonnay/Pinot Noir/Pinot Meunier |
| Alc/vol | 12% |
| Food | Apéritif/Chinese |
| Drink | On purchase |

## Pol Roger Extra Dry White Foil nv ☆☆

Broad, intense, bready nose with underlying apple and lime aromas. Fresh, crisp acidity, attractive, green fruit flavours plus strawberry, honey, toffee apple and nutty hints. Classic and seductive. *Barry & Fitzwilliam*

| | |
|---|---|
| Price | €35–€40 |
| Region | France–Champagne |
| Grape | Chardonnay/Pinot Noir/Pinot Meunier |
| Alc/vol | 12% |
| Food | Apéritif/lobster |
| Drink | 2002–4 |

## Veuve Clicquot Ponsardin Brut nv ☆

Powerful style with rich, red fruit, creamy, toasty and nutty nose. A classic, full-bodied palate, with yeast, citrus, hazelnuts and caramelised fruits and an elegant finish. *Findlaters*

| | |
|---|---|
| Price | €35–€40 |
| Region | France–Champagne |
| Grape | Chardonnay/Pinot Noir/Pinot Meunier |
| Alc/vol | 12% |
| Food | Apéritif/smoked fish |
| Drink | 2002–3 |

The Champagne method, called the **traditional method**, is the most expensive, time-consuming and labour-intensive method of producing a sparkling wine. After the normal first fermentation, the wine is bottled and yeast is added to each bottle, which causes a second fermentation to take place. The wine may be left in contact with the yeast for 15 months to 3 years, or even longer, where it will develop aromas and flavours of biscuits or bread. The yeast is removed from the bottle by a process called 'disgorgement' and the wine is then topped up with a mixture of wine and sugar. Depending on the amount of sugar added at this point, the Champagne will be anything from bone dry to sweet.

### €40–€50

## Bollinger Special Cuvée Brut nv ☆

Classic Champagne with really good bubbles and mousse. Full flavoured and yeasty with a weight of biscuit, almond, lemon and Golden Delicious flavours. *Woodford Bourne*

| | |
|---|---|
| Price | €40–€50 |
| Region | France–Champagne |
| Grape | Pinot Noir/ Chardonnay/ Pinot Meunier |
| Alc/vol | 12% |
| Food | Apéritif/smoked fish |
| Drink | 2002–6 |

The rare wine produced from a single year owes its first allegiance to the characteristics of that particular year. **Vintage Champagnes** can benefit from ageing. The vintages of 88, 89 and 90 were wonderful, but very little remains on the shelves. The 91 vintage was poor and only a few Champagne houses made vintage wines in the years 92 to 94; 95 and 96 were very good years.

## Pommery Grand Cru Brut 95 ☆

Subtle apple and yeasty nose with some nutty aromas. The palate has mineral and chalky elements with good, lemony acidity, citrus flavours and a long, persistent mousse. *Irish Distillers*

| | |
|---|---|
| Price | €40–€50 |
| Region | France–Champagne |
| Grape | Champagne varieties |
| Alc/vol | 12.5% |
| Food | Apéritif/scallops |
| Drink | 2002–4 |

## Ruinart Brut nv

Generous nose of strawberries and cream. Fruity and forward style with lots of strawberry and citrus fruit flavours on the biscuity, nutty palate and a good length on the finish. *Taserra*

| | |
|---|---|
| Price | €40–€50 |
| Region | France–Champagne |
| Grape | Chardonnay/ Pinot Noir/ Pinot Meunier |
| Alc/vol | 12% |
| Food | Apéritif/Japanese |
| Drink | 2002–3 |

## Taittinger Réserve Brut nv

Very fresh and fruity with an apple and lemon core, zesty, honeyed and a little bit spicy, nutty and biscuity. The finish is particularly pleasant and lengthy. *Febvre*

| | |
|---|---|
| Price | €40–€50 |
| Region | France–Champagne |
| Grape | Chardonnay/ Pinot Noir/ Pinot Meunier |
| Alc/vol | 12% |
| Food | Apéritif/Chaource cheese |
| Drink | 2002–3 |

---

*Over €50*

## Bollinger Grande Année 92 ☆

Wonderfully concentrated and charming nose of baked apples and roasted nuts. Fresh on the palate with crisp acidity, apple skin, lemon zest and almond biscuit flavours with a very strong, flavoursome finish. *Woodford Bourne*

| | |
|---|---|
| Price | Over €50 |
| Region | France–Champagne |
| Grape | Pinot Noir/ Chardonnay |
| Alc/vol | 12% |
| Food | Apéritif/salmon |
| Drink | 2002–5 |

---

Bollinger is famous for its **RD** or **recently disgorged** wine—which is a vintage Champagne with many extra years ageing on the lees. The wine is complex, best with food.

## Bollinger RD Extra Brut 88 ☆☆

Developed nose of stewed apples, lemon and yeast. The palate is very dry with crisp acidity and a combination of apple and lemon shortbread flavours with a great finish. Top class elegance. *Woodford Bourne*

| | |
|---|---|
| Price | Over €50 |
| Region | France–Champagne |
| Grape | Pinot Noir/ Chardonnay |
| Alc/vol | 12% |
| Food | Apéritif/chicken |
| Drink | 2002–5 |

---

## Deutz Blanc de Blancs Brut 95 ☆☆

Defined and pronounced nose with bread, walnut, lemons and apples. Very integrated and stylish apple and lemon-flavoured palate with a touch of liquorice and an elegant, lasting finish. *Febvre*

| | |
|---|---|
| Price | Over €50 |
| Region | France–Champagne |
| Grape | Chardonnay |
| Alc/vol | 12% |
| Food | Apéritif/truffles |
| Drink | 2002–6 |

---

## Mumm de Cramant Chardonnay Grand Cru Brut nv

Lemon, apple and sourdough nose. Rich, concentrated palate of lemon and lime, which is quite direct and forceful. Still very youthful but beautifully balanced, it has the structure to last. *Grants*

| | |
|---|---|
| Price | Over €50 |
| Region | France–Champagne |
| Grape | Chardonnay |
| Alc/vol | 12% |
| Food | Apéritif/oysters |
| Drink | 2002–4 |

---

# Rosé

€30–€35

## Montaudon Grand Brut Rosé nv

Cheerful, light and flavoursome. An attractive Champagne with a lovely, salmon pink colour, aromas and flavours of strawberries, a creamy mousse and crisp acidity. *Mitchells*

| | |
|---|---|
| Price | €30–€35 |
| Region | France-Champagne |
| Grape | Pinot Noir/ Pinot Meunier |
| Alc/vol | 12% |
| Food | Apéritif/strawberries |
| Drink | On purchase |

€35–€40

## Moët et Chandon Brut Rosé nv ☆

A classic nose, quite yeasty with nutty hints, toast and red-currant aromas. This is matched by a lively and tangy palate with flavours of burnt citrus fruit, strawberries, nuts and yeast. *Dillons*

| | |
|---|---|
| Price | €35–€40 |
| Region | France-Champagne |
| Grape | Champagne varieties |
| Alc/vol | 12% |
| Food | Apéritif/prawns |
| Drink | 2002–3 |

€40–€50

## Laurent-Perrier Brut Rosé nv

This beautifully balanced classic delivers delicious red fruit, rosehip and bready flavours with lovely crisp acidity and a delightful, persistent finish. *Gilbeys*

| | |
|---|---|
| Price | €40–€50 |
| Region | France-Champagne |
| Grape | Pinot Noir |
| Alc/vol | 12% |
| Food | Apéritif/chicken |
| Drink | 2002–3 |

Over €50

## Taittinger Prestige Brut Rosé nv

Tasty, delicate and elegant classic Champagne with the emphasis on fruit resulting in very fine flavours of cherries, loganberries and raspberries, a lovely spiciness, refreshing acidity and a fine, creamy mousse. *Febvre*

| | |
|---|---|
| Price | Over €50 |
| Region | France-Champagne |
| Grape | Pinot Noir/ Pinot Meunier |
| Alc/vol | 12% |
| Food | Apéritif/prawns |
| Drink | 2002–3 |

## Sparkling

### Under €9

#### Gemina Moscato d'Asti DOC Piemonte 01

Very ripe, floral aromas of rose petal and honey-suckle. Sweet and sugary with apricot jam, tropical fruit and tangerine flavours. *Oddbins*

| | |
|---|---|
| *Price* | Under €9 |
| *Country* | Italy |
| *Region* | Piedmont |
| *Grape* | Moscato |
| *Alc/vol* | 5.5% |
| *Food* | Desserts/plum pudding |
| *Drink* | On purchase |

### €12–€15

#### Jacob's Creek Chardonnay Pinot Noir Special Cuvée Selected Reserve nv

Good intense nose, with burnt walnut, red berry and cherry aromas. Fresh, ripe palate with lemony acidity, tropical fruit flavours and some floral elements. This is a real pleaser with lots of fruit and not too acidic. *Irish Distillers*

| | |
|---|---|
| *Price* | €12–€15 |
| *Country* | Australia |
| *Region* | Cross regional blend |
| *Grape* | Chardonnay/Pinot Noir |
| *Alc/vol* | 11.5% |
| *Food* | Apéritif/party |
| *Drink* | On purchase |

#### Lindauer Brut nv ☆ €

Fresh as a daisy and very elegant, this has a lively citrus, apple and yeasty dough nose and concentrated flavours of citrus fruit, honey and some floral notes. *Grants*

| | |
|---|---|
| *Price* | €12–€15 |
| *Country* | New Zealand |
| *Region* | Marlborough |
| *Grape* | Mainly Chardonnay/Pinot Noir |
| *Alc/vol* | 12% |
| *Food* | Apéritif/Thai |
| *Drink* | On purchase |

> **Cava** *is Spain's traditional sparkling wine. It is made using the traditional, or Champagne, method, with the second fermentation in bottle. The DO rules specify that only the first portion of free-run juice (the finest-quality juice when the grapes are pressed) may be used. Non-vintage wines must rest on their lees in bottle for at least nine months (as opposed to fifteen months in Champagne). Vintage Cava must be aged on the lees for three years.*

## M&S Vintage Cava Brut DO Cava **99 €**

Delicate and refreshing with classic, biscuity aromas and a nice concentration of apple flavours on the palate with zesty acidity and a lingering finish. *Marks & Spencer*

| | |
|---|---|
| Price | €12–€15 |
| Country | Spain |
| Region | Penedès |
| Grape | Cava varieties |
| Alc/vol | 12% |
| Food | Apéritif/brunch |
| Drink | 2002–3 |

## Segura Viudas Brut Reserva DO Cava **nv**

Solid nose full of yeasty bread mix and citrus aromas and a lemon-, melon- and lime-flavoured palate with a nutty influence. *Oddbins*

| | |
|---|---|
| Price | €12–€15 |
| Country | Spain |
| Region | Penedès |
| Grape | Macabeo/Parellada/Xarel-lo |
| Alc/vol | 12% |
| Food | Apéritif/tapas |
| Drink | On purchase |

> **Prosecco** *is the name of the grape variety and of a style of sparkling wine from the Veneto region in north-east Italy. The sparkle generally comes from a second fermentation of the wine in tank and not the traditional method where the second fermentation occurs in bottle.*

## Zonin Prosecco Brut DOC Prosecco di Valdobbiadene **nv**

Fruity, crisp and summery. Very fresh apple nose and a refreshing, fizzy palate with summer fruit salad flavour—apples, melons and kiwis. *MacCormaic*

| | |
|---|---|
| Price | €12–€15 |
| Country | Italy |
| Region | Veneto |
| Grape | Prosecco |
| Alc/vol | 11% |
| Food | Apéritif/Parma ham |
| Drink | On purchase |

### €15–€18

## Freixenet Cordon Negro DO Cava **nv**

This is an elegant, classic and flavoursome sparkling wine with a yeasty and nutty nose and apple, lemon and pear flavours, lots of good bubbles and a persistence of flavour. *Woodford Bourne*

| | |
|---|---|
| Price | €15–€18 |
| Country | Spain |
| Region | Penedès |
| Grape | Cava varieties |
| Alc/vol | 11.5% |
| Food | Apéritif/guacamole |
| Drink | On purchase |

## Gratien & Meyer Brut AC Saumur **nv**

Distinctive substantial aromas, yeasty and floral, with apple and honey. Lots of red apple flavours, mango and kiwi on the palate with a slight doughiness and fresh, limy acidity. *Gilbeys*

| | |
|---|---|
| *Price* | €15–€18 |
| *Country* | France |
| *Region* | Loire |
| *Grape* | Cabernet Franc/ Chenin Blanc |
| *Alc/vol* | 12.5% |
| *Food* | Apéritif/picnic |
| *Drink* | On purchase |

## Jakob Gerhardt Premium Sekt Chardonnay Brut **nv**

Apéritif style, perfect for a wedding or party. It has pleasant, light bubbles and fresh flavours of lemon, apple and pear, good acidity and a slight toastiness. *The Wine Seller*

| | |
|---|---|
| *Price* | €15–€18 |
| *Country* | Germany |
| *Region* | Rheinhessen |
| *Grape* | Chardonnay |
| *Alc/vol* | 11% |
| *Food* | Apéritif/party |
| *Drink* | On purchase |

## Salinger Brut **94** ☆ **€**

A complex wine with honeyed and hazelnut aromas, showing its age nicely. Tangy green fruit and dried orange flavours on the palate with nutty overtones and a long, intense finish. *Dunnes Stores*

| | |
|---|---|
| *Price* | €15–€18 |
| *Country* | Australia |
| *Region* | South Eastern |
| *Grape* | Chardonnay/ Pinot Noir |
| *Alc/vol* | 12.5% |
| *Food* | Apéritif/Chinese |
| *Drink* | 2002–3 |

## Yellowglen Pinot Noir Chardonnay **nv** ☆ **€**

A classy choice, really fresh and elegant with lemon, lime and red berry fruit, freshly baked bread, biscuit and spice, a creamy mousse and very good length. *Gilbeys*

| | |
|---|---|
| *Price* | €15–€18 |
| *Country* | Australia |
| *Region* | Victoria |
| *Grape* | Pinot Noir/ Chardonnay |
| *Alc/vol* | 10.5% |
| *Food* | Apéritif/party |
| *Drink* | On purchase |

### €18–€22

## Bouvet Saphir Brut AC Saumur **99**

Full flavoured with very appealing zingy bubbles. The fresh nose has Granny Smith apples, lemon zest and classic Chenin Blanc lanolin. The palate has crisp acidity and baked apple cake and biscuity flavours. *Le Caveau*

| | |
|---|---|
| *Price* | €18–€22 |
| *Country* | France |
| *Region* | Loire |
| *Grape* | Mainly Chenin Blanc |
| *Alc/vol* | 12.5% |
| *Food* | Apéritif/Japanese |
| *Drink* | 2002–3 |

## Ch. Tour Grise Brut AC Saumur **99** ⚘

Intense, developed nose with pure honey/nectar, apples and lychees. Youthful and easy acidity on the palate with ripe citrus fruits. Possibly best with food. *Mary Pawle*

| | |
|---|---|
| *Price* | €18–€22 |
| *Country* | France |
| *Region* | Loire |
| *Grape* | **Mainly Chenin Blanc** |
| *Alc/vol* | 12% |
| *Food* | **Apéritif/fruit** |
| *Drink* | **On purchase** |

## Cuvée Prestige Monmousseau J.M. Blanc de Blancs Brut AC Touraine **nv**

The Chenin really expresses itself in this rich style with its intense and honeyed nose, very juicy tropical fruit and apple flavours and fresh acidity. *Febvre*

| | |
|---|---|
| *Price* | €18–€22 |
| *Country* | France |
| *Region* | Loire |
| *Grape* | **Chenin Blanc** |
| *Alc/vol* | 12% |
| *Food* | **Apéritif/terrine** |
| *Drink* | **On purchase** |

## Delmas AC Crémant de Limoux **98** ⚘

Very moreish, pleasant style with a toasty, biscuity nose with lemony aromas. Richer palate with ripe pears, lemons and almonds, showing nice age and development with a concentration of fruit. *On the Case*

| | |
|---|---|
| *Price* | €18–€22 |
| *Country* | France |
| *Region* | **Languedoc-Roussillon** |
| *Grape* | **Mauzac/Chardonnay/ Chenin Blanc** |
| *Alc/vol* | 12% |
| *Food* | **Apéritif/smoked salmon** |
| *Drink* | **2002–3** |

## Gran Caus Cava Extra Brut Reserva DO Cava **98**

Yeasty and fruity nose; quite a full bready palate filled out with hazelnuts and citrus, melon and apple flavours, good mousse and nice length. *Approach Trade*

| | |
|---|---|
| *Price* | €18–€22 |
| *Country* | Spain |
| *Region* | **Penedès** |
| *Grape* | **Xarel-lo/Chardonnay/ Macabeo** |
| *Alc/vol* | 12.5% |
| *Food* | **Apéritif/prawns** |
| *Drink* | **2002–3** |

## Musaragno Vino Spumante Brut DOC Prosecco di Valdobbiadene **nv**

Very pleasant, seductive nose of ripe lychees backed up by a fruity palate with tropical flavours and zesty acidity. Ideal for summer drinking. *Select Wines*

| | |
|---|---|
| *Price* | €18–€22 |
| *Country* | Italy |
| *Region* | **Veneto** |
| *Grape* | **Prosecco** |
| *Alc/vol* | 11% |
| *Food* | **Apéritif/antipasti** |
| *Drink* | **On purchase** |

## Parxet Chardonnay Cava DO Cava nv

Fresh lime cordial and some nutty aromas belie
a much bigger, fleshy and rich palate with wonderful orange peel, peach, honey and apricot
flavours, toastiness and fresh, tangy, citrus acidity. *Searsons*

| | |
|---|---|
| *Price* | €18–€22 |
| *Country* | Spain |
| *Region* | Penedès |
| *Grape* | Chardonnay |
| *Alc/vol* | 12% |
| *Food* | Apéritif/smoked salmon |
| *Drink* | On purchase |

> **Méthode Cap Classique** on a South African sparkling wine label indicates that
> it has been made in the same way as Champagne, with the second
> fermentation taking place in the bottle.

## Pongrácz Méthode Cap Classique  nv ☆

Elegant style with some complexity. The aromas are quite burnt showing nuts and caramel
but the palate is very fresh and zesty with lovely
lemon peel, apple and pear flavours. *Febvre*

| | |
|---|---|
| *Price* | €18–€22 |
| *Country* | South Africa |
| *Region* | Stellenbosch |
| *Grape* | Pinot Noir/ Chardonnay |
| *Alc/vol* | 12% |
| *Food* | Apéritif/Indian |
| *Drink* | On purchase |

## Réné Muré AC Crémant d'Alsace nv

Fresh and zesty with lively bubbles and lots of
citrus, apple and grapefruit flavours with uplifting acidity and some yeastiness. *Mitchells*

| | |
|---|---|
| *Price* | €18–€22 |
| *Country* | France |
| *Region* | Alsace |
| *Grape* | Riesling/Pinot/ Chardonnay |
| *Alc/vol* | 12% |
| *Food* | Apéritif/pâté |
| *Drink* | On purchase |

### €25–€30

## Albet i Noya 21 Brut DO Cava 00 🍦

Nicely balanced and lightly elegant with nutty
and lemony aromas. Very tangy fruit flavours to
the fore—limes, mandarin and citrus peel.
*Mary Pawle*

| | |
|---|---|
| *Price* | €25–€30 |
| *Country* | Spain |
| *Region* | Penedès |
| *Grape* | Cava varieties |
| *Alc/vol* | 12% |
| *Food* | Apéritif/tapas |
| *Drink* | 2002–3 |

## Green Point Vintage Brut  97 ☆☆☆ €

Burnt toast with nut and strawberry shortcake aromas followed by rich mouth-filling red berries, honeyed, nutty hints and tons of tangy, fresh, citrus fruits. Excellent mousse and long length of flavour. *Febvre*

| | |
|---|---|
| Price | €25–€30 |
| Country | Australia |
| Region | Yarra Valley |
| Grape | Pinot Noir/ Chardonnay |
| Alc/vol | 12.5% |
| Food | Apéritif/salmon |
| Drink | 2002–3 |

## Huia Brut  97

Very ripe tropical fruit and melon on the nose with some nutty hints and doughiness. The flavours, however, are very vibrant, yeasty and citrusy with crisp acidity and a crisp finish. *Searsons*

| | |
|---|---|
| Price | €25–€30 |
| Country | New Zealand |
| Region | Marlborough |
| Grape | Pinot Noir/ Chardonnay |
| Alc/vol | 12.5% |
| Food | Apéritif/brunch |
| Drink | On purchase |

# Rosé

€22–€25

## Gran Caus Cava Rosado Extra Brut DO Cava 98 ☆

Elegance sums up this lovely Cava with its fantastic aromas of red fruit, white pepper and pomegranate, smooth creamy mousse and developed yeasty and creamy strawberry flavours. A really exciting apéritif. *Approach Trade*

| | |
|---|---|
| Price | €22–€25 |
| Country | Spain |
| Region | Penedès |
| Grape | Pinot Noir |
| Alc/vol | 12.5% |
| Food | Apéritif/prawns |
| Drink | 2002–3 |

> **How to find a specified wine**
> *If your local retailer does not stock a particular wine, contact the importer named in italic after the tasting note (contact details are on pages 274–279) for the name of your nearest stockist.*

# Sweet

This year's sweet wines come from eight different countries and represent some of the main sweet styles available. Each is very different from the other—the only common feature being that they are sweet and not dry. A common misconception is that sweet wines are high in alcohol—this is not always the case and wines such as Eiswein and Tokaji are particularly low in alcohol when compared to the majority of wine. Not all sweet wines are made from white grapes—Maury and Banyuls are examples of red sweet wines.

## Under €9

### Achaia Clauss Imperial Mavrodaphne of Patras
AO Mavrodaphne de Patras **nv**

This is a warm red sweetie with a bright, jewel red colour, aromas of plums, prunes, dates and cinnamon and a rich, spicy and nutty cake-flavoured palate. *Taserra*

| | |
|---|---|
| Price | Under €9 (75cl) |
| Country | Greece |
| Region | Patras |
| Grape | Mavrodaphne |
| Alc/vol | 15% |
| Food | Desserts/chocolate cake |
| Drink | 2002–4 |

## €12–€15

### Lamole di Lamole DOC Vin Santo del Chianti Classico **95**

Rich, round and mouth-filling, this Vin Santo has an attractive nose of caramel and lemon and a palate of toasted nuts and frangipane combined with caramelised fruit flavours and lemony acidity which perfectly balances out the sweetness. *Select Wines*

| | |
|---|---|
| Price | €12–€15 (37.5cl) |
| Country | Italy |
| Region | Tuscany |
| Grape | Trebbiano/Malvasia/ Canaiolo Nero |
| Alc/vol | 16% |
| Food | Desserts/panforte |
| Drink | 2002–5 |

### Mas Amiel AC Maury **98** ☆ €

A biggie calling for some serious reflection. Intense, oxidative nose with dark fruit aromas and a macerated fruit palate with plums, figs, raisins, pepper, liquorice and dark chocolate, noticeable tannins and acidity. *Bubble Brothers*

| | |
|---|---|
| Price | €12–€15 (37.5cl) |
| Country | France |
| Region | Languedoc-Roussillon |
| Grape | Grenache |
| Alc/vol | 15.5% |
| Food | Desserts/chocolate cake |
| Drink | 2002–6 |

## Miranda Golden Botrytis  93

Attractive, slightly maderised and oxidised nose is followed by caramel, fig and tangerine flavours on the palate. Really superb and mouth-filling. *Taserra*

| | |
|---|---|
| Price | €12–€15 (37.5cl) |
| Country | Australia |
| Region | South Eastern |
| Grape | Semillon/Riesling |
| Alc/vol | 10% |
| Food | Desserts/pecan pie |
| Drink | 2002–4 |

## Royal Tokaji Tokaji Aszú 5 Puttonyos  96 ☆ €

Your sweet tooth need look no further. Classic Tokaji with a rich amber colour and intense orange and crystallised citrus fruit aromas. Flavours of orange peel, honey, almonds and cashews on the palate with the essential balance between acidity and fruit. *Findlaters*

| | |
|---|---|
| Price | €12–€15 (50cl) |
| Country | Hungary |
| Region | Tokaj-Hegyalja |
| Grape | Furmint/Hárslevelú |
| Alc/vol | 10.5% |
| Food | Desserts/crème caramel |
| Drink | 2002–5 |

### €15–€18

## Alois Kracher Neusiedlersee Beerenauslese Cuvée 2000 Prädikatswein  00 ☆☆☆ €

Divine classic style of silk, satin and spice. Intense aromas of orange blossom and honey with lovely, spicy nuances. Full-bodied palate with ripe nectarine and orange flavours. *Searsons*

| | |
|---|---|
| Price | €15–€18 (37.5cl) |
| Country | Austria |
| Region | Neusiedersee |
| Alc/vol | 14% |
| Food | Desserts/fruit puddings |
| Drink | 2002–6 |

**SWEET WINE OF THE YEAR**

## Ch. Court-les-Mûts AC Saussignac  97 ☆ €

Attractive golden colour with an intense nose of honey, melon and floral aromas and a quite luscious mandarin and orange peel palate with warm, nutty and honeyed flavours. *Wicklow Wine Co.*

| | |
|---|---|
| Price | €15–€18 (50cl) |
| Country | France |
| Region | Bergerac |
| Grape | Sémillon |
| Alc/vol | 14% |
| Food | Desserts/crème brulée |
| Drink | 2002–6 |

## MR Moscatel DO Malaga  00

Light and elegant with peach, apricot and elderflower aromas and a palate with honey, pineapple and crystallised fruit flavours. It could work really well with poached fruit such as pears. *Approach Trade*

| | |
|---|---|
| Price | €15–€18 (50cl) |
| Country | Spain |
| Region | Malaga |
| Grape | Moscatel |
| Alc/vol | 13% |
| Food | Desserts/fruit |
| Drink | 2002–4 |

€18–€22

## d'Arenberg The Noble Semillon 99

Inviting nose of lemon, honey and caramel with an intense, rich palate of treacle, toffee and lemon marmalade. *Taserra*

| | |
|---|---|
| *Price* | €18–€22 (37.5cl) |
| *Country* | Australia |
| *Region* | McLaren Vale |
| *Grape* | Semillon |
| *Alc/vol* | 11.5% |
| *Food* | Desserts/chocolate puddings |
| *Drink* | 2002–4 |

## Paul Jaboulet Aîné AC Muscat de Beaumes-de-Venise 00

Pleasing golden colour with pink tinges. Floral, peach and apricot aromas and a lively palate with nectarines, candied peel, and grapefruit, and pink peppercorns adding spice. *Gilbeys*

| | |
|---|---|
| *Price* | €18–€22 (75cl) |
| *Country* | France |
| *Region* | Rhône (South) |
| *Grape* | Muscat Blanc à Petits Grains |
| *Alc/vol* | 15% |
| *Food* | Desserts/fruit crumbles |
| *Drink* | 2002–3 |

€22–€25

## Dom. de Durban AC Muscat de Beaumes-de-Venise 00

This sweetie is very rich with fruity and floral aromas and an intense palate with glacé fruits, pineapple, pear and a fine, spicy kick. Sip and savour slowly. *Comans/ Barry & Fitzwilliam*

| | |
|---|---|
| *Price* | €22–€25 (75cl) |
| *Country* | France |
| *Region* | Rhône (South) |
| *Grape* | Muscat Blanc à Petits Grains |
| *Alc/vol* | 15% |
| *Food* | Desserts/fruit salad |
| *Drink* | 2002–4 |

€25–€30

## De Bortoli Noble One Botrytis Semillon 99

Satin smooth with an exotic nose of mango, papaya and pineapple and an elegant, rich palate with honeyed lemons and oranges, hints of botrytis and a delicious, lingering finish. *Febvre*

| | |
|---|---|
| *Price* | €25–€30 (37.5cl) |
| *Country* | Australia |
| *Region* | New South Wales |
| *Grape* | Semillon |
| *Alc/vol* | 10.5% |
| *Food* | Cheese/blue cheese |
| *Drink* | 2002–4 |

## Molino Real Mountain Wine DO Malaga 99

Fruit and nuts combined in one—warm peaches, honeyed cashew nuts and citrus acidity. Forget the dessert trolley and enjoy this on its own. *Approach Trade*

| | |
|---|---|
| *Price* | €25–€30 (50cl) |
| *Country* | Spain |
| *Region* | Malaga |
| *Grape* | Moscatel |
| *Alc/vol* | 12.5% |
| *Food* | Desserts/chocolate puddings |
| *Drink* | 2002–4 |

## €30–€35

### De Bortoli Black Noble nv ☆

Moist fruitcake in a glass! Rich mahogany in colour with aromas of dried fruit, toasted nuts, treacle and molasses and a lusciously sweet palate—figs, orange concentrate, fruit and nut chocolate—with a silky smooth finish. *Febvre*

| | |
|---|---|
| Price | €30–€35 (37.5cl) |
| Country | Australia |
| Region | The Riverina |
| Grape | Semillon |
| Alc/vol | 17.5% |
| Food | Desserts/chocolate cake |
| Drink | 2002–3 |

### Oremus Tokaji Aszú 5 Puttonyos 95 ☆

Very rich and intensely sweet but with counter-balancing acidity. This classic has aromas of citrus fruits and a palate of orange and lemon curd, honey cake and spice. These wines can reputedly live forever but this one is very enjoyable now. *Searsons*

| | |
|---|---|
| Price | €30–€35 (50cl) |
| Country | Hungary |
| Region | Tokaj-Hegyalja |
| Grape | Furmint/Hárslevelú |
| Alc/vol | 11.5% |
| Food | Desserts/sticky toffee pudding |
| Drink | 2002–7 |

## €35–€40

### Louis Guntrum Penguin Eiswein QmP 98 ☆☆

Really sumptuous and unctuous with citrus aromas of lemon, lime and lime blossom and a fantastic, ripe, citrus fruit palate with elegant, floral nuances. Rich and luscious but not a bit cloying due to great acidity.
*Waterford Wine Vault*

| | |
|---|---|
| Price | €35–€40 (37.5cl) |
| Country | Germany |
| Region | Rheinessen |
| Grape | Riesling |
| Alc/vol | 9% |
| Food | Desserts/chocolate puddings |
| Drink | 2002–7 |

# Participating importers' contact details

### Allied Drinks
- JFK Road, JFK Industrial Estate, Naas Road, Dublin 12.
  Tel (01) 450 9777, Fax (01) 450 9699, e-mail anne@allieddrinks.ie
- Windsor Hill House, Glounthaune, Co. Cork.
  Tel (021) 435 3438, Fax (021) 435 4362, e-mail info@allieddrinks.ie
  *Wines are widely available. In case of difficulty in finding a particular wine, email anne@allied drinks.ie*

### Approach Trade Ireland
- South Quay, Carrick-on-Suir, Co. Tipperary.
  Tel (051) 640 164, Fax (051) 641 580.
  *Wines are available direct and in Dublin from Mitchell & Son, On the Grapevine (Dalkey), O'Brien's Off-licences, Michael's Wines (Mount Merrion), Layden Fine Wines (Epicurean Food Hall); in Wicklow from the Wicklow Wine Co., Murtaghs' (Enniskerry); in County Clare from Egan's (Liscannor) and Miles Creek (Kilkee), in Cork from Karwig Wines, in Galway from McCambridges.*

### Henry J. Archer & Sons
- White Walls, Ballymoney, Gorey, Co. Wexford.
  Tel (055) 25176, Fax (055) 25842, e-mail paul.dubsky@oceanfree.net
  *Wines are available from Cullen's, Ballymoney, Gorey, Co. Wexford, Tel (055) 25211; Next Door, Kavanagh House, Enniscorthy, Co. Wexford, Tel (054) 38000; Redmond's, 25 Ranelagh, Dublin 6, Tel (01) 497 1739; Terroirs, 103 Morehampton Road, Donnybrook, Dublin 4, Tel (01) 667 1311.*

### Barry & Fitzwilliam
- Ballycurreen Industrial Estate, Airport Road, Cork.
  Tel (021) 432 0900, Fax (021) 432 0910.
- 50 Dartmouth Square, Dublin 6.
  Tel (01) 667 1755/660 6984, Fax (01) 660 0479,
  e-mail sinead@barryfit.iol.ie
  *Some ranges, such as Michel Lynch, Guigal, McGuigan, Antu Mapu, Chapel Hill, Vendange and Yaldara are widely available. Specialist stores such as O'Donovans (Cork), Redmonds (Dublin 6), DeVine Wine (Dublin 15) and On The Grapevine (Co. Dublin) stock most of the list.*

### Berry Brothers *see* Fields

### Bubble Brothers
- 43 Upper John Street, Cork. Tel/Fax (021) 455 2252
- English Market, Cork. Tel (021) 425 4641,
  e-mail info@bubblebrothers.com, web site www.bubblebrothers.com
  *Wines are available direct and from off-licences and wine merchants.*

### Cassidy Wines Ltd
- 1B Birch Avenue, Stillorgan Industrial Park, Stillorgan, Co. Dublin.
  Tel (01) 295 4157/4632, Fax (01) 295 4477.
  *Wines are widely available.*

## Comans Wholesale

■ Belgard Road, Tallaght Dublin 24.
Tel (01) 451 9146, Fax (01) 451 9772.
*Wines are widely available.*

## Peter A. Dalton Food & Wine

■ Loch Grein, Ballybetagh, Kilternan, Co. Dublin.
Tel/Fax (01) 295 4945, e-mail padwines@indigo.ie
web site www.daltonwines.com
*The wines are available in some SuperValu-Centra stores, some symbols, some
Cheers (Co. Dublin, Roscommon), Deveneys (Dublin), DeVine Wine (Dublin
15), Ashford Food & Wine (Wicklow), Cana (Mullingar), Cuisine de Vendange
(Naas).*

## Edward Dillon & Company

■ 25 Mountjoy Square East, Dublin 1.
Tel (01) 819 3300, Fax (01) 855 5852.
*Most wines are widely available but some only from specialist outlets.*

## Dunnes Stores

■ Head Office, 67 Upper Stephen Street, Dublin 8.
Tel (01) 475 1111, Fax (01) 475 1441, web site www.dunnes-stores.com
*Wines are available only from branches of Dunnes Stores.*

## Febvre & Co.

■ Burton Hall Road, Sandyford Industrial Estate, Dublin 18.
Tel (01) 295 9030, Fax (01) 295 9036, e-mail info@febvre.ie
*Most wines are widely available but some only from specialist outlets.*

## Fields Wine Merchants Ltd.

■ 1B Birch Avenue., Stillorgan Industrial Park, Stillorgan, Co. Dublin.
Tel (01) 295 4422, Fax (01) 295 4452.
*Fields is the wholesale branch of Berry Brothers & Rudd; Berry Brothers' own-
label wines are available only through the shop, others are available through
NOffLA specialists.*

## Findlater Wine Merchants

■ Magna Drive, CityWest Business Campus, Dublin 24.
Tel (01) 413 5500, Fax (01) 413 5550,
e-mail sales@findlaters.com, web site www.findlaters.com
*Most of the wines are widely available, through Superquinn, Pettits, SuperValu-
Centra, the pub off-licence groups, O'Donovans and Molloys, and the top
individual independents and specialists. The Ironstone range may be harder
to find.*

## Gilbeys Wines

■ The Courtyard, St James's Gate, Dublin 8.
Tel (01) 471 4000, Fax (01) 471 4777, e-mail gilbeys.info@udv.com
*Some of Gilbeys' wines are widely available, others only through the NOffLA
outlets, independent specialists, Superquinn and other wine-focused
supermarket off-licences.*

### Gleeson & Co.

- 15 Cherry Orchard Estate, Ballyfermot, Dublin 10.
  Tel (01) 626 9787, Fax (01) 626 0652.
- Greenlawn, Borrisoleigh, Co. Tipperary.
  Tel (0504) 51113, Fax (0504) 51480.
  *Most of the wines are available through independents and specialists, and through wine-oriented symbols and SuperValu-Centras.*

### Grants of Ireland

- Kilcarberry Industrial Park, Nangor Road, Clondalkin, Dublin 22.
  Tel (01) 630 4156/630 4157/630 4121, Fax (01) 630 4124.
- Annerville, Clonmel, Co. Tipperary.
  Tel (052) 72174/72175/72135, Fax (052) 72255,
  e-mail grants@cantrell.ie, web site grantsofireland.ie
  *The wines are all distributed through the multiples; they are also available from the O'Briens chain and specialists such as McCabes and Redmonds.*

### IberExpo

- Unit 12 Portside, Marina Commercial Park Centre Cork.
  Tel (021) 496 1031, Fax (021) 496 1405,
  e-mail iberexpo@aio.ie, web site www.wine-ireland.com
  *Wines are available direct or from specialist outlets.*

### Irish Distillers Group

- 11–12 Bow Street, Dublin 7.
  Tel (01) 872 5566, Fax (01) 872 3109,
  e-mail info@idl.ie, web site jameson.ie
  *Most wines are widely available and others only from specialist outlets.*

### Karwig Wines

- Kilnagleary, Carrigaline, Co. Cork.
  Tel/Fax (021) 437 2864/437 4159,
  e-mail info@karwig-wines.ie, web site karwig-wines.ie
  *Wines are available direct or through the Internet and from Molloy's and some SuperValu-Centra stores.*

### Koala Wines

- 25 Seatown, Dundalk, Co. Louth.
  Tel (048) 4175 2804, Fax (048) 4175 2943, mobile 086 272 8142,
  e-mail rhode@koalawines.com
  *Most wines are widely available but some only from specialist outlets.*

### Le Caveau

- Market Yard, Kilkenny.
  Tel (056) 52166, Fax (056) 52101,
  e-mail lecaveau@eircom.net, web site www.lecaveau.ie
  *Wines are available direct.*

### MacCormaic Vintners

- 116a Terenure Road North, Dublin 6W.
  Tel (01) 490 7928, Fax (01) 490 7930,
  e-mail maccormaicvintners@eircom.net
  *The wines are available from SuperValu-Centra and the symbols.*

### Marks and Spencer

- Mary Street, Dublin 1. Tel (01) 878 2092,
  web site marksandspencer.com
  *Wines are available only from Marks and Spencer outlets.*

## Mary Pawle Wines

- Gortamullen, Kenmare, Co. Kerry.
  Tel/Fax (064) 41443, mobile 087 226 5967,
  e-mail marypawlewines@oceanfree.net.
  *Wines are available from specialist outlets and Superquinn shops.*

## Maxxium

- Rembrandt House, 1 Longford Terrace, Monkstown, Co. Dublin.
  Tel (01) 236 5300, Fax (01) 280 1805, web site www.maxxium.com
  *Wines are widely available. Try Roches, Londis, Supervalu-Centra and O'Brien's.*

## McCabes Wines

- 51–55 Mount Merrion Avenue, Blackrock, Co. Dublin.
  Tel (01) 288 2037, Fax (01) 288 3447,
- Foxrock Village, Dublin 18.
  (01) 289 2689, Fax (01) 289 2167
  e-mail value@mccabeswines.ie web site www. mccabeswine.ie
  *Wines are available from McCabe's.*

## Michael's Wines

- 63 Deerpark Road, Mount Merrion, Co. Dublin.
  Tel (01) 278 0377, web site www.michaels-wines.com
  *Wines are available from Michael's Wines and the Wicklow Wine Co.*

## Mitchell & Son

- 21 Kildare Street, Dublin 2. Tel (01) 676 0766, Fax (01) 661 1509;
- 54 Glasthule Road, Sandycove, Co. Dublin. Tel (01) 230 2301,
  Fax (01) 230 2305, e-mail wines@mitchellandson.com
  web site www.mitchellandson.com
  *Wines are available from Mitchell's wine shops or through the Internet at mitchellandson.com*

## Molloy's Group

- Head Office, Block 2, Village Green, Tallaght, Dublin 24.
  Tel (01) 451 5544, Fax (01) 451 5658, e-mail molloys@indigo.ie
  web site www.molloys.com
  *Wines are available from branches of Molloy's or through the Internet at www.molloys.com*

## Nectar Wines

- Unit G6, Chapelizod Industrial Estate, Dublin 20.
  Tel (01) 623 3846, Fax (01) 623 3884 e-mail sales@nectarwines.com
  web site www.nectarwines.com
  *Wines are available from off-licences and wine shops. Check web site for details.*

## O'Briens Wine Off-Licence

- Group Head Office, Unit 33, Spruce Avenue,
  Stillorgan Industrial Park, Stillorgan, Co. Dublin.
  Tel 1850 269 777/(01) 269 3139, Fax (01) 269 7480,
  e-mail info@obriensgroup.ie
  *Wines are available from branches of O'Briens.*

## Oddbins

- 31–33 Weir Road, Wimbledon, London SW19 8UG.
  Tel (0208) 944 4400, Fax (0208) 944 4411, web site www.oddbins.com
  *Wines are available from branches of Oddbins.*

### On the Case
- 2 St James Terrace, South Circular Road, Dublin 8.
  Tel/Fax (01) 473 0156, e-mail info@onthecase.ie
  web site www. onthecase.ie
  *The wines are available direct and also in Dublin from McCabes, Laydens,
  Claudio's, On The Grapevine, For Goodness Sake, Mortons, Bird Flanagan,
  Swiss Delicatessan, Quinns, and in Co. Meath from The Barrow (Ashbourne).*

### Papillon Wines (Vaughan Johnson)
- 56 North Strand, Fairview, Dublin 3.
  Tel (01) 856 1339, Fax (01) 855 4740, e-mail greg.grouse@oysterinfo.com
  *Wines are available from specialist outlets or from Vaughan Johnson,
  11 East Essex Street, Temple Bar, Dublin 2. Tel (01) 856 1339.*

### River Wines
- Sandpit House, Termonfeckin, Co. Louth.
  Tel (1850) 794 637, Fax (041) 982 2820, mobile 087 207 5970
  e-mail rvrwines@indigo.ie
  *Wines are available by mail order.*

### Searsons Wine Merchants
- Monkstown Crescent, Blackrock, Co. Dublin.
  Tel (01) 280 0405, Fax (01) 280 4771, e-mail sales@searsons.com
  *All the wines listed are available from Searsons in Dublin. Individual wines
  are stocked in Dublin by On the Grapevine, McCabes, The Vintry, Michael's
  Wines, Redmonds, Laydens, Cabot & Co, Gibneys and McHughs and by
  The Wicklow Wine Co, The Wine Centre (Kilkenny), Murtaghs (Enniskerry),
  O'Donovans (Cork), Cabots (Westport), The Vineyard (Galway), DeVine
  Wines (Letterkenny) and Waterford World of Wines.*

### Select Wines from Italy
- 13 Grattan Court, Gorey, Co. Wexford.
  Tel (055) 80955, Fax (055) 80958, e-mail info@select.ie
  web site www.select.ie
  *Wines are available from independent wine shops nationwide.*

### Taserra Wine Merchants
- 17 Rathfarnham Road, Terenure, Dublin 6W.
  Tel (01) 490 4047, Fax (01) 490 4052.
  *Wines are widely available.*

### TDL Distributors
- Naas Road, Clondalkin, Dublin 22.
  Tel (01) 413 0100, Fax (01) 413 0123, e-mail tdl@tdl.ie
  *Wines are widely available.*

### Terroirs
- 103 Morehampton Rd, Dublin 4.
  Tel (01) 667 1311, Fax (01) 667 1312.
  *Wines are available from Terroirs.*

### Tesco Ireland
- Gresham House, Marine Road, Dun Laoghaire, Co. Dublin.
  Tel (01) 280 8441, Fax (01) 215 2116, web site www.tesco.ie
  *Wines are available from branches of Tesco.*

**Vaughan Johnson** *see* **Papillon**

**Waterford Wine Vault**
■ High Street, Waterford. Tel/Fax (051) 853 444,
　e-mail wineshop@waterfordwinevault.com
　web site www.waterfordwinevault.com
　*Wines are available direct.*

**Wicklow Wine Co.**
■ Main Street, Wicklow.
　Tel (0404) 66767, Fax (0404) 66769.
　*Wines are available direct and from Cabot & Co., On the Grapevine (Dalkey),*
　*Michael's Wines, The Grape Escape (Lucan), The Vineyard (Galway),*
　*Murtagh's Wine Shop (Enniskerry), Cabot's House of Wine (Westport).*

**WineKnows**
■ Salatiga, Meany Ave, Dalkey, Co. Dublin.
　Tel (01) 235 1690, Fax (01) 235 3059, mobile 087 967 6248
　e-mail info@wineknows.com
　*Wines are available from Cabot & Co., On the Grapevine (Dalkey),*
　*Berry Brothers (Dublin 2), Wicklow Wine Co., French Paradox (Ballsbridge),*
　*Higgins (Clonskeagh), Jus de Vine (Portmarnock), Le Caveau (Kilkenny),*
　*Cabots (Westport) and other independent wine shops nationwide.*

**Wines Direct**
■ Lisamate, Irishtown, Mullingar, Co. Westmeath.
　Tel (044) 40634, Fax (044) 40015, e-mail info@winesdirect.com
　web site www.winesdirect.com
　*Wines are available by mail order.*

**Wine Online**
■ Unit 4B, Santry Hall Industrial Estate, Santry, Dublin 9.
　Tel (01) 886 7717, Fax (01) 842 3829,
　e-mail anne@wineonline sales@wineonline.ie
　web site www.wineonline.ie
　*Wines are available through the Internet.*

**The Wine Seller**
■ 5 Seapoint Road, Bray, Co. Wicklow.
　Tel (01) 276 5323, Fax (01) 276 1899, e-mail info@the-wine-seller.com,
　web site www.the-wine-seller.com
　*Wines are available direct.*

**Woodford Bourne**
■ 79 Broomhill Road, Tallaght, Dublin 24.
　Tel (01) 404 7300, Fax (01) 459 9342.
　*Wines are widely available.*

# Glossary

*AC:* Appellation Contrôlée, a French wine classification system that certifies a wine as coming from a particular area. The geographical area may be as large as a region (e.g. AC Bordeaux) or as small as a vineyard (e.g. AC Montrachet). Rules of inclusion differ from AC to AC, but they may prescribe any or all of the following over and above the wine's place of origin—grape varieties, density of planting, yield, alcohol level. Wines must be analysed and tasted before being admitted to the AC.

*accessible/approachable:* tasting term meaning that the wine's flavours and texture are familiar or friendly, easily recognised and appreciated; ready to drink.

*acidity:* all wines contain acids of various kinds, including malic, lactic, tartaric, citric (fixed acids) and acetic (the acid found in vinegar). The fixed acids give wines a crispness to the taste and contribute to the ageing process.

*aftertaste:* the flavours left in the mouth after the wine is swallowed or (in a tasting) spat out.

*American oak:* see *oak*.

*aroma:* a somewhat imprecise term, sometimes applied to the entire *nose*, sometimes only to specific easily distinguishable smells.

*austere:* unforthcoming, sometimes harsh, but not necessarily in a derogatory sense; may indicate immaturity.

*balance:* a term of praise when applied to a wine, indicating that the wine's *tannins*, *acidity* and alcohol blend well and complement each other, without any individual element dominating.

*barrique:* an *oak* barrel with a capacity of 225 litres.

*big wine:* a full-bodied wine with an exceptionally rich flavour.

*black fruits:* tasters' term used to refer to dark berry *fruits* such as blackberries, blackcurrants, black cherries, blueberries, etc.

*blend:* a wine made from more than one grape variety, as opposed to a *varietal*.

*blind tasting:* a tasting in which the identities of the wines are unknown to the taster until after tasting notes have been made and scores assigned. All competitive tastings are blind, as are all tastings for this guide.

*body:* the combination of *fruit* extract and alcoholic strength that gives the impression of weight in the mouth.

*Botrytis:* properly *Botrytis cinerea* (noble rot), a fungus that attacks grapes on vines. Depending on weather conditions and the ripeness of the grapes, it will either spoil the harvest completely (in which case it is known as grey rot) or concentrate the sugars in the *fruit* to produce a high-quality, sweet, very long-lived wine.

*bottle:* the standard bottle size is 75 centilitres. A magnum contains two bottles or 1.5 litres. See also *maturation*.

*bouquet:* strictly speaking, this refers only to those mature aromas that develop as the wine ages in the *bottle*, but it is often used to refer to all characteristics of the grape variety on the *nose*.

*buttery:* a rich, fat and delicious character found in some barrel-fermented or barrel-aged Chardonnay wines.

*carbonic maceration:* see *maceration*.

*chewy:* tasting term referring to the texture imparted to wine by high tannins.

*claret:* an English term for a red Bordeaux wine. It comes from the French *clairet*, a wine between a dark rosé and a light red.

*classic:* word used by wine tasters to indicate that a wine is of high quality, showing the correct characteristics for its type and origin, and possesses great style.

*closed:* tasting term which is generally applied to wines which give out very little smell; sometimes referred to as being dumb. Common in very good but youthful wines.

*complex:* a wine with lots of different layers of flavours, often resulting from age or maturation.

*corked:* a wine is corked when it has been spoiled by contact with a contaminated cork. This is the most common cause of wine spoilage and can be identified by the wine's stale, woody, mouldy smell.

*cru:* literally means 'growth', but on a French wine label refers to the status of the vineyard in which the vines were cultivated; the cru classification is in addition to the *AC*. The system is rather complicated and varies from region to region. In the Médoc region of Bordeaux, there are five *grand cru classé* divisions, beginning with *premier cru* (1st growth), *deuxième cru* (2nd growth), and so on down to the *cinquième cru* (5th growth). In St Émilion, there are three levels—*premier grand cru classé* at the top, then *grand cru classé* and *grand cru*. In Burgundy the top vineyards are *grands crus*; *premiers crus* come below them. *Grand cru* is also used in Alsace and Champagne to distinguish particularly good vineyard sites.

*crust:* *sediment* that forms in bottle-aged port.

*Deutscher Tafelwein:* lowest level of wine classification in Germany.

*DO:* Denominación de Origen (designation of origin) is the main quality classification in Spain, similar to the *AC* category in France.

*DOC:* (1) Denominazione di Origine Controllata (controlled denomination of origin) is the main Italian quality category and is broadly similar to the French *AC*. (2) In Portugal Denominação de Origem Controlada (demarcated region) is the highest quality category. (3) Denominación de Origen Calificada (qualified designation of origin) (sometimes DOCa) is the highest quality category in Spain, currently awarded only to Rioja.

*DOCG:* Denominazione di Origine Controllata e Garantita (controlled and guaranteed denomination of origin) is the highest Italian quality category.

*fermentation:* the chemical process whereby the sugar in grapes is converted into alcohol.

*fining:* the process of adding substances such as egg whites, gelatine or clay to a wine, which causes microscopic suspended solids to fall to the bottom, so that after being racked (transferred to another barrel) or bottled, there will be a minimum of *sediment* or cloudiness in the wine.

*finish:* the last flavours a wine leaves in the mouth, especially after being swallowed or (in a tasting) spat out.

*French oak:* see *oak*.

*fruit:* the fruity flavour of a wine.

*grapey:* though all wine is made from grapes, this tasting term refers to a distinctive smell and flavour of grapes usually associated with wines made from the Muscat variety.

*grip:* word applied to describe red wines with firm tannins, which are felt on the teeth and gums.

*hard:* refers to wines with too much tannin and possibly also acidity; ageing with time usually has a mellowing effect.

*IGT:* Indicazione Geografica Tipica (indication of regional typicity) is an Italian quality category similar to the French *VdP*.

*IPR:* Indicação de Proveniência Regulamentada (indication of origin) (also known as *VQPRD*) is a Portuguese category similar to the French *VDQS* and the Italian *IGT*.

*large oak:* see *oak*.

*lees: sediment* that falls to the bottom of a vat of wine after *fermentation* and *maturation*. Most wines are transferred to another container when the lees form; others, especially Muscadet and sparkling wines, are aged on the lees (*sur lie*).

*length:* the length of time a wine's flavours linger in the mouth after sipping. Long length is one of the markers of a quality wine.

*lively:* fresh and full of vitality, bursting with fruit and flavour, often due to some carbon dioxide that may have been intentionally left in the wine on bottling.

*maceration:* the period of *fermentation* of a red wine during which the *must* has contact with grape skins. It is during this process that red wines derive their colour and *tannin*. Rosé wines undergo a very short maceration period of one or two days. Red wines intended to be drunk young sometimes undergo carbonic maceration, in which uncrushed grapes are fermented under a layer of carbon dioxide. This results in a wine light in colour and low in tannin, but high in *fruit* and *aroma*.

*malolactic fermentation:* the conversion of malic into lactic acids as part of *fermentation*. This is a normal process which reduces the *acidity* of a wine. All red wines undergo malolactic fermentation whereas some white wines may not.

*maturation:* the ageing process by which wines develop character and complexity. Maturation is good only up to a point, beyond which the wine will start to decline, but that point differs for each type of wine. A Beaujolais Nouveau will spend only a few months maturing, while tawny port may be a blend of wines aged in *oak* for as long as forty years. The larger the *bottle*, the slower the maturation—half-bottles of wine mature and decline more quickly than whole bottles.

*mousse:* the bubbles in a sparkling wine. Ideally these should be very small and long lasting.

*mouthfeel:* specifically refers to the texture of a wine, as opposed to the *palate*, which also refers to the flavour.

*must:* unfermented grape juice.

*noble rot:* see *botrytis*.

*nose:* the combined smells of a wine's grape varieties' *aromas* and *bottle*-matured *bouquet*.

*New World/Old World:* originally used to distinguish wines made in Europe from those made in Australia, New Zealand and the Americas, but now often applied to wines of any geographical origin as an indication of style. 'New World' style wines are approachable, fruity, bold and have more obvious oak influence; 'Old World' style wines are complex, subtle and refined.

*nv:* non-vintage; a blend of wines harvested in different years.

*oak: maturation* in new oak adds flavours to wine—the smaller the barrel, the greater the effect. Old oak does not have this effect, but it does allow for controlled *oxidation*. Other oak treatments include adding oak chips or oak staves. See also *barrique*.

*off-dry:* containing some residual sugar, but dry enough to be drunk before or during a meal.

*organic:* there is no one accepted definition of 'organic' in relation to wine, as different certifying organisations have different standards. It certainly involves using less chemicals and herbicides in the vineyard as well as the use of alternative and natural measures to control weeds and pests. Full organic viticulture forbids the use of any industrially made compounds.

*oxidation:* a chemical reaction that takes place when wine is exposed to air. Barrel *maturation* allows for slow, controlled oxidation, improving the flavour of the wine. However, if this happens too fast or if the process is allowed to go too far, it transforms the alcohol into acetic acid. Wine that is too oxidised tastes unpleasant and may look brown and smell of vinegar.

*palate:* the flavour and texture of the wine in the mouth; see also *mouth-feel*.

*QbA:* Qualitätswein bestimmter Anbaugebiete (quality wine from a specified region) is the second-highest quality category in Germany.

*QmP:* Qualitätswein mit Prädikat (quality wine with special attributes) is the highest classification for German wines. The classifications, which depend on the sugar levels in the grapes, are Kabinett, Spätlese, Auslese, Beerenauslese, Trockenbeerenauslese and Eiswein.

*Reserve:* in Italy, Portugal, Spain and Bulgaria, a wine labelled 'Riserva' or 'Reserva' must by law be of very high quality and, in the case of Italy and Spain, have undergone a certain minimum ageing, with at least some of it in *oak* barrels. Anywhere else, the word 'Reserve' or 'Réserve' just means that the winemakers think it is one of their best.

*sediment:* solid debris that falls to the bottom of a wine barrel or, in the case of an unfiltered wine, the *bottle*. Wines undergo *fining* or filtration to reduce the amount of sediment left after bottling.

*small oak:* see *oak*.

*soft:* tasting term generally applicable to red wines with very low or not noticeable tannins.

*stainless steel vats:* vessels used in *fermentation*. The use of stainless steel vats, rather than wood or concrete, makes it easier to control the wine's fermentation temperature.

*steely:* tasting term used to describe white wines with lots of *acidity* and very cool refreshing flavours; may be attributed in some cases to stainless steel fermentation or to a minerally character derived from the soil.

*Stelvin:* a form of screwcap specifically designed for bottled wine. An increasing number of producers in Australia and New Zealand have adopted these with the aim of keeping their wines as fresh and clean as possible and avoiding the possibility of the wines becoming *corked*.

*structure:* the sum of the component parts that shape a wine, including *fruit*, *alcohol* and *acidity*, and, in reds, *tannin*.

*supple:* a texture which is easier to sense than to define; generally applied to wines with generous appealing fruit and not too much tannin.

*sur lie:* see *lees*.

*tannin:* a chemical substance found in grape skins and hence in red wines but not whites. The ability of a red wine to improve as it matures depends very much on its tannins, but a wine that is too tannic will taste dry and hard; red wines intended to be drunk young will sometimes be put through a process called carbonic *maceration*, which minimises tannin. Tannins can also be derived from *oak*, stalks and pips. Tannin from pips is the harshest of all.

*terroir:* the complete growing environment of soil, aspect, altitude, climate and any other factor that may affect the vine.

*vanilla:* often used to describe the *nose* and sometimes the *palate* of an *oak*-aged wine, especially a Rioja.

*varietal:* a wine made entirely, or almost entirely, from a single grape variety, as opposed to a *blend*.

*VdlT:* Vino de la Tierra (wine of the land) is a Spanish classification for country wines similar to the *VdP* category in France.

*VdM:* (1) Vino de Mesa (table wine) is the lowest quality category in Spain. Wines are basic and are often a blend of wines from different regions. This category is also used by progressive producers to make wines that don't conform to *DO* rules. (2) Vinho de Mesa (table wine) is the lowest quality category in Portugal.

*VdP:* Vin de Pays (country wine) is the third-highest quality classification of French wine.

*VDQS:* Vin Délimité de Qualité Supérieure (delimited wine of superior quality) is the second-highest classification for French wines, just below *AC*.

*VdT:* (1) Vin de Table (table wine) is the lowest quality category in France. No region or vintage may be stated on the label and the wine is likely to be of basic quality. (2) Vino da Tavola (table wine) is the basic table wine classification in Italy, but is also used by makers of fine wines that do not conform to *DOC* regulations.

*vegetal:* reminiscent of vegetative matter or a vegetable patch.

*VQPRD:* see *IPR*.

*VR:* Vinho Regional (regional wine) is the Portuguese equivalent of French *VdP*.

*vintage:* the year the grapes were harvested. Wines differ from year to year, depending on weather conditions during the vine's growing seasons. Champagnes and sparkling wines, unlike still reds and whites, are more often than not made from *blends* of grapes harvested in different years ('non-vintage'). A vintage Champagne—one made from grapes harvested in a single season—is rare and expensive.

*yeasty:* bread or bakery aromas often evident in barrel fermented white wines but especially in Champagnes and sparkling wines where yeasts stay in contact with the wine after fermentation.

# Index of wines

1ères Côtes de Blaye AC 123, 125
1ères Côtes de Bordeaux AC 121
35 South
—Chardonnay 98
—Merlot 102
35th Parallel
—Nero d'Avola 188
—Primitivo 188

Abadia Retuerta Rívola 236
Abadia San Campio Albariño 229
Abando Crianza 239
Achaia Clauss
—Imperial Mavrodaphne 270
—Peloponnesiakos Pelopas Topikos
      Oenos 178
Aghiorghitiko grape 178–9
Aglianico grape 189, 200
Agramont Crianza 231
Alasia Dry Muscat 182
Albada 231
Albariño grape 229
Albet i Noya
—21 Brut 268
—Collecció Cabernet Sauvignon 240
—Collecció Syrah 241
—Collecció Tempranillo 241
—Lignum 236
—Núria 243
Alella DO 228
Alentejo VR 208, 210
Alfrocheiro grape 208
Alicante DO 232
Allegrini Valpolicella Classico 190
Alma
—Rosé 255
—Garnacha 232
Almargem 207
A. L. Monastrell 232
Aloxe-Corton 1er Cru AC 139
Alsace 114–7
—AC 11, 114–7
——Grand Cru Kessler 116
——Rosacker 116
——Vorbourg 116, 117
Alta Vista
—Chardonnay 57
—Malbec 60
Alto Adige DOC
—Gewurztraminer 185
—Pinot Grigio 184
—Südtirol 185
—Terlano Classico 182
Alto de Terra Andina
—Cabernet Sauvignon Reserve 107
—Chardonnay Reserve 99
Altos de Temporada
—Cabernet Sauvignon Reserve 60
—Malbec Reserve 60
Alvaro Palacios Les Terrasses 11, 242
Amarone DOC 199, 200
Amelia Chardonnay 101

Anges, Domaine des 146
Angove's Classic Reserve Shiraz 76
Anheuser Kreuznacher
—Narrenkappe Grauburgunder
      Kabinett Trocken 174
—St Martin Weissburg. Kabinett
      Halbtrocken 174
Anjou-Villages Brissac AC 145
Anticaia Riserva 190
Antu Mapu Sauvignon Blanc 01 96
Appert, Domaine Jean Louis 138
Aragonês grape 208, 210
Araucano Jacques et François Lurton
—Cabernet Sauvignon 107
—Sauvignon Blanc 99
Arbos Primitivo 186
Arcano Chianti Colli Senesi 186
Archidamo Primitivo di Manduria 188
Argentina 56–61
Argento
—Chardonnay 56
—Malbec 58
Arlaud Roncevie, Domaine 137
Arzuaga Crianza 239
Ascheri Montalupa di Bra 186
Assyrtiko-Athiri grape 178
Asti DOCG 14
Auphilac Blanc, Domaine d' 4
Australia 8, 9, 13, 14, 17, 20, 62–92
Austria 93–5

Babich
—Winemaker's Reserve Pinot Noir 205
——Sauvignon Blanc 203
——Syrah 205
Backsberg Estate
—Chenin Blanc 213
—Merlot 220
Baga grape 209
Bagordi Crianza 239
Baileys
—1920s Block Glenrowan Shiraz 84
—Glenrowan Shiraz 81
Balbas Crianza 239
Balland, Domaine Jean Paul 143
Barbera 58, 81, 190–3, 195–6, 199–200
Barbera d'Alba DOC 191, 193, 195, 200
Barbera d'Asti DOC 190, 199
Barbera Rive 190
Barolo DOCG 198
Barraida DOC 209
Barreyre, Château 121
Barry, Jim, McCrae Wood Shiraz 90
Basa Blanco 227
Bastardo grape 208
Bastet, Château de 147, 148
Beau Rivage, Château 121
Beaune Marconnets AC 140
Beck, Graham, Cabernet Sauvignon 220
Bel Air Chablis 133
Belles-Graves, Château 125

Bellevue Grand Délicatesse, Domaine
 de 167
Bellingham
—Classic Cabernet Merlot 219
—Sauvignon Blanc 212
Bend in the River Dry Riesling 173
Benziger
—Zinfandel 253
—Fumé Blanc 247
Beraut Cuvée Harmonie, Domaine 169
Berengarium 190
Bergerac AC 13, 170–2, 255
Bergerie de l'Hortus Pic St Loup
 Classique 161
Beringer
—Appellation Collection Fumé Blanc
 246
——Zinfandel 249
Bernard, Louis
—Ch. neuf-du-Pape 155
—Côtes du Rhône 153
—Côtes du Ventoux 152
Beronia Tempranillo 236
Berry's
—Alsace Pinot Blanc 115
—Nelson Sauvignon Blanc 202
Bertagna 'Les Dames Hugeuttes',
 Domaine 137
Bertin, Château 124
Bethany Schrapel Family
—Grenache 14
—Cabernet Merlot 84
—The Manse Semillon Riesling
 Chardonnay 64
Bierzo AC 244
Biran, Château de 171
Bironi de Brolio 1141 190
Blanc Cuvée Aliénor, Château Jacques
 127
Blanco Flor 226
Blaufränkisch grape 95
Blewitt Springs Cabernet Sauvignon 77
Blue White Chenin Blanc 213
Boekenhoutskloof Semillon 19
Boglietti
—Dolcetto 194
—Nebbiolo 198
—Roscaleto 200
Boillot Bourgogne 139
Bolla Valpolicella 188
Bollinger Champagne
—Grande Année 262
—RD Extra Brut 262
—Special Cuvée Brut 261
Bonarda grape 192
Bonhomme, Domaine André 132
Bonterra
—Cabernet Sauvignon 251
—Zinfandel 251
Bordeaux 118–129
—AC 119, 120–23, 255
Borie de Maurel Esprit d'Automne,
 Domaine 163
Boscaini Marano 200
Bouchard Père et Fils 140
Bourboulenc grape 146–7
Bourgogne AC 132, 136, 137, 138, 139
—Côte de Nuits-Villages 137
—Hautes-Côtes de Nuits 137

Bouscassé, Château 172
Boutari
—Aghiorgitiko 179
—Naoussa 178
Bouvet Saphir Brut 266
Brau Chardonnay, Domaine de 159
Brau Cuvée Exquise, Château de 165
Brédif, Marc, Vouvray 12
Briante, Château de 137
Brisson, Château 122
Broglia La Meirana 183
Brokenwood Shiraz 85
Brookland Valley
—Verse 1 Cabernet Merlot 81
——Semillon Sauvignon 69
Brouilly AC 137, 138
Brown Brothers
—Barbera 81
—Dry Muscat 64
—Pinot Gris 69
Brun-Despagne, Château 122
Brusco dei Barbi 191
Buecher, Paul, Réserve Personnelle
 Riesling 115
Burgundy 130–40
Buscando grape 238
Bushman 160
Buzet AC 171

Cabardès AC 165
Cabernet Franc grape 79, 83, 85, 120–9,
 144–5, 171, 224–5, 234, 243, 266
Cabernet Sauvignon grape
—Argentina 60–1
—Australia 75, 77–88, 90–2
—Chile 101–2, 104–113,
—France 120–9, 160, 163–5, 168, 171
—Greece 178
—Italy 189, 191, 194, 200
—Lebanon 201
—New Zealand 206
—Portugal 209–210
—Romania 211
—Rosé 254–5
—South Africa 217–25,
—Spain 231–4, 236–7, 238–244
—USA 248–9, 251–3
Cabernet Sauvignon/Shiraz blends 79,
 82, 90, 107, 161
Cahors AC 172
Caladoc grape 243
Calatayud DO 231, 233
California 9, 14, 245–53
Camarate grape 210
Camarsac, Château de 122
Camillona 183
Campillo Reserva 15
Camplazens L'Hermitage, Château 165
Campo Viejo Reserva 236
Campobarro 232
Campuget, Château de 162
Canaiolo grape 186, 198, 270
Canard-Duchêne Champagne 258
Candido Duca d'Aragona 14
Canepa
—Carmenère 107
—Chardonnay 98
—Merlot 103
——Private Reserve 107

Cannonau di Sardinia 'Le Bombarde' 8
Can Vendrell de la Codina Chardonnay
    Xarel-lo 227
Canyon Road
—Cabernet Sauvignon 248
—Chardonnay 245
—Merlot 249
Cape Jaffa Mt Benson Shiraz 85
Capel Vale Sauvignon Blanc Semillon
    69
Cape Mentelle Chardonnay 74
Caraguilhes, Château de 162
Carchelo Syrah 237
Cardeal Reserva 208
Carignan grape 112, 160, 162–7, 236–7,
    242, 256
Cariñena, see Carignan
Carmen
—Cabernet Sauvignon 101
—Chardonnay Reserva 100
—Merlot 101
Carmenère grape 103, 106–7, 109–112
Carpineto Riserva 198
Casa alla Terra 182
Casa Castillo
—Las Gravas 243
—Monastrell 237
Casa Emma 191
Casa Lapostolle
—Cabernet Sauvignon 107
—Cuvée Alexandre Merlot 113
Casa Rossa di Mizzole IGT Verona 8
Casas del Bosque Sauvignon Blanc 100
Cascina Pallerino di Bono Bricco della
    Saluta 191
Castaño Hécula 232
Castelar Crianza 233
Castell del Remei Gotim Bru 237
Castello Banfi 12
Castillo de Chiva 227
Castillo de Molina
—Cabernet Sauvignon Reserve 108
—Chardonnay Reserve 100
Castello Vicchiomaggio La Prima
    Riserva 199
Castilla León VdT 234
Castelão Frânces, see Trincadeira
Catalan VdP 161, 164
Cataldi
—Madonna 188
—Tonì 199
Catena
—Agrelo Vineyards Chardonnay 57
—Lunlunta Vineyards Malbec 60
Cathedral Cellar Pinotage 222
Cattaratto grape 184
Cauvy, Domaine de 160
Cava DO 265, 267, 268, 269
Cave de Rasteau
—Côtes du Rhône 148
—Côtes du Rhône Villages 151
Caves Bonifácio 207, 208
Cazal-Viel Syrah, Domaine 166
Cazelles-Verdier, Domaine 163
Cerasuolo di Vittoria 194
Cesani
—Sanice Vernaccia 185
—Vernaccia 184

Cesari
—Amarone Il Bosco 199
—Ripasso Mara 191
Chablis
—AC 130, 131, 132, 133, 134
—1er Cru 132
——Montmains 134
——Vaucopins 135
Champagne AC 9, 12, 13, 257–263
Champy
—Mâcon-Uchizy 132
—Savigny-lès-Beaune 139
Chandon de Briailles 138
——'Les Vergelesses' 139
Chanson
—Chablis 131
——1er Cru Vaucopins 135
—Viré-Clessé 14, 131
Chapel Hill Irsai Olivér 180
Chapoutier Les Meysonniers Crozes-
    Hermitage 151
Charavin Rasteau, Domaine Didier 150
Chardonnay grape
—Argentina 56–7
—Australia 62–8, 70, 72–5
—Chile 96–101
—France 130–6, 157–9, 169
—Italy 184
—Lebanon 201
—New Zealand 203, 205
—South Africa 213–7, 212
—Spain 226, 227, 229–230
—Sparkling 257–262, 264, 266–9
—USA 245–7
Charpentier Prestige Brut 259
Chartron, Cuvée Jean
—Chardonnay 132
—Pinot Noir 137
Chartron et Trébuchet
—La Chatenière St Aubin 1er Cru 136
—La Chaume Rully 135
Chasse-Spleen, Château 128
Château, see individual name
Châteauneuf-du-Pape AC 153, 154,
    155, 156
Chatelain 142
Chenin Blanc grape 63, 65, 72, 141,
    212–5, 266–7
Cheval-Blanc, Château 19
Cheval Noir 125
Chianti DOCG
—Classico 190, 191, 194, 196, 197, 198,
    199
—Colli Senesi 186
—Rufina 197
Chiarlo, Michele
—Gavi 185
—Valle del Sole Barbara d'Asti 199
Chile 96–113
Chinon AC 144, 145
Chivite Gran Feudo Crianza 233
Cigales DO 235
Cinsault grape 148, 150–4, 160, 162,
    166, 201, 217, 256
CK Vineyards
—Wildwood Canyon Syrah 249
——Zinfandel 249
Clairette 146–7
Clos Clare Shiraz 89

Clos de Cuminaille 155
Clos de la Perrière 136
Clos du Bois
—Chardonnay 246
—Pinot Noir 251
Clos Frantin, Domaine du 140
Clos Godeaux, Domaine du 144
Clos Malverne
—Auret Cabernet Sauvignon Pinotage
 220
—Pinotage 219
——Reserve 219
——Sauvignon Blanc 214
Clos St Landelin, Domaine du
—Gewurztraminer 116
—Riesling 117
—'V' Pinot Noir 117
Cloudy Bay Pinot Noir 206
Cluver, Paul
—Cabernet Sauvignon 223
—Chardonnay 216
—Pinot Noir 223
—Sauvignon Blanc 216
—Weisser Riesling 214
Códax, Martin, Albariño 229
Col di Sasso Sangiovese Cabernet
 Sauvignon 191
Colle Secco Rubino Mont. d'Abruzzo
 191
Colli Euganei DOC 189
Collines Rhodaniennes VdP 164
Collio DOC 184
Colombard grape 62, 169
Columbia Crest
—Chardonnay 246
—Merlot 251
Comté de Mérinville Minervois 163
Comte Lafond Sancerre 143
Comte L. de Ferande Brut 257
Conca de Barberà DO 242
Con Class
—Sauvignon Blanc 11, 226
—Vendimia Excepcional 227
Concha y Toro
—Casillero del Diablo Chardonnay 98
——Merlot 103
——Shiraz 103
—Gewürztraminer 98
—Sunrise Carmenère 103
—Terrunyo Carmenère 112
—Trio Merlot 103
Condado de Haza 241
Condemine Mâcon-Péronne Le Clou,
 Domaine de 131
Condrieu AC 148
Corbières AC 162, 163, 164, 165, 166,
 167
Corbu grape 170
Coriole Redstone 99 85
Corte Sant'Alda 192
Cortese grape 183, 185
Corvina grape 188, 190–2, 195–7,
 199–200
Costers del Segre DO 237, 239
Costières de Nîmes AC 158, 159, 162,
 163, 167
Coteaux
—d'Aix-en-Provence AC 13, 20, 15
—de l'Ardèche VdP 146, 148

—du Languedoc AC 161, 166
—du Verdun VdP 138, 160
Côtes
—de Bergerac AC 171
—de Bourg AC 121
—de Castillon AC 122, 123
—de Gascogne VdP 169, 170, 171, 254
—de Thongue VdP 163, 168
—du Lubéron AC 147
—du Rhône AC 146, 147, 148, 150–3,
 256
—du Rhône des Papes 148
—du Rhône-Villages AC 150, 151
—du Roussillon Villages Tautavel AC
 165, 166
—du Ventoux AC 146, 150, 152
Côte Rôtie AC 156
Couly-Dutheil Clos de l' Echo 145
Counoise grape 154
Countacc! 200
Court-les-Mûts, Château 9, 17, 170,
 171, 271
Cousiño-Macul Antiguas Reservas Cab
 Sauv 111
Craiglee Shiraz 98 89
Crémant
—d'Alsace AC 268
—de Limoux AC 267
Crochet, Domaine Dominique et
 Janine 142
Crochet, Lucien
—Les Chailloux Pouilly Fuissé 134
——Sancerre 144
Crouchen grape 68
Crozes-Hermitage AC 151, 152, 153,
 155
Cudgee Creek
—Cabernet Sauvignon 75
—Colombard Chardonnay 62
Cuilleron Gaillard Villard 148
Cuvée de l'Arjolle VdP 163
Cuvée Orélie 146

Dallas-Conté Cabernet Sauvignon 108
Dalmeran, Château 168
Dampt, Domaine Daniel 132
Danzante
—Merlot 192
—Pinot Grigio 184
—Sangiovese 192
Dão DOC 208
d'Arenberg
d'Arry's Original Shiraz Grenache 13
—The Custodian Grenache 85
—The Dead Arm Shiraz 91
—The Dry Dam Riesling 69
—The Hermit Crab Marsanne Viognier
 69
—The High Trellis Cabernet Sauvignon
 81
—The Last Ditch Viognier 70
—The Stump Jump Grenache Shiraz 77
——Riesling Marsanne 64
da Sousa, José 208
d'Auphilac Blanc, Domaine de, 8
De Bortoli
—Yarra Valley Chardonnay 74
——Pinot Noir 91
——Shiraz 89

de Castris, Leone, Riserva 195
De Ladoucette Pouilly-Fumé 144
Delbeck Heritage Brut 258
De Leuwen Jagt Pinotage 222
Delheim Sauvignon Blanc 214
Delmas 267
de Moor, Alice & Olivier, Bel Air 133
Denogent Macon-Solutré Clos des
    Bertillonnes, Domaine Robert, 134
Depoivre, Bernard, Brut 258
Descendentes de J. Palacios 244
des Lauzes, Château Etienne 162
Deutz Blanc de Blancs Brut 262
di Lenardo
—Father's Eyes 185
—Refosco 189
—TOH! 182
d'Oc VdP 157–61, 164–6
Dolcetto grape 194–5
Dolcetto d'Alba DOC 194, 195
Domaine de, du, des, see individual
    name
Don Melchor 97 113
Donna Lisa Riserva 199
Dornfelder grape 177
Doudeau-Léger, Domaine 141
Douro DOC 208, 209, 210
Duas Quintas 209
Ducret, Pierre 'Clos Marolle' 138
Dumangin Carte d'Or 1er Cru Brut 258
Dumont, L., Brut 259
Duque de Viseu 208
Durand-Laplagne, Château 122
Durban, Domaine de 272
Durbanville Hills Chardonnay 215
Dutschke St Jakobi Shiraz 8–9
Duveau, Domaine 145

Eaglehawk
—Chardonnay 63
—Merlot 75
Edition Deinhimer Riesling Spätlese
    Trocken 174
Edition Kauzenberg Riesling
    KabTrocken 176
Edition Niersteiner Riesling Spätlese
    Halbtrocken 175
Ehrhard, Carl
—Riesling Auslese Trocken 177
—Rüdesheimer Riesling Trocken 174
Eisacktaler Gewürztraminer 185
El Vínculo 241
Enate
—Cabernet Sauvignon Rosado 256
—Chardonnay 2-3-4 229
Entari 231
Entre-Deux-Mers AC 118, 119
Epiré, Château d' 141
Ercavio Tempranillo Roble 231
Eroica see Ste Michelle, Château
Errázuriz
—Estate Merlot 103
——Syrah 108
—Sauvignon Blanc 96
—Syrah Cabernet Sauvignon 101
Esk Valley Merlot Cabernet Sauvignon
    206
Esporão Reserva 210
Estremadura VR 209, 210

Etchart Rio de Plata
—Malbec 57
—Merlot 58
—Torrontés 56
Evans & Tate
—Margaret River Cabernet Merlot 82
——Chardonnay 70
Excelsior Cabernet Sauvignon 222

Faiveley 135, 136, 138, 139
Falesco 194
Fantini 186
—Montelpulciano 187
—Primitivo 187
—Sangiovese 187
Faugères AC 160, 168
Faustino de Autor Reserva 244
Felton Road Dry Riesling 204
Ferngrove Chardonnay 64
Fetzer
—Chardonnay Viognier 245
—Eagle Peak Merlot 250
—Valley Oaks Zinfandel 250
—Viognier 246
—Zinfandel Shiraz 248
Feuillatte, Nicolas, Réserve Brut 260
Fèvre, Domaine William 133
Filliatreau, Domaine 145
Finca Flichman
—Chardonnay 57
—Dedicado 61
—Malbec Reserve 60
—Syrah 59
Finca Las Moras
—Chardonnay Reserve 57
—Malbec Reserve 59
Flagstone Noon Gun White 212
Fleur du Cap Cabernet Sauvignon 220
Fleurie AC 136, 138
Fontalognier, Domaine de 136
Fortia, Château 156
Fourcas-Dumont, Château 126
Fourcas Hosten, Château 126
Fournier 143
Foxwood Bruno's Block Chardonnay
    157
France 114–72 see also individual
    regions
—South 8, 13, 20, 157–68
—South West 9, 169–72
Francis Coppola
—Diamond Series Merlot 253
——Zinfandel 253
—Presents Rosso 251
Franc Lartigue, Château 126
Frappato di Vittoria grape 194
Frascati Superiore DOC 181
Freie Weingärtner Riesling Trocken 95
Freixenet Cordon Negro 265
Friuli Grave DOC 182, 189
Furmint grape 180, 271, 273

Gago 240
Gaillard 164
Gaja 'Promis' 17
Gallo, Ernest & Julio
—Laguna Ranch Chardonnay 247
—Sonoma Selection Pinot Noir 249
——Zinfandel 250

Gamay grape 136–8
Gardiès, Domaine 166
Garganega grape 181–2
Garnacha, see Grenache
Garnacha Blanca, see Grenache Blanc
Garnier et Fils, Domaine 133
Gavi DOCG 183, 185
Gemina Moscato d'Asti 264
Genius Loci Sangiovese 192
Gerhardt, Jakob, Sekt Chardonnay Brut 266
Germany 173–7
Gerovassiliou Syrah, Domaine 179
Gervais Gobillard Brut 5
Gevrey-Chambertin AC 140
Gewürztraminer grape 65, 98, 114–7, 185
Geyser Peak
—Cabernet Sauvignon 252
——Reserve 253
—Chardonnay 247
—Shiraz 252
Gigognan Vigne du Dauphin, Château 153
Gigondas AC 153, 154, 155
Ginestet Mascaron 121
Girardin, Vincent, Domaine
—'Les Gravières', 140
—'Les Murgers de Dents de Chiens' 135
Givry 1er Cru AC 138
Gléon Montanié Cuvée Gaston Bonnes, Château 166
Gobillard Grande Réserve Brut 9, 258
Godello grape 230
Gold Rock
—Chardonnay 70
—Semillon Chardonnay 65
—Shiraz 82
Goldwater Dog Point Sauvignon Blanc 205
Gonzalez Byass Apostoles Palo Cortado 19
Gourgazaud Réserve, Château de 17
Guirlandes Merlot, Domaine des 164
Graciano grape 238, 240, 244
Grain Sauvage 170
Gran Caus 243
—Cava Reserva 267
——Rosado 269
—Rosado 256
Grand Veneur, Domaine 147, 154
Gran Feudo 254
Gratien & Meyer Brut 266
Graves AC 118, 120, 124, 125
Gravières, Château des 120
Greece 178–180
Green Point Vintage Brut 269
Grenache grape 77, 82, 84–5, 88, 90, 148, 150–5, 160–8, 231–3, 235–7, 238–9, 242, 244, 254–6, 270
Grenache Blanc grape 146–7, 228
Grès St Paul, Château 166
Grigio Luna Pinot Grigio 182
Groot Constantia
—Pinotage 222
—Sauvignon Blanc 216
Gros Manseng grape 169–170
Grosset Semillon Sauvignon Blanc 73
Grove Mill Sauvignon Blanc 204

Growers Chenin 65
Grüner Veltliner grape 93
Guelbenzu
—Azul 11, 237
—Evo 242
Guigal 147, 151, 153, 256
Guitian Godello 230
Guldentaler Riesling Spätlese Trocken 175
Guntrum, Louis
—Dornfelder Rotwein Trocken 177
—Niersteiner Rehbach Riesling Spätlese 176
—Penguin Eiswein 273

Half Moon Shiraz 77
Hardys
—Nottage Hill Cabernet Sauvignon Shiraz 82
——Chardonnay 65
——Shiraz 82
—Stamp Cabernet Merlot 77
——Riesling Gewurztraminer 65
—Tintara Cabernet Sauvignon 87
——Chardonnay 74
——Shiraz 87
Harlin, Henri, Brut 257
Hárslevelú grape 271, 273
Hautes-Côtes de Beaune AC 133, 138
Haut-Médoc AC 123, 124, 126, 128
Haut Pougnan, Château 120
Haut Selve, Château 124
Heidsieck, Charles, Réserve Brut 259
Heidsieck Monopole Blue Top Brut 259
Herencia Remondo Viura 226
Hewitson Riesling 74
Hills View Vineyards
—Cabernet Merlot 77
—Chardonnay Verdelho 63
—Shiraz Cabernet 77
Hochar Père et Fils 201
Honey Tree Semillon Chardonnay 65
Hugel
—Blancs 114
—Cuvée Les Amours Pinot Blanc de 'Gentil' 115
—Riesling 115
Hugues le Juste Syrah 161
Huia
—Brut 269
—Pinot Gris 204
—Sauvignon Blanc 202
Hungary 180
Hunter's
—Pinot Noir 205
—Sauvignon Blanc 205
Hutton Ridge
—Cabernet Sauvignon 217
—Cinsault 217
—Merlot 217
—Pinotage 217
—Shiraz 217

Iglesia Vieja Crianza 233
Igneus 242
IGT
—Marche 192
—Provincia di Pavia 187
—Puglia 186, 187, 189

—Rosso del Veronese 4, 195, 197
—Rosso dell'Umbria 193
—Rosso Salento 10, 187, 190, 193, 194, 196
—Sangiovese Daunia 187
—Sicilia 184, 188, 189, 193
—Tarantino 197
—Toscana 13, 184, 186, 189, 191, 192, 194, 199
—Umbria Merlot 194
—Veneto Merlot 193
—Venezie 184, 192
—Venezia Giulia 185
Il Baciale 196
Incanto Fabiano Pinot Nero 187
Inzolia grape 184
Ironstone Shiraz Grenache 82
Irsai Olivér grape 180
Irvine Eden Crest Merlot Cabernet 90
Italy 8, 10, 12, 14, 17, 19, 181–200

Jaboulet, 272
—Dom. de Thalabert 155
—Le Grand Pompée 155
—Les Cèdres 156
—Les Jalets 152
Jacob's Creek
—Cabernet Sauvignon 75
—Chardonnay 63
—Dry Riesling 63
—Reserve Shiraz 82
Jacquinot, Château 122
Jaen grape 208
Jaffelin 133, 138
Jamieson's Run Cabernet Shiraz Merlot 83
Jarrero 237
Jaume, Alain 150, 152
Jerez DO 15
Jindalee
—Cabernet Sauvignon 78
—Chardonnay 65
—Merlot 78
—Shiraz 78
Jolivet, Passcal, 144
Jolys, Château 170
Jones, Trevor, Cabernet Merlot 92
Jonqueyres, Château 122
Jordan
—Chardonnay 216
—Sauvignon Blanc 215
Joy, Domaine de 169
JP Barrel Selection Red Wine 208
Jumilla DO 237, 243
Jurancon Noir grape 172
Jurançon Sec AC 170

Kadette Kanonkop Estate Wine 221
Kafraya Les Breteches, Château 18
Kanonkop Estate
—Pinotage 225
—Paul Sauer 225
Katnook Estate
—Cabernet Sauvignon 83
—Sauvignon Blanc 74
Kattus, Johann, Riesling 93
Kendall-Jackson
—Collage Zinfandel Shiraz 250

—Vintner's Reserve Cabernet Sauvignon 252
Kettmeir Pinot Grigio 185
Kirwan, Château 129
Kleine Zalze Unwooded Chardonnay 214
Kleinrivier
—Cabernet Sauvignon Merlot 218
—Chardonnay 213
—Pinotage 219
—Pinotage Merlot 218
Knappstein
—Cabernet Franc 85
—Riesling 71
Knorhoek
—Cabernet Sauvignon 222
—Pinotage 221
Koehly, Charles, St Hippolyte Gewurztraminer 114
Kofsifali grape 179
Kracher, Alois, Neusiedler see Beerenauslese 271
KWV
—Cabernet Sauvignon 219
—Chenin Blanc 213

L'Abeille de Fieuzal 120, 128
Laborie Estate Cabernet Sauvignon 221
La Buxynoise 134
La Citadelle, Château 123
La Corte
—Negroamaro 196
—Zinfandel 197
La Croix Canat Les Blancs Gateaux, Domaine 143
Lacroix Merlot Saignée Rosé, Château 255
La Couronne, Château 127
Lafleur de Lynch 124
La Freynelle, Château 119
La Gascogne 170
La Gavina Cabernet Sauvignon 194
La Grande Maye, Château 123
La Grande Métairie, Château 118
La Gravière, Château 119
L'Agnet 237
Lalande de Pomerol AC 125
La Mancha DO 231, 235, 241
Lamole di Lamole 194, 197, 270
Lamothe-Cissac, Château 124
L'Amourier 164
Landskroon Shiraz 223
Langhe DOC 198
Lanzaga 240
Lanzerac
—Merlot 223
—Pinotage 223
La Palmeria
—Cabernet Sauvignon/Merlot 102
—Chardonnay/Sauvignon 96
Lapeyre, Domaine Luc,
—Les Clots 167
—Nuit Blanche 158
Laporte Ruscino, Domaine 164
Laroche, Domaine
—Mâcon-Lugny 131
—St Martin Chablis 134
Laroche, Michel
—South of France Chardonnay 159

——Grenache 161
——Merlot 165
——Terret 157
Las Casas del Toqui
—Cabernet Sauvignon 102
——Prestige 108
——Reserve 104
—Chardonnay 97
Latour, Louis 132
Laurent, Miquel
—Bardou 168
—Cabernet Syrah 161
—Chardonnay Viognier 157
—Nord-Sud Syrah 165
—Saga Pegot 168
—Syrah 161
—Viognier 159
Laurent-Perrier Brut Rosé 13, 263
Laurus, Gabriel Meffre 153, 155
La Vendimia 231
L'Avenir Cabernet Sauvignon 221
La Vieille Ferme 147, 150
Lawson's Dry Hills
—Pinot Noir 206
—Riesling 204
La Xarmada Crianza 242
Lebanon 201
Le Cazal Le Pas de Zarat, Domaine 167
Le Chêne, Château 123
Leeuwin Estate Art Series Riesling 71
Lehmann, Peter
—Clancy's 79
—Eight Songs Shiraz 91
—Mentor 91
—The Barossa Cabernet Sauvignon 83
——Chenin Blanc 63
——Riesling 66
——Semillon 66
——Shiraz 83
—Weighbridge Chardonnay 67
l'Enclos Bonis, Château 124
Lenswood Vineyards Sauvignon Blanc 71
Le Prestige, Château du 172
Le Riche
—Cabernet Sauvignon 221
——Reserve 224
Le Rime 184
Les Baux de Provence 168
Les Chailloux see Crochet
Les Goubert, Domaine 154
Les Maîtres Vignerons de Tautavel 165
Lestage Simon, Château 128
Les Terrasses, Alvaro Palacios 11, 242
Les Vignerons Ardèchois Merlot 148
Leyenda 113
Lindauer Brut 264
Lindemans
—Bin 65 Chardonnay 66
—Cawarra Shiraz Cabernet 76
—St George Cabernet Sauvignon 90
Lingenfelder Bird Label Riesling 173
L'Inspiration des Miaudoux 170, 172
Listrac-Médoc AC 126
Live Oak Road Zinfandel 250
Liversan, Château 128
Loire 141–5
Long Mountain
—Merlot Shiraz 218

—Pinotage 218
Los Boldos Grand Cru, Château 113
Los Robles Private Reserve Cab Sauvignon 108
Loudenne, Château 126
Loureiro grape 207
Luenzo 199
Lugana DOC 183
Lussac St Émilion AC 125
Lustau Manzanilla Fino 10

Macabeo grape 265, 267
Mâcon-Lugny AC 131
Mâcon-Uchizy AC 132
Mâcon-Villages AC 131, 134
McCrae Wood Shiraz 90
McGuigan
—Bin 3000 Limited Release Merlot 78
—Bin 4000 Cabernet Sauvignon 78
—Bin 6000 Verdelho 66
—Shareholders' Shiraz 90
—The Black Label Merlot 78
McWilliam's
—Hanwood Chardonnay 66
—Hunter Valley Chardonnay 70
—Inheritance Shiraz Cabernet 79
Madiran AC 172
Madone, Domaine de la 136
Madonna di Como 195
Magnol, Château 126
Mähler-Besse La Coquille 119
Maine-Gazin 'Livenne' Vieilles Vignes, Château 125
Maison Champy see Champy
Malaga DO 271, 272
Malandes, Domaine des 132
Malbec grape 57–8, 60–1, 91, 109, 171, 172
Malleolus 244
Malvasia grape 181, 228, 270
Malvasia Nera grape 187, 194–5, 199
Mamre Brook Cabernet Sauvignon 85
Mandeler Rosengarten Dornfelder 177
Mandilari grape 179
Mantel Blanco Verdejo Sauvignon Blanc 227
Marchesi de' Frescobaldi Rèmole 189
Marchesi di Barolo
—Le Lune 198
—Madonna di Como 195
—Ruvei 195
Margaux AC 127
—Grand Cru Classé 129
Maris, Château 162
Marks and Spencer
—Cava Brut 265
—Chablis 130
Marqués
—de Alella Classico 228
—de Aragon Old Vine Garnacha 233
—de Cáceres 254
——Gran Reserva 242
—de Casa Concha Cabernet Sauvignon 108
—de Murrieta Coleccion 2100 238
—de Riscal Sauvignon 228
—de Valcarlos Crianza 233
Marsannay AC 139
Marsanne grape 64, 69, 146

Martín Códax Albariño 229
Martinez Bermell Merlot 238
Mas Amiel 270
Mas des Bressades Cuvée Tradition 159
Mas Neuf Cuvée Compostelle, Château 167
Massa Maritima DOC 197
Masson-Blondelet Villa Paulus, Domaine 143
Mateus Rosé 15
Maucaillou, Château 129
Mauro 244
Maury AC 270
Mauzac grape 267
Mavrodaphne grape 270
Mavrodaphne de Patras AO 270
Mazer Inferno 195
Mazuelo grape 238, 240, 244
Médoc AC 124, 126, 127
Meffre, Gabriel 153, 155
Melon de Bourgogne grape 141
Mencia grape 244
Menetou-Salon Morogues AC 142
Mercurey AC 139, 160, 162, 163, 164, 166, 167
—La Livinière 13
Merlot grape
—Argentina 58, 61
—Australia 75, 77–9, 81–4, 87, 90–2
—Chile 101–7, 109, 111–3
—France 120–9, 148, 160, 163–5, 168, 171–2
—Italy 192–4
—New Zealand 206
—Romania 211
—Rosé 254–5
—South Africa 217–225
—Spain 234, 237, 238–9, 242–4
—USA 249–251, 253
Mérinville, Château de 166
Merlot de l'Arjolle Synthèse 168
Merrill, Geoff
—Cabernet Sauvignon Reserve 88
—Chardonnay Reserve 73
Meyer-Fonné Pinot Blanc 115
Meyer Gewurtztraminer, Domaine Eugène 116
MezzoGiorno Nero d'Avola 189
Miaudoux, Château 171, 255
Michel, René, et ses Fils, Domaine 18, 133
Millesimato Riserva 189
Miquel, Laurent
—Bardou 168
—Cabernet Syrah 161
—Chardonnay Viognier 157
—Nord-Sud Syrah 165
—Saga Pegot 168
—Syrah 161
—Viognier 159
Mirambelo 179
—High Country Chardonnay 66
—Old Vine Reserve Shiraz 88
Moët et Chandon Brut Rosé 263
Molinara grape 188, 190–2, 195–7, 199–200
Molino Real Mountain Wine 272
Monastrell, see Mourvèdre

Mondavi, Robert Cabernet Sauvignon 252
Monferrato DOC 183, 196, 200
Monmousseau Cuvée Prestige J. M. 267
Monopole Rioja 228
Montagne, Château 123
Montagne-St-Émilion AC 124
Montagny 1er Cru AC 134
Montana
—Pinot Noir Reserve 206
—Vineyard Selection Sauvignon Blanc Reserve 202
Montaudon Grand Brut Rosé 263
Mont Baudie VdP 8
Montecillo
—Crianza 234
—Gran Reserva 240, 242
Montegradella Santá Sofiá 195
Montepulciano grape 187–8, 191, 199
Montepulciano d'Abruzzo DOC 187, 188, 191, 199
Monteregio Riserva 197
Montes Alpha
—Cabernet Sauvignon 111
—Chardonnay 98
—Pinot Noir 104
Montesierra Crianza 234
Montes Sauvignon Blanc 97
MontGras
—Cabernet Sauvignon Reserve 109
—Carmenère Reserve 109
—Merlot Reserve 109
—Ninquén Barrel Select Chardonnay 101
——Barrel Select Red 112
——Chardonnay 100
——Quatro Reserve 109
——Sauvignon Blanc 97
Montravel AC 169
Morgon AC 136
Moro, Emilio
—Finca Resalso 236
—Crianza 241
Moscatel grape 227, 271–2
Moscato grape 264
Moulis AC 129
Moulis-en-Médoc AC 128
Mount Athos 178
Mount Hurtle Grenache Rosé 254
Mount Pleasant Elizabeth Semillon 17
Mourvèdre grape 88, 90, 148, 150–2, 154–5, 160–1, 163–7, 232–4, 237, 243, 256
MR Moscatel 271
Muga Reserva 238
Mumm de Cramant Grand Cru Brut 262
Muré, Réné 268
Murphy-Goode Chardonnay 247
Musar, Château 96 201
Musaragno Brut 267
Muscadet de Sèvre-et-Maine sur Lie AC 141
Muscat grape 64, 93, 158, 182
Muscat Blanc à Petits Grains grape 272
Muscat de Beaumes-de-Venise AC 272
Musella 192

Nalys, Domaine de 154
Navarra DO 231–4, 238, 242, 244, 254–255
Nathanson Creek
—Cabernet Sauvignon 248
—Chardonnay 245
—White Zinfandel 255
Naudin-Ferrand, Domaine Henri 133
Nebbiolo grape 195, 198, 200
Negroamaro grape 186–7, 190, 193–6, 199
Neil Ellis Groenekloof Sauvignon Blanc 215
Nepenthe
—Adelaide Hills Pinot Noir 88
—Lenswood Pinot Noir 89
——Riesling 72
——Semillon 72
Nero d'Avola grape 188–9, 193–4
New Zealand 202–6
Ninth Island Chardonnay 72
Nipozzano 197
Nodoz, Château 121
Norman, Greg
—Cabernet Merlot 87
—Chardonnay 73
Nostros
—Merlot 104
—Sauvignon Blanc 98
Notios 179

Or et de Gueules, Château d' 162
Oremus Tokaji 273
Ornellaia VdT 10
Osca Crianza 238
Oseleta grape 197
Osoti 238
Oude Kaap Cabernet Sauvignon Merlot 218
Oude Weltevreden Chardonnay 217
Oxford Landing Merlot 79

Palacio de la Vega Merlot Crianza 234
Palacio de Muruzabal
—Cosecha Particular 238
—Reserva 244
Palha-Canas 210
Palmela VQPRD 207
Panizzari 192
Parellada grape 229–230, 265
Parxet Chardonnay Cava 268
Pansa Blanca grape 228
Pardon, Domaine 136
Patache d'Aux, Château 126
Pato, Luis 209
Pécharmant AC 171
Pech, Domaine du 171
Pederna grape 207
Peel Estate
—Chenin Blanc 72
—Premium Red 83
—Shiraz 87
Pèlerins, Château des 128
Pellé, Domaine Henry 142
Pellehaut, Domaine de 171, 254
Penedès DO 227, 229, 230, 234, 236, 240–1, 243, 256
Penfolds
—Bin 128 Shiraz 87

—Bin 138 Shiraz Grenache Mourvèdre 90
—Bin 389 Cabernet Shiraz 90
Pepperwood Grove
—Pinot Noir 250
—Zinfandel 14, 248
Periquita grape 207–210
Pernand-Vergelesses 1er Cru AC 139
Perricone grape 193
Perrier, Joseph, Cuvée Royale Brut nv 259
Perrin
—Les Sinards 156
—Réserve 152
Pesquera Tinto 243
Pessac-Léognan AC 119, 128
Petaluma Coonawarra 99 91
Peter Lehmann, see Lehmann, Peter
Petit Caus 234
Petite Syrah grape 243, 253
Petit Manseng grape 170
Petit Verdot grape 124, 126, 128, 224
Pewsey Vale Riesling 70
Peyragué, Château 118
Peyredoulle, Château 123
Picajuan Peak
—Chardonnay 56
—Malbec 59
Pichon, Château 125
Picot, Didier
—Cabernet Sauvignon 160
—Dom. Haut St-Georges 163
—Sauvignon Blanc 157
Piemonte DOC 264
Pierro LTC Semillon Sauvignon Blanc 72
Pinotage grape 217–225
Pinot Bianco, see Pinot Blanc
Pinot Blanc grape 114–5, 174, 182
Pinot Grigio, see Pinot Gris
Pinot Gris grape 69, 174, 182, 184–6, 204
Pinot Meunier grape 257–263
Pinot Nero, see Pinot Noir
Pinot Noir grape
—Australia 86, 88–9, 91
—Chile 104, 106, 112
—France 117, 136–140,
—Italy 187, 196,
—New Zealand 205–6,
—South Africa 223
—Sparkling 257–264, 266, 268–9
—USA 249–251
Pipers Brook Vineyard Pinot Noir 86
Pique-Sègue, Château 169
Plaisir de Merle
—Cabernet Sauvignon 223
—Chardonnay 216
Poliziano 193, 198
Pol Roger Extra Dry White Foil 260
Pomerol AC 128
Pommery Grand Cru Brut 261
Pongrácz Méthode Cap Classique 268
Ponnelle, Pierre 131, 137
Porta
—Cabernet Sauvignon Select Reserve 109
—Chardonnay Reserve 99
—Pinot Noir Reserve 104

Portal del Alto
—Cabernet Sauvignon Gran Reserva 111
——Reserve 109
—Carmenère Reserve 111
—Chardonnay Reserve 100
Portugal 207–10
Pouilly-Fuissé AC 134, 135
Pouilly-Fumé AC 142, 143, 144
Poussan le Haut Chardonnay, Domaine de 158
Prado Enea Gran Reserva 244
Primitivo grape 186–190, 193
Primitivo di Manduria DOC 188
Primum 209
Priorat DO 11, 237, 242
Prosecco grape 265, 267
Prosecco di Valdobbiadene DOC 265, 267
Provence
Prunotto 193
Puisseguin St Émilion AC 122
Pujol, Domaine de 164

Quiltro
—Cabernet Sauvignon Reserve 104
—Merlot 102
Quinta d'Almergem Garrafeira 209
—de Azevedo 207
—de Pancas Cabernet Sauvignon 209
—do Cachão 210
—do Crasto 209
Quiot, Domaine Jerôme, Les Combes d'Arnevel 154

Race, Denis 134
Radici Mastroberardino 200
Ragotière, Château de la 141
Raïmat Cabernet Sauvignon 239
Rasteau, Domaine Martin 151
Raux, Château du 124
Ravaut, Gaston et Pierre 139
Ravenswood Vintners Blend Zinfandel 99 252
Refosco grape 189
Regaleali 184, 193
Régnié AC 136
Reichsgraf von Kesselstatt Josephshöfer
Remelluri 243
Renjarde, Domaine de la 151
Reynella Shiraz, Château 89
Rhône 146–56
Rías Baixas DO 229
Ribatejo DOC 209
Ribaute Cuvée François le Noir, Château de 165
Ribera del Duero DO 236, 239, 241, 243, 244
Ribera del Guadiana DO 232, 233, 235
Ribera del Queiles DO 7
Riesling 18, 63–72, 74, 93, 95, 114–7, 173–7, 185, 203–4, 212, 214, 247, 268, 271, 273
Rimbert Le Mas au Schiste, Domaine 167
Rioja DOC 11, 226, 228, 231, 234–40, 242–4, 254
Rion, Michèle et Patrice, Les Bois Bâtons 138

Riscal Tempranillo 234
Rivaner grape 93
Robert's Rock Chenin Blanc Chardonnay 214
Robertson's Well Cabernet Sauvignon 88
Roblot, Roger, Blanc Prestige 130
Rocca 187, 197
Rockford Local Growers Semillon 20
Roederer, Louis, 1er Brut 260
Rollan de By, Château 127
Romania 211
Rontets Clos Varambon, Château des 135
Rondinella grape 188, 190–2, 195–197, 199–200
Roncée Clos des Marronniers, Domaine du 145
Ropiteau 132, 134
Roquette, Domaine de la 156
Rosemount Estate
—Balmoral Syrah 92
—GSM 88
—Riesling 67
—Show Reserve Chardonnay 72
Rosso di Montalcino DOC 12
Rosso di Montepulciano DOC 193
Rosso di Verona IGT 8
Roty, Joseph 139
Roubaud, Château 163
—Cuvée Prestige 158
Roussanne grape 146–7
Rovit Special Reserve Cab Sauv 211
Royal Tokaji Tokaji 271
Ruby Cabernet grape 217, 221
Rueda DO 7, 226–8
Rufus Stone Sauvignon Blanc 70
Ruinart Brut 12, 261
Rully AC 135
Rust en Vrede
—Estate Wine 225
—Shiraz 224
Ruth, Château de 146, 150

Sacred Hill Semillon Chardonnay 67
Sagramoso 182
Sahateni Vineyards Reserve Merlot 211
St Ahon, Château 123
St Auriol, Château 166
St Andrews Shiraz 92
St Aubin 1er Cru AC 135, 136
St Chinian AC 162, 167, 168
St Cosme, Château de 153
Ste Michelle Eroica, Château 247
St Émilion AC 125
—1er Grand Cru Classé 15
—Grand Cru 126, 127
St Estèphe AC 124
St Gayan, Domaine 154
St Georges St Émilion AC 125
St Julien AC 12
St Hallett
—Barossa Select Semillon 71
— Eden Valley Riesling 71
St Hilaire Chardonnay, Domaine 159
St Joseph AC 152, 155
St Julien AC 8, 128
St Nicolas-de-Bourgueil AC 145
St Véran AC 131, 133

Salauze, Château 160
Salento Rosso 14
Salice Salentino DOC 186, 195, 199
—VQPRD 190
Salinger Brut 266
San Angelo Pinot Grigio 186
Sancerre AC 141–4
San Colombano Riserva DOC 192
Sandalford
—Cabernet Sauvignon 86
—Shiraz 86
Sandalyn Verdelho 5, 9
Sangiovese grape 186–7, 189–194,
       196–9, 251
San Lorenzo de Luca 193
Sanlucar de Barrameda 10
San Pedro
—Cabernet Sauvignon Reserve 105
—Merlot 102
—Merlot Reserve 105
Santa Carolina
—Barrica Selection Carmenère 111
——Syrah 112
—Cabernet Sauvignon 105
—Chardonnay Reserve 99
—Merlot Reserve 105
Santa Ines
—Cabernet Sauvignon 105
—Carmenère 110
—Legado de Armida Cabernet
       Sauvignon Reserve 110
—Sauvignon Blanc 99
Santa Isabel Barbera 58
Santa Julia Tempranillo 60
Santa Margherita Versato 193
Santa Rita
—120 Cabernet Sauvignon 105
—Cabernet Suavignon Medalla Real
       Special Reserve 112
—Carmenère Reserve 110
—Merlot Reserve 106
—Sauvignon Blanc Reserve 100
Santa Rosa Estate Malbec 58
Santenay 1er Cru AC 140
Santo Stefano Vino di Ripasso 195
Sapin, Paul, Cuvée Prestige 133, 137
Sardinia DOC 8
Sarget de Gruaud Larose 12, 128
Sartori 181
Saumaize-Michelin Les Crèches 131
Saumur AC 266, 267
Saumur-Champigny AC 145
Saussignac AC 5, 271
Sauvignon Blanc 70–2, 74, 96–100,
       141–4, 146, 157, 169–170, 183,
       202–5, 212, 214–6, 226–8, 230,
       246–7
Sauvignon Blanc/Semillon 69, 118–9,
Savennières AC 141
Savigny-lès-Beaune AC 138, 139
Scàranto Rosso 189
Schmitt Söhne Riesling 173
Scholtzenhof Petit Chenin 213
Schlumberger Gewurztraminer 116
Séguinot-Bordet, Domaine 131
Segura Viudas Brut Reserva 265
Semellerie, Domaine de la 144
Semillon 64–8, 71–3, 75, 271–3

Semillon/Sauvignon Blanc 69, 72–3,
       118–9, 169–70
Senechaux, Domaine des 154
Señorio de los Llanos Gran Reserva 234
Seppelt Moyston Unoaked Chardonnay
       64
Serentos Soft Press Chardonnay 67
Seuil, Château du 125
Sherry 6, 15
Shiraz see Syrah
Shiraz/Cabernet Sauvignon blends see
       also Cabernet Sauvignon/Shiraz
       blends
       76, 77, 79, 80, 91, 101
Sicilia DOC 194
Sierra Cantabria Reserva 240
Sierra Grande
—Merlot 102
—Sauvignon Blanc 97
Simonassi Lyon Malbec 58
Simonsig Estate
—Chardonnay 214
—Shiraz 221
—Tiara 224
Sipp Mack
—Pinot Blanc 115
—Riesling 116
—Riesling Tradition 116
Sirius 120, 121
Soave DOC 181, 182
Solyss 193
Somerset Hill Unwooded Chardonnay
       73
Somontano DO 229, 234, 238, 256
South Africa 19, 212–25
Spain 226–44
Spier
—Cabernet Sauvignon 219
—Chardonnay 215
—Pinotage 220
Straccali
—Garbino 181
—Tramontano 188
Stratford Chardonnay 246
Strauss, Johann
—Grüner Veltliner 93
— Rivaner 93
Synthèse Merlot de l'Arjolle 168
Syrah/Cabernet Suviignon blends see
       Shiraz/Cabernet Sauvignon blends
Syrah grape
—Argentina 59, 61
—Australia 76–92,
—Chile 103, 108, 112
—France 148, 150–6, 160–8
—Greece 179,
—Lebanon 201
—New Zealand 205
—Rosé 254
—South Africa 217–8, 220–5
—Spain 237, 241–2
—USA 248–253

Tahbilk Marsanne, Château 64
Taittinger
—Prestige Brut Rosé 263
—Réserve Brut 262
Talus
—Cabernet Sauvignon 249

—Chardonnay 246
Tannat grape 171–2, 254
Targé, Château de 145
Tariquet, Domaine du 169
Tatachilla
—Foundation Shiraz 89
—Partners Cabernet Sauvignon Shiraz 79
Taurasi DOCG 200
Taurino Notorpanaro 194
Tempranillo grape 60, 231–7, 238–244
Terlan
—Pinot Bianco 182
—Pinot Grigio 184
Teroldego grape 189
Teroldego Rotaliano DOC 189
Terra Alta DO 236
Terra das Fragas 208
Terra Mater Cabernet Sauvignon 106
Terras Gauda O Rosal 229
Terras do Sado VR 208
Terret grape 157
Tesco
—Frascati 181
—Australian Chardonnay Reserve 67
—Chilean Cabernet Sauvignon Reserve 106
——Sauvignon Blanc nv 97
—Frascati 181
—New Zealand Dry White Wine 202
—Spanish Tempranillo 235
—Viognier 158
—West Coast Chardonnay 245
Teyssier, Château 127
The Crossings Sauvignon Blanc 203
Thomann
—Gewürztraminer 115
—Riesling 114
Tierra Buena Reserve Malbec 59
Timberlay, Château 120, 121
Tinta Barroca grape 209–210, 218
Tinta Câo grape 209
Tinta Francesa grape 209
Tinta Roriz grape 208–9
Toar 197
Tocai Friulano grape 182, 185
Tohu Sauvignon Blanc 204
Tokaji Furmint Mandolas 180
Tommasi Ripasso 196
Tormaresca 189
Toro DO 235, 239, 240
Torres
—Atrium Merlot 239
—Fransola 230
—Viña Sol 229
Torres, Miguel
—Cabernet Sauvignon Rosé 255
—Cordillera 112
—Manso de Velasco 113
—Santa Digna Cabernet Sauvignon 104
Torrontés grape 56
Touraine AC 267
Tour Baladoz, Château 127
Tour Boisée 'À Marie Claude', Château 167
Tour du Pas St Georges, Château 125
Tour Grise Brut, Château 267
Touriga Franca grape 209
Touriga Nacional grape 208–210

Trapiche
—Iscay 61
—Malbec 59
Trebbiano grape 181, 183, 270
Trevallon ,Domaine de 20
Trignon, Château du 147
Trignon Sablet, Château du 151
Trillol, Domaine du 164
Trincadeira grape 207–208, 210
TriVento Malbec 58
Trulli Primitivo 190
Tsantalis Rapsani Epilegmenos Reserve 179
Tyrrell's Old Winery
—Chardonnay 67
—Vat 1 Hunter Semillon 75
—Vat 47 Pinot Chardonnay 75
—Vat 8 Shiraz Cabernet 91

Ugni Blanc grape 147, 169
Undurraga
—Carmenère 106
—Founder's Collection Cabernet Sauvignon 113
—Pinot Noir 106
—Sauvignon Blanc 97
USA
—California 245–53
—Washington State 246, 247, 251
Utiel-Requena DO 226, 230, 238, 255

Vacqueyras AC 150
Valdadige DOC 182
Valdemoya Crianza 232
Valdeorras DO 230
Valdepeñas DO 232, 234
Valderiz 243
Valdipiatta 198
Valencia DO 227
Valette, Domaine 135
Valmoissine Pinot Noir, Domaine de 138
Valpolicella DOC 10, 188, 190, 192, 195, 196
Valtellina Superiore DOC 195
Varière, Château de 145
Varieta Tasca grape 184
Vaughan Johnson's
—Good Everyday Cape Red 218
——Cape White 213
—Sunday Best 220
VdM
–Branco 207
–de Castilla León 236
–Tinto 208
VdT 130, 181, 182, 186, 188, 232, 244
—Castilla León 234
Vega Esteban Tempranillo 235
Vega Ibor Crianza 232
Vega Sauco 235, 239
Vendange Cabernet Sauvignon 248
Veuve Clicquot Ponsardin Brut nv 260
Verdejo grape 227
Verdelho grape 63, 66
Vernaccia grape 182, 184, 185
Vernaccia di San Gimignano DOCG 182, 184, 185
Vidal-Fleury 150, 156
Vignaioli Asti 19

Vignelaure, Château 13
—Domaine 160, 254
Villa Anheuser Riesling Trocken 175
Villa Antinori Riserva 196
Villa Canlungo Collavini Pinot Grigio
    184
Villa Maria
—Private Bin Cabernet Sauvignon
    Merlot 206
——Riesling 15, 203
Villard Estate Reserve Pinot Noir 112
Villiera
—Chenin Blanc 215
—Cru Monro Cab Sauv Merlot 222
Viña 105 235
Viña Carmina 255
Viña Casablanca Sauvignon Blanc 10
Viña Cascarela Sauvignon Blanc 227
Viña de Santa Isabel Reserve Malbec 59
Viña Hermosa Crianza 235
Viña Lidon Chardonnay 230
Viña Mater Tempranillo Reserva 236
Viña Salceda Reserva 240
Viña Tarapacá
—El Tranque Cabernet Merlot 106
—La Cuesta Vineyard Cabernet
    Sauvignon Syrah 107
—Piritas Vineyard Chardonnay 99
Vinho Verde DOC 207
Vino Nobile di Montepulciano DOCG
    198
Vin Santo DOC 270
Viognier grape 69–71, 147–8, 158–9,
    186, 245, 246
Viré-Clessé AC 14, 18, 131, 132, 133
Virginie
—Chardonnay 158
—Syrah 161
—Viognier 158
Vistarenni Vigneto Assolo 196
Viura grape 226, 228
Vouvray AC 12

Waimarie Gimblett Road Chardonnay
    205
Waipara Hills Sauvignon Blanc 204
Wairau River Sauvignon Blanc 203
Wakefield
—Cabernet Sauvignon 79
—Chardonnay 68
—Promised Land Chardonnay 68
——Shiraz Cabernet 80
—Riesling 68
—Semillon 68
—Shiraz 80
—White Clare 68
Walter Filiputti Pinot Grigio 185
Wardy, Domaine
——Ch. Les Cèdres 201
——Perle du Château 201
Warwick Estate Trilogy 224
Waterford
—Cabernet Sauvignon 224
—Sauvignon Blanc 216

Washington State 246, 247, 251
Weandre Stream Shiraz 80
Weingut Schumacher
—Riesling Kabinett 176
—Riesling Spätlese Trocken 176
Wildekrans Pinotage 224
Winkler Jesuitgarten Riesling Spätlese
    Trocken 177
Wither Hills
—Chardonnay 203
—Sauvignon Blanc 203
Wohlmuth
—Blaufränkisch 95
—Muskateller Summus 93
Wolf Blass
—Chardonnay 68
—Merlot 83
—President's Selection Cabernet
    Sauvignon 86
——Chardonnay 73
——Shiraz 86
—Red Label Shiraz Cabernet Sauvignon
    80
—Shiraz 84
Wyndham Estate
—Bin 444 Cabernet Sauvignon 80
—Bin 555 Shiraz 80
—Bin 888 Cabernet Merlot 81
Wynns
—Coonawarra Estate Cabernet 88
—Coonawarra Estate Riesling 69

Xanadu
—Cabernet Sauvignon 87
—Secession 81
—Semillon 73
Xarel-lo grape 227, 265, 267
Xerolithia 178
Xynomavro grape 178–9

Yaldara Cabernet Merlot Reserve 84
Yalumba
—Barossa Bush Vine Grenache 84
—Y Series Merlot 84
——Viognier 71
Yecla DO 232, 233
Yellowglen Pinot Noir Chardonnay 266
Yellow Tail Shiraz 76

Zaca Mesa 9
Zalse Chardonnay 215
Zédé, Domaine 127
Zenato
—Amarone 200
—Ripassa 10, 196
—San Benedetto 183
Zind Humbrecht Wintzenheim Clos
    Häuserer
—Gewurztraminer 117
—Gueberschwihr Riesling 11
—Riesling 117
Zinfandel grape 197, 248–253, 255
Zonin Prosecco Brut 265

# (o'briens
wine off-licence

## special discount for readers of The Wine Guide 2003

Bring this voucher to any O'Briens Wine Off-Licence store and receive 15% OFF any 6 bottles of wine purchased.

Normal discount of 5% applies to a 6 bottle purchase but this voucher entitles you to a 15% discount (an extra 10% off).

See overleaf for list of stores. Terms and conditions apply.

✂ - - -

# (o'briens
wine off-licence

## special discount for readers of The Wine Guide 2003

Bring this voucher to any O'Briens Wine Off-Licence store and receive 15% OFF any 6 bottles of wine purchased.

Normal discount of 5% applies to a 6 bottle purchase but this voucher entitles you to a 15% discount (an extra 10% off).

See overleaf for list of stores. Terms and conditions apply.

✂ - - -

# (o'briens
wine off-licence

## special discount for readers of The Wine Guide 2003

Bring this voucher to any O'Briens Wine Off-Licence store and receive 15% OFF any 6 bottles of wine purchased.

Normal discount of 5% applies to a 6 bottle purchase but this voucher entitles you to a 15% discount (an extra 10% off).

See overleaf for list of stores. Terms and conditions apply.

# o'briens
wine off-licence

| | |
|---|---|
| Bray, Quinsboro Rd: 01 286 3732 | Rathgar: 01 490 9366 |
| Bray, Vevay Rd: 01 286 8776 | Rathmines: 01 496 7811 |
| Greystones: 01 287 4123 | Navan Road: 01 838 4864 |
| Dun Laoghaire: 01 280 6952 | Glasnevin: 01 837 3220 |
| Donnybrook: 01 269 3310 | Templeogue: 01 492 0334 |
| Blackrock: 01 283 1664 | Malahide: 01 845 1237 |
| Sandymount: 01 668 2096 | Navan: 046 73206 |
| Dalkey: 01 285 8944 | Newbridge: 045 449804 |
| Stillorgan: 01 283 6287 | Drogheda: 01 269 3139 |

**Terms and conditions**

No other promotional offers apply. To avail of the discount all six bottles must be purchased at the same time, in one till transaction. Offer available in all O'Briens stores from September 1st 2002 to August 31st 2003. No photocopies or any other kind of reproduction of vouchers will be accepted.

# o'briens
wine off-licence

| | |
|---|---|
| Bray, Quinsboro Rd: 01 286 3732 | Rathgar: 01 490 9366 |
| Bray, Vevay Rd: 01 286 8776 | Rathmines: 01 496 7811 |
| Greystones: 01 287 4123 | Navan Road: 01 838 4864 |
| Dun Laoghaire: 01 280 6952 | Glasnevin: 01 837 3220 |
| Donnybrook: 01 269 3310 | Templeogue: 01 492 0334 |
| Blackrock: 01 283 1664 | Malahide: 01 845 1237 |
| Sandymount: 01 668 2096 | Navan: 046 73206 |
| Dalkey: 01 285 8944 | Newbridge: 045 449804 |
| Stillorgan: 01 283 6287 | Drogheda: 01 269 3139 |

**Terms and conditions**

No other promotional offers apply. To avail of the discount all six bottles must be purchased at the same time, in one till transaction. Offer available in all O'Briens stores from September 1st 2002 to August 31st 2003. No photocopies or any other kind of reproduction of vouchers will be accepted.

# o'briens
wine off-licence

| | |
|---|---|
| Bray, Quinsboro Rd: 01 286 3732 | Rathgar: 01 490 9366 |
| Bray, Vevay Rd: 01 286 8776 | Rathmines: 01 496 7811 |
| Greystones: 01 287 4123 | Navan Road: 01 838 4864 |
| Dun Laoghaire: 01 280 6952 | Glasnevin: 01 837 3220 |
| Donnybrook: 01 269 3310 | Templeogue: 01 492 0334 |
| Blackrock: 01 283 1664 | Malahide: 01 845 1237 |
| Sandymount: 01 668 2096 | Navan: 046 73206 |
| Dalkey: 01 285 8944 | Newbridge: 045 449804 |
| Stillorgan: 01 283 6287 | Drogheda: 01 269 3139 |

**Terms and conditions**

No other promotional offers apply. To avail of the discount all six bottles must be purchased at the same time, in one till transaction. Offer available in all O'Briens stores from September 1st 2002 to August 31st 2003. No photocopies or any other kind of reproduction of vouchers will be accepted.